___ cassettes
∟ discs/disks
___ videos
∟ bks/pamphs

FOURTH EDITION

On the Guard II

THE YMCA LIFEGUARD MANUAL

YMCA
We build strong kids,
strong families, strong communities.

Library of Congress Cataloging-in-Publication Data

On the guard II : the YMCA lifeguard manual / YMCA of the USA.--4th ed.
        p. cm.
    Includes bibliographical references and index.
    ISBN 0-7360-3976-7
        1. Lifeguards--Training of. 2. Lifesaving. 3. Aquatic sports--Safety measures. I. Title:
On the guard. II. Title: On the guard 2. III. Title: On the guard two. IV. YMCA of the
USA.

    GV838.74.O5   2001
    792.2'1'0289--dc21

00-054235

ISBN: 0-7360-3976-7

Published for the YMCA of the USA by Human Kinetics Publishers, Inc.

YMCA Project Coordinator: Laura J. Slane
Acquisitions Editor: Pat Sammann
Managing Editor: Cynthia McEntire
Assistant Editor: John Wentworth
Proofreader: Julie Marx
Indexer: Nancy Ball
Permission Managers: Cheri Banks and Toni Harte
Graphic Designer: Stuart Cartwright
Graphic Artist: Francine Hamerski
Photo Manager: Clark Brooks
Cover Designer: Jack W. Davis
Photographer (cover): Tracy Frankel
Photographers (interior): Tracy Frankel, Rhonda Hole, Laura J. Slane, Ken Nemeth, and John
    Fletemeyer
Art Manager: Craig Newsom
Line Drawings: Four-color line art by Roberto Sabas based on illustrations by Keith Neely;
    additional line art by Keith Neely
Mac Art: Gretchen Walters
Cartoons: Cindy Wrobel and Larry Nolte
Medical Art: Marie Dauenheimer and Kristin Mount
Printer: Maracle Press

Information in chapter 14 is from chapters 2-9 of *YMCA Pool Operations Manual*, Ralph L.
Johnson, 1989, Champaign, IL: Human Kinetics. Chapters 3, 4, 6, and 8 and part of chapters 5
and 7 in *YMCA Pool Operations Manual* are adapted from chapters 5 and 13 in Swimming Pools
(4th ed.) (pp. 65-76, 201-221) by M.A. Gabrielsen (Ed.), 1987, Champaign, IL: Human Kinetics.
Copyright 1987 by the Council for National cooperation in Aquatics. Adapted by permission.

Printed in Canada

10 9 8 7 6 5 4 3 2

Copies of this book may be purchased from the YMCA Program Store, P.O. Box 5076, Champaign,
IL 61825-5076, 800-747-0089

The YMCA of the USA does not operate or manage any lifeguard training programs.

C O N T E N T S

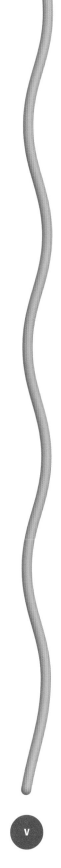

PREFACE

Lifeguarding is a serious and important undertaking. Although much of lifeguarding can be tedious, a matter of watching the same area for hours with little change, at any moment a guard may have to jump into action, quickly and efficiently, to save a life. Lifeguarding is a demanding task, requiring responsible, caring, and capable people who have been well trained in their duties.

On the Guard II is the YMCA's lifeguard training manual. It offers you up-to-date information on how to guard, anticipating and preventing problems before they occur, and taking action to help those in danger when necessary. But this information is always presented with the YMCA's mission in mind: How can we keep people safe in a caring, open way? How can we meet people's needs to have fun and to develop their aquatic skills within legal and moral constraints to keep aquatic environments as safe and pleasant as possible for everyone? The YMCA program tries to develop lifeguards who not only know a lot but also care a lot about lifeguarding and those they are trained to serve.

This new edition brings lifeguarding concepts to life by illustrating them with all-new photos that should give readers even better visual guidance in understanding the key information in this manual. The text is updated, with some changes made in procedures for spinal injury management and scuba rescue. New material has been added on these topics:

- Personal safety on the beach and when riding personal watercraft
- Guarding people with disabilities
- Handling violence and conflicts among patrons
- First aid kits
- Resuscitation equipment, such as suction devices, bag-valve masks, oxygen-powered ventilators, and automated external defibrillators

New appendixes cover the YMCA guidelines for resident camp, day camp, child care, and waterfront operations, as well as waterfront safety and fecal contamination of pools.

Another new addition to *On the Guard II* is a CD-ROM that is bound into the back of the book. It contains video clips for 35 rescue skills. This allows you to watch and review these skills, which are taught in your lifeguarding course.

After an introduction that explains the YMCA's historical involvement in aquatic safety and the lifeguarding requirements and aquatic courses available, *On the Guard II* describes the safety and survival skills every swimmer needs to know. This is followed by chapter 3, in which lifeguards' professional and legal responsibilities are described. The next two chapters cover accident and incident prevention, with specifics on how to lifeguard and pool danger areas, along with suggested rules to protect patrons' safety. That's followed by the information you need to deal with emergencies, including victim recognition and drowning, rescue skills, emergency systems, first aid in aquatic environments, and spinal injury management. The chapters on rescue, first aid, and spinal injury contain step-by-step instructions on how to perform the appropriate procedures.

Chapters 11 and 12 tell you what you need to know for outdoor lifeguarding. Chapter 11 discusses weather and open water dangers and the precautions to take against them; chapter 12 highlights the specialized knowledge required for basic open water lifeguarding. Chapter 13 explains the different aspects and techniques of the growing field of water park lifeguarding, including guarding inflatables.

The next two chapters review some of the job-related responsibilities of lifeguards. The first addresses pool management concerns, such as pool chemistry and filtration and safety inspection; the final one includes guidance on how to seek, obtain, and retain a lifeguarding position and ideas for further training.

Each chapter begins with objectives to guide your reading and ends with review questions to check your knowledge of the main points. Some have special boxes that highlight guidelines or key points of procedures. Most skills and procedures are presented as numbered steps, with illustrations to clarify the instructions.

Seven appendixes contain additional practical information. They include guidelines for prevention of child abuse and for aquatics in camp, childcare, and waterfront settings; additional risk management recommendations; a sample accident report form; information on becoming certified as a United States Lifesaving Association lifeguard; waterfront safety recommendations from the Aquatic Council of AAHPERD; and YMCA of the USA Medical Advisory Committee recommendations for prevention and control of fecal contamination of pools.

As you train at the YMCA to become a lifeguard, you should learn more than just skills. You should grow in both your ability and desire to help others. Lifeguarding is a perfect opportunity to develop leadership and service skills and to make a significant contribution to your community. We hope that as you read this manual and complete your training you develop an appreciation for the value of lifeguarding, for yourself and others.

ACKNOWLEDGMENTS

The YMCA of the USA would like to acknowledge the contributions of the following individuals to *On the Guard II* and the new lifeguard training, collectively known as the Lifeguard Project. Staff leadership for this project was coordinated by Laura J. Slane.

Lifeguard Project Technical Advisory Committee Members

Ronald K. Nelson, Chair	Grand Rapids Metropolitan YMCA, Grand Rapids, MI
Gerald DeMers, PhD	Associate Professor, California Polytechnic State University, San Luis Obispo, CA
Ralph L. Johnson, PhD	Director of Aquatics, Indiana University of Pennsylvania, Indiana, PA
Diane Knight	Garden Ranch YMCA, Colorado Springs, CO
Jay Newell	South Oklahoma City Branch YMCA, Oklahoma City, OK
Nancy W. Reece	Kankakee YMCA, Kankakee, IL
Laura J. Slane	YMCA of the USA, Chicago, IL
Steve Tarver	Suncoast Family YMCAs, Clearwater, FL

Lifeguard Project Field Test Group Members

Fred Doll	Ionia County YMCA, Ionia, MI
Pam Hendricks	Santa Barbara YMCA, Santa Barbara, CA
Ralph L. Johnson, PhD	Director of Aquatics, Indiana University of Pennsylvania, Indiana, PA
Diane Knight	Garden Ranch YMCA, Colorado Springs, CO
Sandra Krol	Rich Port Branch YMCA, La Grange, IL
Jay Newell	South Oklahoma City Branch YMCA, Oklahoma City, OK
Brian Raymond	Sewickley YMCA, Sewickley, PA
Kathy Rhoads	Central Douglas County YMCA, Roseburg, OR
Richard Robinson	International Drive YMCA, Orlando, FL
Kay Smiley	Town North YMCA, Dallas, TX
Debbie Sutton	South Dekalb Family Branch YMCA, Decatur, GA
Steve Tarver	Suncoast Family YMCAs, Clearwater, FL
Cara Telleysh	International Drive YMCA, Orlando, FL
Melinda Vana	Marshalltown YMCA, Marshalltown, IA

Lifeguard Project Reviewers

Joe Ashworth	Jacksonville, FL
Bob Brucker	Phoenixville YMCA, Phoenixville, PA
Karen Bufalino	Aquatic and Physical Education Instructor, Health and Physical Education Department, Quaker Valley School District, Saxsonburg, PA
Paul Cerio	Aquatic Director, University of Nebraska-Omaha, Omaha, NE

Lifeguard Revision Team (for the fourth edition)

Gerald DeMers, PhD	Professor, California Polytechnic State University, San Luis Obispo, CA, and Senior Partner, Professional Aquatic Consultants International
Beth Fugate	Clippard YMCA, Cincinnati, OH
Mindy Hartman	Johnson County YMCA, Buffalo, WY
Teresa Hendrix	Upper Keys YMCA, Key Largo, FL
Theresa Hill	Buehler YMCA, Palatine, IL
Ralph L. Johnson, PhD	Professor and Chairman, Sport Management Department, North Greenville College, Tigerville, SC, and Senior Partner, Professional Aquatic Consultants International
Karen Martorano	YMCA of Metropolitan Detroit, Detroit, MI
Bruce Pearl	Summit YMCA, Summit, NJ
John Wingfield, MS	U.S. Diving, Indianapolis, IN

Special thanks to Dr. Gerald DeMers not only for writing and revising chapter 10 but also for his help, support, and countless contributions throughout this project.

Thanks also to Linda Bump, who wrote the original manual, and to Patricia Sammann, who has provided the developmental editing for all editions.

We also would like to thank the following for their support of the present edition of *On the Guard II:*

- California Polytechnic State University, San Luis Obispo, CA, for allowing the YMCA to use their pool for shooting the pool photos in the book and the video used in the accompanying CD-ROM, and to the students who helped with the shoots

- Mustang Water Slides, San Luis Obispo, CA, for allowing the YMCA to use their pool for shooting the pool photos in the book and the video used in the accompanying CD-ROM

- Adolph Kiefer for his dedication to the promotion of water safety and the contributions of Adolph Kiefer and Associates of equipment for the photo and video shoots

- Aqua Lung, Vista, CA, for supplying equipment used in the photo and video shoots

- A & D Promotions for providing the YMCA with T-shirts for the photo and video shoots

- Marsars Water Rescue Systems for providing equipment for the photo and video shoots

- Big Picture for shooting the video used in the accompanying CD-ROM

- Tracy Frankel for shooting all the technique photos in the book

- Rhonda Hole, John Fletemeyer, and Ken Nemeth for shooting the decorative photos in the book

CHAPTER one

Introduction to YMCA Lifeguarding

YMCA aquatic professionals have led the crusade for improved aquatic safety for over 100 years, and they continue to improve the quality of millions of lives through YMCA instructional aquatic programs. This edition of *On the Guard II* provides personal safety and lifeguard training course material for those developing their aquatic skills.

> **In This Chapter, You Are Introduced To**
> - the importance of aquatic safety,
> - the YMCA's role in promoting aquatic safety,
> - the YMCA's program philosophy,
> - the YMCA's lifeguarding program, and
> - other YMCA aquatic safety programs.

THE IMPORTANCE OF AQUATIC SAFETY

In the past 25 years, interest in aquatic activities has exploded. With greater access to swimming facilities and water parks, people can easily include aquatic activities in their recreation and fitness routines. Enthusiasts are found *on the water*, in activities like rafting, canoeing, sailing, and boating; *in the water*, in recreational and competitive swimming, synchronized swimming, water sliding, and water polo; *under the water*, through skin and scuba diving; and even *above the water*, as in parasailing. The popularity of aquatic activities has generated a new awareness of the need for aquatic education and safety for all age groups.

For those without awareness and proper training, the aquatic environment can be as dangerous as it is fun. And even those who don't participate in water sports may need water safety knowledge. Drowning is the fourth leading cause of accidental death in the United States, claiming about 4,100 lives each year. It's the leading cause of injury death for children age one to two, and, in some states, it's the leading cause of injury death for all those under age 15 (U.S. Lifesaving Association, n.d.). Most drowning victims are nonswimmers who never intended to go into the water. The scenarios include accidents in bathtubs, falling out of a boat, wading too far into the surf, falling off a fishing pier or into a backyard swimming pool, or even plunging into a body of water while inside an automobile.

In addition to those who die by drowning, untold numbers of people are injured in accidents in open water areas and at public, private, and residential pools. For every 10 children who die by drowning, 140 are treated in emergency rooms and 36 are admitted to hospitals for further treatment (U.S. Lifesaving Association, n.d.). Carelessness, rough play, and unsafe head-first entries can lead to injury on pool decks, near starting blocks, and on or around diving boards.

THE YMCA'S ROLE IN AQUATIC SAFETY

The YMCA and other community agencies have taken on the challenge of providing swimming instruction and aquatic safety training for people of all ages. With programs like YMCA Swim Lessons, the national YMCA has developed swimming instruction to address the needs of preschoolers and advanced swimmers alike.

The YMCA has been teaching people to swim for over 100 years. Figure 1.1 traces the development of the YMCA contribution to aquatic safety.

THE YMCA'S PROGRAM PHILOSOPHY

Millions of people learn to swim through YMCA programs every year. But they take away more from those programs than just skills. Every YMCA program should meet the YMCA's mission to put Christian principles into practice to build a healthy spirit, mind, and body for all. To do this, every YMCA program should meet certain program objectives and incorporate the concept of character development.

Program Objectives

In all YMCA programs, the prime objectives are to help participants

- grow personally by developing their self-esteem and self-reliance;
- strengthen and teach positive values;
- improve their personal and family relationships by learning to care, communicate, and cooperate with others;
- appreciate people of different ages, abilities, races, religions, cultures, incomes, and beliefs;

1885–90	The YMCA entered the aquatic arena by teaching individuals to swim.
1906	George Corsan, Sr., revolutionized swimming by teaching people in groups.
1908–09	The YMCA became the first organization to plan and carry out a national aquatic education program.
1909	The YMCA became the first organization to employ national field staff to carry out a national aquatic program.
1912	The YMCA developed the National YMCA Lifesaving Service.
1913	George E. Goss of the YMCA completed a systematic study of lifesaving in the United States.
1929	The YMCA *Lifesaving and Swimming Manual* was published.
1939	The YMCA, in cooperation with Dr. Thomas Cureton and Dr. Charles Silvia, published the first standardized examination of lifesaving and water safety knowledge and attitudes.
1949	The first edition of the *YMCA Lifesaving & Water Safety Instruction* text, written by Charles E. Silvia, was published. It was the first such text to advocate the use of mouth-to-mouth resuscitation.
1965	Charles Silvia's *YMCA Lifesaving & Water Safety Today* was published.
1972	The YMCA Aquatic Safety & Lifesaving Program was launched. It was the first lifesaving program that divided lifesaving into levels (aquatic safety, advanced aquatic safety, senior lifesaving). The YMCA was the first national organization to develop a lifeguard training and certification program.
1974	James Cornforth's *YMCA National Lifeguard Manual* was released.
1986	The first edition of *On the Guard* was released.
1994	*On the Guard II* was released to meet the changing program needs of lifeguards.
1997	The third edition of *On the Guard II* was released.
	The YMCA Aquatic Safety Assistant Course was introduced.
2001	The fourth edition of *On the Guard II* was released.

Figure 1.1   YMCA aquatic safety milestones.

- become better leaders and supporters by learning to work toward a common goal;
- develop specific skills through growth in spirit, mind, and body; and
- have fun.

These objectives, central to the YMCA's philosophy, make YMCA programs different from those offered by any other organization. Through this lifeguarding program, you'll have the opportunity to grow in all of these ways.

Character Development

Another part of all YMCA programs is character development. The YMCA's stated mission is "to put *Christian principles into practice* through programs that build a healthy spirit, mind, and body for all." If we define principles as "a code of conduct; a basis for action" and Christian principles as "positive values," then challenging people to accept and demonstrate positive values is how we put them into practice. Our doing this is called "character development."

Values are the cornerstones that make our society safe and workable. They are the principles of thought and conduct that help distinguish right from wrong and provide a foundation for decision making. Values, which are sometimes referred to as *character*, are the basis of who we are, how we live, and how we treat others. The values we try to impart through character development are these four:

- Caring: to put others before yourself, to love others, to be sensitive to the well-being of others, to help others
- Honesty: to tell the truth, to act in such a way that I am worthy of trust, to have integrity, making sure my actions match my values
- Respect: to treat others as you would have them treat you, to value the worth of every person, including yourself
- Responsibility: to do what you should do, to be accountable for your behavior and obligations

If we believe that values are what makes society good, then it seems likely that inadequately defined values or a lack of values could be the source of many of today's problems: poor work ethics, lack of personal responsibility, lack of trust in our leaders and public officials, crime, violence, and substance abuse. In the long run, character development is an effective strategy that can help solve these problems. It fits the YMCA's continuing long-term goal to help people develop spirit, as well as mind and body.

Living with and acting on good values contribute to the development of a healthy self-esteem and overall personal happiness. The YMCA defines *self-esteem* as the positive valuing of oneself. The YMCA helps children and adults develop self-esteem by providing opportunities for them to become more capable and worthy. By *capable* we mean having practical abilities and competencies. The more capable a person is, the more confident that person is in his or her ability to think and to cope with life's basic challenges. By *worthy* we mean being able to act in a manner that is consistent with those principles a person has been taught are important, such as doing one's best or doing the right thing. As a person becomes more worthy, he or she also becomes more confident of the right to be successful and happy. It makes the person feel more deserving and entitled to assert his or her needs and wants, achieve his or her values, and enjoy the fruits of his or her efforts.

Because we have free will, we always have three choices when we act:

1. We may choose to act in ways that we know will earn and support our self-esteem.
2. We may choose to act in ways that will not earn and support our self-esteem.
3. We may close our eyes to the necessity of maintaining our self-esteem and proceed through life blindly, choosing at random.

Building self-esteem and developing character (values) are connected. When we behave in ways that conflict with what we judge to be appropriate, we lose face in our own eyes and our self-esteem suffers. We feel less worthy. The higher our self-esteem, the more apt we are to strive to make principled choices. Doing this makes us feel more worthy, increasing our self-esteem. We cannot earn self-esteem without values, and we cannot act consistently on our values without being influenced by our self-esteem.

YMCAs can help youth and families develop self-esteem and values by providing participants with sustained relationships with adults, such as YMCA staff members. The YMCA and its staff must convey consistent messages about values, attitudes, beliefs, and behaviors. (Values are not situational; the same values apply in all situations.) To do this, staff behaviors must be consistent with the values, attitudes, and beliefs that they preach.

Lifeguards, like all YMCA staff, must be willing to meet the YMCA's character development challenge and lead by example. Not "walking the talk" is a big problem in teaching character development. Assess your personal ability to lead by example. Once you know where you are and what you want to work on in yourself, you can challenge yourself to improve.

THE YMCA LIFEGUARDING PROGRAM

You probably are reading this book in preparation for becoming a YMCA lifeguard, the initial certification in the YMCA lifeguarding program. However, the program also includes two other levels of certification: YMCA lifeguard instructor and YMCA lifeguard trainer.

YMCA Lifeguard

The YMCA has developed a unique program to prepare skilled lifeguards for a demanding profession. A *lifeguard* by definition has a legal duty to protect the safety of people in an assigned area. Lifeguards have a moral and professional obligation to prevent potential accident situations by enforcing the rules and regulations of their aquatic setting and to react to any emergencies that occur. Lifeguards have a legal duty to respond only if they are on duty at their facility. Should a lifeguard be involved in an accident while off duty, he or she is covered by Good Samaritan laws (see page 46). These laws can't prevent lawsuits, but they do ensure that the lifeguard's actions are compared to the actions expected of others in similar rescue situations with similar training and certification.

To be a proficient lifeguard, you must first know about personal safety and survival skills, which are reviewed in chapter 2. These and other skills necessary for success can be developed in a professional lifeguarding course, such as the YMCA lifeguard training program.

The YMCA lifeguard training program provides a comprehensive education centered on preventing accidents in aquatic environments and is based on research. It focuses on the practical aspects of what lifeguards need to know and on lifeguard and patron safety. Lifeguard training enables you to learn and apply safety principles in your own life, develop leadership skills, learn how to maintain a healthy lifestyle, and improve your decision-making skills.

Besides being advanced-level swimmers, candidates to become YMCA lifeguards should be caring, strong, quick to respond, confident, fit, and intelligent, with good interpersonal skills. The YMCA strives to include all people in their programs, but the hazardous duty of a lifeguard may disqualify some candidates with certain physical or mental conditions from becoming certified. To become certified as a YMCA lifeguard, an individual must be able to accomplish these tasks:

- Remain alert, with no lapses in consciousness.
- Sit for extended periods, including in an elevated chair.
- Move to various locations, including in and around an elevated chair.
- Communicate verbally, including projecting the voice across distances, and communicate swiftly and effectively with emergency personnel over telephone and in person.
- Hear noises and distress signals in an aquatic environment, including in water, understanding that significant background noise exists in aquatic environments.
- Observe all assigned sections of the water area.
- Perform all needed rescues and survival skills.
- Think in the abstract, solve problems, make decisions, instruct, evaluate, supervise, and remember.
- Operate alone as a lifeguard, without other lifeguards for support.

To become a YMCA lifeguard, you must meet the following entrance requirements, complete the course as described, and fulfill all certification requirements. Medical clearance before participation may also be required.

Entrance Requirements

To participate in the lifeguard training program, you must meet the following prerequisites:

- Be at least 16 years old of age by the last day of the scheduled course. Parental consent is required for those under 18.
- Have and maintain current cardiopulmonary resuscitation (CPR) and first aid certifications. CPR certification must include training for administering CPR to adults, children, and infants and obstructed airway maneuver, as well as additional training in two-rescuer CPR, modified jaw thrust, and use of resuscitation-mask and bag-valve-mask resuscitators. First aid certification must include training in victim assessment; treatment for bleeding, shock, burns, specific body area injuries, bites, stings, poisoning, cold- and heat-related conditions, and bone, muscle, and joint injuries; and handling medical emergencies and rescues. For YMCA of the USA courses which require CPR and/or first aid certifications as a prerequisite, appropriate certifications from the following nationally recognized organizations will be accepted: American Heart Association (Health Care Provider course for BLS only), American Red Cross (CPR for the Professional Rescuer), National Safety Council, and American Safety and Health Institute (CPR-Pro Course and Universal First Aid).
- Pass the following swimming test:
  1. Perform a long, shallow front dive, then swim 500 yards, including 100 yards each of sidestroke, front crawl, breaststroke, sidestroke kick with one arm forward, and inverted breaststroke kick with arms on the stomach.
  2. Tread water for at least 2 minutes with legs only.
  3. Surface-dive head-first and feet-first in 8 to 10 feet of water and swim underwater for 15 feet.

The following are presently only recommended prerequisites, but after December 31, 2002, they will be required:

- Have and maintain current certification in oxygen administration.
- Have and maintain current certification in automated external defibrillation (AED).

Course Content

The lifeguard training course includes at least 29 hours of classroom and pool sessions, plus a 2-hour practical experience, that cover these topics:

- The importance of aquatic safety
- Personal safety survival skills and swimming strokes
- Aquatic environments and aquatic science
- Aquatic rescues, including situation assessment, use of a rescue tube or buoy (required for rescue) and other rescue equipment, nonswimming assists, and swimming rescues
- How to handle special situations, such as spinal injuries, rescue breathing, scuba rescue, open water guarding and rescue, search and recovery operations, and first aid procedures specific to the aquatic environment
- Lifeguard responsibilities and administration, including duties, rules, legal responsibilities, emergency procedures, reports, and pool maintenance
- Lifeguarding techniques
- Personal health and safety of lifeguards
- Job searches and additional training opportunities

Certification Requirements

Lifeguard certification is conducted by a certified YMCA lifeguard instructor. To be certified you must complete the course, score 80% or better on each section of a written or oral knowledge test, and correctly perform all skills in a practical skills test. Certification may also include your instructor's subjective judgment about the maturity, attitude, and classroom participation you demonstrated during the course.

Your certification is reported to YMCA of the USA Program Certifications, 101 N. Wacker Dr., Chicago, IL 60606. The certification, which is renewable every 2 years through your local YMCA, is valid only if you keep your certifications in CPR and first aid current.

YMCA Lifeguard Instructor

Certification as a YMCA lifeguard instructor allows you to provide the training necessary for people to become lifeguards. You must take the 18-hour YMCA Lifeguard Instructor course to become certified. The course is based on the content of the *Instructor Manual for On the Guard II*, in addition to this manual.

Entrance Requirements

To participate in the lifeguard instructor course, you must meet the following prerequisites:

- Be at least 18 years old prior to certification.
- Have and maintain current certification as a YMCA lifeguard (including current certification in CPR and first aid). (After December 31, 2002, current certification in oxygen administration and AED also will be required.)
- Have taken one of the following courses: Principles of YMCA Aquatic Leadership, Basic Aquatic Leadership Course, or Fundamentals of Teaching YMCA Swimming.
- Have attended a Program Trainer Orientation course.

Certification Requirements

To be certified you must successfully pass a written or oral knowledge test and correctly perform all skills in a practical skills test. Your certification is reported to YMCA of the USA Program Certifications, 101 N. Wacker Dr., Chicago, IL 60606. The certification is renewable every 3 years through your local YMCA. Completion of this course does not automatically renew YMCA lifeguard certification.

YMCA Lifeguard Trainer

Certification as a YMCA lifeguard trainer prepares you to teach staff and volunteers the certification courses for Principles of YMCA Aquatic Leadership and YMCA Lifeguard Instructor. A 23-hour certification course is based on the *Instructor Manual for On the Guard II* and this manual.

Entrance Requirements

To participate in the lifeguard trainer course, you must meet the following prerequisites:

- Be at least 21 years old prior to certification.
- Have and maintain current certification as a YMCA lifeguard (including current certification in CPR and first aid). (After December 31, 2002, current certification in oxygen administration and AED also will be required.)
- Have and maintain current certification as a YMCA lifeguard instructor and have experience teaching the present lifeguarding program after becoming a certified instructor.
- Have taken one of the following courses: Principles of YMCA Aquatic Leadership, Basic Aquatic Leadership Course, or Fundamentals of Teaching YMCA Swimming.
- Have attended a Program Trainer Orientation.
- Have and maintain current certification as a Program Trainer Orientation Trainer (this certification may be obtained after the Lifeguard Trainer Course).
- Complete a program trainer candidate application. It should include a statement from your executive director verifying that you have taught 300 hours of aquatics, with at least 50 hours of teaching as a certified YMCA lifeguard instructor.

Certification Requirements

To be certified you must successfully pass a written or oral knowledge test and correctly perform all skills in a practical skills test. Your teaching skills will also be observed and evaluated. Your certification is reported to YMCA of the USA Program Certifications, 101 N. Wacker Dr., Chicago, IL 60606. Successful completion of this course automatically renews your YMCA Lifeguard Instructor certification. While there is no renewal for YMCA Lifeguard Trainer certification, you must continue to keep your YMCA Lifeguard and YMCA Lifeguard Instructor certifications current.

If you are interested in becoming a YMCA lifeguard instructor or a lifeguard trainer, consult your local YMCA staff or YMCA of the USA Program Development (800-USA-YMCA).

OTHER YMCA AQUATIC SAFETY PROGRAMS

The YMCA offers five additional aquatic safety programs: YMCA Splash, the Aquatic Safety Course, the Aquatic Personal Safety and Survival Course, the Aquatic Safety Assistant Course, and the YMCA Aquatic Leadership Program.

YMCA Splash

YMCA Splash is an introduction and orientation to swimming and water safety skills. It's primarily for grade-school children and families, but it can be modified for use with older children and adults. Usually it is a 5-day pool or classroom program, but a 1-day specialty course is also a possibility. An optional Parents' Presentation can be used with the 5-day program to instruct parents on the same topics covered in the classes.

The 5-day program, which consists of a 30- to 45-minute lesson each day, includes the following:

- Basic swimming skills
- Backyard pool safety
- Beach safety
- Pool safety
- Boating safety
- Character development
- Family activities
- Parent education

Each participant who completes the course is given a certificate of participation.

Aquatic Safety Course

This introduction to water safety requires no previous training. It is designed to be adapted to the needs of individuals in different aquatic settings, from a corporate fitness program to family backyard pool safety. Nonswimmers are encouraged to enroll and participate, to the extent that they are able, so they can learn about basic water safety.

The Aquatic Safety Course consists of 4 to 6 hours of classroom and water sessions and includes discussions of these topics:

- History and philosophy of the YMCA aquatic safety and lifeguard training programs
- Personal aquatic safety information
- Accident prevention principles
- Basic first aid and rescue breathing
- Nonswimming rescues

Oral or written tests are administered by the local YMCA.

Aquatic Personal Safety and Survival Course

This 8-hour course trains participants in personal safety and survival skills in and around aquatic environments. Classroom and pool sessions address these topics:

- The history and philosophy of YMCA aquatic safety
- Accident prevention principles
- General aquatic information
- Personal aquatic safety information
- Basic survival skills and principles
- Nonswimming rescues
- Basic first aid and rescue breathing

To take the course, candidates must meet the following prerequisites:

- Be at least 11 years old.
- Be able to complete the following swimming test:
    1. Swim 300 yards, including 50 yards each of front crawl, breaststroke, elementary backstroke, inverted breaststroke (legs only), sidestroke left, and sidestroke right.
    2. Tread water for 2 minutes.
    3. Perform head-first and feet-first surface dives.

To receive a certificate of course completion, participants must score at least 80% on a written or oral knowledge test and demonstrate all skills on a performance test. The certificate of successful completion or participation in the course is issued by the local YMCA.

YMCA Aquatic Safety Assistant Course

The purpose of the YMCA Aquatic Safety Assistant Course is to present the knowledge and skills an individual needs in order to recognize and prevent aquatic risks and to assist a lifeguard in responding to an emergency such as an accident or injury. This 16-hour course trains assistants, coaches, and instructor candidates to perform these skills:

- Recognize potential accidents or incidents and prevent them while teaching a class or leading a program
- Recognize potential hazards related to the program and facility and eliminate them or communicate to someone in authority about them
- Use and care for equipment properly
- Recognize and report suspected child abuse
- Assist lifeguards in keeping aquatic activities safe and in following their YMCA's emergency action plan and procedures, including managing the scene of an accident
- Recognize distressed swimmers and try to help them with basic rescue techniques using swimming assists
- Communicate the need for assistance for themselves or others as necessary
- Protect themselves from personal injury while teaching
- Serve as a good role model of Christian values and safe behavior

This certification does *not* include training in lifeguarding, so having an aquatic safety assistant in a program or class does *not* meet the requirement of having a certified lifeguard on duty. The certification only allows the person to assist a lifeguard during an emergency. Certification as an aquatic safety assistant also does not include instruction in how to teach or lead swimming or exercise classes. Such instruction must come through YMCA aquatic specialist instructor courses, for which the Aquatic Safety Assistant Course is a prerequisite.

To take the Aquatic Safety Assistant Course, candidates must meet the following prerequisites:

- Be at least 14 years old.
- Be able to complete the following swimming test:
  1. Swim 100 yards, any stroke.
  2. Tread water for 2 minutes.
  3. Perform a head-first or feet-first surface dive in 4 to 6 feet of water or submerge and touch the hand on the bottom of the pool in 5 feet of water.
- Have and maintain current CPR and first aid certifications (same as lifeguard prerequisites).
- Have the strength and maturity to assist in backboarding procedures.

The YMCA Aquatic Safety Assistant Course is conducted by a certified YMCA lifeguard instructor. To become certified as an aquatic safety assistant, participants must complete the course, score 80% or better on a written or oral knowledge test, and successfully perform all the skills in a practical skills test. Certification may also depend on the instructor's subjective judgment about participants' maturity, attitude, and classroom participation as shown during the course.

To keep this certification current, individuals must renew it every 2 years and keep their CPR and first aid certifications current. To renew the Aquatic Safety Assistant certification, participants must take the written and practical skills tests from a currently certified YMCA lifeguard instructor.

YMCA Aquatic Leadership Program

This course trains young people ages 11 through 15 in various aspects of aquatic leadership and safety. It is for both swimmers and nonswimmers. The course is broken into modules covering the following topics:

- Leadership
- YMCA mission
- Diversity
- Job training
- First aid and CPR
- Facility maintenance
- Healthy lifestyles
- Rescue skills
- Swimming skills
- Character development
- Aquatic safety
- Community service

Participants are given a practical evaluation, and they receive recognition awards for successful completion of the evaluation. Once participants have become certified, they may become involved in any of a number of program activities, including the following:

- Lifeguard in-service (as an assistant)
- Course teaching (as an assistant)
- YMCA Splash (as an assistant)
- Competitions
- Tournament planning
- Mentoring programs (either being mentored or mentoring younger children)

Table 1.1 summarizes the purpose, age levels, course hours, and renewal intervals for the YMCA's lifeguarding and water safety programs.

Table 1.1 Summary of YMCA Lifeguarding and Safety Programs

Course	Purpose	Age	Course hours	Renewal
YMCA Splash	Introduce swimming and water safety skills	Usually grade-school children, but may be preschoolers, teens, or adults	Varies, but primarily 30-minute classes	N/A
Aquatic Safety	Safety for nonswimmers	Teens and adults	4–6 hours	N/A
Aquatic Personal Safety and Survival	Safety for swimmers	Age 11 and up	8 hours	N/A
Aquatic Safety Assistant	Assisting lifeguards	Age 14 and up	16 hours	Every 2 years
Aquatic Leadership	Aquatic leadership	Ages 11–15	Varies	N/A
Lifeguard	Become a lifeguard	Age 16 and up	30 hours	Every 2 years
Lifeguard Instructor	Train and certify lifeguards	Age 18 and up	18 hours	Every 3 years
Lifeguard Trainer	Train and certify lifeguard instructors	Age 21 and up	23 hours	N/A

Review Questions

1. List several types of incidents that lead to drowning deaths or aquatic injuries.
2. What makes YMCA aquatic safety programs different from those of other organizations?
3. List five characteristics of a good lifeguard.
4. What are the certification requirements for the YMCA Lifeguard course?
5. What other certifications must be maintained to keep YMCA Lifeguard certification valid?

two

Aquatic Personal Safety and Survival Skills

Aquatic activities are popular forms of recreation, but they do carry a degree of danger. You should know how to take care of yourself in the water because accidents can happen even to good swimmers.

▷ **In This Chapter, You'll Learn How To**

- use a variety of techniques to stay afloat,
- understand and handle physical conditions that may endanger you as a swimmer,
- perform surface dives and survival strokes,
- perform off-duty rescues,
- follow safe boating procedures,
- follow safe procedures for riding personal watercraft,
- stay safe when rafting or tubing,
- avoid the dangers of low-head dams,
- stay safe when swimming at the beach,
- escape from a submerged vehicle, and
- rescue yourself or others who have fallen through ice.

STAYING AFLOAT

All people who work or play on or in the water owe it to themselves and to their companions to know how to stay afloat in deep water for an extended period. Doing this requires some knowledge of buoyancy and training in how to perform the survival float and how to tread water.

Buoyancy

Buoyancy is the ability to float in water. Three concepts can help you understand how the body floats: Archimedes' principle and specific gravity, vital capacity, and center of mass/center of buoyancy.

Archimedes' Principle

When an object is lowered into water, it pushes away, or displaces, the water that was in that space. Whether the object floats or sinks depends on which is heavier, the object or the water it displaced. This is called Archimedes' principle.

To give you an example, if a 60-pound girl is floating in a water tank as shown in figure 2.1, the amount of water that she displaces weighs 60 pounds. Why is it that a 60-pound girl will float, while a 60-pound stone will sink? The stone is more compact and dense, while the girl has air space in her lungs and soft body parts such as fat. Some lean people do have trouble floating because their bodies are dense, but many can float because the air in their lungs is lighter than the water displaced.

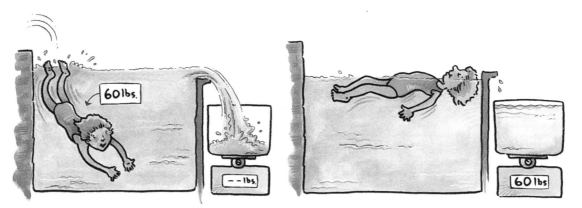

Figure 2.1 Archimedes' principle in action.

A cubic foot of fresh water weighs 62.4 pounds. Any object that weighs more than that per cubic foot sinks in fresh water; if it weighs less per cubic foot, it floats. If the weight is equal to water, the object remains suspended between the surface and the bottom.

To make such comparisons easy, we use the concept of *specific gravity*, which is the ratio of the weight of an object to the weight of fresh water the object would displace if completely submerged. Table 2.1 lists the specific gravities of fresh water, salt water, and the major components of the body: bone, muscle, and fat.

Something with a specific gravity higher than fresh water (1.0) will sink in fresh water; an object with a specific gravity lower than 1.0 will float. The same concept applies to salt water, but because salt water has a higher specific gravity of 1.025 (it weighs more than fresh water), objects are slightly more buoyant in salt water.

Notice in table 2.1 that the specific gravities of bone and muscle are higher than 1.0, so bone and muscle alone would not float in fresh water. If you placed a bone with no visible fat in a pan of water, it would sink to the bottom of the pan.

Figure 2.1 and figure 2.2 reprinted, by permission, from National Council of Young Men's Christian Associations of the United States of America, 1999, *Teaching Swimming Fundamentals*, (Champaign, IL: Human Kinetics), 110, 111.

Table 2.1	Specific Gravities of Water and Body Components	

Element	Specific gravity
Fresh water	1.0
Salt water	1.025
Bone	1.9
Muscle	1.085
Fat	0.78–0.98

People, however, are not made of bone and muscle alone. They also have body fat, with the amount varying from person to person. With a specific gravity of 0.78 to 0.98, fat will float in fresh water. So the more fat people have, the lower their specific gravities are and the more buoyant they are in water. Most people have enough fat to help them stay afloat—only 1 person in 20 is unable to float.

Vital Capacity

Another factor that influences buoyancy is vital capacity, the amount of air that the lungs can hold. For most people, vital capacity plays an important part in floating. By taking a big breath, you expand the volume of your chest, which lowers your specific gravity and makes you more buoyant because air is much lighter than water. You can demonstrate the value of vital capacity by taking a deep breath and floating. Observe your position in the water. Then breathe out as much air as possible and float. What happened? With less air in your lungs, you either floated lower in the water or sank below the surface.

What this means is that you should breathe frequently to maintain your buoyancy; don't hold your breath until you are gasping for air. With greater buoyancy you'll be able to float and swim more efficiently.

Center of Mass/Center of Buoyancy

Center of mass is the point around which your body's weight is evenly balanced. In most people it is located a few inches below the navel. The center of buoyancy, the point around which your body's weight will float, generally is located at chest level in the lungs. By knowing where these centers are (see figure 2.2), you can learn to balance your buoyancy and your stability around them.

You can change your center of buoyancy by adjusting your center of mass. While floating on your back, experiment by slowly raising your arms above your head and bending your knees. (If you move too quickly, you'll create momentum that will cause your feet to sink.) If you find that your legs sink in your floating position, it may help to raise your hands out of the water, moving more weight toward your head. Or bend your legs to bring your feet under your buttocks. These actions cause your center of mass to move toward your shoulders and your center of buoyancy to move toward your hips. These changes make your hips float to the surface.

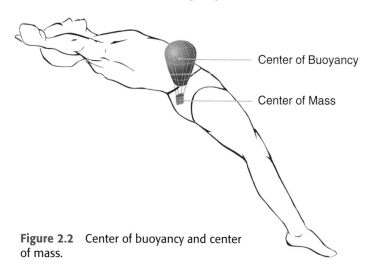

Center of Buoyancy

Center of Mass

Figure 2.2 Center of buoyancy and center of mass.

Resting Stroke

The resting stroke makes use of your body's natural buoyancy to allow you to stay afloat with little effort or use of energy. Since Fred Lanoue developed his program for teaching the survival float in 1936, many variations on the technique have been experimented with and found to be successful.

The resting stroke technique is recommended for situations when you are in warm water and not wearing a personal flotation device (PFD). The method recommended for floating for a long period while wearing a PFD is called the *HELP position*, which is described on page 30.

The resting stroke lets you float in a relaxed position almost endlessly, even without the use of your legs and arms. The most common procedure is illustrated in figure 2.3.

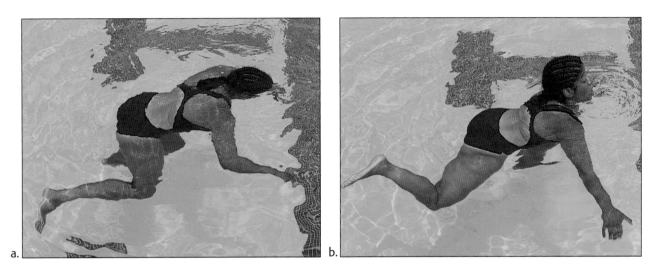

a.   b.

c.

Here's how to do it: After taking a breath, let your body submerge, with your arms and legs relaxed and hanging down. Your back should be near the surface. This position will be easy to assume because the air in your lungs will lift your back up.

Hold your breath only as long as you feel comfortable. There is no need to wait until you desperately need a breath. When you decide to breathe, bring your arms close to the surface, separate your legs as you do when starting a scissors kick, and start exhaling. Press down on the water with your hands, complete the scissors kick, and lift your head above the water to breathe. Only your face should come out of the water. Take a quick breath and return to your relaxed starting position.

Figure 2.3   The resting stroke.

Because your head is submerged in the floating position, you will lose body heat while doing the resting stroke. In cold water and cold air temperatures, this heat loss can lead to hypothermia (described on page 184). Heat loss is less of a concern if the water and surrounding air are warm.

Treading Water

Treading water, shown in figure 2.4, is an important survival skill that should be mastered by everyone. When you tread water, your arms move in a wide in-and-out motion with your palms turned down at a 30- to 35-degree angle. This movement keeps constant water pressure against your hands and lets your body maintain its position in the water.

a.

b.

c.

Figure 2.4   Treading water.

a.

Several types of kicks can be used in treading water. For the single scissors kick, the same leg always goes forward and the other leg always goes backward. As the legs are brought together, they provide a strong upward lift. The double scissors kick is the same, except that the legs alternate their positions forward and back. The breaststroke kick performed vertically and the eggbeater, or rotary, kick (see figure 2.5) provide the most consistent support of all the kicks, although they may be the most difficult for some people to perform. To do the eggbeater kick, alternating legs, you pull one heel toward your seat, turn your toes to the outside, and kick your leg around and to the front. This kick is very similar to the breaststroke kick, but the legs work alternately rather than both at once.

b.

c.

Figure 2.5 The eggbeater, or rotary, kick.

PHYSICAL CONDITIONS THAT MAY ENDANGER SWIMMERS

As a swimmer you need to be aware of physical conditions that can cause you discomfort or put you at risk while swimming. Your ability to react correctly and calmly under these circumstances will greatly enhance your safety and enjoyment.

Panic

Panic is an emotional state in which someone is overcome by a sudden fear and loses the ability to help himself or herself. Panic usually occurs when a person is faced with a seemingly life-threatening emergency. For example, someone who gets a cramp while swimming and does not know what a cramp is or how to release it is likely to panic, which could lead to drowning. Panic is believed to be a major contributor to drowning accidents.

When you are in the water, practice the skills outlined in this chapter and throughout the book. Once they become second nature, you will have the tools to help yourself and others. In an emergency, take a deep breath, call on your knowledge of how to handle the situation, and move forward confidently. You can be in control of any situation.

Ear Squeeze

Ear squeeze is the pain you feel within your ear when you submerge in the water. The increased water pressure is greater in the outer ear than in the middle ear, stretching the tympanic membrane (eardrum) inward and causing pain. Try one of these methods to alleviate this problem (Maas and Sipperly, 1998):

- Pinch off your nose, keep your mouth shut, and attempt to blow out gently through your nose.
- Swallow.
- Reposition your tongue.
- Use a combination of these three methods.

These actions increase the pressure in the throat, which in turn opens the eustachian tube that connects the throat and middle ear, increasing the pressure in the middle ear. When the pressure on the outer ear and middle ear are equalized, the eardrum returns to its normal position and the pain stops.

Be sure to take time to equalize pressure in your ears when you descend in the water. The YMCA Scuba program recommends equalizing pressure at every 2 to 5 feet of descent or whenever necessary to relieve pain or discomfort. Failure to equalize could rupture the eardrum, causing potential hearing loss, loss of balance or orientation, and other complications. It is not safe to swim with such an injury until it is fully healed. It is also unwise to swim underwater when you have a cold or the flu. When your eustachian tubes are clogged, air cannot move through the tubes into the middle ear as you try to equalize, and you could risk a serious ear injury.

Sinus Squeeze

The pressure associated with increasing water depth can cause sharp pain in the sinus area (the upper teeth, cheeks, and above the eyes) as well as the ears when you have nasal congestion. This pain may occur within a few feet from the surface. If you have a bad cold, your sinuses will already be swollen shut. This makes it difficult for your body to equalize the air pressure in your sinuses. We recommend that you not submerge when your sinuses are inflamed, as it may cause severe pain and may damage the sinus membranes. Sometimes nose drops or decongestants can alleviate symptoms, but these remedies can wear off or cause drowsiness. It is best to stay on the surface when you have a severe cold, sinusitis, or any other inflammation of the sinuses.

Cramps

The actual process of how cramps occur is not fully understood. Cramps can be triggered by dehydration or by a lack of sodium (salt), calcium, potassium, or oxygen. The lack of oxygen is one of the most accepted theories for the occurrence of cramps in swimming. Lactic acid builds up in the muscle as a result of the lack of oxygen and causes the muscle to contract beyond its normal range. When enough lactic acid accumulates, the muscle fibers contract and stop functioning, resulting in considerable pain. This condition is called *contracture*.

In the 1930s through the 1950s, cramps were blamed as the major cause of drownings, but they are not life-threatening if you remain calm. As in any situation, panic can cause a swimmer to drown. Most cramps occur in the calf, foot, or hand because they are the body parts most active in swimming. They are also the body parts farthest away from the heart, and as a result they receive oxygenated blood last, which increases the probability of a cramp.

If you experience a cramp, the first thing to remember is to stay calm. If you can, leave the water; it is much easier to release a cramp on land. If you must remain in the water, relax as much as possible.

To relieve the pain of a cramp, you first need to stretch the cramping muscle. The stretching should be slow and steady, not bouncy. Hold the stretch for as long as is comfortable. If the cramp is severe, the pain may initially get worse as you begin to stretch, but it will subside. Continue to stretch the muscle for the prescribed time. If the pain is still evident, continue stretching for an additional period.

After stretching the cramp, if you are still in the water, bend forward as if you were survival floating and massage the cramped muscle gently, massaging it toward the heart, not away from it. This will increase the blood flow to the area and bring more oxygen to the muscles, relieving the cramp.

Once you have released the cramp, don't go right back to swimming. Give the muscle time to recover. If you have been very active in warm weather, you may need to replace body fluids. If this is the case, stay out of the water to rest the cramping muscles and drink plenty of water. Remember, returning to activity too soon will result in a speedy return of your cramp.

Stomach Discomfort

Most everyone has heard that you shouldn't go swimming for an hour after you eat or you'll get a stomach cramp. The time guideline may be common sense, but the warning is not particularly accurate. It appears that drownings that have occurred when people have gone swimming after a large meal have been the result not of cramping but of vomiting the meal and breathing in the vomit.

How soon you can go into the water after a meal depends on several factors:

- How much you ate
- What you ate
- Your physical condition
- How fatigued you are
- The water temperature
- How active you'll be in the water

After eating a large meal, most people don't feel like swimming or participating in any vigorous activity for an hour or more. This is nature's way of keeping the body quiet so that the digestive system can start the process of absorbing the food. Normally when you begin swimming, blood is diverted from your stomach to the muscles that need energy to maintain activity, which slows your digestive and absorption functions.

For young children it is usually wise to establish a minimum resting time between eating a meal and swimming. Older swimmers tend to regulate themselves well; if they feel uncomfortable, they get out of the water or slow their activity. All swimmers should recognize an uncomfortable feeling in the stomach as nature's warning and make appropriate decisions regarding their activity level.

STROKES FOR SURVIVAL SITUATIONS

Several strokes can enable you to swim to safety in a survival situation efficiently, conserving your energy. Because these strokes should be performed with your head out of the water to try to maintain body heat and your arms underwater to conserve energy, the way they are performed in a survival situation differs from the techniques you may have learned in a swimming class.

In a survival situation in which you would need to swim a long distance, first try to find something to help you float—a piece of wood or some other buoyant object. Then decide whether your chances of survival are better if you swim or if you stay in one place and try to conserve body heat (see pages 30–31 for flotation positions that conserve body heat). Water under 70 degrees Fahrenheit quickly cools the body, putting you in danger of hypothermia (see page 184).

Elementary Backstroke

The elementary backstroke (illustrated in figure 2.6) is a very comfortable stroke for most swimmers. Because this stroke requires the head to be in the water, it is recommended for only short distances.

To do the elementary backstroke, initiate the kick by bending your knees, pulling your heels toward your seat, and turning your toes out. As you bend your knees, pull your arms up your sides with elbows down and palms toward the body. Stretch your arms outward slightly above your shoulders. Then kick by whipping the legs out and around, then together, while pulling your arms back to your sides. You might use the following cues to coordinate your stroke: up, out, together.

a.

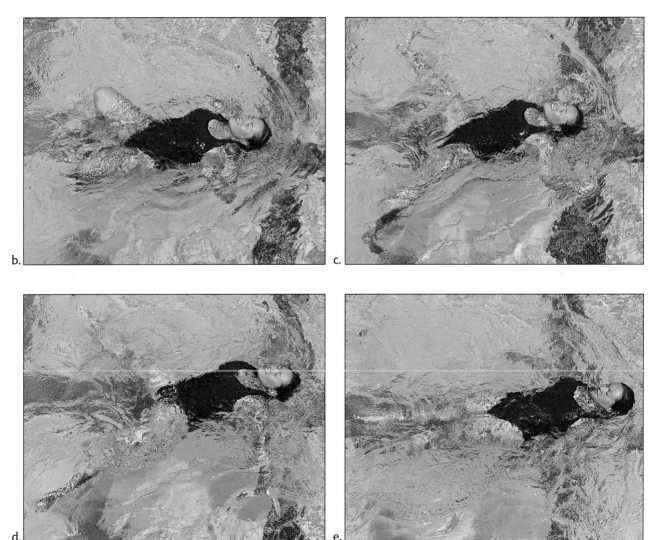

b.

c.

d.

e.

Figure 2.6 Elementary backstroke.

a.

Breaststroke

The breaststroke (see figure 2.7), a useful survival stroke in either calm or choppy water, is initiated from a front glide position in which your arms and legs are both fully extended. Keep your head out of the water and look forward. Keeping elbows high, press your hands outward and downward, moving in a motion that resembles half of a heart. At the end of the pull, press your elbows toward your sides, bring your hands together in front of your chest, and reach again to the front.

To kick in the breaststroke, pull your heels toward your seat and turn your toes out to the sides. Kick the legs together in a circular motion. The coordination of the stroke is pull, kick, and glide.

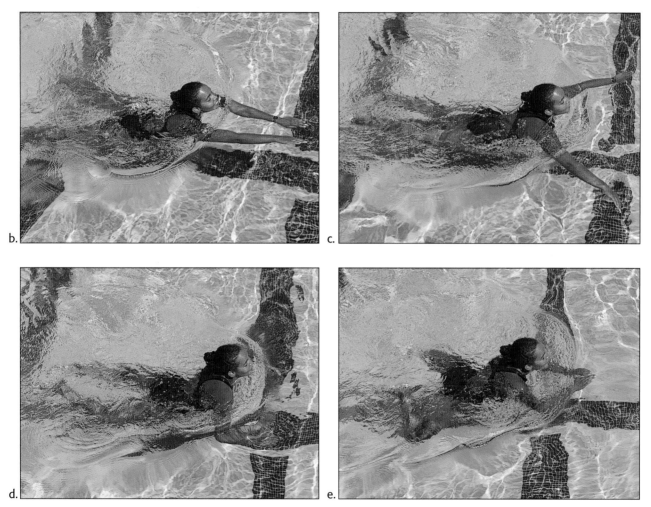

b.

c.

d.

e.

Figure 2.7 The breaststroke.

Sidestroke

In a survival situation, the sidestroke (figure 2.8) should also be done with most of your head out of the water. To begin, assume a glide position on your side, with the bottom arm stretched above your head in the water and the top arm along your side. Lean your head to the side with your ear in the water.

For the stroke, pull your bottom arm down toward your chest, elbow bent, and then turn the arm so the hand is palm up and stretch the arm back to the front. At the same time that you pull with the bottom arm, the top arm recovers. Then bend the elbow, reach with

a.

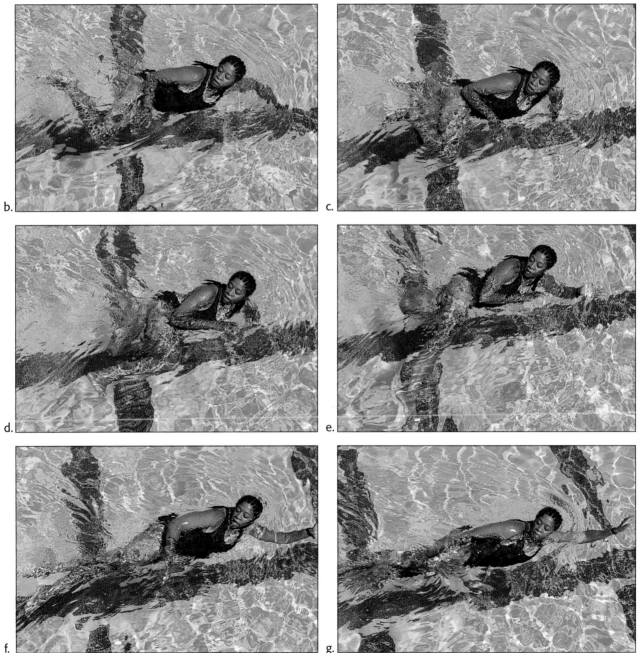

b.

c.

d.

e.

f.

g.

Figure 2.8   The sidestroke.

the top hand toward the opposite shoulder, and push the water toward your feet. The arms work in opposition, that is, while one is stroking, the other is recovering.

The kick follows the top arm: As the arm recovers, the legs recover; as the arm strokes, the legs kick. To kick, pull your heels toward your seat. Stretch your top leg forward and your bottom leg backward, then kick both legs together.

SURFACE DIVES

To get below the surface or away from danger, you may need to use a surface dive. This can be either a feet-first dive or an arm-over-arm dive. The feet-first dive is best used when you are not sure of the water depth or the presence of debris; if you strike something, the feet-first dive is less likely to lead to spinal injury than a head-first (arm-over-arm) dive.

Whenever you perform a surface dive, be sure to equalize your ears regularly and often. Do it first at the surface, then every 2 to 5 feet during descent.

Feet-First Surface Dive

Follow these procedures to execute a feet-first surface dive (figure 2.9):

1. Begin from a vertical position.
2. Stretch one leg forward and one back. With one large kick, snap your legs together and push down on the water as you bring your arms down to your sides. This should bring you up out of the water, and gravity will then pull you downward. Keep your body streamlined.
3. Use a straight arm pulling motion, bringing your arms above your head with palms facing up.
4. If you need to go even deeper, slide your arms back to your sides and repeat the upward lift.

Figure 2.9   Feet-first surface dive.

Arm-Over-Arm Surface Dive

The arm-over-arm surface dive allows you to perform a head-first dive in a continuous motion. Depending on your ability and strength, you can do this dive in either a tuck or a pike position. The tuck position (figure 2.10) requires less strength because it shortens the distance between the hips and feet. The pike position (figure 2.11) allows the legs to go higher out of the water, which speeds the rate of descent. Follow these steps:

1. As your right arm recovers from a crawl stroke, leave your left hand next to your left leg.
2. Reach down toward the bottom with your right hand while simultaneously ducking your head.
3. Pull your right hand back toward your right thigh.
4. Turn your palms down and sweep both hands toward the bottom. This helps lift your legs out of the water. Your hands and arms will end up over your head. Pull both hands back to your thighs for a faster descent. Recover your hands above your head and pull to thighs again, if necessary.

a.

b.

c.

d.

Figure 2.10 Arm-over-arm surface dive from a tuck position.

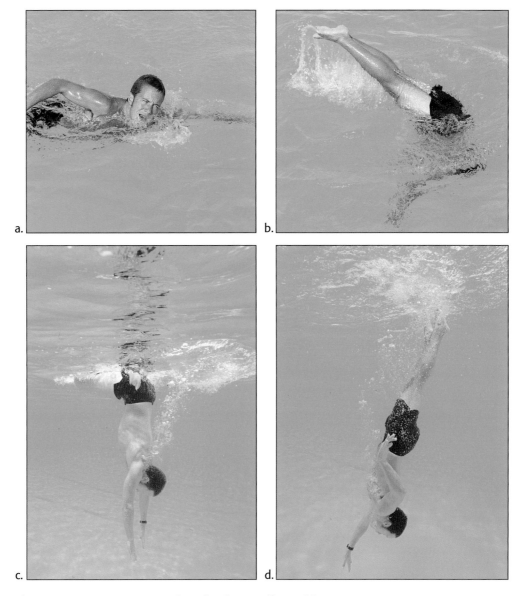

Figure 2.11   Arm-over-arm surface dive from a pike position.

OFF-DUTY RESCUES

Many YMCA lifeguards have asked the question, "How can I rescue a distressed or near-drowning victim in situations in which I don't have equipment?" Such situations can occur during leisure time whenever a lifeguard is near water. You may feel a moral obligation to render assistance in these situations, even when equipment or backup is not available.

Of course, whenever possible, you should swim only in guarded areas. However, this is not always an option, especially during scuba diving, boating, surfing, water skiing, and other aquatic pursuits (unless they are conducted in a formal instruction program such as one that might be offered at a YMCA camp).

The simplest solution is to take a rescue tube or buoy and a pocket mask with you whenever you plan leisure activities around water. If space is limited in your car, boat, or other watercraft, consider taking an inflatable rescue tube, such as the one being used in figure 2.12. Currently two inexpensive models are available, one that can be inflated orally and one that uses a carbon dioxide cartridge for quick inflation.

Figure 2.12 A lifeguard using an inflatable rescue tube.

If you see a distressed swimmer, try to avoid being grabbed by attempting rescue with a reaching, throwing, or wading assist (see chapter 7). Another possibility is a swimming extension rescue using a towel, canoe paddle, ring buoy, tree branch, spare tire, or other similar item. If the distressed swimmer seems panicked, you may be able to get her or him to swim to safety with encouragement. Swim near the distressed swimmer, but not close enough for contact, and coach her or him (Brewster, 1995).

If you are in the water, a distressed swimmer may grab you from in front or behind to stay above water and get air. If this should happen, try to stay calm and react quickly, as it will directly affect your safety. One option is to simply go limp and submerge. Another option is the submerge defense, which is to take a breath and tuck your chin into your shoulder, then find the swimmer's elbow bend and, rotating toward the elbow, submerge using a feet-first surface dive (see figure 2.13). If this is unsuccessful, push up on the pressure point of the swimmer's elbow and push the swimmer away from you; swim away 8 to 10 feet if necessary. Be sure not to surface too close to the person or you could find yourself in danger again.

a.   b.

Figure 2.13 Submerge defense.

(continued)

c.

d.

Figure 2.13 *(continued)*

If you should need to rescue a passive victim on the surface, remember that boaters, water skiers, and scuba divers may have some type of flotation device on them. If they do, you can use it to assist both yourself and the victim.

If you have to rescue a victim who is not wearing a flotation device, try these steps (Brewster, 1995):

- Call for assistance. Get someone to go to the nearest phone and call the emergency medical services.
- Look for a piece of equipment to use in performing the rescue.
- Swim around behind the victim, making sure to remain safely outside arm's reach.
- Check for spinal injury (see chapter 10). If the person does not seem to have a spinal injury, use a single or double armpit tow (see page 139) to bring the victim to a safe place where his or her airway, breathing, and circulation can be assessed and CPR begun if necessary.
- If the victim is clothed, try grabbing the victim's collar and towing him or her, using a sidestroke. You also can use the single or double armpit tow (figure 2.14; also see page 139) to bring the victim to shore. This tow helps keep the victim's head and shoulders supported above the water.

If you feel you are in danger at any time, you should swim away or use the submerge defense and reassess the situation.

Figure 2.14 A double armpit tow.

BOATING SAFETY

Boating is a popular aquatic recreational activity, but it can be hazardous if participants don't take some precautions and don't know what to do if they end up overboard. The following are some basics of safe boating.

Personal Flotation Devices

By federal law, a personal flotation device (PFD), such as a life jacket or vest, is required for each person on board any small craft or boat of open construction. The U.S. Coast Guard is the public agency that establishes minimum standards for PFDs.

Purchase only those personal flotation devices that bear the label "U.S. Coast Guard-approved." Other flotation devices on the market, designed to serve as teaching aids, are good for teaching situations and may be used as aids to assist swimmers, but they should not be relied on as lifesaving devices. U.S. Coast Guard-approved devices have proven and tested buoyancy.

PFDs can be buoyant or inflatable. They come in many sizes and styles, allowing people to choose the ones that are most comfortable and most appropriate for the situation. The Coast Guard approves five types of PFDs (see figure 2.15):

- Type I PFDs are used for off-shore vessels, and are meant for situations in which rescue may be slow in coming. Most commercial craft use these PFDs because they are the most buoyant, are good in rough waters, and can hold an unconscious person in an upright or slightly reclined position.

- Type II PFDs also turn unconscious people to safe positions faceup in the water. However, they are designed for use on inland waters where the water is calm and a speedy rescue is possible.

- Type III PFDs are classified as flotation aids. They do not right someone who is unconscious, but they are very comfortable for the wearer. Many water skiers use this type of vest. These PFDs are best used in calm inland waters and other places where the chances for a rapid rescue are good.

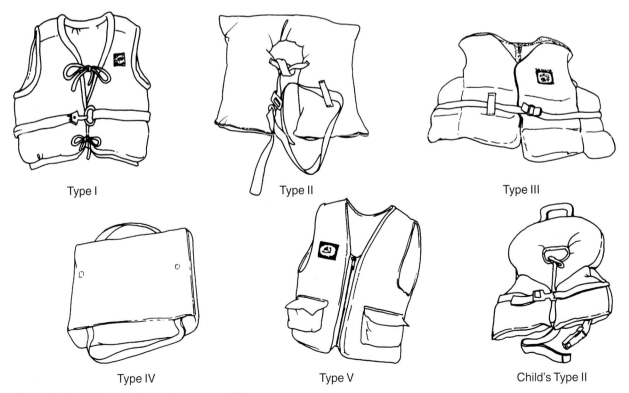

Type I   Type II   Type III

Type IV   Type V   Child's Type II

Figure 2.15   U.S. Coast Guard–approved PFDs.

Figure 2.16   Testing a life jacket.

- Type IV PFDs are throwable devices, such as boat cushions, ring buoys, and other devices designed to be held, not worn. They can be thrown to victims in case of emergency.
- Type V PFDs are designed for special use. The label on the PFD will specify its approved uses. This category of PFD includes whitewater vests, board sailing or wind surfing vests, and work vests.

Besides keeping you afloat, a PFD will keep you warmer in colder water, helping to prevent hypothermia (see page 184). The high-visibility color of your PFD will make it easier for rescuers to find you as well.

Your life jacket should fit properly, with all zippers, straps, ties, and snaps secured correctly. According to the National Safe Boating Council and the U.S. Coast Guard (1997), you can test whether your life jacket fits by putting it on and walking into the water up to your neck, then lifting your legs and tilting your head back to a relaxed floating position (figure 2.16). Your mouth should be out of the water, and you should float without any physical effort. If your jacket rides up, try securing it more tightly to your body. If it still rides up, you may need a smaller life jacket or a different type.

Heat Escape Lessening Posture

If you should fall out of a boat into the water far from land, your first concern should be keeping warm until help arrives. Immersion hypothermia, the cooling of the body from suspension in cold water, is dangerous and potentially life-threatening.

Don't remove your clothes in cold water to help you float. Your clothes serve as insulation against the cold water and help preserve your body heat. Your survival efforts will be aided by doing all you can to keep warm: keeping your head out of the water and protecting the front of your neck (near the carotid artery), your armpits, the front of your rib cage, and your groin. The heat escape lessening posture (HELP) was developed to assist you in protecting these four areas (see figure 2.17). Wearing a PFD that is Coast Guard-approved will enable you to assume this position more easily and effectively than if you're wearing an unapproved device.

Figure 2.17   HELP position.

The HELP position is accomplished in the following way. While wearing a PFD,

- float in a tuck position;
- squeeze your legs together, crossing them at the ankles;
- press your arms against your sides and hold the PFD across your chest; and
- keep your head above water.

When three or more people find themselves immersed in cold water, huddling in a group may help them survive (see figure 2.18). Shared body heat and greater coverage of the heat loss areas, along with moral support, are the advantages of the huddle. The position, however, can be difficult to maintain.

Figure 2.18   Huddle position.

Children are more susceptible to heat loss when immersed. Sandwiching the child between huddling adults will help conserve the child's body heat. The body heat generated by the group should cause the water in the area between them to be slightly warmer, thus prolonging the child's survival.

Rules for Boating

Boating is a fun way to enjoy the water, but it also can be dangerous. Here are some facts about boating accidents:

- Most boating accidents are caused by the operator.
- Fatalities most often involve craft smaller than 16 feet long.
- Most drownings happen to people in boats who don't wear PFDs.
- Drownings usually occur when boaters unexpectedly end up in the water when they fall overboard or the boat capsizes or collides with another object or boat.

Safe boating in large part means using common sense, but it's easy when you're having fun to forget to follow some simple rules:

- If you plan to boat, know how to swim and learn basic first aid, CPR, and boating skills.
- Before you leave shore, be sure you know how to use your craft and what emergency procedures to follow.
- Leave word with someone on shore as to when you are leaving, where you are going, and when you plan to return.
- Stay alert to weather conditions. Listen to a weather report before you leave and take a portable radio with you for periodic checks. If bad weather arises, quickly move to the nearest shore or safe harbor.
- Have everyone in the boat, including children, wear a Coast Guard-approved PFD.

- Closely supervise children in a boat.
- Don't stand up in a small craft.
- Don't boat after dark or in low-visibility conditions without navigation lights.
- Don't overload your craft. Don't exceed the load limit on the boat's capacity plate and be sure to distribute the load evenly.
- Anchor your boat only from the bow. A small boat can be swamped if the anchor is attached to the stern (rear).
- For each nonswimmer, also have a swimmer in the boat at all times.
- Return all equipment to the boathouse. Tell management if any equipment needs repair.
- Don't drink alcohol in or around boats.
- Attend a course on safe boating. Free courses are offered by volunteers from the Coast Guard Auxiliary, the Power Squadron, and the American Red Cross. To find the courses offered in your area, call the BOAT/U.S. Foundation CourseLine, 800-366-BOAT. Your local YMCA also may offer a safe boating course.

If you need more information regarding safe boating or PFDs, contact your local safe boating authority or one of the following:

- Boating Safety Hotline, 800-368-5647
- U.S. Coast Guard, **www.uscgboating.org**
- U.S. Coast Guard Auxiliary, **www.cgaux.org**
- U.S. Power Squadron, **www.usps.org**
- National Safe Boating Council, **www.safeboatingcouncil.org**

PERSONAL WATERCRAFT SAFETY

Personal watercraft are crafts powered by a waterjet pump rather than an external propellor. They are operated by someone positioned on, rather than within, the confines of the hull. Some are for single riders, while others can carry two or more people (Royal Life Saving Society Canada, 1995).

According to the Personal Watercraft Industry Association (PWIA) (n.d.), the U.S. Coast Guard classifies personal watercraft (PWC) as Class A boats (any boat with a hull less than 16 feet in length). This means that PWCs are subject to most of the same rules and requirements as other powerboats. A PWC is a boat, and you're the captain. You are legally in command of a powerboat, and you're bound by the boating rules of the water, as well as the laws and traditions of safe boating. Know the boating laws and regulations for your state.

The PWIA also notes the following:

- Federal regulations require all PWCs to be registered and to have an identification number. When your registration application is approved, you'll receive your certificate of number, title, and validation sticker (if applicable in your state). Follow state and federal guidelines for displaying validation and registration numbers.
- You must have a PFD for each person on board. Choose U.S. Coast Guard-approved PFDs that fit properly and wear them. Coast Guard and state rules also require you to have a fire extinguisher on board.
- Many PWCs have a lanyard connected to the start/stop switch. If your craft has such a switch, it won't start unless the lanyard is attached. Never start your engine without attaching the lanyard to your PFD or wrist. That way, if you fall off, the engine will automatically stop so your craft won't travel far from you and you can swim to it easily.
- It also is recommended that each rider wear eye protection, a wetsuit, footwear, and gloves.

According to the Royal Life Saving Society Canada (1995), most PWC injuries result from collisions caused by rider carelessness, overconfidence, or inexperience. Riding takes practice, so allow yourself plenty of time to learn to operate your PWC. Always use your PWC safely and responsibly, following the manufacturer's directions. (Some manufacturers recommend that you be at least 16 years old before operating a PWC.)

Here are some tips* for safe operation of a PWC (Royal Life Saving Society Canada, 1995):

- Boating and booze don't mix. Alcohol impairs your ability to make good, quick decisions. This ability is critical when you are operating a fast and maneuverable PWC.
- Know your craft. Study the manufacturer's manual and practice handling your craft under experienced supervision and in open water well away from other boaters.
- Take a boating safety course. Learn the common boating rules, regulations, and safe practices.
- Look out. Ride defensively. Collisions with other boats or stationary objects like rafts or docks are the number one cause of PWC injuries.
- Watch the weather. Check the weather forecast before starting out. Be alert for the wave, wind, and cloud changes that signal the approach of bad weather.
- Be prepared for cold water. Cold water robs body heat 25 times faster than air of the same temperature. If you fall off your craft into cold water, reboard immediately.
- Know the area. Do not assume the water is clear of obstructions. Rocks, shoals, sandbars, or submerged pilings can seriously damage your craft or injure those on board. Check marine charts and stay in marked channels.
- Carry safety equipment. Besides having the required PFDs and a fire extinguisher, you also should carry a sound signaling device like a whistle, a tow rope, and, when operating on a large body of water, some small flares in a watertight container.
- Don't ride at night. Most personal watercraft are not made with the navigation lights that the law requires for night riding.

RAFTING AND TUBING SAFETY

Rafting and tubing have become more and more popular as recreation in recent years. Lifeguards are rarely available for such activities, so you must take responsibility for your own safety. Keep the following guidelines in mind:

- Have each person wear a Coast Guard-approved PFD.
- Prepare before you go. Know the area you will be in—its dangers and its calm spots.
- Know and follow the local laws governing rafting and tubing. If you don't know them, contact the local conservation or park department.
- Be sure you have been trained to handle your raft or tube safely. If you have never rafted or tubed before, visit with an experienced person before starting your own expedition. Many park districts and outdoor or wilderness stores offer training or can suggest effective training programs.
- Check your equipment before entering the water.
- Be aware of other watercraft in the area.
- Carry bailers, sponges, extra paddles, a first aid kit, and other safety items.
- Avoid rafting or tubing after heavy rain.
- Avoid alcohol. You need your best judgment to remain safe.

If you end up in river rapids, walk through them if they aren't too strong by keeping your weight low in the water, with your legs apart to form a wide base of support. Don't stand up straight. If you find yourself in strong river rapids, remain calm. Roll onto your back and float downstream, feet-first to protect yourself from head injury. Once you have escaped the rapids, swim to shore. You might need to swim diagonally with the current, rather than directly against it.

*Reproduced with permission of the Lifesaving Society, Canada's Lifeguarding Experts, **www.lifesavingsociety.com**

AQUATIC SAFETY NEAR A LOW-HEAD DAM

The most dangerous hazard on a river is a low-head dam. Water goes over the dam and creates a back current or undertow (figure 2.19) that can pull a boat into the turbulence and capsize it. The current can trap and hold a person or a boat (Pennsylvania Fish and Boat Commission, 2000). The following are dangers as well:

- Shallow water below the dam can quickly become deep when the floodgates are opened. A wall of water is created as the water passes through the gates.
- Currents near hydroelectric power plants are strong enough to pull swimmers into and through the dam.
- Swimmers may surface at the boil line only to find themselves sucked back into the water pouring over the dam (Bechdel and Slim, 1997).
- Swimmers or boaters can be caught in debris or by exposed steel bars on the dam, or they may be seriously injured by being pulled over a dam and trapped in the current at its base.

Watch for low-head dams when you swim or boat in a river. Many dams are not marked, and some are difficult to see from upstream (Pennsylvania Fish and Boat Commission, 2000).

Take special precautions when you swim or boat near a dam. In water near a dam, look for instruction signs and obey them. If there are warning signals, act immediately. Stay away from floodgates or spillways, which should be marked with buoys and patrolled regularly. For your safety, make sure that you don't get too close to the dam.

If you should get caught in currents below a dam, follow these tips (Royal Life Saving Society Canada, 1994):

- Stay calm and don't fight the current.
- Grab onto and hold a large object, such as a rock or a boat, and wait for help.
- Watch for and avoid becoming entangled in debris. Tree branches are particularly dangerous.
- If you are unable to hold onto a large object, you have two choices. One is to swim underwater at the bottom of the hydraulic current and away from the dam. Allow the current to carry you to the dam and to pull you under. When you get to the bottom, you can swim with the downstream current to safety. The other alternative is to try to move to shore along the face of the dam. This may work if the shore is close enough and if someone is there to help you over the dam's vertical section or onto the shore.

Cross section of lowhead dam

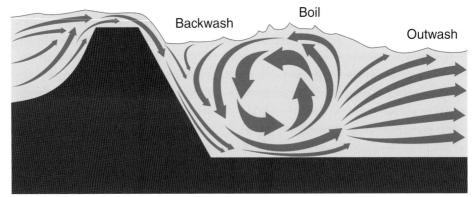

Figure 2.19 Current at the base of a low-head dam.

Illustrated by Ted Walke, Pennsylvania Fish and Boat Commission

BEACH SAFETY*

A day at the beach usually means carefree fun, but lake and ocean waters can hold some serious dangers. To enjoy the beach and protect yourself, follow some common-sense safety rules.

- *Swim near a lifeguard.* USLA statistics over a 10-year period show that the chance of drowning at a beach without lifeguard protection is almost five times as great as drowning at a beach with lifeguards. The USLA has calculated the chance that a person will drown while attending a beach protected by USLA-affiliated lifeguards at 1 in 18 million.

- *Learn to swim.* Learning to swim is the best defense against drowning. Teach children to swim at an early age. Children who are not taught when they are very young tend to avoid swim instruction as they age, probably due to embarrassment. Swimming instruction is a crucial step to protecting children from injury or death.

- *Never swim alone.* Many drownings involve single swimmers. When you swim with a buddy, if one of you has a problem, the other may be able to help, including signaling for assistance from others. At least have someone on shore watching you.

- *Don't fight the current.* USLA has found that some 80% of rescues by USLA-affiliated lifeguards at ocean beaches are caused by rip currents. These currents are formed by surf and gravity. Surf pushes water up the slope of the beach and gravity pulls it back, which can create concentrated rivers of water moving offshore. Some people mistakenly call this an undertow, but there is no undercurrent, just an offshore current. If you are caught in a rip current, don't fight it by trying to swim directly to shore. Instead, swim parallel to shore until you feel the current weaken, then swim to shore. Most rip currents are narrow, and a short swim parallel to shore will bring you to safety.

- *Swim sober.* Alcohol is a major factor in drowning. Alcohol can reduce body temperature and impair swimming ability. Perhaps more importantly, both alcohol and drugs impair good judgment, which may cause people to take risks they would not otherwise take.

- *Leash your board.* Use surfboards and bodyboards only with a leash. Leashes are usually attached to the board and the ankle or wrist. They are available in most shops where surfboards and bodyboards are sold or rented. With a leash, you will not become separated from the flotation device. You also may want to consider getting a breakaway leash. A few drownings have been attributed to leashes becoming entangled in underwater obstructions. A breakaway leash helps you avoid this problem.

- *Don't float where you can't swim.* Nonswimmers often use flotation devices, like inflatable rafts, to go offshore. If they fall off the devices, they can quickly drown. No one should use a flotation device unless he or she is able to swim. Use of a leash is not enough because a nonswimmer may panic and be unable to get back to the flotation device, even with a leash. The only exception is a person wearing a Coast Guard-approved life jacket.

- *Life jackets = boating safety.* Some 80% of fatalities associated with boating accidents are from drowning. Most involve people who never expected to end up in the water, but who fell overboard or ended up in the water when the boat sank. Children are particularly susceptible to this problem, and, in many states, children are required to be in life jackets whenever they are aboard boats.

- *Don't dive head-first—protect your neck.* Every year, people sustain serious, lifelong injuries, including paraplegia, due to diving head-first into unknown water and striking the bottom. Bodysurfing can result in serious neck injury when the swimmer's neck strikes the bottom. Check for depth and obstructions before diving, then go in feet-first the first time. Use caution while body surfing, always extending a hand ahead of you.

---

*Adapted, by permission, from the United States Lifesaving Association, **www.usla.org/copy.html**, 2000, *The Importance of Aquatic Safety and Beach Safety*.

EMERGENCY SITUATIONS

Few people know how to react if a vehicle goes underwater or if a person falls through ice. The following sections teach you what to do in both of these life-threatening situations.

Escaping From a Submerged Vehicle

Although it is not statistically likely that you will ever be involved in a submerged vehicle incident, knowing what action to take if you are is key to survival. Remember that many drownings happen to people who never intended to go into the water.

You can lose control of a small vehicle in as little as 6 inches of water and of a large vehicle in as little as 2 feet of water. During flashfloods, a driver can lose control of the vehicle as soon as two wheels are off the road. This is why you need to pay attention to posted signs indicating high water (Dworkin, 1998).

Generally a vehicle that enters water from a height of 6 feet or less and lands on its wheels will float for an unpredictable time; but once the vehicle begins to sink, it will be underwater in less than a minute. Vehicles stay afloat longer if the windows are up, giving more time for escape or rescue. Once underwater, most vehicles sink at a steep angle and may come to rest on the roof.

Experts recommend that you not open a window as the vehicle descends until the pressure is equalized—when the car is completely submerged and filled with water—because water rushing into the car through the window will force you away from the escape route. You will not be able to get a door open until the pressure is equalized.

In any front-engine vehicle, an air pocket forms as the vehicle descends and is forced into the rear and possibly to the trunk area until the vehicle comes to rest. At that time, the air moves back into the passenger section. Usually the small size of the air pocket has no effect on the ability to open doors and windows.

Studies have shown that people wearing seat belts have a greater chance of surviving initial impact with water. However, after the impact you should unbuckle your belt. If the vehicle is floating in the water, wheels down, the best technique is to escape through an open window before the water rises to window level. If the vehicle sinks too quickly to escape, stay calm, move to the rear of the car to take advantage of the air pocket, and plan an escape by opening the nearest door or window once the pressure has equalized. If young children are in the car, prepare to push them out the opening before you exit.

Be aware that power windows do not operate once the car's engine stops. Car windows can be broken with a spring-loaded centering punch engaged at the bottom margin or with a hammer. If you drive in an area near water, you should keep one of these in the car at all times. The punch can be taped to the steering wheel column.

Before you attempt to rescue people in a submerged vehicle, call or have a bystander call for emergency assistance immediately. As you approach the vehicle, be aware that your clothes could get tangled on bent vehicle parts. If a vehicle has submerged with all the windows up, the best approach may be to break a side window and remove it from the frame. If you are trying to get someone out as the vehicle submerges, be aware of the force exerted by the water entering through the window.

Escaping After Falling Through Ice

Although activities *in* the water become less enjoyable as the seasons change and the temperature cools, winter activities *on* the water draw many enthusiasts outdoors to enjoy skating, hockey, ice fishing, and the like. These activities can be fun and safe as long as participants know the areas they are using and are familiar with the conditions that will make each area safe. It is least risky to use monitored recreation areas where flags are used to signal the conditions of the ice (red means "not safe" and green means "safe"). Do not go out on the ice if you don't know its thickness or if you see water on the ice, slush, cracks or holes, or gray or dirty veins in the ice (Royal Life Saving Society Canada, n.d.).

Ponds, small lakes, and slow-moving streams are generally the safest for ice activities. The ice should be frozen to at least 6 inches to support one or two people and 8 inches for groups (Royal Life Saving Society Canada, n.d.).

Here are some additional tips about ice conditions (Royal Life Saving Society Canada, n.d.):

- Ice is rarely uniformly thick; it tends to vary a lot.
- Snow insulates ice, making the ice under the snow thinner and weaker. It may even melt existing ice.
- Newly formed ice isn't as strong as older ice; however, in the spring, even the older ice begins to lose its consistent thickness with the spring thaw.
- Clear blue, black, and green ice are the strongest types of ice; white, opaque ice is weaker.
- A cold snap with very cold temperatures weakens ice quickly and can cause large cracks within half a day. A warm spell takes several days to weaken ice.

If you or someone with you breaks through the ice, follow these guidelines:

1. Stay calm; don't try to climb out immediately. Thrashing will make it more difficult to escape.
2. Kick behind you to keep your body near the surface in a horizontal position (see figure 2.20).
3. Extend yourself as far as you can on unbroken ice while keeping your lower body as close to horizontal as possible.
4. Work your way carefully onto the ice. If the ice breaks again, keep using this method until you reach stronger ice. Once you are out, stay low and distribute your weight over as much surface area of ice as possible as you move to safety.
5. If you can't climb out, wait for someone to come to your rescue. Keep still and calm. Stay warm by keeping your arms close to your body and your legs together.

Figure 2.20   Kicking to avoid being pulled under the ice.

If you try to help someone who has fallen through the ice, be careful not to fall through yourself. Stay low and try to find something like a branch, rope, or a board to extend to the person in the water (see figure 2.21). If no equipment is available, lie flat on the ice as far away from the hole as possible and grab the person's wrist. Encourage her or him to stay calm and kick to get into a horizontal position. Then you can pull the person up onto the ice. Remember to stay flat on the ice and slide to safety. Once the person is off of the ice, get to shelter immediately and treat for hypothermia (see page 184).

Figure 2.21   Rescuing someone who has fallen through the ice.

Review Questions

1. What is Archimedes' principle and how does it relate to buoyancy?
2. Why is it easier to float in salt water than in fresh water?
3. What is vital capacity? How does it affect buoyancy?
4. Where is a person's center of buoyancy?
5. Name two skills that will allow you to stay afloat with minimum effort.
6. What emotional state commonly leads to drowning?
7. What causes ear and sinus squeeze? How can you avoid them?
8. How do you relieve a leg cramp in the water?
9. How do you decide how long to wait after a large meal before swimming?
10. Name three strokes you can use to move safely with minimal use of energy.
11. What are your options if a distressed swimmer grabs you when you're off duty?
12. Describe the five types of PFDs.
13. If you are immersed in cold water, should you remove your clothes to improve your chance of survival?
14. Describe the HELP position and why it is so valuable.
15. List five safe boating rules.
16. List the nine guidelines for safe rafting and tubing.
17. Why is it dangerous to swim near a dam?
18. When should you open a door or window to escape from a sinking vehicle?
19. After a vehicle sinks, where is the best place for passengers to position themselves?
20. What are the five guidelines to follow if you fall through ice?

three

Lifeguarding Responsibilities

In the YMCA lifeguard training course you learn many skills that help you assist and protect swimmers in an aquatic environment. This chapter helps you understand the important responsibilities you accept when you become a lifeguard.

In This Chapter, You'll Learn About

- the characteristics of a successful lifeguard,
- the responsibilities and role of a lifeguard, and
- the legal responsibilities of a lifeguard.

THE SUCCESSFUL LIFEGUARD

The best lifeguards are good at what they do because of particular personal characteristics. They are people-oriented professionals who share their aquatic abilities to enable others to safely enjoy water activities. A successful lifeguard

- cares about others,
- is strong and fit,
- is a good swimmer,
- is a responsible person,
- knows how and when to have fun, and
- wants to help others.

Are these characteristics true of you? If so, you are on your way to becoming a lifeguard who other swimmers will look up to. If not, think carefully about whether the job of a professional lifeguard is one that you want to pursue.

Once you've learned lifeguarding skills, most of what will determine your success as a lifeguard is your attitude. In this section, we'll look at the attitude a successful lifeguard presents, the physical conditioning necessary, the knowledge required, and the equipment the well-prepared guard brings to any work situation.

Attitude

You must have the right attitude to be a successful lifeguard. Do you really care about people? Are you ready to take on responsibility for the safety of others?

You give managers and patrons clues to your attitude and work ethic by the way you behave in both work and social situations. The image you present greatly influences how much respect observers have for you. Whatever your intentions are, the patrons of your facility will get their impression of your attitude from what they see and hear as you interact with them and with other patrons, peers, and staff. You will always be regarded as a leader, so lead others at your facility by your example:

- Look professional.
- Be well groomed.
- Be punctual.
- Follow the rules. (You can't expect others to follow them if you don't!)
- Be alert at all times.
- Avoid gossiping, joking around, or reading while you're on duty.
- Be courteous; avoid shouting or arguing.
- Direct questions for which you don't know the answer to a supervisor.
- Never report for your shift under the influence of alcohol or drugs.
- Do not abuse your authority.
- Maintain control of your assigned area.
- Cooperate with fellow lifeguards—you are a team.
- Be familiar with your area and its potential hazards.
- Try to prevent accidents before they occur.

Using plain common sense and courtesy will go a long way toward demonstrating that you want to serve patrons and that you are worthy of their respect and trust. It will make your lifeguarding service pleasant, satisfying, and rewarding.

Physical Conditioning and Wellness

By doing a good job, you will help prevent accidents that could require your rescue skills. But when you do need to use them, you need the strength and endurance to carry out the rescue. Regular exercise is vital to maintaining your physical conditioning. The best exercise for a lifeguard is swimming. Try lap swimming, stroke drills, and water

Figure 3.1   Regular exercise, such as weightlifting or swimming laps, will keep you in good physical condition.

games to help you build and maintain your strength, endurance, breath control, agility, and skill at the levels essential for effective lifeguarding (figure 3.1).

Your attentiveness, vigilance, and fitness are crucial to the safety of those who use your facility. Your lifestyle will influence these areas of your preparation. Take some time to evaluate your lifestyle—your personal way of life. The lifestyle you choose affects your social, spiritual, intellectual, physical, and emotional wellness.

Lifestyle Assessment

Here are some questions to help you assess your lifestyle:

1. Do you have good personal relationships?
2. Do you balance your needs with the needs of others?
3. Do you have a purpose to your life—a goal?
4. Are you in good physical condition?
5. Do you regularly spend time doing some kind of physical fitness activity?
6. Do you eat healthy foods?
7. Do you get 7 or 8 hours of sleep every night?
8. Are you sensitive to the feelings of others?
9. Do you control your emotions effectively?
10. Are you overweight?
11. Are you underweight?
12. Do you smoke? Drink? Take drugs?

If you answered no to some of items 1 through 9 and yes to some of items 10, 11, and 12, you may want to consider some changes in your lifestyle. The changes you decide on could be important not only to the patrons of your facility but also to your personal development.

What changes would you like to make in your lifestyle?

Personal Equipment

As a lifeguard, you will need certain equipment to carry out your job and to be comfortable while on duty. Most of the equipment you will need is inexpensive. Some of it may be provided by your employer, but you must take the initiative to have the appropriate lifeguarding equipment with you at all times when you are on duty.

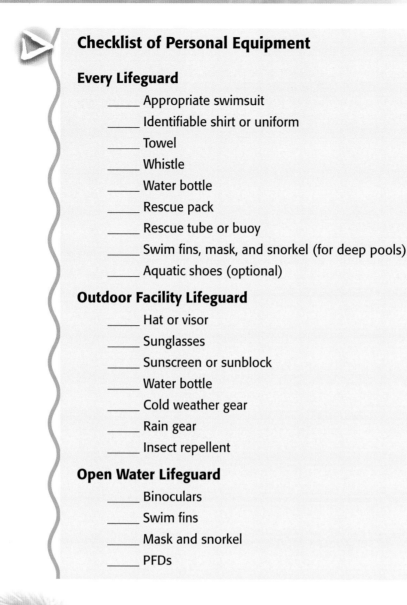

Checklist of Personal Equipment

Every Lifeguard

_____ Appropriate swimsuit

_____ Identifiable shirt or uniform

_____ Towel

_____ Whistle

_____ Water bottle

_____ Rescue pack

_____ Rescue tube or buoy

_____ Swim fins, mask, and snorkel (for deep pools)

_____ Aquatic shoes (optional)

Outdoor Facility Lifeguard

_____ Hat or visor

_____ Sunglasses

_____ Sunscreen or sunblock

_____ Water bottle

_____ Cold weather gear

_____ Rain gear

_____ Insect repellent

Open Water Lifeguard

_____ Binoculars

_____ Swim fins

_____ Mask and snorkel

_____ PFDs

You should always report for work properly attired in a *swimsuit* that is comfortable and practical. An *identifiable shirt* or *assigned uniform* is important so that patrons can identify you as a lifeguard and to protect yourself from the sun if you are working outdoors.

The well-prepared guard also has a *towel* at the station. You may need this towel as a rescue aid, or you may need to towel off after being in the water. (Your towel can also reduce the embarrassment of a patron who loses a suit after diving or going down the water slide!) And of course a towel helps pad the seat on your lifeguard stand.

Every lifeguard needs a *whistle*, preferably on a wrist strap to keep it close at hand. Your whistle is your prime communication tool; you may even want to have two or three whistles at your disposal. Test your whistle before you go on duty to make sure it's working. We recommend that you not use other guards' whistles; germs and viruses can be transmitted through such shared implements.

One thing you should *not* wear when lifeguarding is sharp or loose jewelry. This includes jewelry for pierced parts of the body. If you have to rescue someone, such jewelry can pose a danger to the victim or to you.

Stay hydrated by keeping a *water bottle* nearby at all times. You'll be sitting or standing for long periods of time in places where you won't have access to drinking water.

You need to always be prepared to begin emergency first aid. Your *rescue pack*, including protective equipment—a resuscitation mask (see page 173), latex gloves, gown, and eye shield or goggles—and minor first aid supplies, is essential. You need the protective equipment to protect yourself from the transmission of blood-borne diseases (see pages 168–172). You may want to put these items in a fanny pack to keep them at your fingertips on land. During water rescues, be sure to bring your resuscitation mask.

Always have a *rescue tube* or *buoy* with you. This equipment is essential for any water rescue you might be called on to perform. Protect the extra line from the rescue tube by holding it in your hand, so it can't get tangled on the chair. Additional items that may help you during a rescue if your pool is deep are *fins*, a *mask*, and a *snorkel*.

Many lifeguards work in *aquatic shoes*, which can be worn in or out of the water. On the deck, they help protect your feet from hot and irregular surfaces and from scrapes, cuts, and stones; they also provide additional traction on slippery surfaces. In the water, the shoes do not interfere with your ability to swim, and in open water they can protect your feet from unseen dangers.

If you are a lifeguard outdoors, you are exposed to the harmful effects of the sun. Too much exposure to the sun may cause skin cancer. You'll want a wide-brimmed *hat* or *visor* to protect you from the sun's rays and from the glare of the sun off of the water. *Sunglasses* also help cut down on glare and reduce your blind spots; in addition, they protect your eyes from damage by ultraviolet rays. (Use them indoors as well when there's lots of glare.) When you choose sunglasses, look for a pair that filters out 99 to 100% of both UV-A and UV-B rays. Lens colors of gray, brown, or amber and polarized lenses can help reduce glare and eye fatigue.

Your sun protection will be complete if you add a *sunscreen* or *sunblock* to your equipment. The American Cancer Society recommends a sun protection factor (SPF) rating of at least 15. Remember, you not only get direct sun rays but also reflected sun. Reapply sun protection frequently during your shift, especially if you have been in the water (figure 3.2).

Figure 3.2 Reapply sunscreen frequently, especially after you have been in the water.

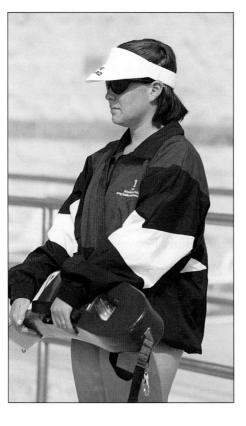

Figure 3.3 A long-sleeved jacket will protect you from the elements on cool or rainy days.

Every day, especially on hot, sunny days, bring a filled *water bottle* to work with you and drink water regularly to keep from becoming dehydrated. Other days will not be bright or sunny. Cool temperatures, wind, and rain can make you miserable if you aren't prepared. Have a *sweatshirt* and *sweatpants* available for cold days and *rain gear* (a coat, slicker, or rainsuit) for rainy days (figure 3.3).

Insect repellent should also be a part of your equipment. You don't want anything to interfere with your ability to concentrate on monitoring the swimming area assigned to you. Using repellent may help you avoid the discomfort of multiple insect bites and swarming gnats or mosquitoes.

If you are lifeguarding on the open water—a river or lake or the ocean—you will need *binoculars* because visibility is limited. With binoculars you can scan your area for trouble. If rescue is required, *swim fins* will cut down on the time it takes to reach a victim. (Fins also help speed underwater rescue in pools with deep water or diving wells.)

Other equipment needed for open water lifeguarding includes a *mask* and *snorkel* to make searching underwater for victims easier and *PFDs* if you are required to use a boat for patrolling or rescuing.

Get a special bag to carry your lifeguarding equipment. Having this equipment will make you well prepared for duty.

LIFEGUARD RESPONSIBILITIES AND PROFESSIONALISM

Your primary responsibility as a lifeguard is to protect the safety of all swimmers in your area, first by preventing accidents and second by responding to an emergency quickly and efficiently to minimize the danger to those involved. You meet this responsibility by

- having the skills in accident prevention, decision making, and rescuing to do your job,
- being in good enough physical condition to use your skills,
- knowing about your area of responsibility,
- being able to communicate that knowledge to your patrons, and
- enforcing the rules.

In addition to the skills and knowledge you must develop to be a good lifeguard, you must accept responsibility for your actions. As a professional lifeguard, you are part of a highly trained team, and your actions reflect on your whole organization, including your coworkers. Swimmers who come to your facility will notice your behavior whether you are on or off duty.

When you accept the responsibility of being a lifeguard, you also accept the legal and moral consequences of your actions and decisions. This is not a responsibility to be taken lightly. When you agree to protect the public's safety, you are accountable for your knowledge and your actions. (See the "Legal Responsibilities" section later in this chapter.)

As a lifeguard, you are part of a team, contributing to your facility's operation. The impression you make on patrons is important. If you look and act professionally, with confidence and authority, it makes your facility look professional, too. The way you greet patrons, how you sit or stand and hold your equipment, and your alertness on the job all affect how patrons respond to you. To reinforce a professional image and to carry out your responsibilities, try to make the following duties habit:

- Report to work on time as scheduled. Be in uniform and at your position when your shift begins.
- Have the appropriate equipment at your station (see page 42).
- Check your area for hazardous conditions when you arrive at your station.
- Be professional, alert, courteous, and diplomatic. When you interact with patrons, follow the four YMCA values of caring, honesty, respect, and responsibility.
- Stay alert to observe signals from other guards.
- Know and practice the proper emergency procedures for your area.
- Avoid socializing while on duty.
- Scan your area at all times.
- Enforce all facility rules. Be courteous but firm. Report a persistent problem to the head guard or manager.
- When enforcing a rule, briefly explain the reason behind the rule as well as the danger the rule infraction presents. Remember that your first responsibility remains protecting swimmers in your assigned area.
- Keep patrons from congregating on walk areas around lifeguard stands.
- Refer detailed inquiries to the head guard or manager.
- Safeguard the lives of your patrons first, but also ensure their comfort and pleasure. Don't tolerate recklessness or rough play.
- Clear all swimmers from the water during an electrical storm.
- Keep the swimming area clean and ready for inspection at all times.
- In open water areas, be alert for dangerous marine life.
- If you are working at open water, be familiar with bottom conditions and knowledgeable about the use of small craft for rescue.
- Know how to use all lifeguarding, rescue, and first aid equipment, and keep it ready and in good repair.
- Practice rescue skills regularly.
- Secure the area by locking all doors and gates when a lifeguard is not on duty.

CHILD ABUSE PREVENTION GUIDELINES

Child abuse, which includes nonaccidental physical injury, neglect, sexual molestation, and emotional abuse, has become a critical national concern. It is important that you, as an employee, never abuse children yourself or become involved in a situation in which you could be accused of abuse. To assure this, follow these commonsense suggestions:

- Don't ever be alone with a child unobserved by other staff.
- Don't socialize with or become involved in activities (babysitting, weekend trips) outside of your job with children who are patrons.
- Don't ever use physical punishment.
- Don't verbally or emotionally abuse children.
- Don't ever deny a child necessities, such as food or shelter.

Your employer should give you more training in guidelines for child abuse prevention and in procedures related to reporting signs of child abuse. Appendix A contains "Child Abuse Identification and Prevention: Recommended Guidelines for YMCAs."

LEGAL RESPONSIBILITIES

In addition to developing physical skills to be a good lifeguard, you must accept responsibility for your actions. As a professional lifeguard, you accept the duty to provide a safe environment in which patrons of your facility can enjoy aquatic activities. This means that you must maintain the pool and surrounding area to meet basic health and safety codes, provide adequate supervision for all areas in the facility, provide appropriate direction to patrons regarding the rules, anticipate potential hazards and act to reduce the resulting risks, provide necessary emergency first aid, and proficiently perform the skills described in this lifeguarding manual.

Because the possibility exists that actions that you take (or don't take) may result in legal action against you and your facility, you need to know some basics about your legal responsibilities as a lifeguard. In this section, we briefly explain the legal process, common situations for which you might have liability, the defenses that might be used in a liability case, and the importance of accurate record keeping. We begin with some definitions of common legal terms.

Common Legal Terms

Take some time to familiarize yourself with the following legal terms, applied here to lifeguarding. They will be important to your understanding of the legal responsibilities of being a professional lifeguard.

duty: A duty is a legal obligation to act in accordance with a prescribed standard of conduct in order to protect others from unreasonable risk.

breach: If a patron is owed a duty and the lifeguard does not perform it, the lifeguard is said to have breached the duty.

common law: Under this general principle of law, which all states follow in the absence of a specific law, an individual owes no general duty to help another person in danger, even if the individual has the skills and ability to provide assistance. But the doctrine of common law is negated when a lifeguard is *on duty*. A lifeguard on duty must help a person in danger or may be considered negligent if an injury occurs.

ordinary standard of care: The performance considered by law or practice within a profession as the action likely to be taken by an average, reasonable, and prudent professional is the ordinary standard of care.

negligence: Actions that fall below the standard of care established by law for the protection of others against unreasonable risks are considered to be negligent. Such actions could be an unintentional breach of a legal duty, causing foreseeable damage that could have been avoided had the individual performed his or her duty.

liability: An individual can be held legally responsible for actions or lack of action intentionally designed to harm another as well as for negligent acts that harm another.

proximate cause: When a reasonably close causal connection is drawn between the failure to provide a legal duty and an injury, the breach is considered a proximate cause.

Good Samaritan laws: These statutes provide protection from legal liability to a trained person acting in good faith while off duty to provide emergency medical assistance at the scene of an accident or emergency. Good Samaritan laws differ from state to state, and lifeguards should know the law for their state.

nuisance: Anything that causes hurt, inconvenience, annoyance, or damage is considered a nuisance.

plaintiff: The plaintiff is the individual or group of individuals claiming a wrongdoing and filing a lawsuit.

defendant: The defendant is the individual or group of individuals accused of committing a wrong.

The Legal Process

Following any accident there is a possibility that the victim, or a relative of the victim, will initiate action against the aquatic facility and the lifeguards on duty at the time of the accident. The process usually follows the same general path, illustrated in figure 3.4.

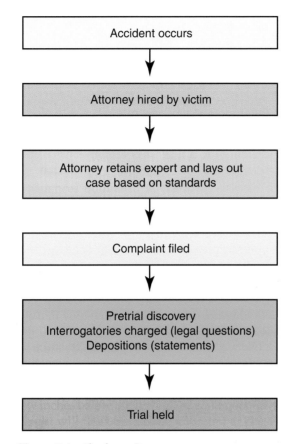

Figure 3.4 The lawsuit process.

In our society, a lawsuit can be brought against anyone for any reason, so the filing of a complaint doesn't mean a facility or lifeguard is guilty of any wrongdoing. It means rather that the plaintiff's attorney has gathered information on the case and that the plaintiff is willing to present the case to a court for a decision.

Before a trial, attorneys for the plaintiff and for the defense continue to gather information and to secure sworn testimony from experts on the standard of care for the particular situation under examination. This is called pretrial discovery. The plaintiff must prove that the defendant's actions caused the injury sustained and that the injury was foreseeable and therefore preventable.

Such court cases may be heard by a jury or by a judge alone. In either situation, both sides of the case are presented. After a deliberation or discussion period, the judge or jury decides whether the defendant is guilty of the charges and, if so, what damages should be awarded.

Aquatic Liability

Most lawsuits concerning aquatic activities involve a perceived wrong. Liability arises when an injury results from a lifeguard's either failing to perform an action that should have been performed or performing an incorrect action. Most lawsuits filed against aquatic facilities focus on two elements that give rise to liability: negligence and nuisance. Because specific laws regarding aquatic liability vary from state to state, we will consider general principles in this section. Check with the appropriate departments in your local government to learn about the laws governing aquatic facilities in your area.

Negligence

In the law of negligence, the person bringing suit—the plaintiff—must prove

- that the defendant owed a duty to the plaintiff,
- that the defendant breached that duty,
- that the plaintiff suffered some injury or loss, and
- that the injury or loss was caused by the defendant's breach (proximate cause).

All four elements must be proved for the lawsuit to advance.

Negligence can take many forms. *Willful negligence* is performing an action intended to cause someone harm. Unintentional acts of negligence that cause harm are considered *slight*, *ordinary*, or *gross negligence*, depending on their severity. Examples of unintentional negligence include failure to foresee a potential hazard, carelessness, poor judgment, excitement, inattention to duty, inexperience, ignorance, stupidity, and forgetfulness.

In your role as a professional lifeguard, you assume a legal duty to provide the services you were trained to provide to each patron of your facility while you are on duty. That doesn't mean that you ensure the safety of patrons. Rather, it means that if an accident occurs while you are on duty, you must function competently. In other words, as a lifeguard, you must respond by providing the standard of care outlined by the organization that certified you and that is expected of professional lifeguards. If you perform according to those standards, you would not be found negligent.

Two common types of negligence are not responding to constructive notice and not fulfilling the ordinary standard of care. The facility owner should know of any potentially dangerous conditions that may exist, regardless of whether or not he or she has actual knowledge of them. In other words, if an employee or a patron sees a hazardous condition but fails to report it to the owner, the owner is considered to have *constructive notice* because he or she should have been aware of the condition. If an injury occurs because of this hazardous condition, the owner can be held liable due to negligence.

In any pool facility, the owner must ensure the following conditions:

- Chemical and storage areas are safely and properly used.
- Rescue equipment is in good working order and readily available.
- Ladders and diving structures are safe and in good repair.
- Lighting, including underwater lighting, is safe and adequate.
- Pool water is disinfected, and pH levels are correctly adjusted.
- Water is clear.
- Water depth is clearly marked at all places, especially in shallow and deep water.
- Regular checks are made for hazards such as broken glass, equipment that has not been put away, or cracked cement around posts supporting the diving structure and lifeguard chairs.

You also can be found negligent if you do not fulfill the *ordinary standard of care* you owe a patron; you are obligated to use the care that circumstances would indicate to a prudent and careful person. Negligence would be based on the plaintiff's demonstrating that your actions fell below what could be expected of other similarly trained individuals in similar circumstances.

Nuisance

Nuisance is not the same as negligence. Rather, in the legal sense, a nuisance is something that causes hurt, inconvenience, annoyance, or damage. The operation of a swimming facility is not by itself a nuisance if it is done without disturbing the surroundings. Large floodlights, loud music, and inadequate parking, however, could be judged nuisances.

Liability Defenses

To avoid legal liability, you must exercise reasonable care. Although there are numerous ways to be held liable for an injury, the only sure way to avoid liability is to see that an injury doesn't occur. By taking the appropriate actions to ensure the safety of your patrons and by adhering to state and local regulations for aquatic facilities, you will be doing as much as you can to prevent accidents.

Many organizations suggest that you obtain liability insurance for your lifeguarding activities. Most facilities have liability insurance to protect themselves and their employees, and many personal general liability insurance policies include such liability coverage. Take time to learn about the insurance available to you before you accept any lifeguarding position.

If a liability suit against an aquatic facility should come to trial, the following are some types of defenses that the defendants might use.

Governmental or Sovereign Immunity

In some states, government employees involved in liability actions can claim immunity because of their positions as "agents" of the state.

Assumption of Risk

In the assumption-of-risk defense, the defendant combats the plaintiff's charges by claiming that the plaintiff assumed or accepted a certain level of risk by entering the aquatic facility and by participating in the activity that led to the injury. For example, a patron who dove from the diving board and hit her head on the end of the board could be said to have assumed that risk by deciding to attempt a dive.

Contributory Negligence

The contributory-negligence defense is somewhat weak in that it admits negligence. However, it also places some of the burden on the plaintiff, indicating that he or she contributed to the overall negligence. If, for example, a patron was injured by participating in rough play in the shallow end of the pool, the lifeguard might admit negligence by not having stopped the activity. However, the lifeguard would claim that the plaintiff contributed to the cause of the injury by knowingly participating in an activity that was against the facility rules.

Comparative Negligence

This defense, too, admits some degree of guilt on the part of the lifeguard. In deciding the award to be given to the plaintiff, the judge or jury would assign relative amounts of negligence to the lifeguard and to the injured party. Say, for example, a lifeguard had cleared the water because of an impending electrical storm and a patron sneaked back into the water and was struck by lightning. Under the comparative negligence defense, the plaintiff might be awarded no damages because the lifeguard fulfilled her or his initial duty by clearing the water. Although it might have been negligent not to have noticed that the patron went back into the water, the plaintiff bore greater negligence by not obeying the lifeguard.

Last Clear Chance

In many accidents, the injured party could have stopped some action before the injury occurred. If the plaintiff had a clear chance to avoid the accident and did not, the lifeguard might not be found negligent.

Record Keeping

In many facilities, patrons must sign waivers of liability. By signing such forms, they agree that they will not hold the facility liable for injuries they receive while participating in specific activities. These waivers do not remove liability resulting from faulty or damaged equipment or any intentional or willful negligence by staff.

Other records that may be of use in aquatic facilities include staff manuals, emergency plans, posted rules governing the facility, accident and incident reports, and chemical safety logs. These records can establish the standard of care that your facility provides, and they include information that will be vital to your defense in the event of a lawsuit. Be sure you complete these records systematically and file them carefully. If you usually keep excellent records but cannot provide them for a particular situation, you would appear to have failed to meet the standards your organization has set. It is not generally necessary to keep records for longer than 5 years.

Review Questions

1. Describe a healthy lifestyle.
2. List the personal equipment a well-prepared lifeguard has on-site.
3. Why is it important to use sun protection?
4. List the lifeguard duties that should become habits.
5. Name some precautions you can take to ensure you are not involved in or accused of child abuse.
6. Describe the Good Samaritan law.
7. Describe the legal process when a lawsuit is initiated.
8. Define liability and explain why it is of concern to aquatic facilities.
9. Define negligence and list the four elements required to determine it.
10. Could a pool owner be liable if a patron is injured when a piece of equipment breaks but the owner didn't know it was in poor condition?
11. What is the ordinary standard of care?
12. Define nuisance.
13. Name five types of liability defenses.

Lifeguarding Procedures

As a lifeguard, you are responsible for patrons' safety and well-being while they are in the swimming area. This means that you must continuously make decisions about what actions to take to prevent trouble and be constantly vigilant while you are on duty.

In This Chapter, You'll Learn About

- the decision-making skills you'll use daily as a lifeguard,
- how to perform the duties of a lifeguard, and
- how to handle special lifeguarding situations.

DECISION MAKING

For every decision you make, there is a consequence. For instance, say you are driving and see your gas gauge is near empty. You can decide either to fill up at the nearest gas station or to try to make it to your destination on the gas you have. If you fill up, it will cost you some money, but you won't have to worry about running out of gas on a deserted road. If you don't fill up, you could end up on foot!

The Decision-Making Model

As you make a decision, systematically follow some simple steps to ensure that you have considered the possible consequences. The *PACA* model may help you:

- P: What is the *problem* or situation?
- A: What are the *alternatives*?
- C: What are the *consequences* of each alternative, positive and negative?
- A: What is the *action* or decision?

Learn the acronym *PACA* to remember the steps. Now try this exercise to sharpen your decision-making skills.

Decision-Making Exercise

On a piece of paper, describe a situation in which you are faced with an important decision. Using that example, answer the following:

- Describe the problem or situation.
- List ways to resolve the problem or situation. Try to list at least three.
- List the advantages and disadvantages of each alternative.
- Make your decision and write a brief justification. Explain how you plan to follow through on your decision.

Preparation

Because each of us is responsible for the decisions we make, we need to think through what may happen as a result of our decisions. This is especially true when you take on the role of a lifeguard. Choosing to intervene and the action you take may mean the difference between someone's safety and a serious injury or death.

As a lifeguard, you may have little time to make critical decisions. Often you'll have only seconds to respond. This fact makes it important to think through what to do in certain situations *before* you need to take action. The emergency drills and in-service training at your facility will help prepare you, but it is also important that you, personally, consider what to do in given situations. For example, how would you react if someone

- broke a minor rule that might endanger someone else's safety, like sitting on a ladder or running on the deck?
- looked frightened, unsure, or tired while swimming or diving?
- was reported missing?
- was breaking a major rule, perhaps pushing or dunking another patron?

When you think about what to do, it's not enough to tell yourself, "I'd just talk to him" or "I'd blow my whistle and ask her to get out of the pool." In the real-life situation, you might find you had forgotten to prepare for crucial actions. You need instead to know each step you would take and what you would say. Try this system of accident prevention to guide you in planning ahead.

Q-1-2 Accident Prevention System

As a lifeguard, you are always watching for potential problems in order to act on them before they become emergencies. But if you have to intervene over and over again, it becomes annoying to both you and the patrons. So how can you enforce the rules without blowing your whistle constantly?

One solution is to learn to use the Q-1-2 system, which works with children and adults alike. There are three advantages to using this system:

- It helps you be consistent and fair.
- It reduces the stress and emotion of enforcing rules.
- It allows you to remain focused on your assigned area.

Let's look at each step of this three-part system.

Q: Question

The process begins before someone actually violates a rule or does something potentially dangerous. You will frequently notice people who appear to be preparing to do something that might put them or someone else in danger, like one of these:

- A person walks very tentatively to the edge of the diving board or deep end.
- A swimmer starts across the pool but then returns, struggling and gasping for air.
- Someone floats a kickboard a few feet from the deck and appears to be preparing to jump onto or over it.
- A patron on the deck says to another, "Race you to the deep end."
- Someone is sneaking up behind another person.
- A person is walking faster than normal.

Although no one in these situations has violated a rule or done anything dangerous, the potential is clear. The first step, *Q*, is to ask the person a question (figure 4.1). Ask him or her to come stand beside you, then ask your question without looking away from your assigned area or having to shout.

Questions are used not to accuse but to help make sure people have enough information about the situations they are in. The following questions might be useful in the scenarios just described:

- Have you ever jumped off the board before? Can you swim across the pool? Would you show me?

Figure 4.1 The first step is to ask the person a question.

- Have you ever had swimming lessons? Can you stand up in that depth?
- Were you going to jump on the kickboard? Do you know what would happen if you landed on it?
- How are you going to race? In the water? On the deck?
- Were you going to push the person you were sneaking up on?
- Did you know we have a rule against running on the deck? Do you know why?

Sometimes the question itself gets the point across. However, be sure you listen to the answer. If it does not indicate that the person is aware of the potential problem, give more information or instructions:

- You need to be able to swim across the swimming pool before jumping off the diving board. Wait until the break, and I'll let you try.
- Maybe you should swim in the shallow end for now.
- Do not jump on or over the kickboard.
- There seem to be too many people in the pool for you to race now.
- You cannot push (dunk, splash) another person, even if it's your friend and you are playing a game.
- The deck is wet. Please walk a little slower.

Step Q Key Points

- Watch for situations where you think someone is about to do something unsafe or against pool rules.
- Ask the person to come to where you are.
- Ask a question to determine if the person was about to do something unsafe or against the rules.
- Give more information or instruction.
- Watch your area of responsibility at all times.

1: Warning

The second step of the system is used when you see someone do something unsafe or against pool rules. First, call the person to your side so you do not have to shout or look away from the water (figure 4.2). Next, tell the person what you saw. This may sound silly; what you saw might have been obvious. But people sometimes don't realize what they have just done. Also, you want to be certain the person knows what you are warning her or him about.

Because this will be the offender's one and only warning, use simple, direct statements using this format.

- I saw . . .
- That is . . .
- Please . . .

Here are some examples of how this would work:

- *I saw* you jump off the side of the diving board. *That is* dangerous because it is too near the deck. *Please* jump off the end of the board.
- *I saw* you running. *That is* unsafe because the deck is wet. *Please* walk.
- *I saw* you dive into shallow water. *That is* very dangerous because you may hit your head and injure your neck. *Please* dive only in the deep end.
- *I saw* you chewing gum in the pool. *That is* unsafe because you may choke. *Please* get rid of the gum.
- *I saw* you enter the pool without taking a shower. *That is* against our pool rules because it makes the water dirty. *Please* shower before entering the pool.

Figure 4.2 The second step is to issue a warning.

Always make simple, direct statements, without emotion. They are all statements of fact and do not need discussion. People often will want to argue in their defense, but try to avoid long discussions. You can listen, but maintain your focus on the water. Make it clear to the one being given the warning that if the undesirable behavior is repeated, you will have to ask the person to leave or to take a time-out (see next section).

Step 1 Key Points

- State the warning using "I saw . . . ," "That is . . . ," and "Please . . ." statements.
- Don't argue with the patron.
- Watch your area of responsibility at all times.
- Make it clear that a repetition of the undesirable behavior is not acceptable and may mean the patron must leave or take a time-out.

2: Time-Out

If an adult repeats the behavior you have warned about, inform someone in management so he or she can ask the patron to leave the pool area (see the next section) (figure 4.3). With children, direct them to take a time-out from the pool instead. Giving a time-out means removing the child from the water and from the company of others to a chair for a short period. (Whether a teen is given a time-out depends on your facility's guidelines and your own judgment.)

Again call the offender to your side. Then, without emotion, say, "I saw you run (push, jump off the side of the board) again. Please go to the time-out chair for 5 minutes. Then come back to see me."

The purpose of time-out is not public humiliation but to have the child think about proper behavior. The time-out chair should be away from the edge of the pool and out of the sun but in sight of a lifeguard or other staff member. It would be good to have the pool rules posted in the time-out area so the offender can think about what he or she should be doing more than what was done wrong.

Keeping track of the time should be the responsibility of the child, not the lifeguard. An easy way to assist in time-keeping is to give the youngster an inexpensive plastic stopwatch or kitchen timer. Start the watch or timer and hand it to the child with instructions to bring it back when it says 5:00 (or whatever time you choose).

Figure 4.3 If the problem persists, ask someone in management to talk to the patron.

When a child returns to you from the time-out chair, ask for a description of what to do in the future in the same situation. Ask why what you recommended is better. (Basically, you are asking for a repeat of the warning you gave.) If the person cannot answer appropriately, explain the warning and ask for it to be repeated to you.

Step 2 Key Points

- Ask an adult to leave the pool area.
- Send a child to the time-out chair with a timer for a specified period.
- After the time-out, ask the child to tell you what he or she should do in the future in the same situation.

Asking a Patron to Leave

If an adult performs an undesirable behavior after a warning, or if a child does so after one or more time-outs, inform management so the head guard, manager, or assistant manager can meet with the patron and ask her or him to leave the premises voluntarily. If a minor is involved, the parent or guardian should be contacted. File an incident report afterward. To ensure consistency among lifeguards and the support of management, the issue of dismissing people from the facility should be discussed and procedures determined at staff meetings.

What if a child repeats the same behavior after a time-out? Every facility will have different rules, so be sure you know the steps your facility has established to enforce them consistently. However, unlike before, every repeated behavior need not be treated the same way. Not showering before swimming may earn a time-out; dangerous behavior may merit removal from the area.

Exceptions

The Q-1-2 system is designed to be fair and consistent, but exceptions will arise. The system is only a tool—you should use it, not allow it or swimmers to use you. Your judgment should always overrule the system when needed.

For example, a swimmer may do several different things that merit warnings but never repeat the same behavior to earn a time-out. Explain to the child that you have seen the several offenses and you want the child to take a time-out. After the child returns from time-out, ask for a list of the things that have received warnings.

A regular young patron who receives a warning one day and repeats the behavior the next day should go to time-out without a new warning. You may reasonably hold higher expectations for those who use a facility regularly.

Remember, regardless of what occurs, maintain a professional attitude. Treat patrons courteously and focus on the behavior to be corrected, not the individual. *Never* shout or use abusive language or physical violence.

HOW TO GUARD

The quality of any facility is due in large part to the commitment management makes to its patrons and staff. All facility managers should be committed to providing a safe and fun environment for patrons, ensuring that

- there are enough lifeguards on duty to serve the patrons,
- the lifeguards are certified, and
- lifeguards are positioned at waterside to assist swimmers.

The capacity of the facility is important in determining the number of lifeguards needed on duty. Each facility should have a minimum of one certified lifeguard on duty when it is open. Beyond that, state and local ordinances prescribe supervision requirements, and many facilities set their own stricter standards. These standards should be based on the following conditions:

- Size and shape of the pool
- Equipment in the pool areas (slides, inflatable objects, etc.)
- Bather load
- Skill level of swimmers
- Activity or activities in the pool area (on deck and in the water)
- Changes in glare from the sun
- Number of high-use or high-risk areas
- Ability to handle emergencies properly and effectively
- Meeting or exceeding compliance with applicable state and local codes

The standards should be written up and included in the facility's lifeguard manual and/or the facility's administrator's manual.

The management is also likely to divide the facility into zones for particular activities, such as diving, wading, and perhaps ball playing. These zones help both patrons and lifeguards know what behavior is appropriate for each area.

The management of your facility should also make a commitment to you and provide a safe working environment. They ought to have completed the planning necessary to ensure that emergency procedures are established in writing, equipment is available and in good repair, and lifeguards are stationed in appropriate areas to reduce accidents. Such preventive steps help protect patrons from injury and the facility and lifeguards from liability in the case of an accident (see chapter 3 for your legal responsibilities as a lifeguard). The management must also ensure that its policies and procedures protect your safety. You, then, must meet your duty to provide professional lifeguard services.

Supervision Systems

It is important that you know what area of the facility you are responsible for at all times. If just one person on a large staff neglects his or her area, a serious accident may be the result.

A number of factors influence what is considered a proper supervision system:

- Size and shape of the facility
- Demographics of the population using the facility
- Number of people in the water

- Number of lifeguards available
- Aquatic experience of swimmers and guards
- Environmental conditions
- Lighting conditions
- Types of activities
- Positioning of guards
- Placement of lifeguard chairs or towers

The most common systems are entire-area coverage or zone coverage. An emergency coverage plan should also be formulated.

Entire-Area Coverage

In entire-area coverage, a single lifeguard supervises the entire swimming area (figure 4.4). The system works best when the swimming area is small and there are few swimmers. Entire-area coverage has both advantages and disadvantages:

Figure 4.4 One lifeguard supervises the entire area.

Advantages

Few lifeguards are required.

The lifeguards understand their responsibilities.

Disadvantages

Lifeguards may be responsible for a large area.

Lifeguards tend to concentrate on boundaries rather than entire swimming area.

Lifeguards get little change of pace.

Although entire-area coverage is suitable for small pool settings with no obstructions, it would be difficult to use in a large, complex facility. If it becomes necessary to cover a large swimming area in this manner, consider closing some sections of the facility and concentrating the swimmers in a manageable area. When a single guard is on duty, additional trained staff need to be available to assist in emergency situations.

Zone Coverage

In zone coverage, the swimming area is broken into smaller units, or zones, with one lifeguard responsible for each. The zones should overlap to assure complete coverage (see figure 4.5 for an example).

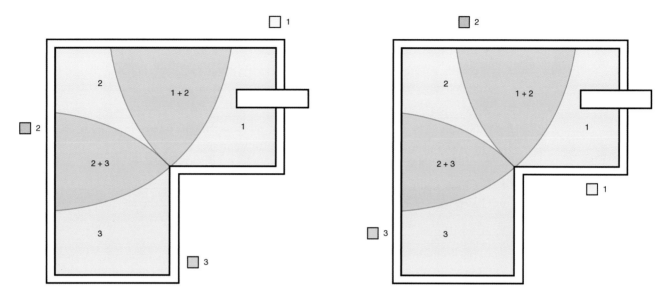

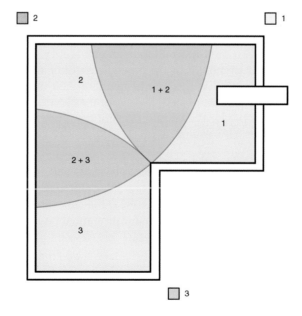

Figure 4.5 Example of zone coverage.

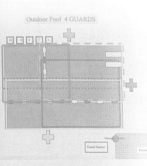

Outdoor Pool 4 GUARDS

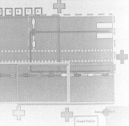

Outdoor Pool 5 GUARDS

Several factors should be considered in designating zones for a facility:

- Zones should not require a lifeguard to scan more than 180 degrees. Some state codes are more restrictive, limiting guards to scanning 90 degrees or less.
- Zones should minimize blind spots.
- High-risk areas should overlap into the areas of responsibility for two guard positions, ensuring double coverage.
- Each zone should be set up so it's possible for a lifeguard to both scan the area within 10 seconds and reach any point in the zone within 10 seconds.

Zone coverage is usually accompanied by a rotation system, discussed later in this section. Zone coverage has its own advantages and disadvantages:

Advantages

Guards concentrate on limited areas.

There is double coverage in overlap areas.

Rotation keeps lifeguards refreshed.

Guards can interact with patrons more easily.

Disadvantages

More lifeguards are required.

Confusion about areas of responsibility may result in areas being unguarded.

This system allows the greatest flexibility for management and the greatest definition of area for lifeguards.

Emergency Coverage

Every facility needs an emergency coverage plan. Whenever there are two or more lifeguards and one must enter the water, the other lifeguards on duty must shift their responsibilities to cover larger areas. The guards remaining out of the water will probably have to move to new positions to cover the pool or waterfront effectively and to perform emergency procedures. If your facility uses entire-area coverage, there must be assistance nearby so you can call for help in an emergency.

All lifeguards should know the procedures for emergency coverage. Management is responsible for seeing that all staff are aware of their responsibilities, and an emergency coverage diagram is to be posted. If you or other lifeguards are unsure of your responsibilities, ask. Your preparation could prevent an injury or accident.

Scanning

According to Fenner, Leahy, Buhk, and Dawes (1999), the ability to scan for long periods of time is a lifeguard's most valuable contribution to drowning prevention. *Scanning* here means observing, recording, and assessing the condition of the patrons in the pool in the areas you have been assigned. Your scanning must be constant, vigilant, and systematic.

You must be positioned where you have a clear, unobstructed view of your assigned areas (Lifesaving Society, 1993). If your facility is using zone coverage, each guard must know the area assigned to every lifeguard station in the facility. Management should post a diagram of the zone coverage system so you can learn the zones and any accompanying high-risk areas or blind spots. Pay extra attention to the high-risk areas (see pages 78–91 for common high-risk areas); your vigilance will pay off. If you have a blind spot in your area, ask your supervisor if you may adjust your position to make that section more visible to you. If that is not possible, ask the manager about making additional coverage arrangements.

In zone coverage, be sure to look at the lifeguard in the station next to yours at the beginning and end of each scanning sweep. This visual contact will help both of you feel confident that help is nearby. You will also be able to keep track of potential problems by communicating with that guard. Include the area beneath your lifeguard chairs in your scan; that high-risk area is sometimes difficult to monitor.

Scan your assigned areas with a systematic, sweeping pattern. Use all your senses to monitor what is happening so you can anticipate and spot trouble (Lifesaving Society, 1993):

- *Vision:* Watch the flow of activity, monitor the position of other guards, or look for changing weather conditions.
- *Hearing:* Listen for unusual sounds such as people arguing or breaking equipment, or for sounds made by occurrences outside your field of view (like thunder). Also listen for signals from other guards or patrons. Swimmers who become fatigued, suffer a cramp, or become injured may call for help.
- *Smelling:* Notice if you can smell liquor on patrons' breath, chemicals from spillage or leakage, or smoke from a fire.
- *Touching:* Feel the sun's heat, the roughness or suppleness of surfaces, drops of rain, or strong winds.

Practice developing and improving your perception skills. As you scan, watch for patrons who are doing things such as the following:

- Violating rules
- Behaving unusually
- Looking panicky
- Swimming underwater repeatedly
- Showing signs of drowning (see chapter 6)
- Engaging in horseplay
- Thrashing at the surface
- Doing what appears to be the jellyfish float
- Swimming long distances or many widths underwater
- Having breath-holding contests

Note patrons' size, swimming proficiency, comfort, and facial expressions. Chapter 6 provides more on victim identification, and chapter 5 covers handling rule infractions.

Use whatever scanning pattern is effective for you. Be sure to scan above and below the surface of the water, including the bottom of the pool, each time you scan your area. (If you are lifeguarding in an open water area, do not scan bottom to top. For the most part you'll be unable to see below the surface, so concentrate your efforts strictly on the top.) Use many different patterns—horizontal, vertical, circular, and triangular. Here are some additional strategies you can use to organize and sort your sensory input (Lifesaving Society, 1993):

- *Head counting:* Notice the changes as you count the swimmers in your zone during each scan.
- *Grouping:* Sort swimmers into groups by age, gender, risk potential, or some combination of these categories. Monitor changes.
- *Mental filing:* On each sweep, build swimmer profiles based on their ability, skill, or activity. Track changes in behavior or activity on each scan.
- *Profile matching:* Measure what you see against characteristics of types of victims (see chapter 6 for more on these characteristics).
- *Tracking:* Track the progress of patrons who have submerged (from the diving board or the surface) and those who fit a high-risk profile (see chapter 6 for types of people who may be at risk).
- *Counting seconds:* If you are guarding open water and visibility is poor, count 20 seconds whenever you see a swimmer go underwater. If that swimmer does not reappear at the surface after 20 seconds, stand up in your chair or tower and count 10 seconds more. If the swimmer still does not reappear, activate your emergency plan and enter the water.

Figure 4.6 While scanning, swivel your head and look directly at each area.

As you scan, swivel your head to look directly at each area (figure 4.6). Stop your eyes momentarily every 10 to 15 degrees to detect details (Fenner, Leahy, Buhk, and Dawes, 1999). In swimming pools, your goal is to scan your entire area in 10 seconds and to strive to be able to respond to help a swimmer in distress in 10 seconds or less. This is called the *10 × 10 reaction*. It's based on a worst case scenario, which would be a 5- to 9-year-old child who could remain active at the surface for up to 10 seconds. To continue to scan in 10-second intervals, you must stay alert and attentive; even a brief distraction can cause you to miss important information that might prevent an accident or aid a victim.

According to Fenner, Leahy, Buhk, and Dawes (1999), fatigue can cause your scanning ability to deteriorate. Many of the conditions under which you guard can fatigue you, such as dehydration, physical and mental fatigue, eyestrain, hunger, and exposure to sun and wind. Come to work well-rested and avoid medications (prescription and nonprescription) that affect your alertness. Follow these tips to help maintain your alertness:

- Drink enough water.
- Maintain good posture.
- Use adequate protection against the sun and wind.
- Rotate tasks or areas so you get sufficient breaks from being on duty.
- Adjust your position to offset glare, whether you are indoors or outdoors. Wear sunglasses that are polarized and that allow clear peripheral vision.

In single-guard facilities at which you are not able to rotate your position, talk to your supervisor to make sure you receive the support you need to stay alert.

When you feel fatigue setting in, try some of these tips for maintaining mental alertness:

- Count swimmers in your zone.
- Check high-risk patrons (see chapter 6) and hazardous areas.
- Change your posture by leaning forward or backward, standing, or stepping to the right or left of the chair. You may want to change every few minutes.
- Mentally rehearse a rescue.
- Visually check other guards.

Following a system when you guard ensures that you thoroughly observe your assigned area.

Lifeguarding Steps

When you lifeguard, scan your assigned area while you are on duty, following these guidelines:

- Guard bottom to top in pools; guard the surface in open water.
- Strive to achieve the 10 × 10 reaction.
- Scan your area continually.
- Start and end each scan with a visual check of the adjacent guard.
- Maintain vigilance
- Know every lifeguard zone.
- Pay extra attention to high-risk areas.

Assess the state of the patrons in your zone (see chapter 6) to determine if there is a need for some action on your part. If so, take action, either by enforcing rules using Q-1-2 or initiating a rescue. When you perform a rescue, resuscitate the victim if necessary. Remove the victim and monitor her or his condition until emergency medical personnel arrive. After you have assisted the emergency medical personnel, complete an accident report (see chapter 8).

To summarize:

1. Scan your zone continuously while you are on duty.
2. Assess the state of the patrons.
3. Determine if there is a need for action and, if so, either enforce rules (using Q-1-2) or initiate rescue.
4. If rescue is needed, rescue the victim and resuscitate if necessary.
5. Remove the victim from the water and monitor her or his condition until emergency medical personnel arrive.
6. Assist emergency medical personnel.
7. Complete an accident report.

Rotation Systems

When there are two or more lifeguards, you should rotate regularly. Rotation relieves the boredom of watching the same area for an entire day, keeping guards alert and letting the management easily shift zone responsibilities when necessary. Rotation also distributes the most and least enjoyable areas among all guards.

Most rotation systems are set up on a time schedule. A lifeguard returning from break usually initiates the rotation, temporarily putting one extra guard on duty until the rotation is complete. Between rotation cycles, the guard who rotates off duty gets a short break. In some facilities the guard may be rotated not to a break but to another task, such as picking up trash or checking chemical levels.

Staff also may be rotated at a prearranged signal. This type of rotation is usually set in motion by a change in the number of swimmers in an area. The signal should be given only by the head lifeguard or another guard assigned to that duty by the management. An individual guard should not make such a rotation decision.

Rotation systems can be designed in different ways. Figure 4.7 illustrates a generic approach to rotation triggered by a guard returning from break.

If your facility uses elevated lifeguard stands, one guard replacing another on a stand must scan as the second guard climbs down (figure 4.8). Once on the ground, that guard must scan the assigned area until the new guard is in position on the elevated stand.

If there are not enough lifeguards on duty to provide an extra guard for the rotation, guards should exchange positions in a prearranged order, watching the zones as they switch. One guard would move to replace another, and the guards would exchange any necessary information about the potential hazards. The relieved guard would then move to the next assigned position, and so on.

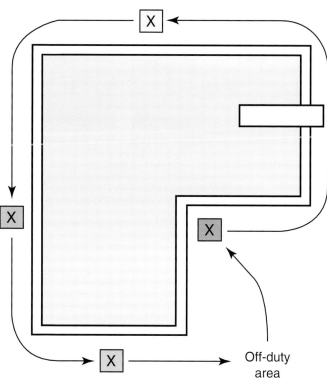

Figure 4.7 Example of a rotation system.

a.

b.

c.

d.

e.

f.

Figure 4.8   The replacement guard scans the water as the other guard climbs down from the lifeguard stand. Once on the ground, the other guard scans the water while the replacement guard climbs onto the stand.

Whatever system is in operation at your facility, the following guidelines for rotation are important:

- Rotate regularly.
- Rotate systematically.
- Move the lifeguard from the most demanding position to either a break period or a less-demanding spot.
- As you rotate, keep alert to potential problems and patron needs.

Lifeguarding Locations

Where you stand, sit, or rove is as important as determining the area that you supervise. The location of the sun and the placement of windows at an indoor facility have a definite effect on where lifeguards and lifeguard stands should be placed. Your location governs how well you can see your assigned area and how quickly you can react to an emergency.

You may be stationed either in an elevated chair (or tower) or on the ground as a roving lifeguard. Each position has different advantages. For example, from an elevated area you can see what is going on in the pool much better than from the ground. At ground level, waves or other swimmers may obscure some patrons. It's also more difficult at ground level to see distressed or actively drowning victims, who may be changing from a horizontal to a vertical position and making little progress in moving toward the edge of the pool. However, on the ground you are closer to patrons, making it easier to give them advice, cautions, or reprimands.

Towers and Elevated Chairs

Both towers and elevated chairs will give you a better viewing point than a station on the ground (figure 4.9). Elevated lifeguard stands are the best for supervising the swimming area, but be sure to scan the areas next to and beneath the chair, which are blind spots where accidents can happen.

Figure 4.9 Elevated chairs provide a better viewing range.

Chairs or towers must be placed appropriately if guards are to be able to scan effectively. Lifeguarding chairs should be located at pool side and should face all entrances. They should be placed according to the zone coverages used. The height of the chairs should be appropriate for effective vision. If a chair is not placed properly, guard in a roving position until the chair can be moved.

On a tower or chair, keeps all of your equipment within easy reach in case of an emergency. Rather than storing it on the ground, mount it on the tower or the elevated chair. Have a rescue tube or buoy with you at all times. Protect the extra line from the rescue tube or buoy so it doesn't get tangled on either you or the chair.

In addition to having your equipment at the top of an elevated lifeguard station, you will need to practice getting down from the station. Depending on the height of the station and the depth of the water, you may jump or climb down. When jumping from any height, look before you leap!

Check the area beneath you to avoid landing on a patron or injuring yourself. When you do jump, grasp any equipment you are taking with you tightly, being careful of lines that can get caught. You want to maintain control of your rescue equipment at all times. Finally, bend your knees when you land; landing with locked knees can be very painful and can cause serious injury to your knees and back. Practice getting down from the tower or chair until you can do it fluidly. Every second counts in an emergency.

If you intend to jump directly into the water, you must know that the water is deep enough for jumping safely. In traditional pools, that should be easy. In a wave pool, you must time your jump so you hit the water at the peak of the swell. In a river, the depth and speed of the water change with rainfall or drought. Know the conditions in your area before you jump from a tower or an elevated chair into the water.

Roving Lifeguards

Lifeguards who patrol the area by walking around the perimeter find it easier to handle public relations and courteously discipline patrons. These guards are also able to provide educational tips to patrons because they are more accessible (figure 4.10). Many times roving guards are assigned to shallow water areas so they can carefully supervise the water and the surrounding deck or beach. Roving guards should carry a rescue tube or buoy so that it is ready for use. Roving guards may also serve as a communication link between lifeguard towers, particularly at beaches.

Figure 4.10 A roving lifeguard can interact with patrons more easily

Guard Communication Systems

Communication is very important to your success as a lifeguard. Not only do you need to communicate well with the patrons of your facility, you must be able to do the same with the other members of your lifeguarding team. Several communication systems exist for lifeguards:

- Whistle signals
- Hand signals
- Rescue equipment signals
- Flags
- Radios
- Telephones
- Megaphones

Your facility will select one or more of these systems, and you and all of the other lifeguards should be familiar with them.

Whistle Signals

Patterns of whistle blows can be used to signal particular situations. One common signal system is the following:

- One short blast—used to get swimmers' attention
- Two short blasts—used to get other lifeguards' attention
- One long blast—used to initiate emergency procedures

Hand Signals

Lifeguards frequently use hand signals to communicate with patrons and other lifeguards. Some examples are illustrated in figure 4.11. These signals are frequently accompanied by whistle signals. Be sure to hold your signal a few seconds to be sure it has been seen.

a.

b.

c.

d.

e.

Figure 4.11 Common hand signals: *(a)* used to give direction; *(b)* lifeguard needs help; *(c)* used at water slides to stop staff from sending sliders down the slide; *(d)* activity can resume; *(e)* lifeguard taps her head when she needs another guard to watch her area temporarily.

Rescue Equipment Signals

Some signals can be made using a rescue tube or buoy (see figure 4.12). Rescue equipment held vertically and moved from side to side means assistance is needed. Rescue equipment held horizontally over the head means the situation is under control.

a.   b.   c.

Figure 4.12   Rescue equipment signals: *(a)* urgent, additional help needed; *(b)* additional help needed, but less urgent; *(c)* situation under control, no additional help needed.

Figure 4.13   A megaphone can be useful at a crowded facility.

Flags

Flags are not used in most swimming pools, but they are used at some waterfront areas and are common at water slides and water parks. Waving a red flag means danger, or stop sending water sliders down the slide. Waving a green flag indicates that all is well.

Radios

Two-way and CB radios are most frequently used in large waterfront areas where visual contact is more difficult. These radios are for lifeguarding business only, not socializing.

Telephones

Phones are important for use in emergencies. Emergency numbers should be listed on or posted by the telephones. If cell or cordless phones are used, a standard phone also should be available in case the cell or cordless phones do not work. Phone use should be restricted to business or emergency use only.

Megaphones

A *megaphone* is a cone-shaped device used to intensify and direct the voice. Using a megaphone can be helpful when a facility is crowded (figure 4.13).

Group Swimming Safety Check Systems

Most camps and youth organizations use one or more safety check systems to account for all individuals quickly. These systems keep lifeguards aware of the number and location of swimmers in the water; they are especially useful in lake or river environments where visibility is limited. Failure to enforce the system undermines its value.

Four of the most common safety check systems are the buddy system, the tag board (or roll call) system, the cap system, and the pool check. Each is useful for a different purpose. Although management will decide which system you'll use, you may be asked to give input. And for any system to work, swimmers must be informed of the procedures. You are likely to play a major role in that educational process.

Buddy System

In the buddy system, every swimmer is assigned a "buddy" of similar ability. If there is an uneven number of swimmers, one set of buddies may be a triad. Buddies are required to stay close to each other at all times. Then, if one buddy is having difficulty, the other buddy can signal for help.

At a predetermined signal, different from all other signals used by the staff, swimmers "buddy up"—they stop, join hands with their buddies, raise their arms high, and remain stationary (figure 4.14). Such positioning lets staff members count groups and account for all swimmers. At a second sounding of the signal, buddies may drop hands and continue their activities.

It is important that you test this system frequently so that partners remain close together. If any buddies have strayed too far apart when you signal to "buddy up," warn the violators that another instance of being away from a buddy will result in time out of the water (see page 55). Consistent enforcement of the system rules, along with other swimming rules, will make the buddy system work for you and your facility.

Figure 4.14 At the signal, buddies join hands, raise their arms, and remain still while the lifeguard counts groups.

Tag Board and Roll Call Systems

The tag board and roll call systems work in the same way—swimmers are accounted for before they enter the water and after their swimming period is over. With the tag board system, each person gets a tag with his or her name on it. Swimmers hang their tags on a pegboard as they enter the water and remove them when they leave the water, both under the watchful eye of a lifeguard or camp staff member. A variation of this system uses color-coded tags with a different color on each side (figure 4.15). One color indicates swimmers are in the water, the other that they are out. At the end of each swimming period, the group leader can easily check to see that all swimmers have left the water.

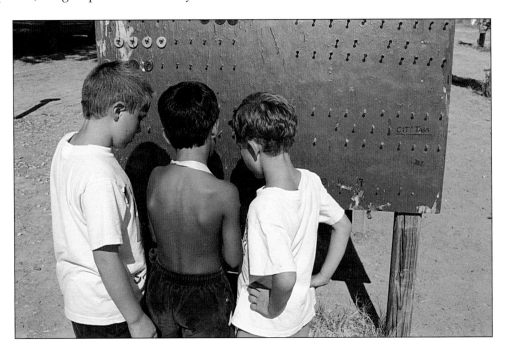

Figure 4.15 Different colored tags indicate swimmers who are in or out of the water.

If a tag is unaccounted for, an immediate search is started. For the safety of all swimmers, the group leader must enforce the rule that each individual is responsible for her or his own tag. Spot-checking swimmers is a good way to test whether they are following the rules and placing their tags correctly on the board as they enter the water. Identify a swimmer and look to see that the tag is displayed appropriately. If it is not, summon the swimmer and discuss the rules.

The roll call system (figure 4.16) operates on the same principle of checking attendance before and after the swimming session, but no equipment is necessary. The group leader simply takes attendance by calling names aloud before the swimmers enter the water and immediately after they exit. If someone doesn't respond, a search is started immediately. One drawback of the roll call system is that the time between roll calls could be the time during which a swimmer becomes missing.

Cap System

This system allows lifeguards, staff, and swimmers to differentiate between different swimming skill levels by looking at what color bathing cap, headband, or wristband a swimmer is wearing. The system can be used with either of the other safety check systems. The following color coding is widely used.

- Nonswimmers and beginners wear red.
- Intermediate swimmers wear yellow.
- Advanced swimmers wear blue or green.
- Leaders and lifeguards wear white.

The advantage of this system is that a lifeguard can easily spot red or yellow in an area reserved for advanced swimmers and act quickly to move that person to a safer area.

Figure 4.16 In the roll call system, the group leader calls attendance before swimmers enter the water and after they exit.

Pool Check

The widely-used pool check system is designed for busy periods when lifeguards want to be sure that they can account for all swimmers. On a specified signal, all swimmers are asked to leave the water or sit on the edge of the pool. This system allows the lifeguards to periodically check that no one is on the pool bottom and provides the swimmers with a rest period.

Pool checks can be annoying to patrons if overused. However, if they are necessary to ensure safety, carry them out. To make checks less objectionable, consider coupling them with announcements for all patrons, brief swimming tips, or the beginning of special activities.

Special Guarding Situations

You will undoubtedly experience many different lifeguarding situations during the course of your service. Some are more common than others. Spend some time considering how you should react to each of the following situations. If you are likely to confront one of them, seek out any additional training you might need.

Classes

When you are assigned to lifeguard during a class, your role is simply to provide lifeguarding services. In any class situation, watch every swimmer, just as you would during a free swim period. Assess the comfort and skill level of each one and use that information to guide your attention. Be sure to keep all class members grouped together (the instructor should help). They need to hear instructions and you need to know where they are and that they are practicing the skills for their class.

Day Camps and Day Care

In day camp and day care situations, when possible, give children a skill test and divide them into groups by skill level for swimming activity. Your job will be a little easier when you know that the swimmers are of similar abilities. A common swim test is to ask those children who want to swim in deep water to first swim across the shallow end to the wall, using any style. Those children who can do this successfully are then escorted to the deep water, where they are asked to jump in, surface, swim 40 feet on the front, and stop. They then must turn over, tread water for 10 to 15 seconds, then turn onto their backs and return to the starting position, either on their fronts or on their backs.

If the group is not divided, it might be a perfect chance to institute one of the group-swimming safety check systems just described. Select the one that will let you keep track of swimmers most easily. Working with these young swimmers is an excellent opportunity to teach them water safety.

Review the rules frequently with children (figure 4.17); repetition will help them learn and understand the rules. Train camp or day care staff to assist you in teaching the rules and watching their groups. Be sure that staff have learned the rules and know your facility's emergency system. However, make it clear to staff that you, as the lifeguard, are in charge of the swimming activity.

Figure 4.17 With children, review the rules frequently.

Clear the water periodically. While the water is empty, scan the pool bottom. In a waterfront situation, check attendance carefully. These "out of the water" checks are good teaching opportunities and give swimmers a chance to rest.

In working with a group of only young children, you might find it useful to stand on the deck near them. You'll be closer should anyone become frightened or need help in the water, and you'll be close enough to begin teaching these young swimmers the rules. Be sure, however, to check with your facility manager before independently changing your position based on the group using your area.

For guidelines for aquatics in day camps and day care, see appendix B.

Competitive Events

The most common activities a lifeguard at a competitive event will become involved in are assisting distressed swimmers or divers, controlling crowds, maintaining safety, and responding to potential spinal injuries. It is important that you establish communication with the meet director so that any incident is handled effectively.

Although you may feel that there is no possibility of needing to go into the water to assist a swimmer during a swim meet, you must be prepared. You should arrive at this assignment dressed as you would for a shift at a crowded pool. You'll still need rescue equipment available in the usual places. If an incident does occur, you want to be able to react efficiently and effectively. Stay alert and be ready to respond.

Rental Groups

Groups that rent a facility for a party need special attention. Some patrons assume that the rules are relaxed because they are the only ones at the facility.

The management of your facility should have a signed agreement with any rental group that clearly states the rules and enforcement policy and procedures. These rules should be enforced just as they are during a regular swim session. Be sure to review any special agreements the management might have made.

When the group arrives at your facility, learn who is in charge. That person will be your contact should any incidents occur. Next, review the rules with the group. Remind them that the rules are to ensure their safety. If the group doesn't follow the rules, they will be asked to leave and risk not being able to use the facility in the future.

If a group brings their own lifeguards to your facility, have those lifeguards meet with the facility guards to discuss facility rules, emergency procedures, and hazards specific to your facility. Conversely, if a group from your YMCA is visiting another facility and brings lifeguards, those lifeguards should learn that facility's rules, emergency procedures, and hazards before anyone enters the water.

Language Barriers

You may face a situation in which a swimmer doesn't speak the same language as you. With our country becoming more ethnically diverse, there is probably another lifeguard or a patron who can translate. Get to know those around you who can help. If there is no one to translate, use common hand signals to communicate.

People With Disabilities

Under the Americans with Disabilities Act (ADA), people with disabilities must have access to all facilities and must receive equal opportunity to use them. Furthermore, they must be treated by the same standards you treat other patrons. Those with disabilities are people first! Aquatic facilities must determine how to work with each person with a disability.

Disabilities can be categorized in many ways. Perhaps the most common divisions are

- sensory disabilities (blindness, deafness),
- physical disabilities,
- developmental disabilities (may be either physical or mental), and
- mental disabilities.

People with sensory disabilities rely on their nondisabled senses to receive communication. For example, people who cannot see rely on their hearing, and those who cannot hear rely on sight. Practice giving instructions using just your hands and no words. Then use your voice and no hand signals. If your facility has deaf patrons, consider developing a vocabulary of sign language signals and having a board to write on available.

Swimming is a common therapeutic activity for people with physical and developmental disabilities. Some of these individuals may have difficulties communicating or moving that could place them in danger. So they can participate in aquatic activities safely, you need to learn how to handle emergencies involving people with disabilities.

People with physical disabilities may not have sufficient buoyancy, strength, flexibility, or agility to navigate certain areas of your facility safely. Give these individuals a little extra attention, especially if they are moving into areas requiring more skill.

People with developmental disabilities may have excellent physical skills. Your obligation with these patrons is to help them understand and follow the rules of the facility. People with communication deficits may have no trouble swimming or understanding the rules. They may have difficulty understanding what you are trying to communicate because of impaired senses, or they may have difficulty expressing their questions or concerns to you.

So what can you do to be effective in these situations? First, be alert enough to notice anyone with a disability who is at your facility. Medic alert tags may indicate those who have disabilities. Talk with disabled patrons about the facility and about their needs. Most people with disabilities are happy to discuss their situations if you approach them in a supportive, professional manner. Be sure that people with a developmental or communication disability understand the rules and policies of the facility. Work with them and their companions to ensure that they understand. If one of them asks you a question, work hard to understand it and provide an answer that he or she can understand.

You can use the same rescue techniques that you will learn in chapter 7 to provide assistance to people with disabilities, but be flexible. You may need to be somewhat inventive. If someone does not have a right arm for you to grab, you'll have to do the rescue using the left arm. Or a swimmer may not be able to see the equipment you are extending—how can you get her or him to grab it? Once you know about a patron with a specific disability, think through how you will assist him or her should the need arise. Plan ahead and use whatever works!

Tips for Working With Individuals Who Have Disabilities

Here are some tips to assist you in dealing with individuals who are deaf or blind, or who have developmental, physical, or cognitive disabilities (American Red Cross, 1995).

Patrons Who Are Deaf

- Get the patron's attention before you speak by gently tapping his or her shoulder or waving your hand where he or she can see it. You may have to ask people to help you make contact with patrons who are hearing impaired, especially if you are trying to enforce rules from a distance.
- Maintain eye contact.
- Be especially calm and patient.
- Determine if patrons can read lips. Even if they can, they probably will understand only 30 to 40 percent of the conversation (or less). Lip-reading is more difficult if the person who is talking has serious orthodontic problems, a foreign accent, or a beard or mustache.
- Face patrons while you are speaking to them.
- Speak slowly and clearly. Even if the patrons cannot read lips, speak as you gesture or use signs.
- If possible, use an interpreter who can communicate in sign language.
- Try pantomiming, using broad gestures.
- Do not shout; if patrons have even partial hearing and are wearing hearing aids, you could distort their hearing.
- Use written messages. Patrons who have been deaf since birth may not understand some grammatical combinations, so keep it simple.

Patrons Who Are Blind

- Determine if patrons also have hearing impairment.
- Do not shout.
- Maintain touch contact by lightly resting your hand on a patron's forearm.
- Explain things in detail.
- If a patron can walk and needs to be led, lead him or her by standing one step ahead and one step to the side, letting the patron rest a hand on the inside of your bent elbow. Walk forward slowly, alerting the patron to any obstacles.
- Identify the source of any strange noises.

Patrons With Developmental Disabilities

People with developmental disabilities may appear confused or disoriented. When speaking with such patrons, use the following guidelines:

- Determine the patron's level of understanding by asking questions.
- Speak as you would to adults, but at an appropriate developmental level.
- Wait for a delayed response when it is a patron's turn to answer or respond; have patience.

- Evaluate the patron's understanding by asking a few questions, and re-explain if necessary.
- Listen carefully.
- Do not hesitate to ask patrons about their disabilities.
- Speak slowly and distinctly.
- Use the word "disability" instead of a slang word to describe patrons' conditions.
- Be aware that some people with Down syndrome can hold their breath underwater for long periods of time. If you have a patron with this syndrome, find out how long she or he can hold her or his breath (Lepore, 2000).

Patrons With Physical Disabilities

People may have many different kinds of physical disabilities. Try to become familiar with individuals and their abilities, especially if you will be transporting them within the facility or helping them enter and exit the water. If equipment is required to assist them, know where the equipment is located and how to use it. Use the following guidelines when working with patrons who have physical disabilities:

- Try to look beyond physical impairments and relate to each patron as an individual.
- Do not be afraid to tactfully ask patrons about their capabilities.
- When possible, let patrons ask for assistance. Respect their right to indicate what help is needed.
- Try not to categorize patrons by expecting only stereotypic behavior or achievement.
- While some broad generalizations can be made regarding disabling conditions, remember that individuals will vary greatly both in how they manifest conditions and in their own capabilities.
- When assisting patrons in and out of the water, ask them how they would like you to assist. They will tell you where to support them and what lift method is comfortable for them.
- To prevent accidents during entries and exits, watch for hazards such as wet spots. Keep in mind that patrons may have some difficulty with balance (Lepore, 2000).
- Show empathy to patrons, trying to understand how they feel, rather than sympathy.
- Be considerate. Speak directly to people with disabilities, not through family members or peers.
- Allow patrons to keep prosthetic devices and aids, including wheelchairs and crutches, within reach.
- Do not ignore patrons' obvious needs, but don't overdo assistance.
- Be aware that people who have physical disabilities may not be very stable in the water when they are using flotation devices, especially tubes around their chests. Many of these people may not be able to lift their heads above water after falling face-first into the water (Lepore, 2000).
- People with cerebral palsy or other neurological disabilities may find it difficult to change from a vertical to a horizontal position in the water. This may cause a problem. For example, if they are swimming in the deep end and must stop to avoid running into other swimmers (becoming vertical), they may have difficulty starting up again and become exhausted by treading water. People with neurological disabilities also may have difficulty turning over

from front to back or recovering to a stand from the prone position (Lepore, 2000).

Patrons With Cognitive Disabilities

- Be aware that many people with cognitive impairments are impulsive. They will not obey rules because they cannot "apply" to themselves the rules they have been told, or they are hyperactive and cannot control their outbursts. Remind them of the rules in a positive manner every time they come to the pool (Lepore, 2000).

Reproduced, by permission, from the American Red Cross, 1995, *Head Lifeguard* (St. Louis, MO: Mosby Lifeline).

Review Questions

1. List the four steps to making good decisions.
2. Define the parts of the Q-1-2 system and give an example of each part.
3. What is the difference between entire-area coverage and zone coverage? List two advantages and disadvantages of each.
4. Name four strategies to follow while scanning.
5. List four things you can you do to help stay alert while you're lifeguarding.
6. Describe a typical rotation system.
7. Why is rotation important?
8. List the advantages and disadvantages of towers and elevated chairs and roving lifeguards.
9. What are the seven communication systems for lifeguards?
10. Name two signals that you can use with your rescue tube to communicate to other lifeguards.
11. List and describe four group swimming safety check systems.
12. Describe how you would guard differently in a class, at a day camp, and during a swim meet.
13. What options do you have for communicating with someone with a communication disability?
14. Briefly describe how you would handle lifeguarding where someone with a disability swims.
15. Name three things you can do to improve communication with one of the following groups: patrons who are deaf, patrons who are blind, or patrons with developmental disabilities.

CHAPTER *five*

Rules and Regulations

To prevent aquatic accidents you need to be familiar with your state's bathing code, your swimming facility, and the hazards within your facility. You also need to establish rules that minimize these dangers and then consistently enforce them.

In This Chapter, You'll Learn About

- establishing and communicating rules in your facility,
- common rules for high-risk locations, and
- enforcing the rules.

ESTABLISHING AND COMMUNICATING RULES

In most facilities, the management tries to keep the number of rules for patrons to a minimum to keep the atmosphere as enjoyable as possible. When additional rules are found to be needed, the management must consider both the safety and enjoyment of patrons. Any rules must be realistic, specific, and understandable.

Once the rules are established, the lifeguard must enforce them among patrons. The first step to enforcing the rules is communicating them. The most logical way to inform the users of a facility of the rules is to post them in the swimming area. Fences, lifeguard stands, and diving boards are all appropriate spots to mount signs. Copies of the rules can be handed out with pool passes or perhaps listed in a facility newsletter.

COMMON RULES FOR HIGH-RISK LOCATIONS

Certain areas of any aquatic environment can be more dangerous than others. Lifeguards must closely supervise the areas where accidents occur most frequently (see figure 5.2). In the following section, each area's potential dangers are described along with some suggested safety rules. (For more on safety and water play elements, see chapter 13.)

Entrance

Wanting to get into the water as quickly as possible often leads swimmers to run at the entrance to the pool (figure 5.1). A wet and slippery deck poses a high risk, and one swimmer can easily collide with another.

Suggested rule:

Walk, don't run.

Figure 5.1 The entrance to the pool can be a hazardous area.

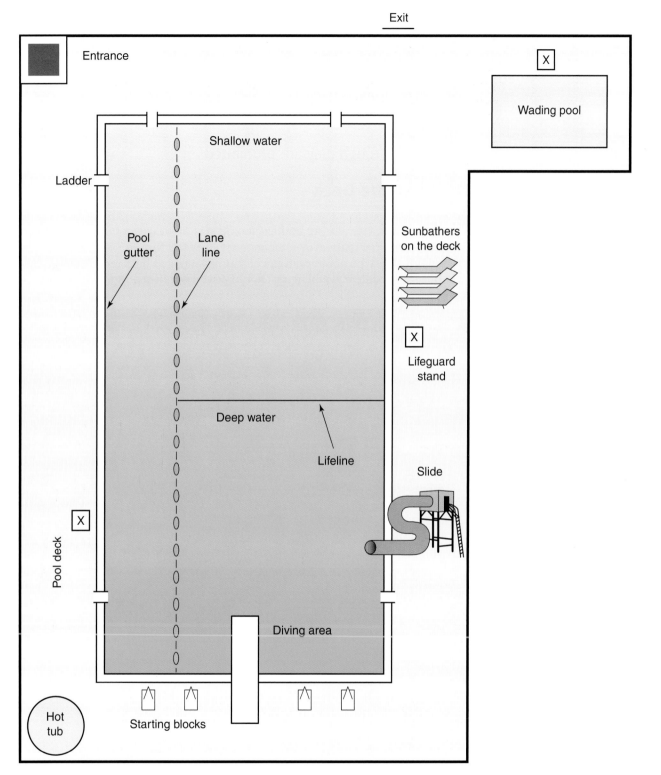

Figure 5.2 High-risk areas in a swimming facility.

Pool Deck

Running and rough play are the primary concerns on the pool deck. Many falls are the result of runners skidding or bumping into other patrons. Nonswimmers also can be knocked into the water by people running on the deck. Good-natured rough play often escalates, causing participants or bystanders to be pushed or knocked to the ground or into the water. This behavior detracts from the enjoyment of others at your facility.

Suggested rule:

> Pushing and rough play are prohibited.

Sunbathers on the Deck

Sunbathers lying too close to the pool's edge can cause swimmers walking around the pool to stumble or trip. Generally sunbathers should stay at least 6 feet from the edge to allow adequate room for swimmers to enter and exit the water (figure 5.3). A 2- to 4-inch-wide safety stripe around the pool perimeter at this distance can help remind patrons to observe this rule. Breakable or metal items should not be permitted in the deck area.

Figure 5.3 A special deck area for sunbathers will keep them away from the edge of the pool.

Suggested rules:

> Sunbathe at least 6 feet from the edge of the pool.
>
> Only plastic containers and toys are allowed in the pool, observation deck, and locker/shower areas.

Ladders

Ladders (figure 5.4) should be used only for getting into and out of the pool; other uses can pose hazards. People who sit on the ladders to talk block access for tired swimmers. Other dangers include swimmers who use the ladders to pull themselves underwater and back to the surface; they risk getting caught in a rung, shoved off the ladder, or stepped on. Slippery ladders are dangerous when swimmers swing on them or dive from them. If swimmers swim between the ladder and the wall, they risk being caught, either on the surface or underwater.

Figure 5.4 Ladders should be used for entering and exiting the pool only.

Suggested rules:

Use ladders only for getting into or out of the water.

Only one swimmer on the ladder at a time.

Pool Gutters

Pool overflow gutters or troughs pose several potential dangers. Nonswimmers may use the gutters to travel from shallow to deep water, traveling along the side of the pool hand over hand when the guard is looking the other way. Danger can arise when the nonswimmer is pushed away from the wall or attempts to climb out of the water and traps a knee or elbow in the gutter. If you spot a nonswimmer moving along the gutter, have her or him climb out of the water on the nearest ladder and walk back to shallow water.

Prohibit patrons from standing on the gutters or climbing into them. Arms, hands, legs, or feet can get wedged into the gutter and cause an injury, particularly if the patron loses balance.

Small children also enjoy jumping into the water and turning to grab the gutter for support. Mistimed turns result in many cut chins, so stop this activity immediately.

Suggested rules:

Nonswimmers must stay in shallow water.

Use a ladder to get out of the pool.

Jump into the pool well past the gutter.

Lifelines

Lifelines mark the break between shallow and deep water (figure 5.5). The chief danger to watch for is small children or weak swimmers who edge into deep water by pulling themselves along the lifelines. If they are pushed or otherwise lose a grasp on the lines, nonswimmers may be in water over their heads and consequently in danger. Swimmers should not sit or hang on lifelines; a lifeline submerged under the weight of a chatting swimmer is much more difficult for the distressed swimmer to find. Be sure to keep the lifelines strung tightly enough to be visible and to support panicky swimmers. They should be strong enough and strung tightly enough to support an adult with his or her head above water, with the rope not submerging more than a foot.

Figure 5.5 Lifelines separate shallow water areas from deep water areas.

Suggested rules:

Nonswimmers must stay in shallow water.

Keep off the lifelines.

Use lifelines only for temporary support.

The Water

Any water area is potentially hazardous if swimmers are not careful. Flotation devices like inner tubes and plastic toys can be dangerous if a nonswimming user floats into deep water or the device deflates and traps the person in it. If someone tries to get out of a flotation device, she or he may experience difficulty. These swimming aids are even more dangerous on crowded days when swimmers may accidentally bump into them, causing the user to fall away from the flotation device. They also obstruct the lifeguard's view of the bottom of the pool.

Many parents buy swimming aids for their children and perhaps gain a false sense of security from them. Parents must supervise their children at all times, whether or not the children are using swimming aids. But keep in mind that parental vigilance doesn't mean that you don't have to keep watch on those children as well.

A second general concern in any aquatic facility is patrons who enter the water at an unsafe depth. Consider a nonswimmer going down a ladder unknowingly into deep water or a skilled swimmer diving at a steep angle into the shallow end of the pool. You can decrease the probability that someone will enter the water not knowing the depth by pointing out depth markers to patrons.

Depth markers should appear on every side of the pool and on the deck. In some pools a contour depth line shows all swimmers exactly how deep the water is in relation to their height. The contour line, generally on a fence or wall, provides a profile of the pool depths. Patrons can easily stand next to the contour line to determine the point in the pool where it is safe for them to enter.

A third general concern is underwater swimming and other breath-holding activities. Underwater swimmers may be jumped on, possibly receiving back injuries. Another common problem for underwater swimmers is blacking out from hyperventilation. Swimmers may take a series of deep breaths before swimming across the pool underwater. This decreases the amount of carbon dioxide in the blood, and because carbon dioxide tells the brain when to breathe, the reduction interferes with the breathing process. In effect, a swimmer can black out—and possibly drown—because he or she doesn't breathe when necessary. (For additional information on hyperventilation, see page 188.)

Do not allow swimmers to swim underwater or to hold their breath during recreational periods. If you see someone performing these activities, intervene, using the Q-1-2 system. Such activities might include the following:

- Hyperventilation
- Hypoxic breathing
- Swimming multiple lengths or widths underwater
- Performing multiple sprints without taking breaths between strokes
- Breath-holding games or contests

Suggested Rules:

Only Coast Guard-approved PFDs permitted.

Adult supervision required for all children.

Breath holding and prolonged underwater swimming is prohibited.

Shallow Water

The primary dangers in shallow water are diving and dunking. Even an experienced diver may hit the bottom, causing injuries to the fingers, hands, head, neck, or back. Depths should be marked at regular intervals and at changes in water depth and contour to alert divers to the conditions. Standing front dives should be performed in no less than 9 feet of water. (See appendix C for YMCA guidelines on diving and diving water depth.)

Dunking is also a common activity for playful children and adults. The unsuspecting swimmer may ingest water and become scared or be injured hitting the side or bottom of the pool.

Suggested rules:

Diving allowed only in marked areas.

No dunking or rough play.

Deep Water

Those who are most in danger in deep water (figure 5.6) are nonswimmers and underwater swimmers. The nonswimmers can be spotted moving to the deep water along the gutter, on the deck, or from the diving board. Before entering the water, they may look very apprehensive and usually have their arms folded or wrapped around themselves. Prevent nonswimmers from getting into the deep water.

Patrons should take a swimming test before being allowed to swim in the deep water. A common swim test is to ask those patrons who want to swim in deep water to first swim across the shallow end to the wall, using any style. Those who can do this successfully are then escorted to the deep water, where they are asked to jump in, surface, swim 40 feet on the front, and stop. They then must turn over, tread water for 10 to 15 seconds, then turn onto their backs and return to the starting position, either on their fronts or on their backs.

Masks, fins, and snorkels may lure poor swimmers into deep water by providing false security. Keep a close watch on anyone using such equipment (if your facility allows it).

Figure 5.6 Deep water can be extremely dangerous to nonswimmers or underwater swimmers.

Goggles, while safe in water up to 5 feet deep, should not be worn at greater depths. The pressure on the eyes may cause discomfort or injury.

Allow diving from the deck only where the water is more than 9 feet deep.

Suggested rules:

Nonswimmers must stay in shallow water.

Deep diving starts are prohibited.

Diving from the deck is allowed only where the water depth is more than 9 feet.

Starting Blocks and Platforms

Starting blocks and platforms (figure 5.7) pose a significant hazard, especially to the inexperienced swimmer. No one should be allowed to dive from a starting block or platform except in a competitive program or under proper supervision during instruction. Your management should check local and state bathing codes for guidelines on placement of the blocks and the water depth required. They also need to check with their insurance carrier regarding the regulations that carrier requires. The YMCA of the USA recommends that diving blocks be placed in the deep end, with a water depth of at least 5 feet.

If starting blocks or platforms cannot be removed during recreational swims, the YMCA suggests they be capped and that warning signs be posted to stop patrons from using them. (Also see "Competitive Swimming Starting Blocks," page 197, and appendix C.)

Figure 5.7 Starting blocks and platforms should be marked off unless they are needed for a competitive event or program.

Suggested rules:

No sitting, playing, jumping, or diving from starting blocks or platforms.

Starting blocks are for competitive swimming program use only.

Slides

Slides, which continue to become more popular in swimming facilities and water parks, are another high-risk area. Pools with slides should have at least one lifeguard whose main responsibility is the slide area.

All sliders should enter the water feet-first in a sitting position to avoid head injuries. Watch carefully that each slider returns to the surface and clears the area before the next person begins. Insist that the area at the bottom of the slide be kept open to avoid injuries from swimmers being hit by the slider. Also be aware that outdoor slides can get hot enough to cause burns, particularly on hot days. All slides should have a water spray to keep sliders safe. See chapter 13 for more on slides and aquatic attractions.

Suggested rules:

Swimming is prohibited in the slide area.

Move away from the bottom of the slide immediately.

Use the ladder only to get onto the slide.

One person on the slide at a time.

Go down the slide feet-first in a sitting position. Head-first sliding is prohibited.

Recreational Springboard Diving Areas

Diving off a 1-meter board (figure 5.8) may be done either in a separate well or in an area of the pool that is at least 11 feet, 6 inches deep. In either case, you need to give these diving areas special attention and enforce the rules consistently. Many accidents associated with diving can be prevented by an alert lifeguard. Some of the many causes of diving accidents include the condition and arrangement of the equipment and diving areas, the visibility into the water, numerous weather factors, and the depth and distance to the upslope of the pool bottom.

Check the diving boards regularly throughout the day. Restrict the fulcrum setting to keep the board "stiff" for recreational use. Watch each diver return to the surface and exit the diving area before another diver approaches. Watch also for rough play on and around the boards. See appendix C for more information on diving and risk management. We recommend that your facility follow the safe diving practices put forth by United States Diving.

Figure 5.8 Recreational diving off a 1-meter springboard should be closely supervised.

Do not allow recreational use of a 3-meter board or tower. Such equipment should be used only by participants in a supervised program with specially trained diving instructors.

Suggested rules:

Use the ladder to mount the diving board.

Hanging onto or under the board is prohibited.

Only one diver on the board at a time.

Sitting on the guardrails is prohibited.

Wait for the previous diver to swim clear before diving.

Only one bounce allowed.

Dive off the front of the board only.

Hands must enter the water first in head-first dives.

Swim to the ladder immediately after diving.

Swimmers are not allowed in the diving area when the board is open for use.

No fancy dives.

Platforms, 3-meter boards, and towers are closed during recreational swims.

Lifeguard Towers and Equipment

Lifeguard towers and stands (figure 5.9) present a hazard because they attract young swimmers, who often gather at the foot of a stand, potentially obscuring the lifeguard's view. Be sure to scan the water under and around towers in your range of vision. Older patrons may enjoy socializing with the lifeguards. Keep your conversations brief and continue to monitor your area.

Ring buoys and other safety devices may prove equally attractive and dangerous. A ring buoy, like any flotation device, could prove dangerous as a floating aid to a foolhardy nonswimmer. Such equipment is to be used only by trained personnel.

Figure 5.9 Be sure to check the area around your lifeguard tower or stand for curious swimmers.

Suggested rules:

> No climbing on guard towers.
>
> No sitting below guard towers.
>
> Emergency equipment for lifeguard use only.

Wading Pools and Zero-Depth Entry Pools

The reason most facilities decide to add wading pools (figure 5.10) or zero-depth entry pools is to provide a safe haven for nonswimmers to enjoy the water. Parents often supervise their nonswimming children in these areas, but sometimes they become involved in conversation and don't notice that a child is experiencing difficulty. Do not be lulled into thinking that your responsibility is covered by parents' supervision of their children.

Wading pool or zero-depth entry pool accidents are typically the result of rough play by older siblings or nonswimmers who are old enough to be in the main pool. They run and splash, creating an environment in which people can be knocked under the water or onto the deck, and you should warn them to stop.

Figure 5.10 Wading pools provide a safer area for nonswimmers to enjoy the water, but they should still be monitored carefully.

Others who frequent wading pools or zero-depth entry pools are adults who want to sit in shallow water or to watch the children play. On very hot days such pools may become congested, and a wet deck combined with crowded conditions makes slipping and falling into the pools or on the surrounding deck a real danger.

Suggested rules:

> Running or rough play is not allowed in the pool area.
>
> All nonswimming children must be accompanied by an adult.
>
> No diving.

Spas and Whirlpools

Spas (figure 5.11) are relatively new additions to aquatic facilities. If your facility has one, you'll need to learn your state's codes for it and add this area to your list of danger zones. The most common physical hazards of a spa area are drowning, falling, and electrocution. The drownings and falls are often attributed to medical conditions or to the use of alcohol in the area. Electrocutions result from the use of electrical devices in the area.

Figure 5.11 The most common hazards in a spa are drowning, falling, and electrocution.

When people who are overheated from vigorous exercise or have just used a sauna get into a spa, the danger of heat-related illness increases greatly. People should cool down properly after exercising before they enter the spa, and vigorous exercise should not be allowed in the spa.

Spas attract even people who know they should stay away. Be sure that you post the rules of the whirlpool or spa prominently and enforce the rules rigidly.

Suggested rules:

Do not use the spa alone.

Spa use is not recommended immediately after intense physical activity or after sauna use.

Aerobic exercise in the spa is prohibited.

Enter and exit the spa slowly and cautiously.

Pregnant women, patrons with cardiovascular or respiratory problems, and children under 5 should avoid using the spa.

Older children must be accompanied and supervised by a responsible adult.

Limit use to 10 minutes.

Diving or jumping is prohibited.

Underwater submersion is prohibited.

Food or drink is not allowed in the spa area.

Shower before entering the spa.

Body lotions, oils, or suntan products are not allowed in the spa.

For additional information about whirlpool or spa management, see chapter 14 and the *YMCA Pool Operations Manual* (2nd ed.).

SPECIAL SITUATIONS

Although every facility has rules of conduct, some patrons inevitably try to test those rules. As an employee of a recreational facility, you are responsible to ensure that one patron doesn't endanger the safety or well-being of others. This section is designed to help you handle those situations. Your management may also post emergency contact phone numbers in the pool office should you need additional assistance.

Crowd Control

If an accident occurs, you may be put in charge of moving the patrons from the accident area. Moving the patrons will allow staff to deal with the situation without onlookers. Stay composed and be respectful as you move patrons to a prearranged area, such as a locker room or another part of the facility or grounds. Remind everyone to remain calm, as the situation is being taken care of by the facility's trained staff.

If you are in a single-guard situation, be sure your facility has an emergency plan for you to obtain assistance with crowd control immediately when it is needed.

Theft

The management of your facility will probably post conspicuous notices regarding responsibility for loss of personal property. However, you should be alert to any theft. If an incident is reported to you, notify the manager or assistant manager so he or she may contact law enforcement officials.

Do not accuse a person of theft. Present your evidence to the law enforcement authorities and let them make any charges. You could be charged with making a false accusation if you act hastily and have no proof of your claim. Make sure you fill out the appropriate incident report form and obtain statements from witnesses before they leave the scene.

Sexual Activity

Do not permit inappropriate sexual behavior in your facility. Diplomatically control these situations from the start of the swimming season.

Indecent Exposure

Exposing oneself in public is a crime in most areas. If someone indecently exposes himself or herself, suggest that the person cover up immediately. If your request is ignored or if the behavior is repeated, contact the management and police.

Disregard for Lifeguard Authority

Working at a facility that your friends frequent can put you and them in an awkward situation. You are duty-bound to enforce the rules of the facility, no matter who violates them. It may help to explain that to your friends if they are causing problems.

Anyone who disregards the lifeguard's authority is creating a risk, and you must not allow patrons to ignore your instructions. Summon the manager or assistant manager with a prearranged signal, such as a raised, clenched fist, to assist you in these instances. Repeated disregard of authority is grounds for banning offenders from the facility. If necessary, contact local authorities to escort a troublemaker from the scene.

Conflicts or Disturbances

Use your customer relations skills when situations arise. In a conflict, you can use the problem-solving process (PACA) to find solutions and get needs met, as long as people communicate honestly and listen to one another. When you are trying to resolve such situations, keep the following guidelines in mind:

- Keep your emotions in check and stay calm. Remember that the conflict is not about you, and don't take it personally.
- Listen actively and acknowledge what is being said. Use "I" statements and re-state what they said to be sure you understand them correctly.
- Be respectful.
- Speak for a purpose; don't just talk to hear yourself talk.
- Ask each party to state the problem, their feelings, and what they want.
- Maintain control of the situation and the process of resolution.

You may be able to resolve a situation in one of the following ways (American Red Cross, 1995):

- Allow one party to decide that the argument is not worth the trouble and "give in" to the other person's position.
- Have both parties apologize without necessarily implying that they did or said anything wrong, or have them take equal responsibility for the conflict.
- Have each party consent to give up something to resolve the conflict.
- Reduce tension surrounding the conflict by making light of the situation in ways that do not offend those involved.
- Use a technique that relies on chance to resolve the issue, such as flipping a coin or choosing a number between 1 and 10.
- Get the parties to agree to wait for a better time in which to handle the conflict.

If a situation arises between patrons in the pool or pool area and you cannot resolve it quickly, call for an off-duty lifeguard or your supervisor, who can either deal with the patrons or change places with you. Your facility should have a prearranged signal to alert other lifeguards or your supervisor of such situations so your zone in the pool remains covered.

If you are having difficulty getting patrons to resolve their dispute, be sure to involve your head lifeguard or supervisor. The head lifeguard or supervisor should separate the two individuals and ask them to move to different areas, then talk with each of them separately. If the situation escalates, contact the police for assistance. Be sure to complete an incident report form after any disturbance.

Violence

The first step in dealing with violence in the pool area is to make sure your facility has a plan to minimize the chances of violence occurring and has put that plan into place. One part of the plan should be to influence patrons' behavior by having staff members who appear and behave professionally. As a lifeguard, you should command authority in the facility. Your attitude, behavior, and appearance will all affect patrons' perceptions of your authority.

Another part of the plan should be to post the rules and enforce them consistently and effectively. Everyone who enters your facility should know the rules. Signs listing the rules should be placed at the facility's entrance and in multiple locations within the facility. You, as an employee, should be able to explain to patrons why the rules exist.

Your facility's emergency plan should include procedures for preventing or dealing with violent acts. Staff should know and practice these procedures, just as they do other emergency procedures.

If you suspect a violent act may happen, notify your supervisor right away. If a violent act clearly is about to happen, contact your supervisor and the authorities immediately. Do not intervene or confront those involved, and do not approach anyone with a weapon; instead, retreat and follow your facility's procedures. Your priority should be the safety of your patrons, as well as your own.

Once authorities arrive, listen to their instructions and let them take charge. Identify those who were involved in the violence, and inform them that they are either not allowed back in the pool at all or only after a certain period of time.

Following a violent incident, staff members should reopen the pool only when guards are mentally prepared to resume their duties.

Substance Abuse

People who are abusing substances such as alcohol or other drugs should not be in or around aquatic areas; their lack of judgment and reduced physical abilities could easily endanger both them and other patrons. Be aware of signs or behavior patterns that are characteristic of substance abuse:

- Unusual tiredness
- The odor of alcohol, tobacco, or other drugs
- Unsteadiness and lack of coordination
- Unusual detachment from the group
- Unusual changes in mood or attitude
- Unexplained lack of interest in normal activities
- Unusual giddiness
- Preoccupation with drug-related clothing, signs, or other paraphernalia
- Obvious slurring of words
- Public use of alcohol, tobacco, or other drugs

If you suspect that a patron in your area is under the influence of alcohol or other drugs, watch her or him carefully and request that the manager or assistant manager join you. If the manager agrees that the patron is acting suspiciously, he or she should ask the patron to leave. Encourage the patron to have someone take him or her home and not drive. Your manager may authorize calling a taxi or providing other transportation assistance. If the person will not leave, contact the police. Once the person has left, document the behavior on an incident report form. The manager may inform the parents of youthful abusers.

Concern for Younger Patrons

If you think you see signs of child abuse or neglect or of drug abuse in children, notify your manager or the appropriate staff member and explain what you have observed. That staff person can then contact the child's parents and take whatever steps are deemed appropriate and necessary, including referrals to agencies and services. (See appendix A for "Child Abuse Identification and Prevention: Recommended Guidelines for YMCAs.")

Problems Unique to Your Facility

Although the section you have just read may provide some basis for your decision making, each facility has its own unique difficulties and its own rules. And to a large degree lifeguards must make their own decisions about what constitutes a potentially dangerous situation. Study the layout of your facility and the rules that have been made to govern it. If you see potential problem areas, bring them to the attention of the management. Then assist in the creative process of establishing rules that will preserve a safe and fun environment.

ENFORCING THE RULES

Rule enforcement is always difficult. No one likes to play watchdog, and no one likes to be corrected. But you must enforce the rules to meet your responsibility of providing a safe environment in which patrons can have enjoyable aquatic experiences.

Discipline is needed whenever someone's behavior

- could result in injury to self or others,
- could result in damage to property, or
- infringes on the comfort and enjoyment of others in the area.

A few guidelines will help you enforce the rules at your facility:

- Know all rules and the procedures for enforcing them.
- Use a short blast of your whistle to get patrons' attention.
- Be consistent, enforcing the same rule in the same way for everyone. Don't make exceptions for friends, fellow employees, or adults. Also, enforce the rules in the same way each and every day.
- React immediately. Blow your whistle as soon as you detect a rule being broken. The patron will know what behavior has drawn your attention.
- Be specific. If there is a question over what behavior is prohibited, be specific in describing your concern. For example, you may say, "I saw you running on the deck. As you know, that is against the rules because you may run into another swimmer and knock someone down." You have pointed out the incorrect behavior and indicated why it was a problem.
- Provide alternative behaviors if you can. You might encourage the runner on the deck to take a group to the grassy recreation area, where there is room for such activities.

By following these guidelines, you should be able to gain the respect and cooperation of those who use your swimming facility. And each time you enforce the rules, you gain experience in how to deal with people successfully.

Your primary responsibility is to guard your area. Enforcing rules is one part of that duty. You must never stop scanning the water. If a rule enforcement discussion is lengthy or is taking your attention away from your assigned area, signal for assistance.

Review Questions

1. Why are rules needed in a facility?
2. How are rules communicated to patrons?
3. List the high-risk locations at a pool.
4. What are the dangers of deep water?
5. How is the hazard related to starting blocks minimized?
6. Name five suggested rules related to recreational springboard diving areas.
7. How should you respond when someone disregards your authority as a lifeguard?
8. List six guidelines for resolving conflict situations.
9. Name two possible ways of resolving a conflict situation.
10. What should you do if a violent act is about to happen?
11. What three general types of situations require disciplinary action?
12. List six guidelines for effective enforcement of the rules.

Victim Recognition and Drowning

A major part of a lifeguard's job is to be alert in order to prevent accidents or incidents. To do this effectively, you must know who is potentially a victim and recognize victims when they do get into trouble.

It is also true that, despite your best efforts to stop problems before they begin, you may at some time be faced with a situation in which a patron is at serious risk of drowning. For such a situation, it's essential that you understand what drowning is and how it works.

▶ **In This Chapter, You'll Learn**

- how to recognize potential and actual victims and
- the stages and types of drowning.

VICTIM RECOGNITION

The first step in executing an effective rescue is to detect the need for action. As a trained professional, you can reduce the anxiety of identification by learning to look for potential victims and by analyzing options before potential accidents occur. By doing this, you can determine what option is best for you. Identifying potential victims early is the key to your success as a lifeguard.

Types of Victims

According to the Royal Life Saving Society Canada (Lifesaving Society, 1993), people who become victims may be in many different conditions. They may be exhausted, injured, panicked, unconscious, not breathing, or vomiting. They may even be calm but unable to help themselves due to trauma, cramps, or poor swimming skills. Your task is to recognize people in these states and to help them by removing them from danger and doing no further harm.

As patrons arrive, observe them for clues as to their swimming ability and familiarity with the water (Richardson, 1997). Watch people who fall into the following categories closely:

- People of age extremes—the very young and the very old
- People of weight extremes—very heavy or very thin
- Pale people—their pallor may signal a lack of exposure or experience in outdoor aquatic activities
- Parents holding children—their skills may not be strong enough to support both themselves and a child
- Unstable or intoxicated individuals—their movement and behavior patterns may be impaired
- People using flotation devices—use of such aids may signal lack of comfort in the water
- Physical impairment—disabilities may signal limited ability to maneuver in and around the water
- Improper dress or equipment—may mean they are unfamiliar with the situation

According to Richardson (1997), these categories will help you identify patrons who may have problems, but it does not mean that they necessarily will. Once they enter the water, their behavior may either confirm or negate your suspicions.

Signs of Trouble

Because you may be called at any time to make a decision about how to react to an aquatic emergency, learn to detect signs of trouble. Although you should observe swimmers before they enter the water for clues about their abilities, once swimmers are active, other signs will help you identify potential victims.

Early Warning Signs

Swimmers likely to become victims often display a variety of warning signs:

- Weak stroke—head low in the water, little over-arm recovery, or a weak kick demonstrates a lack of ability
- Hair in the eyes—swimmer may be too concerned with keeping the head out of the water to push hair out of the eyes
- Glassy, empty, anxious-looking eyes—the facial expression preceding exhaustion
- Two heads together—a possible double-drowning situation

- Hand-waving—a sign of needing help
- Moving toward rocks or a pier—swimmer may be caught in a current
- Erratic behavior—any activity out of the ordinary
- Clinging to objects for security—swimmer may be too tired to swim to safety
- Neutral to negative buoyancy—means little air remains in lungs; the person may sink in seconds
- Inability to respond verbally—may indicate struggling to stay afloat or swallowing water

Being able to identify potential victims is crucial for a lifeguard; however, not everyone displaying one or more of these signs will be involved in an accident. Taking such an extreme position could lead to unnecessary tension and an embarrassing situation following an overreaction. Stay relaxed; keep a vigilant watch over your area, but let your common sense keep your responsibility in perspective.

Distressed Swimmers

According to Pia (1997), a distressed swimmer (figure 6.1) is someone who is under great physical or mental stress or strain in the water. To identify distressed swimmers, observe and evaluate swimmers' breathing, arm and leg motions, body position, and movement in the water. Characteristics of distress may include

- waving the arms,
- shouting for assistance, and
- kicking to maintain an upright position, making little or no forward progress.

A distressed swimmer can assist in his or her own rescue by following instructions, grabbing extended rescue equipment, keeping afloat, and kicking.

Figure 6.1 A distressed swimmer.

Drowning Victims

Drowning victims may be passive or active. A passive victim is unconscious and displays no active movements. Such a victim is usually found facedown or submerged in the water. An active victim (figure 6.2), thrashing or showing signs of panic and fear, is more dangerous to rescue without risking harm to yourself. Such a victim may continue to struggle even after submerging until she or he loses consciousness. Active victims can easily become passive victims if they are allowed to thrash around for a long time. Actively drowning individuals are suffocating, unable to keep their mouths above water (Pia, 1997).

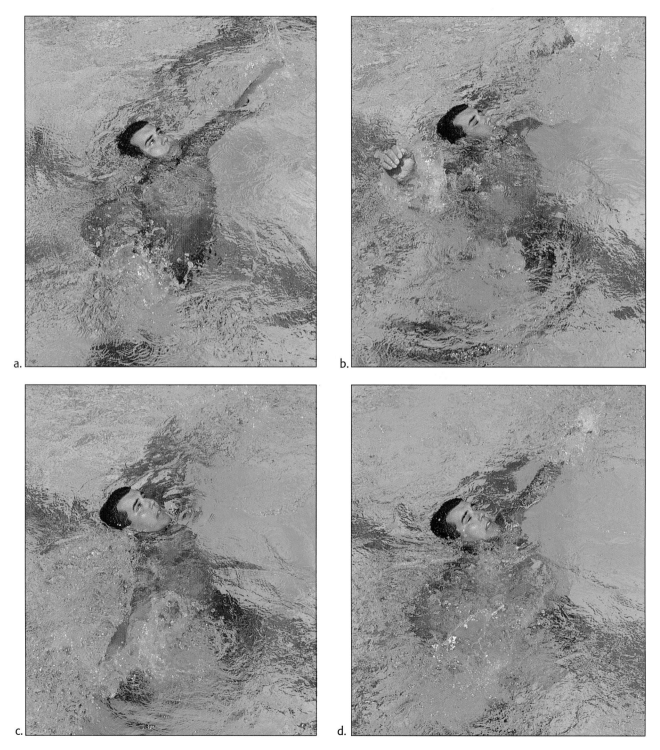

a.   b.   c.   d.

Figure 6.2   An actively drowning victim thrashes in the water, trying to keep his mouth above water.

Nonswimmers or exhausted swimmers are the usual drowning victims. (You will learn more about the physical aspects of drowning in the next section.) Actively drowning swimmers display the instinctive drowning response (IDR), unlearned behavior that individuals display to attempt to avoid perceived or actual suffocation in the water (Pia, 1997). Unlike distressed swimmers, they are unable to call for help. They are expending all of their energy trying to keep their heads above water and breathe. Characteristics include

- the inability to call for help,
- head back and the body low in the water,
- arms extended out from the sides and moving up and down ineffectively in an attempt to keep the face above water to facilitate breathing,
- little or no support from the kick, and
- an upright (vertical) position facing the nearest source of assistance.

Drowning victims (figure 6.3) are more difficult to spot than distressed victims because they cannot call attention to themselves. But it is critical to identify a drowning victim quickly—it takes as little as 20 to 60 seconds to slip below the surface. (An adult may struggle for up to 60 seconds, but a child may submerge in 20 seconds.)

Figure 6.3   It can take as little as 20 to 60 seconds for a drowning victim to slip below the surface of the water.

Because the underwater struggles of a drowning victim can be mistaken for swimming movements (Pia, 1997), you need to observe swimmers closely. If it seems that an underwater swimmer is not making progress to the surface, you need to enter the water immediately to rescue the victim. Keep in mind that the victim will be unable to assist in the rescue.

It can be difficult to see a submerged victim under the water, so you will have to scan the bottom of the pool vigilantly (figure 6.4).

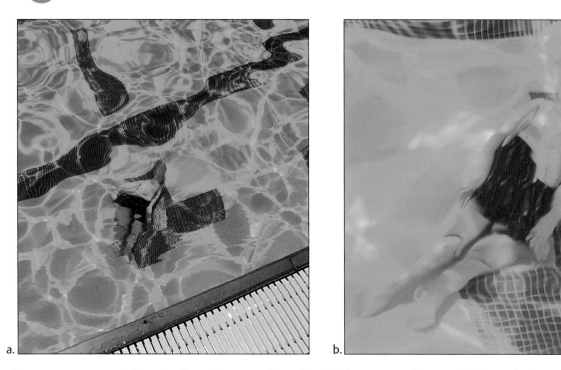

Figure 6.4 Because of the reflection of the water, it can be difficult to see a submerged victim at the bottom of the pool.

DROWNING

Drowning is asphyxiation (cutting off of the air supply) due to blockage or reflex spasm of the trachea (commonly called the *windpipe*), usually caused by water, which stops breathing. Drownings can be either passive or active.

In a passive drowning, the victim does not struggle on the surface because he or she is unconscious, incapacitated, or dead. Various situations and physical conditions can result in a passive drowning:

- Heart attack (cardiac arrest)
- Head injury
- Shallow-water blackout (due to hyperventilation)
- Stroke
- Epilepsy or other types of seizures
- Alcohol abuse or drug overdose
- Hypothermia or hyperthermia (see chapter 9)

You will have no warning of passive drownings, which is one of the reasons you must keep alert. Assume that any individual who is facedown or on the bottom and has made little or no motion for 20 seconds is an unconscious victim, and take action immediately.

Active drownings may arise for any number of reasons. In most situations, victims panic. *Panic* is an uncontrolled and incapacitating fear that strikes when someone thinks she or he has lost control. Severe panic destroys all sense of logic and reason. Self-preservation becomes the top priority, even at the expense of friends and loved ones.

The behavioral pattern of an actively drowning victim takes the following form:

- Struggle for air
- Cessation of movement accompanied by limited exhalation and frequent swallowing of water

- Violent struggle for survival
- Uncontrolled efforts to take in air accompanied by convulsions and disappearance of reflex actions
- Death

People who are actively drowning usually progress through defined stages, which we will now describe.

The Stages of Active Drowning

The active drowning process has been divided into four stages. Although the names given to the stages differ, the concept of each stage is basically the same.

Before examining the specific stages of drowning, let's take a brief look at the body structures involved. In the normal throat (see figure 6.5), the glottis is the top edge of the beginning of the trachea that connects to the lower part of the throat. The glottis is covered by the epiglottis, a flap of skin that acts as a barrier to prevent foreign material from entering the trachea, which carries air from the throat into the lungs. The esophagus, which is next to the trachea, carries food and liquids from the throat to the stomach.

What is called the *reflex closure of the glottis* is the involuntary (automatic), controlled process of swallowing. As water enters the mouth, the tongue blocks the back of the throat. The glottis then closes, blocking the airway, the tongue drops, and the water passes the trachea into the esophagus and to the stomach. During the drowning process, this reflex is disrupted.

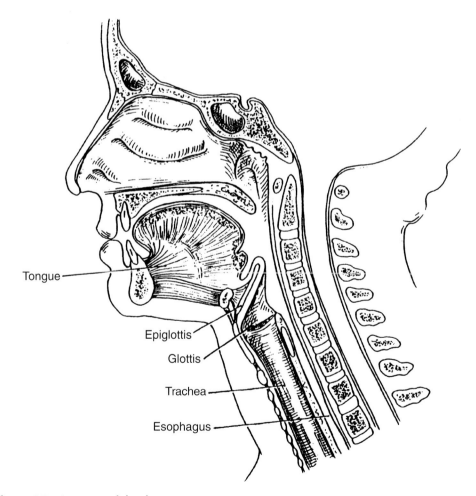

Tongue

Epiglottis

Glottis

Trachea

Esophagus

Figure 6.5 Anatomy of the throat.

Stage I: Initial Apnea

Apnea means the absence of breathing. In drowning, the glottis closes by a reflex action, but unlike during eating or drinking where the air supply is resumed immediately once the food or drink passes the glottis, the water stays in the mouth and throat, cutting off all air to the lungs. No water enters the lungs in this stage, however. During this step, the victim's panic increases. Struggling to get air, he or she may not call for help!

The time span of the first stage varies significantly, from seconds to minutes. Physiologically, the following occurs:

1. The blood pressure rises and the adrenalin flow increases due to panic and the self-preservation instinct.
2. The victim begins to struggle in an attempt to keep the head above the water.
3. The victim swallows water into the stomach, filling some of the available air space in the body and diminishing buoyancy.
4. The victim gradually sinks. Each attempt to raise the head above water is less successful because of fatigue and the extra water in the stomach.
5. The brain begins to degenerate because it does not get enough oxygen to function properly (a condition called *hypoxia*).
6. The lack of oxygen causes an excess of waste chemicals in the blood, making the blood more acidic (acidosis) and causing muscles to fatigue and stop functioning.

Stage II: Dyspnea

Dyspnea refers to difficulty in breathing and occurs when the glottis begins to relax partially. Air and water begin to enter the trachea. Because the victim has swallowed water into the stomach and is growing weaker from struggling, the body and head will be lower in the water and more water will be swallowed. This time water flows down the trachea into the lungs. If rescued during this stage, the victim would suffer from a condition called *aspiration pneumonia* resulting from breathing water into the lungs.

On the surface of every air sac (alveolus) in the lungs is a chemical known as *surfactant* that reduces the strength of the alveolus's membrane, allowing for the easy exchange of oxygen to and carbon dioxide away from the blood (figure 6.6). In drowning, the water ingested into the lungs washes away the surfactant, making the exchange of gases more difficult and creating another complication to resuscitation.

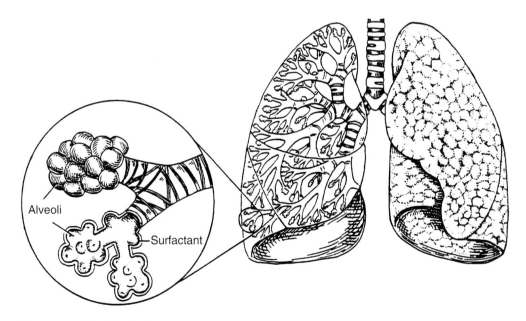

Alveoli

Surfactant

Figure 6.6   Alveoli in the lungs.

Because there are over 700 million alveoli in the lungs, many survive the wash-away to help exchange gases as long as they are exposed to the air. The mixture of water and surfactant causes a pink froth at the mouth of some victims. Resuscitation of victims in this stage may be quite difficult because of the decreased exchange of oxygen and carbon dioxide.

During dyspnea the victim experiences the following:

1. The failure of the swallow reflex causes the aspiration of water into the lungs. Although normally no one can intentionally take water into the lungs, by this stage the protective mechanism of the body has failed.
2. The influx of water into the stomach and lungs may cause vomiting.
3. Frothing may occur at the mouth because of the mixture of surfactant and water in the lungs.
4. Brain hypoxia continues, and very little rationality remains.
5. Acidosis continues to cause a severe chemical imbalance in the blood.

Stage III: Terminal Apnea

As soon as the victim becomes unconscious and stops breathing, he or she has entered the third stage. Terminal apnea is respiratory arrest, in which breathing ceases. Water will be present in the lungs, making air exchange during resuscitation efforts very difficult.

During this stage the following occurs:

1. Brain hypoxia continues.
2. Acidosis continues.
3. In some cases, lack of oxygen to the brain causes convulsions in which the entire body becomes rigid and the victim jerks violently and involuntarily.
4. In some cases, the sphincter muscles may relax, in which case the victim will urinate, defecate, or both.

Stage IV: Cardiac Arrest

Cardiac arrest occurs when the heart ceases to function and pump blood. Depending on the circumstances, the third and fourth stages of drowning may occur simultaneously, with the heart and lungs stopping together. But because the heart can continue to beat up to 5 minutes after the lungs have stopped, rescue breathing alone can revive victims who have been underwater for a short time. Once the pulse has stopped, CPR must be used to revive the victim.

Drowning victims experience two types of death: clinical death and biological death. *Clinical death* occurs first; it is defined as the point at which both breathing and pulse have stopped and the body is in respiratory and cardiac arrest. Clinical death is generally considered to last about 4 minutes from the time the heart stops beating. The lack of oxygen causes the pupils of the eyes to dilate (widen) and the skin to become cyanotic (blue). This blue color is especially noticeable in the lips and the beds of the fingernails. If you begin CPR within the first 4 minutes, there is a good chance that no brain damage will occur.

Biological death is the point at which irreversible brain damage begins and the most sensitive parts of the brain start to die. Without oxygen, brain cells begin to die within 4 to 6 minutes. Longer periods of oxygen deprivation result in loss of more and more brain cells. Dead brain cells cannot regenerate like skin and bone; once dead, they are gone.

You can see why it is critical to reach a drowning victim and begin CPR as soon as possible. CPR maintains minimal circulation and respiration in order to sustain life until advanced medical care can begin.

In cold water, bodily functions are slowed significantly. As a result, less oxygen is needed to maintain the body, and a good portion of the oxygen available is used by the brain. Because of the slowed depletion of oxygen, cold-water drowning and near-drowning victims experience a delayed onset of biological death.

Progression of Stages

Figure 6.7 summarizes the stages of active drowning and provides an approximate timeline for their occurrence.

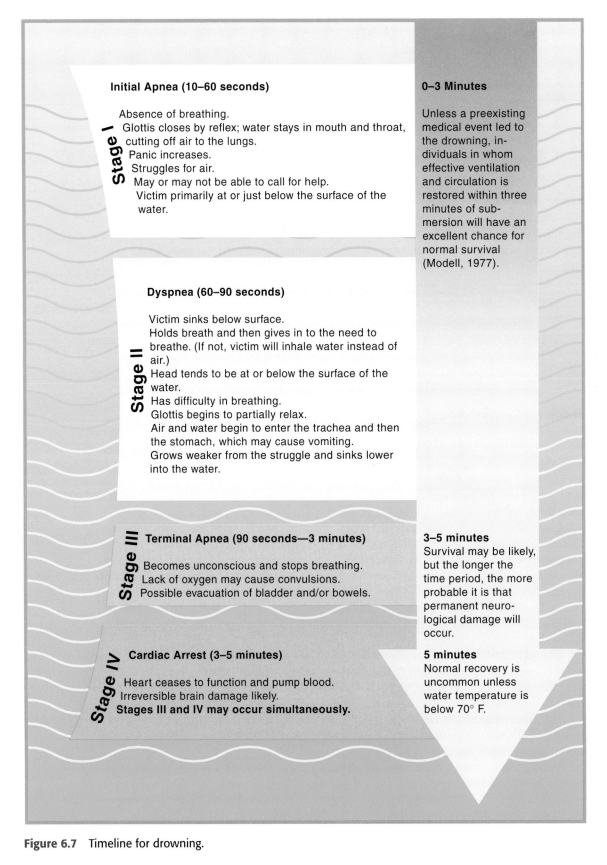

Initial Apnea (10–60 seconds)

Stage I

Absence of breathing.
Glottis closes by reflex; water stays in mouth and throat, cutting off air to the lungs.
Panic increases.
Struggles for air.
May or may not be able to call for help.
Victim primarily at or just below the surface of the water.

Dyspnea (60–90 seconds)

Stage II

Victim sinks below surface.
Holds breath and then gives in to the need to breathe. (If not, victim will inhale water instead of air.)
Head tends to be at or below the surface of the water.
Has difficulty in breathing.
Glottis begins to partially relax.
Air and water begin to enter the trachea and then the stomach, which may cause vomiting.
Grows weaker from the struggle and sinks lower into the water.

Stage III Terminal Apnea (90 seconds—3 minutes)

Becomes unconscious and stops breathing.
Lack of oxygen may cause convulsions.
Possible evacuation of bladder and/or bowels.

Stage IV Cardiac Arrest (3–5 minutes)

Heart ceases to function and pump blood.
Irreversible brain damage likely.
Stages III and IV may occur simultaneously.

0–3 Minutes

Unless a preexisting medical event led to the drowning, individuals in whom effective ventilation and circulation is restored within three minutes of submersion will have an excellent chance for normal survival (Modell, 1977).

3–5 minutes
Survival may be likely, but the longer the time period, the more probable it is that permanent neurological damage will occur.

5 minutes
Normal recovery is uncommon unless water temperature is below 70° F.

Figure 6.7   Timeline for drowning.

Factors that affect how much time can pass between submersion and successful resuscitation before permanent neurological damage or death occurs include the following (Modell, 1997):

- Whether the victims entered the water with lungs maximally deflated or maximally inflated
- Whether the victims had preexisting diseases that limit rescuscitation
- The temperature of the water to which they were exposed
- Whether the victims were mentally or physically impaired

Other factors that may be involved include the use of drugs or alcohol, age, level of swimming ability, fatigue, and physical conditioning.

If no one saw the victim's initial submersion, it may difficult to determine how long the victim was drowning before resuscitation or what caused the submersion to occur.

Types of Drowning

Not all drownings happen in the same way. Various situations and environmental conditions can cause different results.

Wet and Dry Drownings

Between 80 and 90% of all drownings are wet drownings—the glottis opens at the second stage (dyspnea) and allows water to enter the lungs, making the lungs wet. The remaining drownings are dry drownings, in which the glottis stays shut from the first stage (initial apnea) and allows no water to enter the lungs.

Laryngeal Drowning

There are two forms of laryngeal drowning. In the first, the swimmer may aspirate vomit into the lungs, choke, and drown. This has been found to be a possible cause in some drowning accidents in which the victim had eaten a big meal immediately before swimming (supporting the idea of waiting an appropriate time after eating before swimming). The second type of laryngeal drowning, called a secondary drowning, occurs after the victim has been pulled out of the water. The epiglottis and the larynx have a reflex spasm, causing the victim to be unable to breathe. This can occur up to 24 hours after a near-drowning incident, so current EMS procedures recommend hospitalizing victims of near-drownings.

Saltwater and Freshwater Drowning

As far as the lifeguard is concerned, there is no significant difference in the method of reviving a victim of saltwater or freshwater drowning. When a victim drowns in salt water, the water in the blood diffuses through the membranes of the alveoli because the salt (sodium) content of the water is much higher than that of the water in the blood. Because sodium attracts water, the water in the blood is drawn into the lungs.

In an extreme case, the victim's blood volume can drop almost 40%. This drop is critical. As water is drawn from the blood, it gets thicker and the red blood cells cannot carry their full capacity of oxygen to the tissues.

In freshwater drowning, the imbalance of sodium is the opposite. Water enters the lungs and is drawn through the membranes of the alveoli into the blood because the sodium content of the blood is higher than that of fresh water. In an extreme case, where fresh water has very little sodium, water can be drawn in over several minutes so that the blood volume of a victim doubles. This blood dilution causes severe chemical imbalances, resulting in irregularities in body functions. Imbalances of sodium, potassium, chloride, magnesium, and other salt components in the blood are caused by the dilution, and these imbalances contribute to spasms of the heart muscle called ventricular fibrillation, a precursor to cardiac arrest, in 80% of freshwater drowning cases.

As red blood cells fill up with water in freshwater drowning, another problem arises. In some cases when the water content of the red blood cells becomes too great, the cells will explode (experience hemolysis) and no longer be able to carry oxygen. If enough red blood cells suffer hemolysis, oxygen transportation is significantly reduced.

Buoyancy of a Drowned Body

Whether a drowned body will float or sink depends on the victim's original buoyancy and on the amount of water taken into the lungs and stomach. Positively buoyant victims will float (figure 6.8); negatively buoyant victims will sink. If the victim was borderline buoyant or nonbuoyant, the amount of air in the lungs—the vital capacity—may change the body's ability to float. As the body descends, the lungs are squeezed of their residual volume (the air that remains in the lungs). This causes the body to descend faster as it goes deeper. Air bubbles from the victim may appear on the surface for quite some time.

Figure 6.8 A body may float, depending on the victim's original buoyancy and the amount of water taken in during drowning.

Most bodies will eventually surface if they are not held down in some way as the body decomposes and carbon dioxide and other gases are created. This process is slowed in cold water.

Review Questions

1. What signs can alert you to the potential for trouble before a swimmer enters the water? After a swimmer is in the water?

2. Describe the difference in how a distressed swimmer and an actively drowning victim behave. Why is this difference important?

3. Define passive drowning and give at least four examples of causes of passive drowning.

4. What are the four stages of active drowning?

5. What is the difference between clinical death and biological death? Why is the distinction important?

6. What is the difference between wet and dry drownings?

7. What are the two forms of laryngeal drowning?

8. What factors determine the buoyancy of a drowned body?

CHAPTER *seven*

Rescue Skills

Lifeguards must be prepared to identify a trouble situation, determine what type of rescue or assist is needed, and execute the rescue. Your ability to identify the emergency, analyze the options, make a decision, and carry out the rescue will determine whether you are successful. In a recent research study by Porter (1997), the YMCA's rescue procedures were shown to be most efficient compared to those of other major lifeguard programs.

 In This Chapter, You'll Learn the Details of Performing Rescues.
- Rescue equipment
- Nonswimming assists
- Water entries
- Approaches
- Rescues using a rescue tube or buoy and in-water rescue breathing
- Multiple-victim rescues
- Rescue towing
- Water exits

RESCUE EQUIPMENT

You will learn how to make a variety of rescues in your lifeguarding course. In each one you should use a piece of rescue equipment. The most common pieces of rescue equipment are pictured in figure 7.1 and described here:

Figure 7.1   Rescue equipment: *(a)* a shepherd's crook; *(b)* a reaching pole; *(c)* a ring buoy; *(d)* a rescue bag.

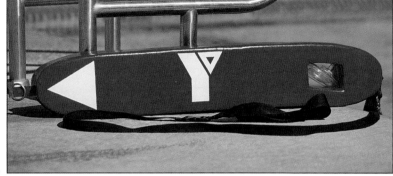

e.

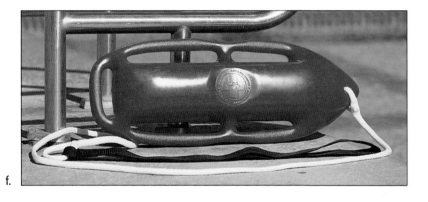

f.

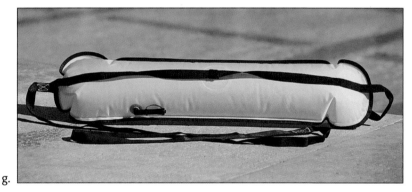

g.

Figure 7.1 Rescue equipment *(continued)*: *(e)* a rescue tube; *(f)* a rescue buoy; *(g)* an inflatable rescue tube. The strap connects to the tail of the tube or buoy.

- *Shepherd's crook and reaching pole.* The shepherd's crook and reaching pole are lightweight wood, aluminum, or fiberglass rods 10 to 15 feet long. The shepherd's crook has a blunt hook on one end that is large enough to place around an unconscious victim. Both the shepherd's crook and pole can be used to assist a conscious victim.

- *Ring buoy.* The buoyant ring buoy usually weighs no more than 2-1/2 pounds and is used primarily on lakefronts and in pools. The ring buoy is attached to a 40- to 50-foot line for use in throwing assists. The ring buoy is generally effective only with a distressed swimmer.

- *Rescue bag.* Used most frequently in moving water, the rescue bag is a self-contained throwing device with a 75-foot rope coiled inside a bag. The weight of the rope and the bag as they are thrown is sufficient to enable rescuers to be accurate in their throws. The rescue bag does not provide flotation and should be used with distressed swimmers.

- *Rescue tube.* A rescue tube is one of the most versatile pieces of equipment used by lifeguards. It can be used for reaching to a struggling victim, towing an active or passive victim, or supporting the rescuer. Although sizes and shapes vary, a typical rescue tube is made of buoyant molded foam, 3-1/2 inches by 5-1/2 inches by 40 to 54 inches. All have a line with a loop attached to one end (the *tail*). The line may vary in length depending on the depth of the water in which it will be used.

- *Rescue buoy.* The rescue buoy is made of a lightweight, hard plastic and is buoyant. It has molded handles along the sides and end and, like the rescue tube, a tow rope attached to one end. The buoy can also be used in a reaching assist or as a buoyancy aid for victims. You cannot, however, use it to support an unconscious victim without maintaining contact with the buoy and victim. The buoy is used predominantly in surf rescues.

- *Inflatable rescue tube.* An inflatable rescue tube may be used for water rescue when people are camping, backpacking, canoeing, or engaging in other outdoor aquatic activities. It is easier to carry than a normal rescue tube. The tube can be inflated and deflated either manually or with an automatic CO_2 inflater. An inflatable rescue tube also can be helpful in multiple victim situations.

Remember, using rescue equipment reduces the risk of harm to you and to the victim. The equipment provides support for both of you, conserves your energy, and makes it easier to tow the victim to safety.

NONSWIMMING ASSISTS

A safe way to perform a rescue is to use one of several assists from a stable position. These include reaching, extension, and throwing assists from the pool deck or pier and wading assists in water no higher than chest deep.

Figure 7.2 An extension assist from the deck.

Reaching and Extension Assists

Reaching assists, although limited to rescues only a few feet from the side of the pool or dock, play an important role in lifeguarding. These rescues are recommended only for distressed swimmers and in situations in which your safety as the responding lifeguard is endangered. To perform a reaching assist out of the water, lie on the pool deck or dock to establish a stable position. Spread your legs apart to increase stability, keeping your center of mass centered over a wide base. Extend *one arm only* over the water. Your goal is to grasp the victim's wrist or upper arm.

Reaching rescues can also be made in the water. Maintaining eye contact and distance from the victim, slip into the water. Establish a firm grasp on a ladder, the side of the pool, or a dock support. Then extend your other arm or a leg to the victim. When extending the arm, be sure you grab the victim before she or he grabs you. If you are caught off guard, you may be pulled away from your anchor and become a victim yourself.

If a victim is too far away to use a reaching assist, consider an extension assist (figure 7.2). Traditional lifeguard equipment or a towel, clothing, or a piece of lumber can be used for a quick extension rescue. Remember to establish a firm base of support with your legs spread and your weight low and away from the victim so you aren't pulled into the water. Distressed victims can grab the extended equipment (although they may not do so). Be prepared for a sharp tug at the object.

As you learned in chapter 6, a drowning victim will probably not grasp the extended reach pole or assisting device. In this instance, keep the object within reach of the victim, slide it under the victim's armpit, or press it against the victim's side. This will generally cause the victim to grab the object. Do not try to jab the victim with the object; it may cause additional injury.

Once the victim has a firm grasp of the object, maintain your position with your weight shifted away from the victim; pull him or her in slowly, hand over hand. Communicate with and reassure the victim as you bring him or her to safety.

Extension assists can also be made in the water (figure 7.3). While maintaining eye contact and distance from the victim, slip into the water. Grasp a ladder, the side of the pool, or a dock support firmly, then extend the object to the victim.

Figure 7.3 An extension assist in the water.

Throwing Assists

If the distance to a distressed victim is beyond the range of an extension assist, and if the necessary equipment is available, the next option is the throwing assist. (Remember, throwing assists will not be effective with an actively drowning victim because he or she will not be able to respond.) The key to success is throwing accuracy, and the key to accuracy is preparation and practice. A rescue bag, a ring buoy with a line, a heaving line (a line with a weighted knot on the end), or a heaving jug (a line tied to a plastic gallon jug with a small amount of water in it for weight) are all acceptable throwing devices.

To perform a throwing assist, as illustrated in figure 7.4, follow these steps:

1. Hold the neatly coiled rope in your open hand with the throwing device in your throwing hand. Be sure the coils lie side by side to avoid any tangling. Secure the rope by standing on it, with a knot stopping the rope from slipping through. Step on the rope with your forward foot, which should be on the side opposite to the throwing arm.

2. Throw the rescue device underhand and let the rope feed freely from your open hand. Throw the device past the victim's head, then pull it to her or him. If you are on a river, throw upstream from your victim and allow the current to carry the device back to the victim. If the wind is strong, compensate for it in aiming your throw.

Figure 7.4 A throwing assist.

3. If your throw is unsuccessful and the device moves away from the victim, plant your feet and pull in the rope, letting it drop on the ground in front of you. Do not recoil the line; it wastes precious time. Simply throw the device again as soon as possible. Always be careful to avoid rocks, branches, or anything else that could tangle the line.

If you are using a rescue bag, remove the knotted end and leave the rest of the rope coiled inside the bag. Do not stand on the rope. Rather, hold onto the knot with your nonthrowing hand. Be sure to leave 4 to 6 feet of slack. The rest of the throwing procedures are the same. If your first throw is inaccurate, do not restuff the bag. The water gathered in the bag as you tow it back to shore will provide the necessary weight to guide your second toss.

Wading Assists

A wading assist is more dangerous than the other nonswimming assists because you must enter the water. A wading assist should be used when the victim is too far away for a reaching or extension assist, is too close to warrant a throwing assist, and is in water that allows you to go no farther than chest-high water. Safe wading assists follow these steps:

1. As you enter the water, take a rescue tube or buoy to extend toward the victim.
2. Move into water no deeper than your chest.
3. Assume a stable position with one foot forward and one foot back and your weight shifted away from the victim.
4. Extend the nose end of the rescue device to the victim.
5. After the victim has grabbed the device, slowly walk to safety, holding on to the tail end (*not* the rope). Talk to the victim as you bring him or her to safety.

Nonswimming Rescue Guidelines

In making any nonswimming rescue, let the following principles guide you:

1. React calmly and quickly, following your emergency plan (see chapter 8).
2. Maintain visual contact with the victim at all times.
3. Find a piece of rescue equipment appropriate for the situation. Almost any object can be used as an aid for reaching, extension, and wading assists.
4. Establish a firm base for your rescue. Keep your weight low and away from the victim to avoid being pulled into the water or the victim's grasp (if you are already in the water).
5. Establish communication with the victim. You may get the victim to assist in her or his own rescue, and you may reduce the victim's anxiety.
6. Bring the victim to safety. Ask whether there is any pain and, if so, where. Keeping possible injuries in mind, help the victim exit the water.
7. Provide any necessary first aid or call for assistance.
8. Complete the appropriate accident or incident reports.

If you keep these principles in mind, you'll find nonswimming assists safe and valuable tools.

WATER ENTRIES

When a nonswimming rescue isn't possible, you will need to swim to the victim. Before you enter the water, plan your rescue and make sure the strap of your rescue tube or buoy is in place so you won't lose your equipment. Take a resuscitation mask with you in case in-water rescue breathing (page 124) becomes necessary. Activate the EMS and use your communication system to call for backup help.

You have several choices for entering the water. In a given situation, you will need to determine which of the methods described here is most appropriate. Whatever method you use, always maintain eye contact and communicate with the victim.

Compact Jump

To enter water at least 5 feet deep from a height of 3 feet or more, use a compact jump (see figure 7.5).

1. Hold the rescue tube or buoy horizontally under your arms and against your chest.
2. Jump into the water with both feet parallel to the water surface and knees bent. Hold the access strap in your hand.
3. As you hit the water, your knees should be bent slightly to absorb the shock. Allow your rescue tube or buoy to lift you to the surface.

Keep in mind that you will lose sight of the victim when you go underwater. Remember where you last saw him or her so that you can go there if for some reason you can't locate the victim when you surface.

Stride Jump

In water over 7 feet deep and from a height not more than 3 feet, you can enter the water quickly and maintain eye contact using a stride jump (see figure 7.6).

1. Hold your arms out to your sides with your hands slightly above your shoulders.
2. Lean forward and step out away from the edge.
3. As your body enters the water, force your legs together using a scissors kick and bring your arms forward and down to slow the jump and keep your head above water.

Figure 7.5 The compact jump.

Where you hold the rescue tube or buoy during the entry depends on rescue conditions. If the victim is a short distance away, hold the rescue equipment against the chest and under the arms. If the victim is farther away, drop it to the side and the rear. If many people are in the water where you enter, hold the rescue equipment at your side or against your chest. When you begin your approach stroke, your rescue equipment should be close to you but should not interfere with your stroke.

a.   b.

Figure 7.6 The stride jump.

Shallow Dive Entry

When time and speed are crucial, a shallow dive might be the most appropriate entry. In this entry, you sacrifice visual contact momentarily for greater momentum. Before deciding to use the shallow dive entry, you should know the water depth to be sure that you will not be injured. The YMCA recommends a minimum depth of 9 feet for a diving entry from the deck. Rescuers trained to do shallow dives may use this dive only if the water is at least 5 feet deep. Also check the water conditions before diving. Seaweed, floating debris, rocky terrain, and pollution may make a shallow dive dangerous and thus inappropriate.

Execute a long shallow dive (see figure 7.7). As you enter the water, propel yourself to the surface by steering up with your arms and head. Reestablish visual contact with the victim as quickly as possible.

Bring your rescue tube or buoy with you to the victim. Simply release the apparatus to the side before you enter the water.

Figure 7.7 Shallow dive entry.

Waveless Entry

When the victim is fairly close to your point of entry or when waves created by jumping or diving into the water could cause additional injury, you should select a waveless entry. This entry is for shallow water.

1. Move to a location close to the victim.
2. Sit on the side of the pool or dock. Put your rescue tube or buoy on the deck or in the water next to where you will enter.
3. Support your weight on your hands and arms and slowly slide into the water, maintaining visual contact with the victim.
4. Retrieve your rescue tube or buoy.

Once you are in the water, slowly wade toward the victim to avoid creating waves. Figure 7.8 illustrates this waveless entry.

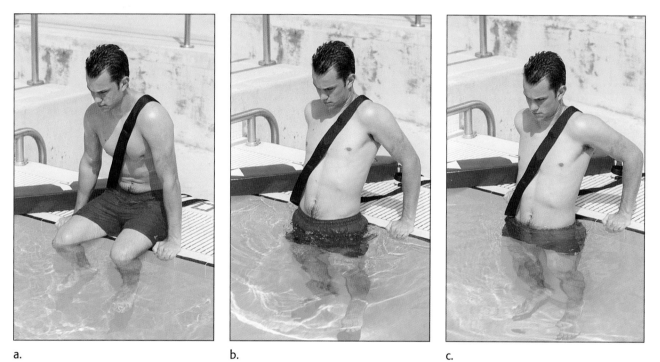

a.　　　　　　　　　　b.　　　　　　　　　　c.

Figure 7.8　Waveless entry into shallow water.

A waveless entry for deep water or as an alternative for shallow water calls for the following steps (see figure 7.9):

1. Sit on the edge of the deck. Put your rescue tube or buoy on the deck or in the water.
2. Place one hand on the deck near your leg.
3. Reach across your body with the other hand and place it on the deck or on the lip of the pool gutter.
4. As you lower yourself into the water, you will be turning 180 degrees to face the side of the pool. Maintain visual contact with the victim as much as possible.
5. Grab your rescue tube or buoy.
6. Swim toward the victim using a waveless, underwater stroke, such as the breast-stroke or sidestroke.

a.   b.   c.

Figure 7.9   Waveless entry into deep water.

Surf Entry

To perform a surf entry, do the following (Brewster, 1995):

1. From a sloping shoreline, run into the water using high-stepping strides. Run as far as possible before beginning to swim. Do not run and dive into the water.
2. Reach swimming depth by doing surface dives under incoming waves or porpoise dives in waves that are too large to jump over or through. Remember to keep your hands and arms extended to protect your head and neck.

Regardless of whether the slope of the beach is steep or long and gradual, running and surface diving or porpoising will be quicker until water depth allows for fast, effective swimming.

APPROACHES

After you enter the water, you have to get to the victim as soon as possible. The stroke you choose will be based on five factors:

- The distance to the victim
- The number of people in the swimming area
- The concentration of people between you and the victim
- The condition of the victim
- Your strength and condition

Approach Strokes

Your goal is to reach the victim as quickly as possible with an adequate reserve of energy to enable you to perform a safe rescue and tow the victim to safety. In all cases, you need to have your rescue equipment, usually a rescue tube or rescue buoy, on and ready to assist you.

If the victim is severely injured or not breathing, use the fastest possible stroke to reach him or her. If you suspect the victim has a spinal injury, use an approach that creates few waves.

If the victim is near once you've entered the water or if you need to weave between people separating you from the victim, turn the rescue tube on edge and place your hand at the center on top or grasp the rescue buoy on the long side handle (figure 7.10).

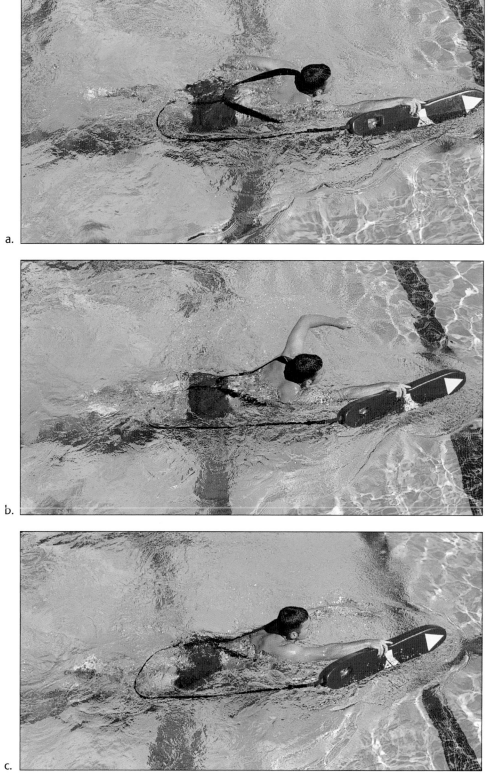

a.

b.

c.

Figure 7.10   The single arm approach crawl.

Point the nose of the tube or buoy in the direction you are swimming. Swim to the victim using a single arm pull breaststroke, modified crawl stroke, or a combined stroke using the breaststroke kick and a single arm crawl. This positioning will let you manipulate the apparatus and move relatively quickly. It will help you get around swimmers in a crowded pool and over lane lines. In any instance, keep the apparatus in front of you. Keep the line end of the apparatus (the tail) pointed toward your armpit. If lane lines are between you and the victim, hold the tube in one hand and stroke over the lane line, pushing the lane line down as you go over it.

For longer distances, unless there is a possibility that the rescue tube or buoy will become caught on something behind you, allow the line to trail behind while you approach the victim. The crawl stroke allows the quickest approach. If speed is essential, you may place your face in the water. Turn your head to the side to breathe; then rotate your head forward to look at the victim before putting your face in the water again. When you are about 15 feet from the victim, keep your head up and your eyes on the victim.

When you approach the victim, you must prepare yourself for contact, regardless of whether the victim is active or seemingly passive. Pause and position yourself for proper execution of the rescue.

If you dragged the rescue tube or buoy behind you during the approach, stop approximately 9 feet from the victim and retrieve the rescue equipment by grabbing the line and pulling it toward you. During this process be sure to keep your eyes on the victim.

RESCUES USING A RESCUE FLOTATION DEVICE (RFD)

Any time you enter the water you need to take a rescue flotation device (RFD) secured to you with a shoulder strap. Generally the rescue tube or buoy is the most helpful. Having one of these pieces of equipment with you provides an added measure of security. It serves as a flotation aid to assist you in performing the rescue and in positioning the victim for rescue breathing.

If you are right-handed, be sure to place the shoulder strap so it hangs from the shoulder of your left arm to the opposite hip. If you then hold the rescue equipment in your right hand, the line will not interfere during the rescue. (If you are left-handed, reverse the placement.)

This section and the next describe rescues using RFDs under nine conditions:

- Front, active victim
- Rear, active victim
- Injured, conscious victim on the surface
- Front, passive victim
- Rear, passive victim
- Active victim just below the surface
- Passive victim just below the surface
- Submerged victim
- Multiple victims

All instructions are written for right-handed individuals. If you are left-handed, reverse the instructions accordingly.

Front, Active Victim

For an active drowning victim approached from the front (figure 7.11), pause and ready yourself about 6 feet away. In most situations you'll have the tube or buoy in one hand or under your arms. If the tube is trailing behind you, tread water and grab the rescue tube or buoy line, pulling the apparatus to you as you continue to look at the victim. If you are using a rescue tube, bring it in front of you and turn it on edge. Hold the rescue tube with one hand at the nose of the tube and the other hand in the center. If you are using a buoy, turn it on edge and hold it with one hand on the top handle and the other on the nose. Keep the equipment between you and the victim at all times.

a.

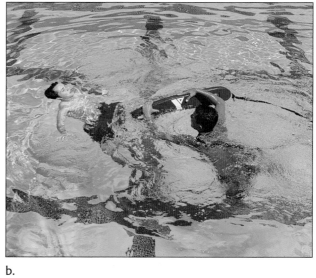

b.

c.

d.

e.

f.

Figure 7.11 Rescuing an active victim from the front.

To extend the tube or buoy to the victim, press the nose across the front of the victim and under one arm. Once the victim grabs the apparatus, continue to give reassurance. If the victim does not grab the equipment, remove your hand from in front of the tube or buoy and quickly place it on top of the victim's upper arm. Push the arm down on the tube or buoy to help the victim hold on to the device by trapping the victim's arm over it. You may even have to remind the victim to hold onto the equipment or hold the victim's arms around it yourself. Holding the victim's elbow and the equipment, use a rescue kick to move the victim to safety. Upon reaching shallow water, the side of the pool, the deck, or a boat, be sure to assess the victim's condition.

If the victim grabs you in a way that places you at risk, take a quick breath and submerge, pushing the rescue tube up and into the victim (figure 7.12). Swim away underwater. When you surface, reassess the situation and make another approach if necessary.

a.

b.

c.

d.

Figure 7.12   Avoiding a distressed victim.

Rear, Active Victim

The approach from the rear to an actively drowning victim uses the same technique as in a front active rescue. About 6 feet from the victim, pause and ready yourself. Then proceed with the rescue as described for the active victim from the front, pushing the nose of the tube or buoy across the victim's back and underneath the victim's arm (figure 7.13). Take your hand off the nose and place it on the victim's upper arm. Press the arm down, trapping the tube, and tow the victim to safety.

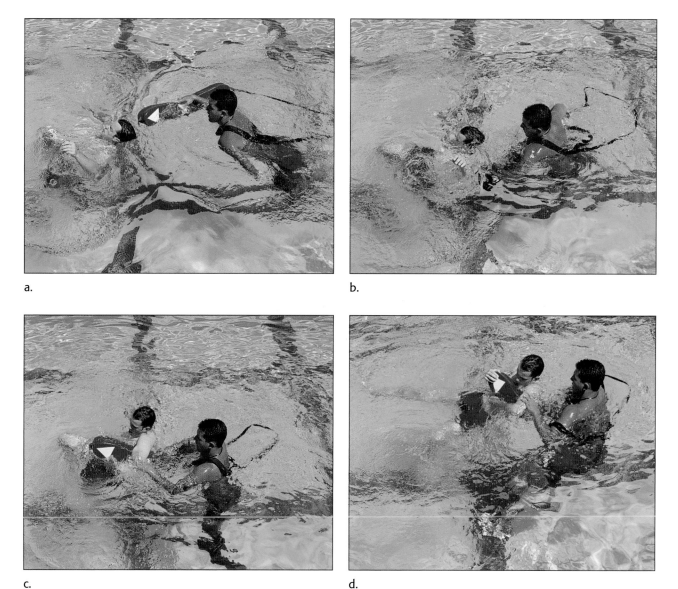

a.

b.

c.

d.

Figure 7.13 Rescuing an active victim from the rear.

Injured, Conscious Victim on the Surface

Many variables must be considered when an injured, conscious victim must be rescued. You must consider the type of accident that just occurred and determine if the victim needs assistance in swimming to the side of the pool. You will need to modify your rescue methods to suit the conditions of the injury, in order to provide adequate support to the victim and to avoid moving the injured body part. (If a spinal injury is suspected, perform the rescue techniques discussed in chapter 10.)

Figure 7.14 Rescuing a conscious victim with an injury to an upper extremity.

Begin by trying to identify what area of the victim's body has been injured. How the injury occurred and how the victim moves in the water after the accident can give you clues. Sometimes it will be fairly easy to determine which part of the victim is injured, but in some instances it will be more difficult. In any situation in which you do not know the extent of the injury, perform the rescue that will best support the victim and limit movement. If the injury involves upper or lower extremities, use the following rescue procedures.

Upper extremity. An upper extremity injury could be one to the shoulder, upper arm, elbow, lower arm, wrist, or hand. After a traumatic injury to an upper or lower extremity, victims may be dazed, disoriented, incoherent, and/or unable to move efficiently. They may be able to support themselves fairly well, or they may have a great deal of difficulty staying afloat, perhaps struggling to stay at the surface or alternating between surfacing and submerging. If such a victim is having difficulty swimming to the side of the pool, enter the water with a rescue tube as previously discussed. For your own protection, always keep the rescue tube between you and the victim.

Perform either a front or a rear active victim rescue. As it is best to keep the injured extremity as motionless as possible, determine which body part is injured and place the rescue tube under the victim's armpit on the opposite side of the injury (figure 7.14). Hold on to the rescue tube and tow the victim to safety. This procedure provides good flotation for the victim and allows him or her to avoid moving the injured limb.

Lower extremity. A lower extremity injury could be to the hip, upper leg, knee, lower leg, ankle, or foot. A victim with an injury to the lower extremity may be able to scull with the arms but may have difficulty kicking. Because of the water's resistance, any leg movement can be extremely painful.

Enter the water as previously described. Approach the victim with the rescue tube in front of you. Extend the rescue tube to the victim or place the tube under the victim's arm, as previously described. Instruct him or her to place the rescue tube against the chest and under an armpit. Grab the rescue tube and tow the victim to safety (see figure 7.15).

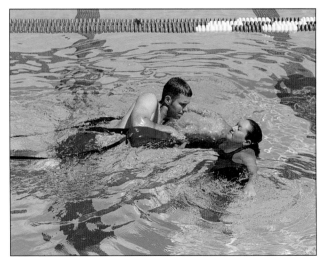

a.

b.

Figure 7.15 Rescuing a conscious victim with an injury to a lower extremity.

If the victim is unable to hold the rescue tube, place the rescue tube against your chest and under your armpits. Swim to the rear of the victim and reach under his or her armpits. Support the victim in a comfortable position and swim him or her to safety.

Front, Passive Victim

In this situation, the victim is not struggling, and you have determined that there are no signs of spinal injury. (With signs of spinal injury, follow the procedures described in chapter 10 instead of these.) The victim is floating facedown. Carrying your RFD and resuscitation mask, quickly move to about 6 feet from the victim and ready yourself. Maintaining visual contact, bring the rescue equipment to your side.

To perform this approach with a rescue tube, take the following steps (see figure 7.16):

1. Place the tube between you and the victim so that it crosses the front of your body.
2. Place your left hand on the center of the tube.
3. Reach over the tube with your right hand while submerging the tube slightly with your left hand. Reach your right hand to the underside of the victim's right wrist.
4. Grasp the victim's wrist with your thumb on top. Turn the victim faceup by pulling the arm down and then back up toward the surface (draw a *U*). Simultaneously, with the opposite hand in the center of the tube, push down to submerge the tube while pulling the victim's wrist just past your ear and pulling him or her onto the tube.
5. Once the tube is under the victim's back, release your hold on the wrist. Place your right arm over the victim's upper arm and place your right hand on top of the tube between it and the victim's back to hold the tube in place. Pull your other hand from under the victim.
6. If you are in choppy water or far from safety, grab one end of the tube's fastener in each hand and secure the tube. If you are in calm water and close to safety, there is no need to secure the tube.
7. Move to the right side of the victim's head and get your resuscitation mask ready to use. Place your left hand on the victim's forehead and tilt it back to check the airway and breathing.
8. Tow the victim to the side of the pool or to shallow water. If the victim is not breathing, hold the resuscitation mask in place with the thumb and middle finger as you tow. Bend the valve toward you with your index finger until it reaches 90 degrees. Begin with two full breaths and then give one breath every 5 seconds.

a. b.

(continued)

Figure 7.16 Rescuing a passive victim from the front using a tube.

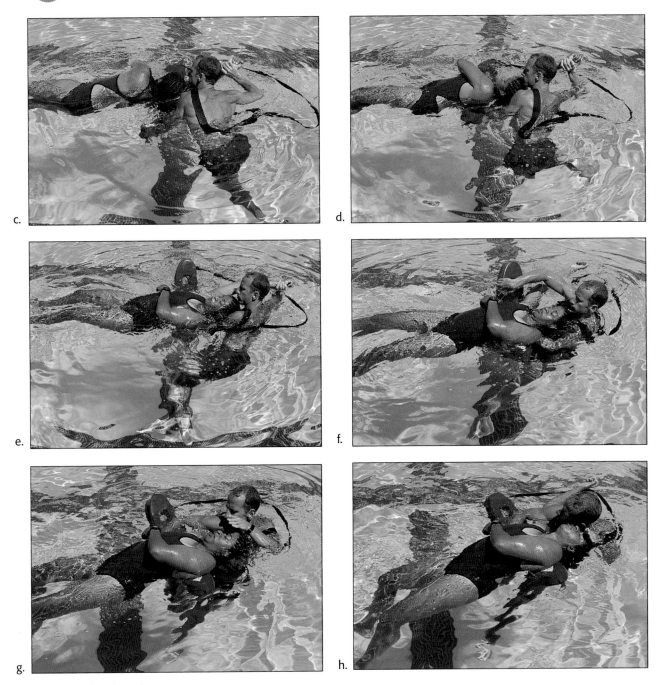

Figure 7.16   *(continued)*

To use a rescue buoy for this approach and rescue (see figure 7.17), come to about 6 feet from the victim and ready yourself. After checking for and finding no signs of spinal injury, do the following:

1. With your right hand, bring the buoy nose end first to a position between you and the victim. Then place your left hand over the buoy, grasping the hand grip with fingers on the outside and the thumb inside.

2. Reach over the buoy and grab the underside of the victim's right wrist with your right hand. Turn him or her faceup with the technique described previously while simultaneously submerging the buoy and pulling the victim onto it.

3. When the buoy is under the victim, release the victim's wrist, move to the right side of the victim's head, and place your right hand over the victim's

right arm. Grab the handgrip of the buoy with your right hand and stabilize the victim.

4. Pull your left hand out from under the victim's back and tilt the victim's head back with your left hand and assess for breathing.

5. Tow the victim to the side of the pool or to shallow water. If the victim is not breathing, hold the resuscitation mask in place with the thumb and middle finger as you tow. Bend the valve toward you with your index finger until it reaches 90 degrees. Begin with two full breaths and then give one breath every 5 seconds.

To determine whether the victim is breathing, tread water hard enough so you can place your ear close to the victim's mouth to listen for breathing sounds and see if the chest is rising and falling. Do not submerge the victim's head or turn it toward you, but look, listen, and feel for breathing for 5 seconds.

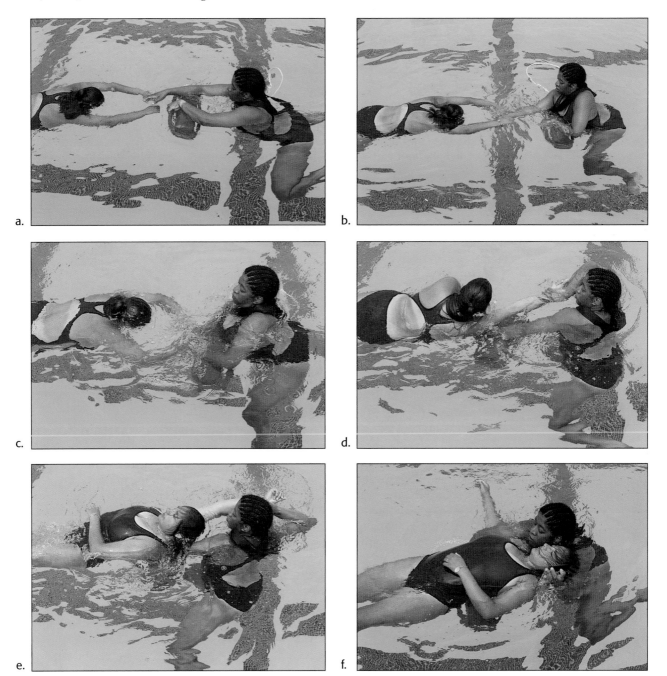

a.

b.

c.

d.

e.

f.

Figure 7.17 Rescuing a passive victim from the front using a rescue buoy.

(continued)

Figure 7.17 *(continued)* g.

If the victim is breathing, tow her or him to safety. If not, and conditions allow, follow these steps to provide rescue breathing for a victim with no signs of spinal injury (figure 7.18; see chapter 10 for rescue breathing procedures for those suspected to have spinal injuries):

1. After the victim is level, use your left hand to turn the head. Pull the corner of the mouth down to let any water run out.
2. Release the corner of the victim's mouth and place the heel of the left hand on the victim's forehead, tilt it back, and check for breathing.
3. If the victim is not breathing, take out your resuscitation mask and be sure the dome is pushed out and the one-way valve is attached to the valve. Rinse it in the water and shake it to remove excess water.
4. Position the resuscitation mask over the victim's nose and mouth, making sure you maintain a good seal at the edges so air and water do not leak. Tilt the head back to open the airway. Provide rescue breathing as you learned it.
5. You should be able to feel the air move into the victim's lungs. If not, reposition the victim's head and try again.
6. Vomiting is very common during resuscitation; expect it to occur. If vomiting occurs, turn the victim's head away from you, wipe the vomitus away from the victim's mouth, and resume rescue breathing.
7. Tow the victim to the side of the pool or shallow water. If the victim is not breathing, hold the resuscitation mask in place with the thumb and middle finger as you tow. Bend the valve toward you with your index finger until it reaches 90 degrees. Give one breath every 5 seconds.

After giving the first two full breaths, check the victim's pulse at the neck (carotid pulse) for 5 to 10 seconds. If the victim has no pulse, tow him or her to shore or the deck and begin CPR. If the victim has a pulse, continue rescue breathing as you tow the victim.

If the distance is great or if conditions don't allow you to perform rescue breathing, move to shallow water or safety. Once in shallow water or on land, begin rescue breathing. If CPR is needed, remove the victim from the water as soon as possible and begin CPR. Continue until emergency personnel arrive on the scene to relieve you. Any immersion victim who required resuscitation must be transported to the hospital.

As you learn how to do rescue breathing, practice often. It is a difficult but important skill to master. Keep your resuscitation mask with you at all times so you have it when you need to make an emergency response.

Note: The YMCA conforms to the standards established by the Emergency Cardiac Care Committee of the American Heart Association, which specifies that rescue breathing should be started as soon as possible (here being as soon as the victim is contacted in deep water).

Victim assessment and rescue breathing can be accomplished in waist-deep water with the same technique used with a rescue tube in deep water and without a tube in shallow water.

a.

b.

c.

d.

e.

f.

Figure 7.18 Rescue breathing while using a rescue tube.

a.

b.

c.

Rear, Passive Victim

In this approach you come up from behind a victim who is facedown in the water. Swim quickly to about 6 feet from the victim, pause, and ready yourself for the rescue. Check for signs of spinal injury. If you see such signs, follow the procedures outlined in chapter 10. If signs of spinal injury are not present, follow these steps for use with a rescue tube (see figure 7.19):

1. With the right hand, bring the tube into position crossing in front of your body so the tail of the tube is on your right side.

2. With your left hand on the center of the tube, submerge the tube as you reach across with your right hand and grab the victim's right armpit. Your fingers should be in the victim's armpit with your thumb on the back of the victim's arm.

3. Pull the victim over the tube until it reaches a position below the shoulder blades. Then place your right arm over the victim's upper arm and place your right hand between the top of the tube and the victim's back (if the tube is not clasped) to secure the tube in place. Pull your other hand from under the victim.

4. Evaluate the distance from safety. Grasp the ends of the tube and secure them together, if desired, while towing the victim to safety.

5. Move to the right side of the victim's head. Place your left hand on the victim's forehead to tilt the victim's head back to check for breathing.

6. Tow the victim to the side of the pool or to shallow water. If the victim is not breathing, hold the resuscitation mask in place with the thumb and middle finger as you tow. Bend the valve toward you with your index finger until it reaches 90 degrees. Begin with two full breaths and then give one breath every 5 seconds.

d.   e.

Figure 7.19   Rescuing a passive victim from the rear using a rescue tube.

When using a rescue buoy for a rear, passive rescue, swim to about 6 feet from the victim, pause, and ready yourself. After checking for and finding no evidence of spinal injury, follow these steps (see figure 7.20):

1. With your right hand, bring the buoy nose end first to a position between you and the victim. Then place your left hand over the buoy, grasping the hand grip with fingers on the outside and the thumb inside.

2. Push the buoy underneath the victim with your left hand and pull him or her over the buoy toward you with your right hand.

3. Move to the right side of the victim's head.

4. Take your right hand and move it so it is over the victim's upper arm and under the back, gripping the buoy handle.

5. With the left hand on the victim's forehead, tilt the victim's head back and assess for breathing.

6. Tow the victim to the side of the pool or to shallow water. If the victim is not breathing, hold the resuscitation mask in place with the thumb and middle finger as you tow. Bend the valve toward you with your index finger until it reaches 90 degrees. Begin with two full breaths and then give one breath every 5 seconds.

a.

b.

c.

d.

e.

f.

Figure 7.20 Rescuing a passive victim from the rear using a rescue buoy.

Active Victim Just Below the Surface

Approach from the front or rear and swim to either side of victim. Pause and ready yourself about 6 feet from the victim. If you suspect the victim has a spinal injury, follow the procedures outlined in chapter 10; if not, then do the following (see figure 7.21):

1. Place the rescue tube or buoy so it is between you and the victim. Reach over the tube or buoy and grab the victim's wrist or forearm. Pull that arm up, over, and around the top of the tube or buoy to keep the victim afloat on the surface.

2. Keep the rescue tube or buoy between you and the victim at all times.

3. Follow all other procedures for rescuing an active victim.

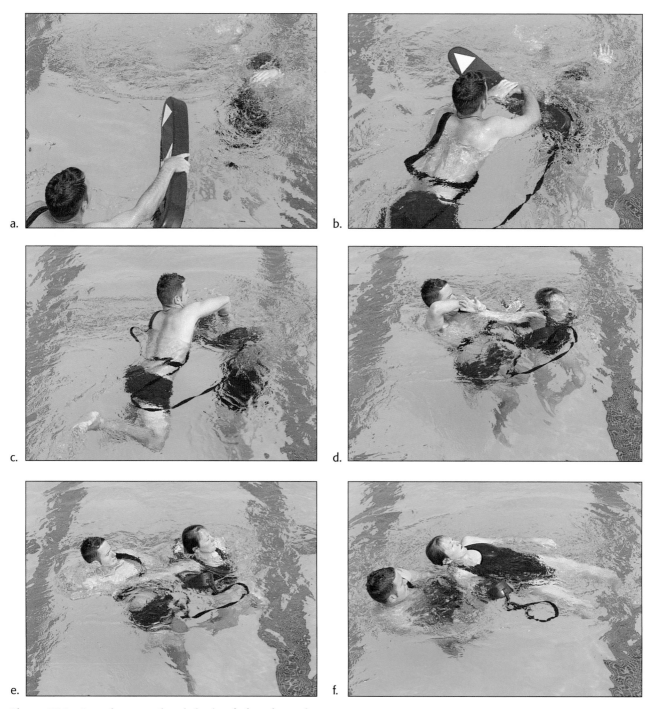

a.

b.

c.

d.

e.

f.

Figure 7.21   Rescuing an active victim just below the surface.

Passive Victim Just Below the Surface

Either a front or a rear approach can be used with a passive victim just below the surface. Pause and ready yourself about 6 feet from the victim. Again, if you suspect the victim has a spinal injury, follow the procedures in chapter 10; if not, then follow these steps (figure 7.22):

1. Place the rescue tube or buoy between you and the victim. For a front approach, reach over the tube and underwater to grab the victim's wrist. For a rear approach, reach over the tube or buoy and down underwater to grab the victim's armpit.

2. Pull the victim to the surface and onto the tube.

3. Follow all other procedures for rescuing a passive victim approaching from the front or rear.

If you can't reach the victim this way, try the procedures for a submerged victim.

a.

b.

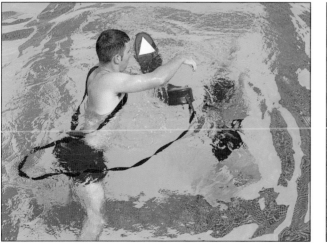

c.

d.

(continued)

Figure 7.22   Rescuing a passive victim just below the surface.

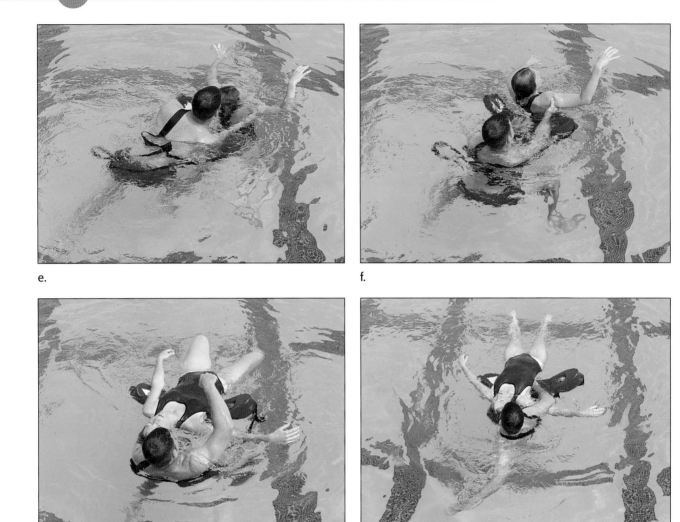

e.

f.

g.

h.

Figure 7.22 *(continued)*

Submerged Victim

Speed is crucial in rescuing a submerged victim (figure 7.23). Use a surface dive, either feet-first or arm-over-arm (described on pages 24–25).

Dive feet-first under the following conditions:

- The water is murky.
- You are not sure of underwater obstructions.
- You don't know the depth of the water.

Choose the faster and more accurate arm-over-arm surface dive when these conditions prevail:

- The water is clear.
- You know the area in which you are diving is safe for diving.
- You know the water is deep enough to safely dive head-first.

Swim quickly to the approximate place where the victim was last seen. Bubbles on the surface can be a clue to where the victim is submerged. If you suspect the victim has a spinal injury, use the rescue procedures described in chapter 10. Otherwise make a surface dive, leaving the rescue tube or buoy on the surface. If the victim is submerged too deeply for you to reach her or him with your rescue tube still attached to your shoulder, remove the strap. Approach from the rear and grasp the victim by the armpit. Bring him or her to the surface with a single or double armpit tow. Once on the surface, position the victim on the rescue equipment as described for the passive victim with an approach from the rear. Be sure to check the ABCs and, if necessary, maintain rescue breathing while towing the victim to the side of the pool or to shallow water.

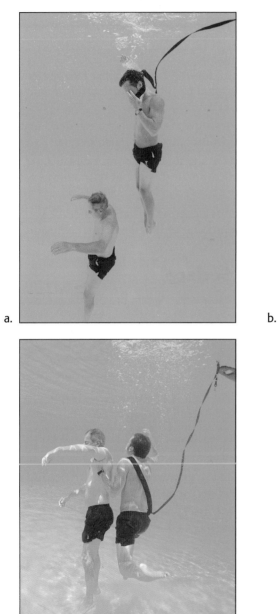

a.

b.

c.

d.

Figure 7.23　Rescuing a submerged victim.

MULTIPLE-VICTIM RESCUES

It's possible that you will encounter situations in which more than one person is in distress or near drowning. Multiple-victim near-drownings do occur, although two-victim incidents happen more often than those involving three or more people. Some of the situations in which one or more victims might grab nearby swimmers are the following:

- At a beach, victims might be knocked over by a wave, lose contact with the bottom due to waves or swells, lose an inflatable support, or step off into a hole or into deeper water.
- At a pool, victims might jump or be pushed into deep water, walk from shallow water into deep water in a pool that has no lifeline indicating the water depth, become tired while swimming across the pool width in deep water, or lose an inflatable support.

To rescue multiple victims, follow these principles:

- Have multiple lifeguards available to provide the best response. If only one is available, do extensive planning and rehearsal before and during the swimming season to ensure successful rescues under these conditions.
- Have an inflatable rescue tube available. A single rescuer can handle two victims, but a situation with three or four victims will require an inflatable tube.
- Have rescue tubes with clasps on the ends so the tube can be fastened around the first victim. He or she probably will not be able to stay afloat without this assistance.

Rescue techniques for multiple victims will vary depending on whether the victims are on the surface or on the bottom and on the number of lifeguards available and the number of victims.

Multiple-Victim Rescues on the Surface

Here are procedures for multiple-victim rescues with one or two lifeguards and two or more victims.

One Lifeguard, Two Victims

After assessing the situation, you may see victims who are face to face, one victim holding onto another one from behind, or one victim holding onto another from the side. Take the following action (figure 7.24):

1. Blow your whistle, use an airhorn, or push the pool alarm button to indicate the beginning of a multiple-victim rescue procedure. This should summon another lifeguard to cover your zone.
2. Enter the water and determine which victim is on top (this usually is the person who initiated the situation). Approach the top victim from behind. Place the rescue tube on edge. Grab the tube approximately 6 inches from the nose end with one hand (this gives you good control over the tube when submerging it).
3. With your free hand, grab the armpit of the top victim (right hand to right armpit or left hand to left armpit).
4. As you lift up on the victim's armpit push down on the tube. Thrust the tube between the two victims. Grasp both ends of the tube and clasp the tube around the top victim, providing flotation.
5. Swim around to the other victim and assist him or her in reaching the rescue tube, or approach victim two from behind, extend your hands under that victim's armpits, and grab hold of the rescue tube.
6. Tow or push both victims to the side of the pool, the dock, or the beach using a breaststroke or inverted breaststroke kick.

a.

b.

c.

d.

e.

f.

g.

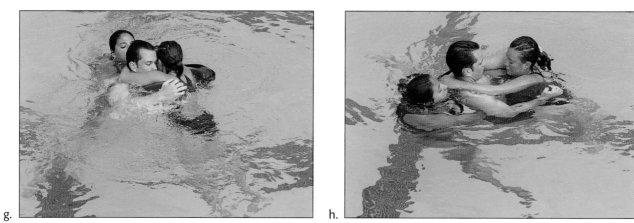
h.

Figure 7.24 A multiple-victim rescue with one lifeguard and two victims.

Two Lifeguards, Two Victims

When a second lifeguard is available, perform the rescue of two victims this way:

1. Signal the start of the multiple-victim/multiple-rescuer procedure.
2. Enter the water and approach the victims.
3. If you are the first lifeguard to reach the victims, determine which victim is on top (the original victim). Insert the tube between the two victims and clasp the tube ends together behind the victim on top.
4. The second lifeguard to arrive should then approach the second victim and extend the tube while instructing the second victim to grab it.
5. If the second victim does not or cannot grab the rescue tube, the second lifeguard should follow the procedures for a front or rear active rescue, depending on which direction the second victim is facing.

One Lifeguard, Three or More Victims

A situation with three or more victims requires both a primary and a secondary rescue tube. An inflatable tube would be a useful secondary tube. Two models are available, one that is inflated orally and one that uses a carbon dioxide cartridge to inflate. The one with the cartridge is probably the better one for these situations. It can be stored in a large fanny pack or attached with hook-and-loop tape to the sash or rope on the primary tube.

Follow these procedures to rescue three or more victims (figure 7.25):

1. Signal the start of the multiple-victim rescue procedure.
2. Enter the water and approach the victims. Determine which two victims you can insert your primary tube between.
3. Clasp the ends of the tube together behind the victim whose back is nearest to you. Remove the sash from your neck so you can move to the other victims without getting tangled.
4. Retrieve the inflatable tube from your fanny pack or primary rescue tube, inflate it, and extend it to the third victim. If there is a fourth victim, tow the third victim on the inflatable to the fourth victim, and allow these victims to be supported by the inflatable tube.

a.

b.

Figure 7.25   A multiple-victim rescue with one lifeguard and three victims.

c.

d.

e.

f.

g.

h.

Figure 7.25 *(continued)*

Two Lifeguards, Three or More Victims

When two lifeguards are available, rescue three or more victims like this (figure 7.26):

1. Signal the start of the multiple-victim/multiple-rescuer procedure.
2. Enter the water and approach the victims.
3. If you are the first lifeguard to reach the victims, attempt to determine which victim is on top (the original victim). Insert the tube between the first two victims, then clasp the ends together behind the victim on top.
4. The second lifeguard to arrive should follow the procedures for a front or rear active rescue for the third victim or, if the situation involves four active victims, attempt to insert the tube between the two remaining victims.
5. If the two remaining victims become separated, use the appropriate approach (front or rear active or passive) to the third victim, then tow the third victim and tube close to where the fourth victim (if there is one) can grab hold of and be supported by the tube.
6. If the second lifeguard has an inflatable tube, he or she can use it to rescue the fourth victim.

a.

b.

c.

d.

Figure 7.26   A multiple-victim rescue with two lifeguards and three victims.

e.

f.

g.

h.

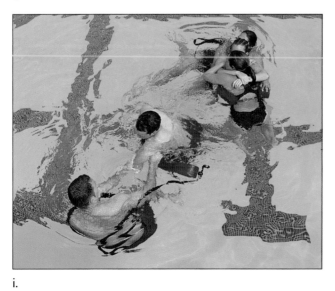

i.

j.

Figure 7.26 *(continued)*

Multiple-Victim Rescues of Submerged Victims

If it becomes necessary to rescue more than one submerged victim from the bottom, you will need the help of either another lifeguard or of individuals who are certified in CPR. Follow these steps to recover multiple victims from the bottom:

1. Signal the start of the multiple-victim/multiple-rescuer procedure.
2. Enter the water with another lifeguard as soon as possible. Approach the victims on the surface to the point where they are directly beneath you, then surface dive to the bottom. If your tube line isn't long enough to reach the bottom, remove the rescue tube sash from your shoulder before diving.
3. Each of you should place your victim in a single or double armpit tow, then swim the victim to the surface.
4. Assess for breathing and provide rescue breathing, if needed. If the distance to the pool deck or the beach is short, continue towing the victim to safety. Use one of the water exits (see page 140) to remove the victim from the water quickly. If the distance is long, you should try to retrieve your rescue tube and attach it around the victim for additional support before towing.
5. Since the victims were on the bottom, they probably need rescue breathing and/ or CPR. Begin the procedure with a resuscitation mask immediately upon getting them out of the water.

If a second lifeguard isn't available, but one or more people with CPR certification are, you may have to rescue and tow the victims to safety one at a time. Those who have CPR certification can then care for them while you rescue the others.

RESCUE TOWING

Two techniques can be used to tow the victim to safety: the rescue stroke and the armpit tow.

Rescue Stroke

The rescue stroke (figure 7.27) is used to tow a victim. It consists of a one-arm pull with a scissors, breaststroke, or rotary kick.

Figure 7.27　Rescue stroke.

Armpit Tow

If a victim is breathing, is truly passive, and has no evidence of a spinal injury, you can tow her or him to shore using a single or double armpit tow (figure 7.28). If you have clasped the rescue tube around the victim, tow by grasping either the tube or the victim's armpit. Grab the victim as close to the armpit as possible (right hand to right armpit or left hand to left armpit) with your thumb on the outside of the arm and keep the tube or buoy between you and the victim. For the single armpit tow, use any rescue stroke that allows you to keep visual contact with the victim and swim to safety quickly. For the double armpit tow, grab both of the victim's armpits and kick to safety.

Figure 7.28 The armpit tow.

REMOVING VICTIMS FROM THE WATER

Once you have brought a victim to safety, you have to get him or her out of the water as quickly as possible to start emergency first aid. The type of exit you use is influenced by conditions such as terrain, proximity to medical assistance, your own size and strength, the assistance available, and the victim's size, condition, and injuries.

While the water generally is good support for an injured extremity, it becomes challenging to provide support and stabilization while removing the victim from the water. Depending on the extent of the injury, you may or may not need assistance in exiting the water. Consider issues such as these:

- Will additional movement of the injured part cause further damage?
- Could further injury result if I do not assist the victim in exiting the water?
- Would it be better to move to shallow water before exiting the pool?
- How much pain is the victim currently having?
- What is the victim's level of consciousness?
- How many others are able to assist?

These and many other variables will dictate your actions in removing the victim from the water. You may even decide that additional professional assistance is necessary and allow EMS to perform the removal from the water.

Get feedback from the injured victim to help you decide what you can do to assist. Once you have towed the victim to the side of the pool and he or she is floating with the assistance of a rescue tube, ask additional questions to determine the extent of the injury such as the following:

- Do you know what happened?
- Do you have pain anywhere? How much pain do you have?
- Do you feel light-headed? Are you nauseated?
- Can you feel your arms and legs? Can you move your arms and legs?
- Are you having difficulty breathing?
- Do you feel weak?
- Are you cold?

The answers to these and other questions can help you decide how to approach removing the victim from the water. Whatever procedure you use for removing the victim from the water, follow these guidelines:

- Call EMS.
- Take charge.
- Protect yourself from blood-borne pathogens.
- Provide support that will eliminate movement of the injured extremity.
- Ensure that the extrication process will not cause further injury.
- Do not allow the victim to place any pressure or weight on the injured extremity.
- Work in unison with the victim and assistants.
- Give specific directions to others who may assist in the extrication.
- Identify a location for the victim following removal from the water. The location should be out of the sun, away from a crowd, and close to the first aid facilities.

Lower the victim to the ground carefully to reduce the chance of additional injury. Provide cushioning whenever possible. If CPR is necessary and the ground slopes, be sure that the victim's legs are higher than the head to facilitate blood flow back to the heart.

The two types of removal discussed here are water exits and board lifts. Assess your situation to determine which one of the many methods of removal is most appropriate.

Water Exits

Some of the ways you can assist victims in exiting from the water include the supporting assist, the one-person drag, the one- or two-person lift, and the ladder exit.

Supporting Assist

If a victim is conscious but very weak, assist him or her to safety. Stand next to the victim, pull the near arm across your shoulder, and secure it by grabbing the wrist with your far hand. Your free arm should support the victim's waist. You should be able to walk the victim to safety (see figure 7.29).

Figure 7.29 The supporting assist.

One-Person Drag

The one-person drag is probably one of the quickest and most efficient ways to carry an unconscious person from an open body of water. After you have ruled out the possibility of a spinal injury, reach around from behind the victim under the armpits and grab your wrist with the other hand to lock your grip. Walk backward, dragging the victim's feet. Be careful to lift the victim primarily using your legs and arms to avoid injuring your back.

If you are smaller than the victim, you may have difficulty reaching all the way around and grasping your wrist. If you cannot easily maintain a tight grip, you may find it more secure to grasp the victim's wrists (your right hand to the victim's right wrist and your left hand to the victim's left wrist) and cross the victim's arms slightly, as shown in figure 7.30.

If you are the second rescuer on the scene, you can assist the first rescuer who is performing a one-person drag. Simply lift the victim's legs from the knees, with one leg on each side of your body. From this position, called a *two-person carry*, you can move the victim to safety much more quickly. Again, lift primarily using your legs and arms.

Figure 7.30 The one-person drag, grasping the victim's wrists.

One- or Two-Person Lift

This lift is used primarily in deep water. It is best performed as a two-person lift, but it can be done by one with some modifications (explained later). Although generally two rescuers are required to lift an adult victim, a one-person lift can be done safely, depending on the size of the victim and the strength of the rescuer. For the one-person lift, if the victim is not breathing, provide rescue breathing while holding onto the side of the pool or deck. Position a breathing victim next to the side of the pool or deck facing the wall or deck. Position yourself to the rear of the victim.

Reach under the victim's arms and grab the side of the pool to support the victim. You can also support the victim on your knee. Lift the victim's hands onto the deck, one on top of the other, then get out of the water. If the distance between the deck and the water level is too great for you to lift yourself out of the water while maintaining control of the victim's hands and keeping her or his head out of the water, call for additional help.

After you have positioned yourself on the deck, grab the victim's wrists and lower the victim before lifting to gain momentum and make the lift easier. Do not submerge the victim's face. Keep in mind that the victim's head may be leaning forward. Take care to lift the victim straight up to protect the head from possible injury. Lift with your legs, not your back, to protect yourself.

If the victim is too heavy for one rescuer to lift, a second rescuer assists (see figure 7.31). Each rescuer takes one of the victim's wrists and upper arms, and with coordinated movements the rescuers lift the victim onto the deck. For a large victim, one or two assistants may be needed in the water to push the victim up while those on the deck lift.

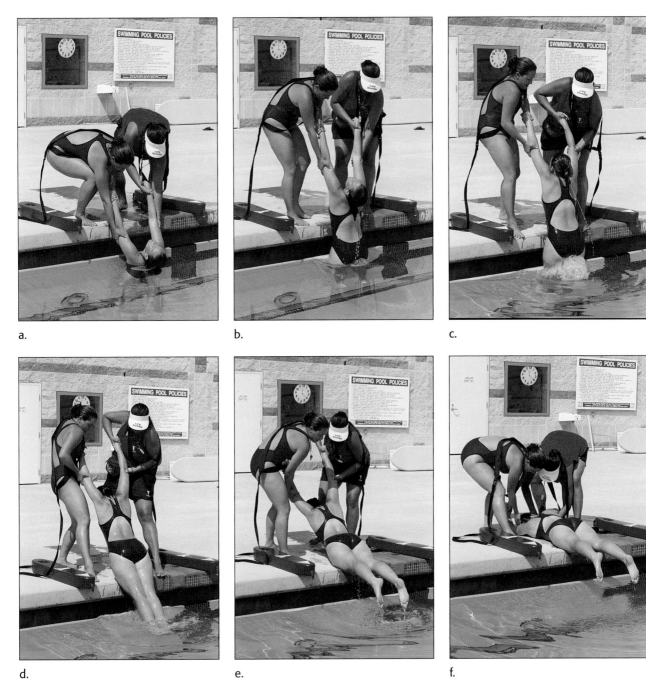

a.

b.

c.

d.

e.

f.

Figure 7.31   Two-person lift.

As the victim clears the deck at mid-thigh or lower, step back and lower the victim slowly to the deck (figure 7.32). Place your foot under the victim's face to prevent it from hitting the deck. Roll the victim onto his or her back to begin emergency procedures. Be sure that the victim is completely out of the water and lying horizontally. If the victim's legs are in the water, you will not be able to perform CPR or use an automated external defibrillator successfully.

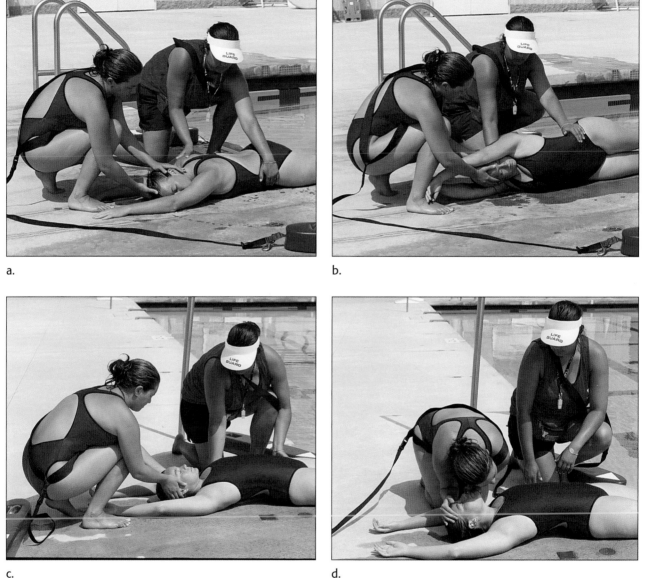

a.

b.

c.

d.

Figure 7.32 Lower the victim to the deck, roll the victim over, and begin emergency procedures.

Ladder Exit

Use a ladder exit when a victim has an upper extremity injury. Transport the victim to a ladder in shallow or deep water, then do the following (figure 7.33):

1. Instruct the victim to step onto the ladder with both feet and grab the pool gutter or the ladder railing with the hand of the uninjured extremity.
2. Position yourself behind the victim, then reach around the victim with both arms and grab the lip of the gutter or the ladder.
3. Squeeze your arms against the victim to stabilize her or him on the ladder.
4. Position your chest close to or against the victim's back or hips as you climb up the ladder with the victim.

Others on deck may assist by holding on to the victim to ensure safety. They also may help in stabilizing the victim's injured part during the climb out of the water. Remember that any movement of the extremity may cause further injury; avoid it if at all possible.

a.

b.

c.

d.

Figure 7.33 Ladder exit.

Board Lifts

A board lift is a good alternative for removing a victim from the water. It is especially effective when victims are difficult to remove because they are unconscious or have a lower extremity injury. A board lift also will be needed in cases of spinal injury; see chapter 10 for the appropriate procedures for spinal injuries.

Unconscious Victim Board Lift

You will find it difficult to remove a limp adult victim from the water without further harming him or her. One way to remove a victim without causing abrasions or contusions during the lift is to use a backboard to remove the victim from the water. Follow this procedure (figure 7.34):

a.

b.

c.

d.

Figure 7.34 Board lift with an unconscious victim.

(continued)

Figure 7.34   *(continued)*

1. As you transport the victim to the side of the pool, have another rescuer on deck grasp the victim's wrists and stabilize her or him. The victim will be facing the side of the pool with her or his head out of the water. The rescuer on deck will be holding the victim's wrists, right hand to left wrist and left hand to right wrist.

2. Exit the pool and retrieve a backboard. Remove the straps and head restraints from the backboard.

3. From the deck, submerge the board next to the victim.

4. Have the rescuer holding the victim turn the victim so the victim's back is toward the board.

5. As you hold the top of the backboard with one hand, grasp one of the victim's wrists with the other hand. The rescuer who has been holding the victim will then support the victim's other wrist with one hand and grasp the top of the backboard with the other. Begin the lifting action as soon as the victim is on the board. If done too slowly, the board may slide out from under the victim.

6. Both of you lift the backboard and victim simultaneously onto the deck. During the lift, slide the backboard against the edge of the pool, step back, and lay the board and victim on the deck.

Conscious Victim With a Lower Extremity Injury Board Lift

Removing a victim with a lower extremity injury from the water can be complicated, as the victim probably cannot climb the ladder without additional movement of the injured body part. Give the victim support that restricts or completely eliminates movement of the extremity. Use the following removal procedure to help restrict movement and make this process more comfortable for the victim (figure 7.35):

1. Stabilize the victim in the water at the side of the pool. Allow him or her to continue to hold onto the rescue tube or the pool edge.
2. Turn the victim so his or her back is to the pool wall. Then have a rescuer on deck grasp the victim's wrists (right hand to right wrist, left hand to left wrist). The victim should also grab the rescuer's wrists, if possible.
3. Retrieve a backboard, remove all straps and the head restraint, and then submerge the backboard. From the deck, guide it, foot-end first, straight down into the water until the top end is adjacent to the victim's head. Angle the foot-end of the board toward the pool wall to help control the board as you submerge it.
4. The rescuer holding the victim moves the victim in front of the backboard.

a.

b.

c.

d.

(continued)

Figure 7.35 Board lift of victim with an injury to a lower extremity.

e.

f.

g.

h.

Figure 7.35 *(continued)*

5. As you hold the top of the backboard with one hand, grasp one of the victim's wrists with the other hand. The rescuer who has been holding the victim will then support the victim's other wrist with one hand and grasp the top of the backboard with the other.

6. Both of you pull the backboard and the victim simultaneously up and onto the deck. Do not do this too slowly, as the backboard may start to slip to one side if this transition is not performed soon enough.

As the two of you pull the backboard onto the deck, rest the underside of the board against the edge of the pool and slide it onto the deck. This will make a smooth transport during the lift onto the deck.

The backboard will have some buoyancy, perhaps a lot. Be sure that you have positioned the backboard squarely behind the victim before you slide the victim and the board onto the deck. Assistants in the water may help keep the backboard in position behind the victim. Before you lift, make certain that the injured extremity will not slide off the backboard during the lift from the water.

Review Questions

1. Name and describe seven pieces of rescue equipment.

2. List three things in your aquatic environment that could be used in an extension assist.

3. Why is it important to keep your weight shifted away from the victim in a reaching, extension, or wading assist?

4. Where should you aim in a throwing assist?

5. List and describe the five entries. When would you use each?

6. Why is it important to ready yourself upon reaching a victim?

7. Why must you use rescue equipment in each rescue?

8. Describe the following rescues: active victim from the front, active victim from the rear, passive victim from the front, and passive victim from the rear.

9. Describe how to position a victim for rescue breathing using a rescue tube or buoy for additional support.

10. How do you rescue a partially submerged victim?

11. When should you perform a feet-first surface dive? An arm-over-arm surface dive?

12. How do you rescue a deeply submerged victim?

13. Describe how to rescue two victims with one and with two lifeguards and how to rescue three or more victims with one and with two lifeguards.

14. Describe how to rescue multiple victims who are submerged.

15. Describe how to tow a passive victim.

16. Describe the supporting assist and when to use it.

17. Describe the one-person drag and when to use it.

18. Describe the one- or two-person lift and when to use it.

19. How do you prevent back injury to yourself when performing lifts and drags?

eight

Emergency Systems

It is likely that emergencies and potential emergencies will arise at your facility on occasion. Being prepared for common emergencies will help reduce the guesswork involved in reacting to them and the amount of stress you experience.

In This Chapter, You'll Learn How to Respond to Emergencies by Examining

- types of emergencies,
- preparation for emergencies,
- steps for creating an emergency policy,
- emergency plans,
- how to complete accident and incident reports,
- how to use injury charts, and
- crisis control responsibilities.

TYPES OF EMERGENCIES

Seven specific groups of emergencies are presented in this section:

- Medical
- Water
- Missing persons
- Environmental
- Chemical
- Mechanical
- Facility

As you read this section and the rest of this chapter, consider how you and your facility would handle various emergency situations. Your facility should have an emergency plan for each category of emergency. If your facility does not have one for a particular type, suggest to management that they use the principles presented later in the chapter to preplan a course of action for that type.

Medical Emergencies

Medical emergencies can be divided into two general situations: life-threatening and potentially life-threatening. In life-threatening emergencies, death probably will occur if no action is taken. Such emergencies require immediate advanced first aid, such as CPR, and transportation to a medical facility. In potentially life-threatening emergencies, death is less certain but such conditions still require immediate action. Outside emergency medical assistance may still be needed, including transport to a medical facility. Here are some examples of life-threatening and potentially life-threatening emergencies:

Life-Threatening Emergencies

Cardiac arrest	Uncontrolled bleeding
Drowning/near-drowning	Poisoning
Cessation of breathing	

Potentially Life-Threatening Emergencies

Seizure	Obstructed airway or respiratory emergency
Heart attack or angina	Allergic reaction
Spinal injury	Asthma attack
Loss of consciousness	Diabetes or insulin shock
Fracture	Cut or laceration
Reaction to extreme heat or cold	

There are undoubtedly other medical emergencies that you could list. Staff should discuss how to handle such emergencies at your facility.

Water Emergencies

By the time you finish this lifeguarding course, you should have the skills to handle a wide variety of water emergencies. Through in-service training, the staff at your facility should collaborate to develop the emergency procedures you need to react effectively and efficiently. Be sure you have plans to cover

- drownings and near-drownings,
- severe injury in the water and spinal injury in the water,
- cardiac or respiratory emergencies in the water, and
- missing persons.

Missing Persons

If a missing person is believed to be in the water, the situation is life-threatening. If she or he is believed to be out of the water, the situation is less critical. In any instance, you must assist in efforts to locate the missing person. See chapter 12 for a complete discussion of search and rescue techniques.

Environmental Emergencies

Chapter 11 provides some information concerning storms and signs of approaching bad weather. It is important that facility personnel know the policy and procedures for a variety of weather-related situations:

- Thunderstorms and lightning
- Hurricanes
- Tornadoes and high winds
- Heavy rain and hailstorms
- High and low temperatures
- Reduced visibility (due to fog, haze, dust, blowing debris, or other causes)
- Earth tremors or earthquakes

Chemical Emergencies

Pool operators should be very careful in handling the chemicals used to keep the water properly balanced for recreation. Unfortunately, accidents occur that can create potentially hazardous conditions. Each facility should have procedures for handling a variety of chemical emergencies:

- Liquid gas or chlorine leaks due to tank ruptures, leaks, or spills resulting in serious or fatal injuries
- Pool-acid spills resulting in caustic vapors and skin irritations
- Explosion of flammable chemicals (for example, chlorinated granulates or bromine)
- Imbalance in water chemistry (for example, cloudiness, or improper pH or chlorine level, irritating swimmers' skin or eyes)

For more information on pool chemistry, see chapter 14. Be sure you have read the material safety data sheets on chemicals, available from your manager.

Mechanical Emergencies

Various potential mechanical hazards exist depending on the type of facility you work at. Your facility should have procedures to handle

- structural failure,
- filtration system failure,
- lighting failure, and
- equipment malfunctions (slides, wave pool, diving boards).

Facility Emergencies

Not all emergency situations that affect your facility will occur within the pool area. Be sure you know your facility's provisions for handling a variety of emergency situations:

- Structural fire on the grounds
- Brushfire on the grounds
- Bomb threats
- Electrical outages
- Chemical explosion on the grounds or nearby, presenting danger from fire or fumes
- Fire nearby, presenting danger from flames or smoke

PREPARING FOR EMERGENCIES

The most successful emergency responses are a result of effective teamwork, reducing the risks for both lifeguards and patrons and increasing the speed and efficiency with which an emergency situation can be handled. All facilities should have plans and an in-service training program for handling a variety of emergencies. Evaluating staff performance after an emergency is useful in helping staff identify hazardous areas, refine their responses, and acknowledge their successes.

Your emergency team includes lifeguards, law enforcement officials, fire department personnel, emergency medical staff, civil defense officials, and the members of a variety of other local organizations. The involvement of each group makes your emergency plans more efficient and more effective.

Facility Layout

Another key to quick and successful emergency response is knowing the layout of your facility. That may sound simple enough, but knowing the easiest way for medical personnel to reach each area is vital in an emergency. Plan for emergency access—don't leave finding the best route for emergency personnel to chance! Determine ahead of time the shortest and safest routes for paramedics to reach all locations at your facility.

Consider the following factors:

- The length and width of the backboard (page 207) and ambulance gurney
- Stairs
- Sharp corners and narrow hallways
- Locked doors or other obstacles

Once you have planned the shortest and safest access routes for emergency personnel, make sure that these routes are kept clear at all times. The excitement of an emergency situation may make clearing the routes difficult when it is most important.

Your facility should arrange in-service training sessions with outside emergency personnel to practice your procedures. During these practice sessions you can determine whether you have selected appropriate access routes. Those routes, along with the locations of fire alarms, fire extinguishers, telephones, first aid areas, and tornado areas, should be posted for all staff and patrons.

Equipment Assessment

Your equipment and supplies should be examined every day as part of your opening procedure. Every facility should have a variety of lifeguarding and emergency medical equipment, including an adequate supply of the following:

- Shepherd's crooks or reaching poles
- Ring buoys
- Rescue tubes or buoys
- Backboards and straps
- Head immobilizers and cervical collars (see page 208)
- Telephones and posted emergency telephone numbers
- First aid kits (including resuscitation masks, protective glasses, rubber gloves, and gowns)
- Blankets

Every locale has different codes specifying the requirements for the equipment needs of recreational facilities. Contact your state, county, and local health departments for lists of the apparatus they require.

Safety equipment that is broken, in poor repair, or locked in a room is of little use in an emergency. And the equipment is valuable only if all staff members know where it is stored and how to use it. Most facilities should schedule regular staff in-service training sessions to ensure that lifeguards can react effectively to a variety of emergency situations.

Emergency Medical Procedures

All personnel should be aware of the needs and procedures of the emergency medical system (EMS) personnel who respond to emergencies. Ignorance or misunderstanding of these needs and procedures may cause increased danger for the injured individual and may expose the facility to increased legal liability.

EMERGENCY POLICY GUIDELINES

The YMCA encourages all facilities to document emergency procedures before any emergency occurs. Having trained, knowledgeable personnel can only enhance the quality and safety of your aquatic program. If you work for a facility that does not have these procedures documented, strongly encourage the management to take these steps:

- Specify an emergency team leader and define this leader's responsibilities and limitations.
- Specify the personnel who should be involved in an emergency response and assign specific duties.
- Specify a chain of command.
- Select one spokesperson for the facility and direct all questions to that person.
- Establish a sequence of emergency steps.
- List emergency phone numbers.
- Prepare a written script for calling in emergencies and post it by the phone.
- Define the procedures for moving and transporting victims.
- Instruct lifeguards in the importance of and procedures for completing accident and incident reports (described later in this chapter).
- Schedule regular emergency procedure training and practice sessions.

It is vital that the emergency procedures be practiced frequently and systematically. Only through practice will reactions be refined and procedures fully understood. Practice also makes the emergency situation less stressful as all team members become familiar with their responsibilities. The more comfortable team members are when responding to their duties during an emergency, the more effective and efficient they will be. When you practice emergency action plans, evaluate your own performance and identify areas for improvement.

EMERGENCY PLANS

Emergency plans include six fundamental steps:

1. Initial reaction and assessment
2. Initiation of the primary response by the lifeguard, including calling EMS
3. Initiation of any necessary secondary response by other team members leading to resolution of the emergency (including providing first aid)
4. Notification of designated personnel (Staff should be instructed not to comment on the emergency situation to any witness, bystander, or reporter. Only those specified in the chain of command should be given information.)
5. Completion of the necessary incident or accident report
6. Investigation of the incident

The manner in which each of these steps is completed varies with the specific situation. Figures 8.1 and 8.2 are sample emergency plan flowcharts for single-guard emergency reaction and multiguard staff reaction, respectively.

The sample plans provided in this chapter, meant only as a guide, are for multiguard facilities. Each facility must determine which guards perform which duties. Single-guard facilities must establish a procedure for the lone guard to signal for immediate assistance or know how to recruit assistance from other adult patrons. Reponsibilities for the guard and assistant under those circumstances must be carefully defined.

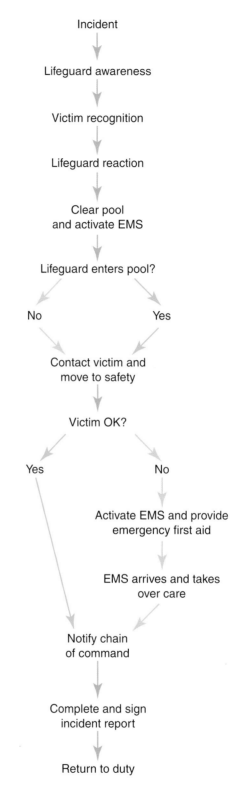

Incident

↓

Lifeguard awareness

↓

Victim recognition

↓

Lifeguard reaction

↓

Clear pool
and activate EMS

↓

Lifeguard enters pool?

No ← → Yes

Contact victim and
move to safety

↓

Victim OK?

Yes ← → No

Activate EMS and provide
emergency first aid

↓

EMS arrives and takes
over care

Notify chain
of command

↓

Complete and sign
incident report

↓

Return to duty

Figure 8.1 Single-guard emergency plan flowchart.
Based on a flowchart prepared by the Klamath County YMCA Pool Administrators.

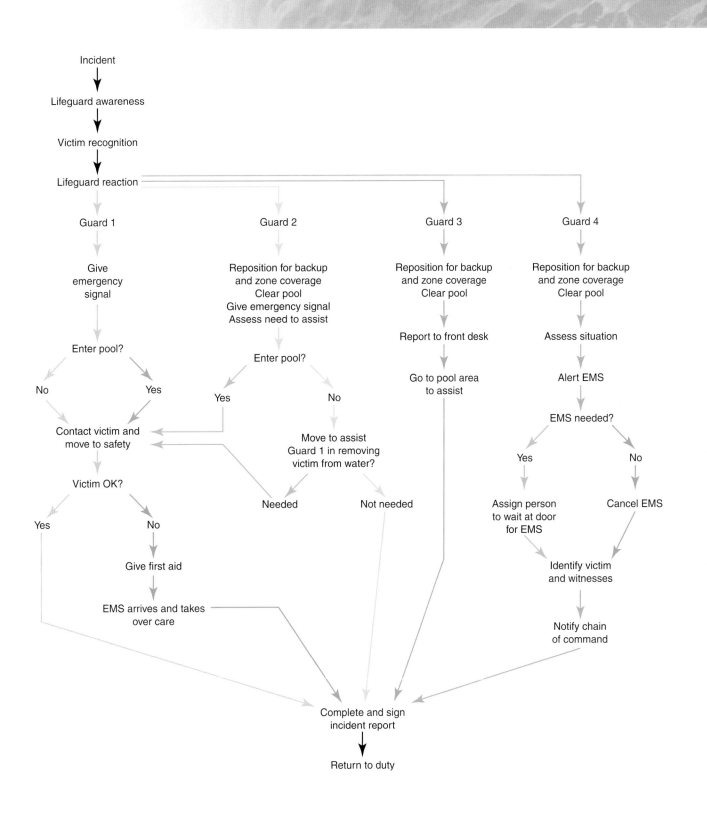

Figure 8.2 Multiguard emergency plan flowchart.

Your facility should have written procedures for handling emergencies. Be sure you are familiar with the procedures and your responsibilities. Your in-service training and practice sessions will help you feel comfortable in responding.

Sample Pool Evacuation Plan

Each facility must have a plan for evacuating the pool area. In all emergencies, quick and organized action is important. This plan is appropriate for a weather emergency.

1. Signal other lifeguards to initiate the evacuation plan.
2. Signal swimmers to clear the pool.
3. Remain on post until all swimmers have left the water.
4. Assist other staff in directing patrons to a shelter or designated area.
5. Reassure patrons of their safety.
6. Report to management for further instruction or assignment.
7. Assist as necessary.
8. Assist in completion of the incident report form.

Sample Emergency Plan for a Life-Threatening Medical Emergency

Follow this procedure for providing first aid for a heart attack victim requiring prompt attention:

1. Signal another guard to cover your area while you initiate first aid. If you are the only lifeguard, call for assistance using your preplanned emergency signal.
2. Assess the situation, call for EMS assistance, and provide the emergency first aid necessary.
3. Notify those in the chain of command.
4. Complete an accident report and file it with the appropriate person before returning to duty.
5. Review your actions with the manager.

Sample Emergency Plan for a Near-Drowning

The procedure for handling a water rescue situation at a multiguard facility is outlined here. Figure 8.2 illustrates one way that responsibilities can be divided.

1. Signal other guards to initiate emergency procedures. While you react, they will supervise your area, assist in the rescue or removal of the victim from the water, send for any first aid equipment or EMS assistance necessary, and control onlookers. If necessary, they will evacuate the pool.
2. Assess the situation and determine what rescue skills and equipment are necessary.
3. Carry out the rescue.
4. Begin any necessary first aid.
5. Calmly notify those on the chain of command of the accident; they in turn should notify emergency contacts (relatives or other designated individuals).
6. Complete and file an accident report.
7. Return to duty as soon as possible.

Sample Emergency Plan for a Missing Person

It is essential to have and practice an emergency plan for finding a missing person. A variety of different search and rescue techniques can be used for open water areas (see chapter 12). For a missing person search at a pool, take the following steps:

1. Signal the other guards to initiate emergency procedures.
2. Signal an immediate pool check.
3. Clear the pool.
4. Get an accurate description of the missing person, including age, race, height, weight, color of hair, color of clothing, and where he or she was last seen. Keep the person giving this description in a designated area to be available whenever necessary.
5. Do a visual search as quickly as possible.
6. If the missing person has become a drowning victim, complete the rescue and begin emergency first aid immediately. Arrange for EMS assistance.
7. If it is determined that the missing person is not a drowning victim, swimmers may return to the water while the following steps are taken in order:
    a. Check all facilities, including washrooms, locker rooms, gymnasiums, and any related facility on the grounds.
    b. Check the missing person's home by phone.
    c. If the person is not found, notify those on the chain of command, who should in turn notify emergency contacts.
    d. Notify law enforcement officials. This is the duty of the manager or the head lifeguard.
8. Complete the necessary accident or incident report.
9. Return to duty as soon as possible.

ACCIDENT AND INCIDENT REPORTS

As a professional, you are responsible for your decisions. In the case of an emergency, completing accident and incident reports is often the only way to substantiate your procedures and actions if they are ever questioned. Complete the reports carefully as soon after the emergency as possible. Accurate detail is critical. An accident report is used any time first aid is required; an incident report is used for any other situation, usually one in which a lifeguard, staff member, or outside agency is called into action (such as discipline problems or theft).

In an accident that requires you to provide first aid, your responsibility does not end when the injured person is delivered to the appropriate medical care provider. You must follow your facility's procedures for reporting and recording the accident. Copies of this report should be made and sent to the appropriate authorities. Be sure to keep a copy for your own records.

A sample Accident Report Form is included in appendix D. This sample should serve as a guide; amend it to meet the unique needs of your facility. From the form or other records, the following information should be provided:

- Names, titles, employment numbers, years of experience, locations of assignments, hours on duty, and lunch periods of employees involved
- Date, type, and amount of training for each involved employee
- Time, location, and nature of the accident
- Number of persons involved in the accident
- Weather and water conditions
- Number of people present at the pool or beach where the accident occurred
- General comments of importance in evaluating the situation
- Plan or sketch of the area showing any unusual conditions and assignment of personnel if deemed necessary (should be prepared by the supervisor and the lifeguard)
- Names, addresses, and phone numbers of witnesses to the accident

These questions should also be answered:

- How did the employee become aware of the accident?
- How soon did the employee respond to the emergency situation?
- What did the employee do in response to the emergency situation?
    —Did the guard have to enter the water to effect a rescue?
    —How far did the guard have to swim?
    —What action did the guard take to help the victim?
    —What rescue equipment was used by the guard?
    —What did the guard observe about the victim's condition?
    —Did the guard observe signs of spinal injury? If so, what were they?
    —Did the guard need assistance with the rescue?
    —Did anything interfere with the rescue?
    —Did the guard do everything possible to help revive the victim?
- Was the victim identified? By whom?
- What were the factors contributing to the accident?
    —What was the victim doing at the time of distress?
    —Could the victim swim?
    —Had the victim disregarded rules or orders given by the lifeguard?
- What first aid was administered?
- Was CPR necessary? Was effective circulation noted in carotid pulse or skin color?
- Were police, emergency squad, and ambulance called? At what time?
    —How soon did they respond?
    —What action did they take?
    —Was rescue breathing continued? By whom?
    —When did the EMS personnel or doctor take over?
    —When did the EMS personnel or doctor make a declaration of the victim's condition?
    —Was the victim removed from the beach or pool area? At what time?

Because some incidents require less emergency action, your facility may not have a form for reporting them. Minor incidents, such as a patron running on the deck, do not require a report. If you have asked a patron to leave the facility or if an outside agency has been contacted, it is wise to prepare a report describing the situation, those involved, and the actions taken. Your facility will define when you need to complete such forms.

INJURY CHART

One way to improve your facility's ability to prevent and react to injury situations is to determine what injuries occur and where. An injury chart can be an effective tool for gathering that information. The chart is a diagram of the supervised area, complete with all pieces of equipment, diving boards, ladders, lifelines, depth markings, lifeguard stations, fences, recreation areas, and auxiliary facilities. Each time an accident occurs, it is noted on the chart with a code.

Your facility may have a code system for listing all the types of injuries sustained. A letter, number, or symbol may be assigned to each injury. Figure 8.3 illustrates an injury chart in which the injury is signified by a number and the location on the body by a letter.

From this chart facility managers and staff can learn about the common accidents and injuries at the facility and where they are likely to occur. They can then plan the actions to be taken to prevent future accidents: establish new rules, repair equipment, install additional safety equipment, reposition lifeguards, add additional staff, or limit access to an area.

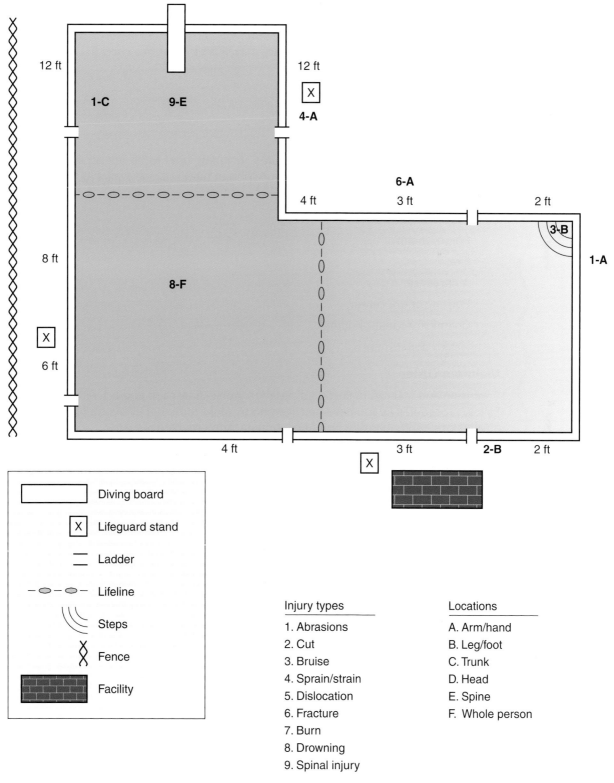

Figure 8.3 Injury chart.

CRISIS CONTROL

Having emergency procedures in place is the first step to managing crises. However, it also helps to be prepared for handling people's reactions to those crises and to think about how to stay calm and reasonable during stressful situations.

Checklist for Crisis Management

In handling any emergency situation, be sure you know the elements of crisis management shown in this checklist. Your facility may wish to post this checklist in the guard room and at the front desk.

Checklist for Crisis Management

Be Prepared

Know your facility's emergency procedures, including how to fill out an incident report, and review them regularly. Make sure phone numbers are available for the following people or agencies:

Supervisor/manager:

Police/sheriff:

Fire:

Ambulance:

Poison control center:

Chemical accident hotline:

Health department:

Maintain Order

Confusion and fear can make a bad situation worse. Stay calm and act with authority. Follow procedures as you have practiced them. Make sure that everyone present is in a safe place and unharmed before continuing with emergency plans.

Notify the Chain of Command

Report the incident to your supervisor or another designated manager as soon as possible. If necessary, call for emergency personnel or information.

Protect Your Facility

Make no statements to anyone about the incident; only the media spokesperson should discuss it publicly. File your incident report as soon as you can, using your facility's standard form. Include separate documentation of witnesses' statements.

Return to Your Post

Resume regular operations as soon as possible. This helps calm patrons and staff and reduces negative speculation about the event.

Learn From the Experience

With other staff, review how the incident was handled. Discuss the event, determine the causes, evaluate your responses, and consider what other actions you could have taken. This lets you offer ideas for improving safety, express your emotions about the occurrence, and help improve emergency procedures.

Dealing With the Media

Be prepared for media involvement in any emergency involving a large facility or when an accident or incident has been reported to EMS personnel or the police. Your facility should have a crisis communications plan for handling the media. Although most reporters wish you and your facility no ill will, sensationalism sells news. So it is good practice to use care in making statements about emergencies.

Because public perception is very important to most facilities, it is important to convey appropriate information to all interested parties. Facility policy and legal responsibilities should outline what information is released.

The facility's crisis communications plan should designate a spokesperson to make all media contacts and public statements. All other staff should refrain from answering questions or making comments. Some patrons may ask seemingly innocent questions about events at the facility or about the situation itself. All too often the "patron" turns out to be a media or legal representative trying to obtain information that may or may not be relevant to the incident.

It may help to have a standard statement, such as this one: "The accident is under investigation, and a statement will be released by our spokesperson shortly. Thank you. Now I must return to my job." Once you have made the statement, move on and answer no more questions.

Staff Post-Traumatic Distress

Any time you are involved in a rescue, you are subject to great stress as a result of your duty to react to the emergency and the danger you face in doing so. Well-trained professionals generally can respond to emergencies without stress interfering with rescue efforts. It is vital that you remain calm while carrying out emergency procedures. That is why practice is so important.

After the emergency is over, however, especially one in which a severe injury or death occurred, you may feel emotionally drained. Discussing your feelings, fears, and reactions within 24 to 72 hours of helping in an emergency helps prevent later emotional problems. You may want to talk with a trusted friend, a mental health professional, or a member of the clergy. Bringing out your feelings quickly helps to relieve personal anxieties and stress (National Safety Council, 1997).

The following actions also may help reduce the psychological effects of a rescue:

- Complete the accident or incident report. This is part of your responsibility.
- Think through your actions and emphasize the things you did well.
- Get some physical activity as soon as possible. It will remove you from the stressful situation and give you an opportunity to relax.
- Be aware that authorities are not trying to assess blame as they gather information about the accident; their questions are just part of the necessary "system." Be as objective as possible.
- Don't isolate yourself. Talk with supportive others to voice your feelings in a safe environment. Remember to be supportive of others if they are in a similar situation.
- Eat a healthy, balanced diet to significantly improve your ability to cope (National Safety Council, 1997).
- Try to maintain a normal life schedule, including schoolwork, socializing, and lifeguarding.

If you feel that the stress may overwhelm you and you think you need help in dealing with it, seek professional services or support groups. In an extreme case, you might be able to make use of the critical-stress teams many communities have to help firefighters, police officers, and other rescue workers address their psychological trauma.

An accident involving a death or serious injury may take considerable time to re-solve. If you were prepared and acted according to your facility's emergency procedures, you performed your legal duty. Cooperate with the authorities and, if you need to, seek help in managing your reaction to the trauma you have experienced.

Review Questions

1. What is the difference between a life-threatening and potentially life-threatening emergency?

2. What seven major types of emergencies should any facility be pre-pared to handle?

3. Why is teamwork important in an emergency response?

4. Why is it important to work with your local EMS unit in preparing for emergencies?

5. List three issues you should consider in preparing for emergencies.

6. What 10 steps should be included in creating an emergency policy?

7. List the six steps common to any emergency plan.

8. What is the difference between an accident and an incident?

9. What is an accident report, and why is completing this report impor-tant?

10. What is an injury chart, and what important information does it contain?

11. Name the six points made in the checklist for crisis management.

12. How do you as a lifeguard respond to questions regarding a major accident at your facility?

13. Name three action steps you can take to control trauma or stress following an emergency.

nine

First Aid in Aquatic Environments

Because you must complete first aid and CPR courses before pursuing your lifeguard certification, this chapter does not provide guidelines for first aid treatment of all possible injuries in the aquatic environment. It focuses instead on handling both common and life-threatening situations.

In This Chapter You'll Learn About the Following Elements of First Aid Specific to Lifeguarding:

- What should be included in a first aid kit
- Medical alert tags and their value
- How to protect yourself against hepatitis and the human immunodeficiency virus (blood-borne pathogens)
- How to contact the emergency medical system
- The first aid devices that can be used in managing respiratory and cardiac emergencies
- How to recognize and provide first aid for
    - a heart attack,
    - severe bleeding,
    - three types of hyperthermia,
    - hypothermia,
    - an allergic reaction,
    - an asthma attack,
    - an epileptic seizure, and
    - hyperventilation.

In lifeguard training we spend a lot of time on accident prevention and procedures for responding to the most severe accidents and incidents. However, most of the accidents that occur around swimming areas are minor, due to the diligence and professionalism of the lifeguards on duty. Common types of accidents include the following:

- Slips and falls
- Cuts and abrasions
- Bites and stings
- Burns (primarily sunburn)
- Broken bones
- Problems caused by medical conditions, such as diabetes or epilepsy

You need to know first aid skills well in order to assist people with these types of injuries.

FIRST AID KITS

Your facility should have a fully-equipped first aid kit available for care of aquatic injuries (figure 9.1). Staff should inventory the supplies regularly and often and should replace missing or consumed materials immediately. Here is a list of the items that should be available in the kit (Lifesaving Society, 1993):

Figure 9.1 A first aid kit should be available, and the contents should be inventoried regularly.

- Blankets, plastic sheets, towels, pillows
- Bandage scissors, forceps, tweezers, safety pins
- Dressing and bandages of assorted sizes
- Adhesive tape of various widths
- Needles for removing splinters
- Cotton swabs
- Mild antiseptic soap solution
- Antiseptic wipes
- Disposable drinking cups

- Mineral oil, calamine lotion
- Antibiotic ointment
- A flashlight or penlight
- Glucose, sugar, or candy
- Cold packs
- Triangular bandages
- A spineboard and stretcher, a head and neck immobilizer, straps, and cervical collars (in four sizes: small, medium, and large adult, and large child)
- An aspirator (oral suction unit) with an extra plastic cartridge
- Latex rubber gloves
- A resuscitation mask
- A biohazard waste bag and cleanup kit, including a face shield, two pairs of gloves, a gown, and booties
- A first aid text
- Incident/accident reports, paper, pencils
- Emergency telephone numbers

In addition, we recommend that your facility have the following equipment and have staff members who are trained to use it:

- Oxygen equipment (tank, mask, nasal cannula)
- Automated external defibrillator (AED)

Finally, we recommend that you have a portable basic first aid kit available to you at your lifeguard stand.

MEDICAL ALERT TAGS

Medical alert bracelets and tags (figure 9.2), whether simple or flashy, serve a very important purpose. They provide you and the emergency medical team with medical information about the injured person. Speedy, accurate assessment is important to providing quality emergency care.

Figure 9.2 A medical alert bracelet.

Most medical alert tags list details about the wearer's condition, allergies, and regular medications, covering areas like this:

Abnormal EKG	Glaucoma
Allergies (allergen is listed)	Hypertension
Alzheimer's/memory-impaired	Hypoglycemia
Angina	Medications (specific medications or
Asthma	categories of medications are listed)
Bleeding disorder	Pacemaker
Blood type	Seizure disorder
Diabetes (insulin-dependent or	Special needs (contact lenses,
non-insulin-dependent)	organ donor, living will)

Some tags provide a phone number to call for current medical information about the person. Look for these pieces of jewelry around the wrists, ankles, or necks of swimmers at your facility.

If you notice a patron with a medical alert tag, take some time to talk about it; most wearers are happy to discuss their special needs with you. They can help you prepare to assist them in an emergency.

PROTECTING YOURSELF FROM HEPATITIS AND THE HUMAN IMMUNODEFICIENCY VIRUS

You can contract many illnesses through direct contact with an injured, ill, or drowning individual's body fluids, such as blood or saliva. These illnesses are caused by *blood-borne pathogens*, microorganisms that live in human body fluids. Two of the most serious illnesses are the hepatitis B virus (HBV) and the human immunodeficiency virus (HIV), both of which can be life-threatening. The blood-borne pathogens can be transmitted to others through blood, saliva, nasal discharges, vomitus, tears, urine, or fecal matter in salt or fresh water (as in lakes or rivers) or improperly treated swimming pool water. That's why it is important that you understand what these illnesses are and how to protect yourself from exposure.

Hepatitis

Hepatitis is an infection or inflammation of the liver that is usually caused by a virus. The virus and resulting infection can take two forms. Type A, formerly called infectious hepatitis, is usually spread by fecal contamination of food, such as when an infected food preparer doesn't wash his or her hands after using the toilet. Type B, formerly called serum hepatitis, is spread by contact with blood or other body fluids. It is Type B that is of concern for you as a lifeguard.

The hepatitis B virus is carried in the blood and other body fluids of the infected person. Once contracted, the virus may be present for years, so any time you come in contact with another person's blood or body fluids, you risk contracting hepatitis B.

Hepatitis B infections are prevalent among intravenous drug users, prostitutes and others with multiple sexual partners, homosexuals, recipients of blood products (such as those with hemophilia or dialysis patients), and health care workers in contact with blood products and body fluids.

The symptoms of hepatitis B may include fatigue, nausea, vomiting, jaundice (a yellow coloration of the skin and eyes), dark yellow urine, and light-colored stools. The infection is generally severe and can lead to liver failure and death. A victim who survives the initial infection is likely to develop a long-term phase of the illness called *chronic hepatitis*.

During this long-term phase, the infected person is essentially free of symptoms but can still infect others with the virus. Anyone exposed to the blood or body fluids of a suspected high-risk individual should seek immediate medical advice and consider a preventive injection of hepatitis B immune globulin.

Anyone at high risk for exposure to hepatitis B should seek medical advice and consider the hepatitis B vaccine. The vaccine has been proven very successful in preventing people at high risk from contracting the disease.

Human Immunodeficiency Virus

Acquired immune deficiency syndrome (AIDS) is a condition in which the elements of blood that control the immune system are damaged, leaving the body susceptible to opportunistic infections. AIDS is one of the manifestations of the human immunodeficiency virus (HIV). You can have this virus (be HIV-positive) without having the symptoms of AIDS.

Like hepatitis B, HIV is contracted through contact with blood and body fluids. Casual contact, coughing, and sneezing do not transmit the disease, nor can it be transmitted through the water in a swimming pool. HIV can be contracted through

- sexual contact,
- contact with contaminated blood or body fluids,
- use of contaminated needles (as is common among intravenous drug users), and
- the placenta and body fluids during pregnancy or birth.

Fortunately, outside the body the virus is not particularly hardy. As soon as the fluid has dried or been exposed to heat, the virus dies. A solution of 10% household bleach in water also kills the virus. As household bleach has a limited shelf life of 60 to 90 days, keep the supply fresh and replace it as needed.

AIDS has a variable incubation period (the time from infection to the appearance of symptoms), ranging from several months to over 7 years. There is currently no known cure for AIDS, so it is vital to protect yourself from contracting the virus. Become aware of the universal precautionary procedures (described next) and follow them every time you have the potential to come in contact with the blood or body fluids of another person.

Protecting Yourself

To protect yourself from contracting hepatitis or HIV through contact with contaminated blood or body fluids, follow the universal precautionary procedures developed by the Centers for Disease Control as a result of research into the transmission of blood-borne diseases. (See list on page 170.) Your facility should have steps for cleanup and disposal of medical waste as well.

When you are involved in a rescue or cleanup that might put you in contact with an individual's body fluids, wear at least one pair of latex gloves and learn how to take them off using the following procedures:

1. Grasp the top or wrist part of one glove, being careful to touch only the glove.
2. Pull the glove down toward the fingers, turning it inside out. Continue to hold onto the glove.
3. Insert one or two clean fingers into the top of the other glove. Be careful not to touch the outside surface.
4. Pull the glove off, turning it inside out while pulling it over the first glove. Now the first glove taken off is inside the second glove, both turned inside out.
5. Discard the gloves into a red plastic medical waste bag with the biohazard symbol on it.
6. Dispose of the medical waste bag (biohazard waste bag) in accordance with the protocols established by your department of health, local hospital, EMS service, or local municipal code.

Universal Precautionary Procedures

1. Use a barrier. The use of gloves, masks, face shields, mouthpieces, gowns, and other barriers protects you from contact with the blood and body fluids of a victim. Assume all victims are infected.

2. Wash your hands. Good hygiene also reduces your risk. Wash your hands with soap and warm water after you come in contact with another person's blood or body fluids—even if you were wearing gloves.

3. Clean up. Clean surfaces that have been exposed to blood or body fluids with a mixture of household bleach and water. Combine 1 part bleach with 10 equal parts of water. Wear protective gear during the cleanup procedure.

4. Keep sharp objects separate. It is unlikely that you will use any sharp objects, such as scalpels or hypodermic needles, with any victims you'll see, but sharp debris on the beach can pierce the skin and cause bleeding. Dispose separately of any sharp object with blood on it. Medical facilities have labeled red containers designed specifically for such hazardous material; some pool facilities have similar containers.

5. Avoid contamination. Don't allow swimmers to share towels contaminated with blood or body fluids. Instead place the soiled linen in a separate, plastic-lined laundry bin.

6. Launder or dispose of soiled linens separately. Bloody linens should be stored separately and double-bagged in plastic. Laundry personnel should handle the parcel as infected material and wash the linens in detergent with hot water.

7. Cover wounds. When someone receives a cut, scratch, or other open wound at your facility, require him or her to cover it. This procedure not only helps that person remain free of infection, it decreases the probability of other patrons coming in contact with that patron's blood.

8. Provide CPR using a barrier. There is a very low risk of contracting the AIDS virus through contact with saliva. However, the use of a breathing bag or resuscitation mask reduces your exposure to AIDS and other diseases by decreasing mouth-to-mouth contact. (Resuscitation masks for rescue breathing and CPR are described on page 173.)

9. Protect yourself. If you have an open wound, avoid providing first aid to a victim with an open wound if at all possible. If you must provide first aid, wear gloves.

Note: Adapted from guidelines provided by the U.S. Public Health Service, Centers for Disease Control.

When performing a water rescue, begin assessment of the victim and resuscitation in the water with a resuscitation mask and change to a bag-valve-mask resuscitator when the victim is brought out of the water. When performing a water rescue, assume that all blood and body fluids are infected. Follow these steps:

1. Attempt to determine during the approach if blood is visible in the water.

2. If the victim is bleeding and active, avoid swimming in the blood-contaminated water if possible. Approach from the front if blood is visible behind the victim. If blood is visible in front and the victim does not appear to be in danger of submerging, swim around behind and use a rear active approach.

3. Avoid contact with the bleeding victim as much as possible during the approach and while towing an active victim. Avoid swallowing water.

4. During rescues of both passive and active victims, keep the routes of entry into your body (eyes, ears, nose, and mouth) above water at all times.

5. During in-water resuscitation, wash away as much blood or body fluids from the victim as possible before applying the resuscitation mask (United States Lifesaving Association, 1995).

6. If you are the single guard at your facility, you will not be able to avoid direct contact when assisting a conscious victim or removing a passive victim from the pool or waterfront. If two or more lifeguards are available, your accident management procedure should be structured so that a second lifeguard equipped with barrier protection is ready to assist you in removing the victim from the water. You (the rescue guard) should then apply the necessary precautionary barriers (as described in the universal precautionary procedures) before assisting with first aid or resuscitation.

7. When you provide medical treatment, do the following (United States Lifesaving Association, 1995):
   - Use mechanical ventilation whenever possible.
   - Use disposable resuscitation masks.
   - Use oxygen with disposable masks.
   - Wear gloves for handling bleeding victims.
   - If bleeding is profuse, especially from an artery, wear a mask, goggles, and a gown and gloves.
   - Wash your hands with soap and water after providing care.

8. When first aid and/or CPR has been completed and the EMS personnel have taken the victim to the hospital, wash your hair and entire body with soap and water. Rinse your mouth with an antiseptic mouthwash if you performed resuscitation with a resuscitation mask.

The pool area and pool equipment will need to be disinfected after an incident in which body fluids were released. These are the appropriate procedures for disinfection:

- The best defense against contamination of swimming pools and spas from exposure to blood-borne pathogens is sustaining appropriate free chlorine or bromine levels. The best range for a pool is 1.5 to 3.0 ppm (parts per million) of free residual chlorine or 2.0 to 6.0 of free residual bromine. For spas, a free chlorine residual of 3.0 to 5.0 ppm or a free bromine residual of 6.0 to 10.0 ppm is necessary.

- If blood contaminates the pool deck, coping, or walkways made of cement, granite, rock, or other porous surface material, they will have to be disinfected. Mix 4 ounces of calcium hypochlorite or 16 ounces (one pint) of sodium hypochlorite with 1 gallon of water. Be sure that either type of chlorine is fresh. Before applying the solution, clear the area of aquatic staff members and pool patrons. Put on at least gloves, and, if the contamination is extensive, goggles and a gown (United States Lifesaving Association, 1995). Then apply the solution on all contaminated surfaces with a garden sprayer and let it stand for five minutes. Rinse the surface with water from a hose toward a swimming pool deck drain. Repeat applying and rinsing the solution, and allow the surface to dry completely before permitting anyone to walk on it or use it in any way. This same procedure can be used to sanitize diving boards, starting blocks, and wood surfaces.

- To disinfect grass, dirt, and sand surfaces contaminated by blood, mix a solution of chlorine and water using 4 ounces of fresh calcium hypochlorite or 16 ounces (one pint) of sodium hypochlorite with 1 gallon of water. Wear gloves, and, if the contamination is extensive, goggles and a gown. Apply the chlorine solution until the area where the blood spill occurred is thoroughly saturated with the chlorine solution. Rope off the area and prohibit sunbathing or other uses of the area until the area is completely dry. If the contaminated area consists of dirt or sand, turn it over with a shovel and rake it. Saturate the sand or dirt again, and continue to prohibit use of the area until it dries and is raked a second time. As grass will be killed by the chlorine solution, waterfront and outdoor pool operators may want to remove small quantities of sod and dispose of it in medical waste bags to be incinerated. Be sure to decontaminate any shovels, rakes, brooms, or other tools used in the cleanup with the same strength chlorine solution, and rinse them thoroughly.

- Any personal equipment used in rescue, first aid, CPR, or oral suction that is reusable must be properly sanitized before it is used again. This includes, but is not limited to, rescue tubes, rescue buoys, masks, fins, snorkels, backboards, straps, head immobilizers, and hard cervical collars. These items should be cleaned with a quaternary ammonia disinfectant. Be sure to follow the instructions on the label. Disposable equipment such as resuscitation masks and first aid materials must be disposed of in medical waste bags.

Your facility should give you additional training on blood-borne pathogens that includes the following elements:

- The OSHA standard for blood-borne pathogens
- The epidemiology and symptomatology of blood-borne diseases
- The modes of transmission of blood-borne pathogens
- An exposure plan (for employee training and facility precautions), including the points of the plan, the lines of responsibility, and how the plan will be implemented
- Procedures that might cause exposure to blood or other potentially infectious materials at your facility
- The use and limitations of control methods at the facility to control exposure to blood or other potentially infectious materials
- The use and limitations of personal protective equipment available at your facility and who should be contacted concerning the following:
  —Postexposure evaluation and follow-up
  —Signs and labels used at the facility
  —The hepatitis B vaccine program at the facility
  —Where to locate a copy of the OSHA standard

HOW TO CONTACT AND ACTIVATE THE EMERGENCY MEDICAL SYSTEM

In many areas of the country you can summon emergency medical assistance by dialing 911. Check to see if your community uses this system. If not, ask management to prominently post emergency phone numbers near all telephones at your facility.

If you do not make the call to the EMS yourself, be sure to delegate that task to another lifeguard or to a responsible adult. The caller has a crucial role in providing information to the medical team being dispatched. A script should be posted next to the phone with these guidelines for communicating with the EMS:

- Give your name, location, and telephone number to initiate the conversation.
- Explain what type of accident has occurred and what types of injuries have been sustained.
- Describe each victim's symptoms and what first aid has been provided.
- Answer honestly any questions asked of you. If you don't know an answer, say so. Do not guess! Someone's life is at stake.
- Wait for the EMS operator to tell you to hang up the phone, then wait until he or she has disconnected before you do hang up. This will ensure that the EMS has gotten all of the information needed from you before you are disconnected.
- Wait by the phone momentarily to see whether a follow-up call is made.

Never transport a victim yourself; wait for the EMS. If a victim's condition were to worsen while en route to the hospital in your car, you couldn't provide the necessary assistance, but paramedics could. You will also be protected from potential legal action regarding transportation by using emergency medical services rather than your vehicle. In a remote area, exceptions may be necessary depending on the type of emergency. Follow the emergency plan set up by your facility.

FIRST AID DEVICES*

To become a YMCA lifeguard, you will have to complete a professional level CPR course. We also recommend that you take courses on oxygen administration and the use of an automated external defibrillator (AED) (these courses will be required after December 31, 2002). Part of those courses is instruction on the proper use of various first aid devices related to airway management, oxygen administration, and the use of an AED.

Airway Management

As you may have already learned in your CPR course, several devices can help you with airway management: resuscitation masks, bag-valve masks, and manual (hand) suction devices. These should be inspected daily to ensure that they are "rescue ready."

Resuscitation Masks

Figure 9.3 shows examples of resuscitation masks. Mouth-to-mask ventilation can deliver an adequate volume of air to a victim if you ensure a tight mask seal on the victim's face. Resuscitation masks, in general, offer some protection from infection. Certain types of masks have an inlet that allows oxygen tubing to be attached to the mask. All masks must fit well, have a one-way valve, be made of a transparent material, have an oxygen port, and be available in infant, pediatric, and adult sizes.

Masks vary in size and complexity from the simple face shield to the bag-valve mask. Each type of mask has distinct advantages and disadvantages. Since it is unlikely that you will have the option of choosing the mask you prefer in an emergency, you should learn how to use all types correctly.

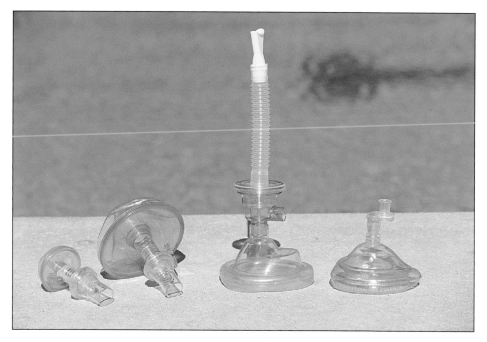

Figure 9.3 Resuscitation masks.

* Adapted, by permission, from the American Academy of Orthopaedic Surgeons and National Safety Council,1999, *Professional rescuer CPR*, (Boston, MA: Jones and Bartlett Publishers), pp. 47-48, 50-54.

Follow these steps when performing mouth-to-mask rescue breathing on land:

1. Position yourself at the victim's head.
2. Open the victim's airway using the head-tilt/chin-lift or jaw-thrust maneuver (see chapter 10 for jaw-thrust instructions).
3. Place the mask over the victim's mouth and nose.
4. Using both hands, grasp the mask and the victim's jaw. Press down on the mask with your thumbs while lifting up on the jaw with your fingers. This will create a good seal on the mask and face.
5. Place your mouth over the mouthpiece and perform rescue breathing.

Bag-Valve Masks

The *bag-valve mask* (BVM) is a hand-held device with three main components: a bag, a valve, and a mask (see figure 9.4). The bag is self-inflating. When you squeeze it, it automatically reinflates. The valve is a one-way device that prevents the victim's exhaled air from entering the bag. The mask is similar to that used in mouth-to-mask rescue breathing. The BVM is used in conjunction with an oral or nasal airway. The BVM delivers a higher concentration of oxygen than a resuscitation mask alone, approximately 90 to 100% when attached to an oxygen source. Even without supplemental oxygen, the BVM provides approximately 21% oxygen, which is also greater than the 16% provided by mouth-to-mouth or mouth-to-mask rescue breathing.

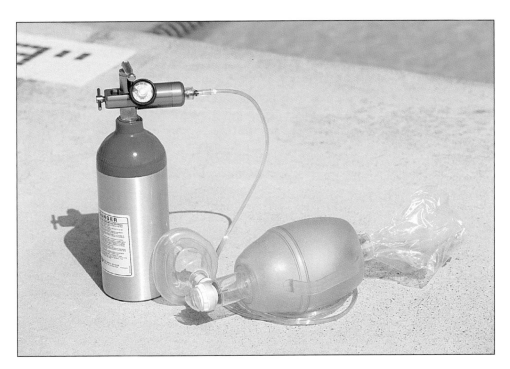

Figure 9.4 A bag-valve mask.

To use the BVM effectively, you must practice this skill regularly. The best results are achieved when two rescuers use the device. One rescuer maintains an open airway and mask seal, while the second rescuer squeezes the bag (figure 9.5). The bag should be squeezed smoothly, not forcefully. Forceful compression of the bag, like forceful rescue breathing, will result in air entering the victim's stomach instead of the lungs.

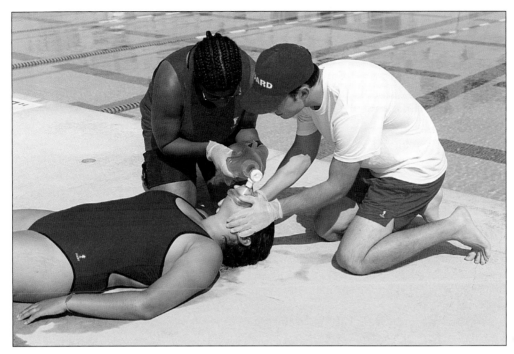

Figure 9.5 Two rescuers using a bag-valve mask.

Manual Suction Devices

Victims who have vomited, been underwater, inhaled fluid or debris, or who are bleeding from the nose or mouth are in danger of an airway obstruction. You cannot maintain an open airway or begin rescue breathing until the airway is clear so that air exchange can occur. Suction devices such as the one shown in figure 9.6 can help you remove airway obstructions.

Although suction units can be mechanical, manual devices often are more common because they do not require batteries or an electrical source. Manual suction devices are always ready to work and require minimal servicing. Suction is applied by inserting the tip of the device into the victim's mouth and squeezing its handle to create a vacuum that withdraws debris.

Follow these steps when suctioning:

1. Turn the victim's head to the side. If you suspect a spinal injury, roll the victim onto his or her side while keeping the neck and body from twisting.

2. Open the victim's mouth and wipe away any large debris with your gloved fingers.

3. Measure the distance from the corner of the victim's mouth to the earlobe so that you will know the correct depth to insert the end of the suction tip. Inserting the catheter too deeply and attempting to suction is likely to stimulate the victim's vomiting (gag) reflex.

4. Turn on the suction device and suction for no longer than 15 seconds. Suction as you slowly withdraw the catheter from the mouth.

Figure 9.6 Manual suction device.

Oxygen Administration

In situations in which a victim needs oxygen, you can use an oxygen-powered ventilator to provide it. An oxygen-powered ventilator works similarly to a BVM, but instead of squeezing a bag to force air into the victim's lungs, you press a button or trigger. An oxygen-powered ventilator is attached to an oxygen cylinder. Like a BVM, an oxygen-powered ventilator can deliver between 90 and 100% oxygen. The advantages of using an oxygen-powered ventilator include the ability to deliver a high oxygen concentration, protection from disease, and easy use. The disadvantage is that an oxygen source is needed to power the device. Once the oxygen is depleted, the device can no longer be used. Because the oxygen is delivered under a higher pressure, you must be careful not to overinflate the victim's lungs or cause gastric distention. Consult your local protocols regarding the use of oxygen-powered ventilators in your area.

Automated External Defibrillation

The normal pacemaker in the heart is the *sinus node (SA node)* (see figure 9.7). Approximately every second it emits an electrical impulse that travels along pathways through the atria, causing them to contract. This signal is received at the *atrioventricular node (AV node),* which separates the atria and ventricles. The AV node acts as a relay station between the atria and ventricles. Below the AV node, the pathway divides into two main branches, which serve the two ventricles. When the electrical impulse reaches the *purkinje fibers* in the ventricles, it causes the muscular walls of the ventricles to contract. This ventricular contraction forces blood to surge from the heart throughout the body, resulting in a characteristic pulse.

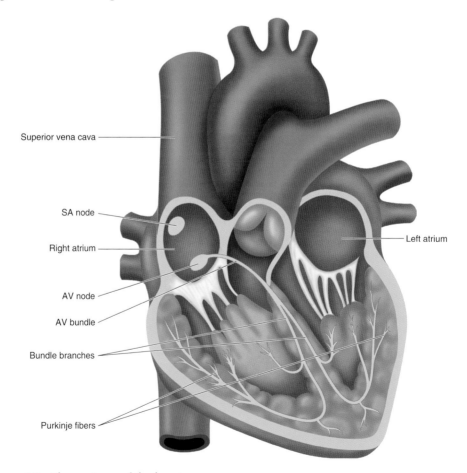

Figure 9.7   The anatomy of the heart.
Reprinted, by permission, from Wilmore and Costill, 1999, *Physiology of Sport and Exercise 2nd Edition* (Champaign, IL: Human Kinetics), 209.

More than half of the individuals who die from sudden cardiac arrest each year do so as a result of an abnormal heart rhythm known as ventricular fibrillation. *Ventricular fibrillation (V-fib)* occurs when irregular electrical impulses originate from multiple sites in the ventricles. The heart muscle reacts erratically, trying to respond to too many signals. The result is a chaotic ventricular rhythm that results in the fibrillation, or quivering, of the ventricles, which does not produce blood flow from the heart.

Another abnormal electrical rhythm is *ventricular tachycardia (V-tach)*. In V-tach, the heart beats at a rapid rate of between 150 and 200 beats per minute. At this rate, it is unable to pump enough blood out because of ineffective contractions.

It has been determined that the most important factor for survival from cardiac arrest is early defibrillation. *Defibrillation* is a process whereby a DC electrical current is passed through the heart to momentarily stop all electrical activity. After this occurs, normal pacemaker cells will take command of the heart's electrical activity and produce a coordinated, regular heartbeat. By applying defibrillator pads to the chest and admininstering a shock, you may be able to reestablish a normal cardiac rhythm.

The time from collapse to defibrillation is the most crucial factor in determining survival. The earlier defibrillation can be performed, the greater a victim's chances of survival. After a victim spends 8 to 10 minutes in cardiac arrest, damage may be so extensive that survival is no longer possible.

While not all cardiac arrest victims will need defibrillation, most adults in cardiac arrest will be in ventricular fibrillation, which can be corrected by defibrillation. For this reason, national efforts have been made to advocate the placement of lower-cost and easier-to-use automated defibrillators in the hands of the people most likely to be at the scene when victims need them. These defibrillators, known as *automated external defibrillators (AEDs)*, are now being placed in stadiums, shopping malls, factories, schools, aircraft, and police and fire vehicles so that they can be used quickly when the need arises.

Many different models of AEDs exist (see figure 9.8). The principles are the same for each, but displays, controls, and options vary. Some models have screens that display the rhythm and provide visual and verbal prompts. Others have a screen displaying only visual prompts. Some have no screen at all. There are also different combinations of recording devices for documenting and transferring patient information. Some devices automatically analyze the rhythm, whereas others require the operator to press a button to begin analysis. Consult the manufacturer's recommendations for your specific model before using it.

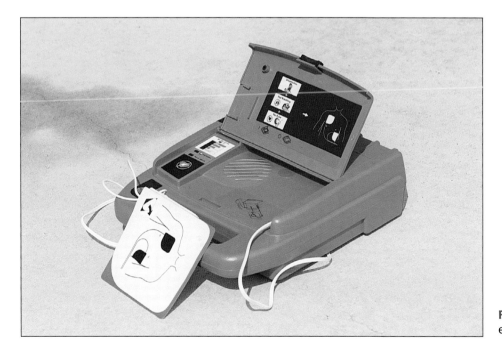

Figure 9.8 An automated external defibrillator.

To use an AED, you must have a victim who is unresponsive, not breathing, and pulseless (figure 9.9). Remember the ABCs: Determine unresponsiveness, check for breathing and provide two initial ventilations if the victim is not breathing, and check for a pulse. If the pulse is absent, begin CPR until the AED is available. When two rescuers are at the scene, one should set up the AED while the other performs CPR. If you are alone and have an AED, you should apply the AED before starting CPR.

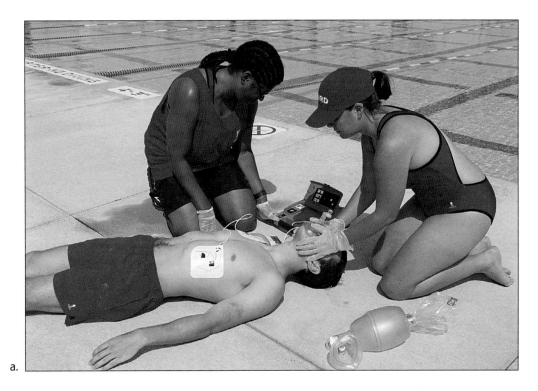

a.

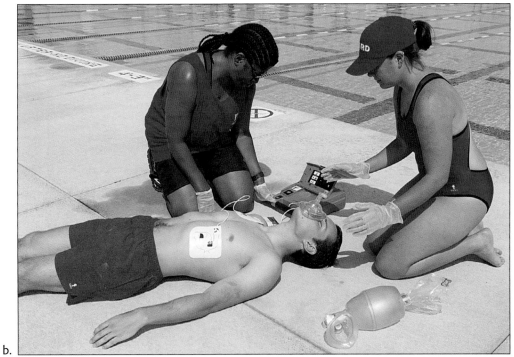

b.

Figure 9.9   Using an AED to revive a victim.

When using an AED, DO NOT

- use alcohol to wipe the victim's chest before placing the pads.
- attach the pads to, or defibrillate anyone with, a pulse.
- defibrillate a victim lying on a metal or other surface likely to conduct electricity.
- depress the shock button or analyze the rhythm until everyone is clear of the victim.
- defibrillate a victim younger than 8 years old or under 90 pounds. (Check with manufacturer's specifications and local protocols.)
- defibrillate a victim while he or she is wearing a nitroglycerin patch.

Summary of First Aid Devices

Airway Management

Manual Suction Devices

You cannot maintain an open airway or begin rescue breathing until the airway is clear. Airway obstructions may be caused by anatomical conditions or by foreign material such as food, fluid, or vomitus. Suction units are available to help remove foreign material. Whatever type of suction device you use, you must understand the machinery and not suction too deeply.

Resuscitation Masks

Mouth-to-mask ventilation can deliver an adequate volume of air (16% oxygen) to a victim while protecting you from the transmission of disease.

Bag-Valve Masks (BVMs)

The bag-valve mask is a hand-held device consisting of a self-inflating bag, a valve, and a mask. It provides 21% oxygen when used alone, and it can supply 90 to 100% oxygen when attached to an oxygen source.

Oxygen Administration

Oxygen-Powered Ventilator

An oxygen-powered ventilator works similarly to a BVM, but instead of squeezing a bag to force air into the victim's lungs, you press a button or trigger. An oxygen-powered ventilator is attached to an oxygen cylinder, and it can deliver between 90 and 100% oxygen. The advantages of using an oxygen-powered ventilator include the ability to deliver a high oxygen concentration, protection from disease, and easy use; the disadvantage is that an oxygen source is needed to power the device.

Automated External Defibrillation

The single most important cardiac arrest survival factor is early defibrillation, which can be accomplished with an automated external defibrillator (AED). The indications for use of an AED are that the victim is unresponsive, not breathing, and pulseless. Once turned on and attached to the victim's bare chest, the AED will analyze the heart rhythm and advise you whether you need to deliver a shock. If no shock is advised by the AED, but the victim still does not have a pulse, perform CPR until advanced cardiac care personnel arrive.

HEART ATTACKS

Heart attack is one of the leading causes of death in the United States. The American Heart Association estimates that each year a million and a half Americans will have heart attacks and almost a third of them will die as a result.

Heart attacks are caused by blood clots or blockages in the blood vessels that supply blood to the heart. You may hear heart attacks referred to by several names: coronary, cardiac, coronary occlusion, coronary artery thrombosis, or myocardial infarction. Each refers to the same life-threatening condition.

A person who is having a heart attack could lose consciousness or die immediately. More likely, he or she will exhibit several or all of the following symptoms:

- Shortness of breath
- Chest pains radiating into the neck and shoulders and down the arm
- Profuse sweating
- Pale, sweaty skin
- Squeezing pressure in the chest
- Indigestion

If any combination of these symptoms lasts longer than 1 or 2 minutes, encourage the person to seek immediate medical attention. It is not unusual for someone to refuse to see a physician or go to the hospital; if this occurs, document your recommendation and the refusal. It is still a good idea to contact the EMS. Most services do not charge for responding to such calls, and, once on the scene, EMS personnel may be able to convince the person to be transported to a medical facility. Any time you are unsure of what action to take, act in favor of the patron and request additional assistance.

You may be required to provide emergency first aid until medical assistance arrives at your facility. If the person is still breathing, take the following steps:

- Keep the person calm and as comfortable as possible.
- Assist the person in taking heart medication if she or he has such medication.
- Monitor the person's condition.
- Be prepared to begin CPR or to administer an AED or oxygen if necessary.

SEVERE BLEEDING

Aquatic injuries can be accompanied by severe bleeding, which can be life-threatening if not controlled quickly. Blood coming from an open wound, or external bleeding, can be escaping from capillaries, veins, or arteries. Capillary bleeding is slow and oozing; it is the easiest to bring under control. Blood flow from veins is steadier but is still more easily stopped than flow from arteries. An artery, if completely severed, may seal itself off, but if it is only torn, it may bleed rapidly and spurt.

To control bleeding, take these steps, in this order:

1. Apply direct pressure to the wound using sterile gauze or, if it is not available, any clean cloth. Use latex or vinyl gloves or any other barrier material you can find to protect yourself from the victim's blood. If no barrier materials are available and the bleeding must be stopped quickly, apply pressure with your bare hands. In either case, be sure to wash your hands with soap and water afterward. Increase the amount of pressure if bleeding doesn't stop.

After applying pressure, cover the wound dressing if possible with a pressure bandage, such as a roller bandage that covers both the dressing and areas below and above the wound. Never remove a dressing; removal may restart the bleeding. If a dressing becomes blood-soaked, place another dressing on top of it.

2. If bleeding continues, keep applying pressure and elevate the limb above the heart. This will reduce blood pressure and slow the bleeding, which will aid blood clotting. Do *not* elevate a limb if it is broken.

3. If bleeding still has not stopped, try putting pressure on one of two pressure points (places where an artery is accessible for compression): the brachial point, which is located in the upper arm; and the femoral point, which is located in the groin. Try this only if you are trained to use pressure points because it works only if you apply pressure to the exact location.

Once the bleeding is under control, the wound can be cleaned. Open wounds can become infected if not cleaned and treated properly. Table 9.1 lists the types of open wounds, their causes and symptoms, and first aid for each type.

Table 9.1 **Open Wound First Aid**

Type	Causes	Signs and Symptoms	First Aid
Abrasion (scrape)	Rubbing or scraping	Only skin surface is affected Little bleeding	Remove all debris Wash away from wound with soap and water
Incision (cut)	Sharp objects	Edges of wound are smooth Severe bleeding	Control bleeding Wash wound
Laceration (tearing)	Blunt object tearing skin	Veins and arteries can be affected Severe bleeding Danger of infection	Control bleeding Wash wound
Puncture (stab)	Sharp pointed object piercing skin	Wound is narrow and deep into veins and arteries Embedded objects Danger of infection	Do not remove impaled objects
Avulsion (torn off)	Machinery Explosives	Tissue torn off or left hanging Severe bleeding	Control bleeding Take avulsed part to medical facility

Note: From National Safety Council, *First Aid CPR, Level 1,* © 1991 Jones and Bartlett Publishers, Boston. Reprinted by permission.

Internal bleeding cannot be seen from the outside, but it is accompanied by symptoms such as these:

- Blood coming from the mouth, rectum, or vagina (nonmenstrual blood) or seen in the urine
- Visible bruises or cuts
- A rapid pulse
- Sweaty, cool skin
- Pupil dilation
- Nausea and vomiting
- Abdominal pain or tenderness, rigidity, or bruising
- Chest bruising or rib fractures

If you suspect internal bleeding, call EMS immediately. Then give first aid for internal bleeding, following these steps:

1. Watch the person's breathing and pulse.
2. Be prepared for vomiting. Don't give the person any liquids; if vomiting occurs, place the person on his or her side for drainage.
3. Raise the legs 8 to 12 inches and keep the body warm.

HYPERTHERMIA

Heat cramps, heat exhaustion, and heatstroke are three progressively more severe forms of hyperthermia, or overheating. In each heat illness, environmental conditions cause the body's core temperature to increase, giving rise to a variety of symptoms. When the temperature and humidity are high, heat-related problems become more common. Figure 9.10 illustrates the combinations of heat and humidity that are the most dangerous.

		Air temperature (°F)										
		70°	75°	80°	85°	90°	95°	100°	105°	110°	115°	120°
Relative humidity	30%	67	73	78	84	90	96	104	113	123	135	148
	40%	68	74	79	86	93	101	110	123	137	151	
	50%	69	75	81	88	96	107	120	135	150		
	60%	70	76	82	90	100	114	132	149			
	70%	70	77	85	93	106	124	144				
	80%	71	78	86	97	113	136					
	90%	71	79	88	102	122						
	100%	72	80	91	108							

☐ Risk of heat exhaustion
☐ Risk of heatstroke
☐ High risk of heatstroke

Figure 9.10   Heat and humidity chart.
Note: Numbers within chart show equivalent temperatures. Shaded areas indicate when exertion may be dangerous. Reproduced with permission of *The Walking Magazine,* copyright © 1987, Raben Publishing Co., 711 Boylston St., Boston, MA 02116.

Heat Cramps

Heat cramps are extremely painful muscle cramps caused by the loss of electrolytes and salt in the body through sweat. These cramps are usually associated with exertion. A person suffering from heat cramps will generally exhibit some or all of the following symptoms:

- Muscle cramps (usually in the legs and abdomen)
- Sweaty skin
- Increased heart rate
- Exhaustion
- Dizziness

Heat cramps are not a life-threatening condition, but the person will want and need immediate attention. To care for someone experiencing heat cramps, take the following action:

- Get the person out of the heat.
- Provide water.
- Apply moist towels to the forehead and cramp to aid in cooling.
- Avoid massage—it will not help and may damage muscle tissue.

In most cases the cramp sufferer will not need to see a physician. However, if the person experiences faintness and recurring cramping, care by medical personnel is advisable.

Heat Exhaustion

The most common heat-related illness, heat exhaustion, is also due to excessive electrolyte and water loss through perspiration. The symptoms of heat exhaustion include

- profuse sweating,
- cool and clammy skin,
- dilated pupils,
- pale coloring,
- increased heart rate,
- weakness,
- nausea,
- thirst,
- fainting, and
- anxiety or apathy.

Any bout with heat exhaustion requires medical attention because the condition can easily escalate to heatstroke. There are several things you can do to assist someone with heat exhaustion while awaiting medical assistance:

- Get the person out of the heat.
- Provide water (only if the person is conscious).
- Lay the person down.
- Loosen restrictive clothing.
- Cool the body with moist, cold towels.

There are several locations where cold towels will speed the cooling process. Figure 9.11 illustrates where towels should be placed to most effectively provide cooling.

Figure 9.11   Placement of moist, cold towels for efficient cooling.

Heatstroke

With extreme overexposure to the heat, a person may experience heatstroke. In this condition, the body's temperature regulation system essentially shuts down and the heat generated is recycled in the body, causing other body systems to malfunction. It is vital that you learn to recognize the symptoms of heatstroke and move quickly to assist anyone who develops it. Contact EMS immediately.

The symptoms of heatstroke vary some, depending on whether the person initially suffered heat exhaustion and how quickly you noticed the problem. The skin may be dry if the person was inactive or if the sweat has already dried. The skin may be sweaty if the person was active and you noticed the problem before the sweat dried. The key here is that the person with heatstroke will no longer be able to sweat. Many or all of the following symptoms are typical:

- Dry or sweaty skin
- Inability to sweat
- Increased then decreased heart rate
- Increased temperature
- Hot, red skin
- Rapid, shallow breathing that may then slow
- Constricted pupils
- Headache
- Confusion
- Disorientation
- Unconsciousness
- Seizure

If you notice a number of these symptoms, don't take any chances—summon medical assistance immediately. Heatstroke can be fatal!

Heatstroke is an extremely critical condition—almost 60% of those who develop it die, even under medical supervision. Your actions truly can mean the difference between life and death. While you are waiting for the EMS to arrive, provide the following first aid:

- Establish the ABCs.
- Do *not* give fluids.
- Get the person out of the heat.
- Lay the person down.
- Loosen any restrictive clothing.
- Cool the body immediately using ice packs or sheets soaked with ice water.
- Monitor body temperature and ABCs.
- Be prepared to handle convulsions if the body temperature drops very rapidly.

HYPOTHERMIA

Hypothermia is exactly the opposite of hyperthermia: The body temperature is decreased by environmental conditions. People can lose body heat in outdoor recreational pursuits, typically during the winter, but perhaps the most common cause of hypothermia is being in cold water for an extended period (immersion hypothermia). Because water cools the body 25 to 27 times faster than does air, hypothermia can occur even in warm weather. In water at 72 to 78 degrees Fahrenheit, unconsciousness can occur in 3 to 12 hours. In very cool water, the arms and legs will cool rapidly. It takes 10 to 15 minutes before the vital organs and brain begin to lose heat. Figure 9.12 illustrates the effects of cold water on the length of time someone immersed can survive. The heat escape lessening posture (HELP) described on page 30 was developed to slow heat loss and increase survival time.

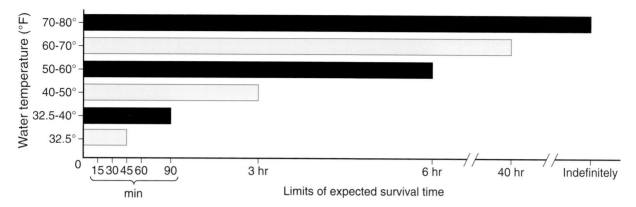

Figure 9.12 Water temperature as a determinant for survival time.
Data from *Fishermen, Hunters, & Campers: Tips for Safe Boating* by United States Boating Institute.

Watch children carefully; their smaller size makes them more susceptible to heat loss in immersion. The major arteries are closer to the skin, allowing quicker cooling of the blood.

Levels of Hypothermia

The symptoms of hypothermia vary greatly with the severity of the exposure and heat loss. The generalized symptoms of hypothermia include these:

- Initially intense shivering
- Rigid muscles
- Reduced coordination
- Slow and labored breathing
- Bluish tinge to skin, lips, and nailbeds
- Reduced blood flow to hands and feet
- Dilated pupils
- Loss of logic
- Difficulty speaking
- Disorientation
- Glassy stare
- Slow and irregular pulse
- Amnesia
- Eventual loss of consciousness

If you notice these symptoms, do not delay first aid; hypothermia can cause complications even after someone is out of the water. Table 9.2 compiles data on the severity of symptoms and the corresponding core body temperatures.

Table 9.2 **Levels of Hypothermia and Their Signs and Symptoms**

Level	Signs and Symptoms
Normal (98.6° F)	No symptoms
Mild (94–95° F)	Alert; hyperventilating; strong, uncontrolled shivering
Moderate (90–93° F)	Conscious, but not thinking clearly; impaired speech; inability to grasp with hands; clumsy
Severe (86–90° F)	May or may not be conscious; ability to think severely reduced; cold to the touch; rigid muscles; uneven pulse; skin may turn blue
Very severe (81–85° F)	Usually unconscious; rigid muscles; slowed breathing and pulse
Critical (below 80° F)	Unconscious; no reflexes; shallow or no breathing; cardiac arrest due to cardiac arrhythmia

Note: Adapted from the U.S. Coast Guard (1977) and Canadian Red Cross Society (1983).

Emergency First Aid

Immediately upon identifying someone with hypothermia, contact EMS personnel. Then help the person remove any wet clothing; getting dried off is important so that the air does not continue cooling the body by evaporating the water. The rest of the first aid you will give centers on providing warmth. Take these steps:

- Move the person near a fire or heater if available.
- Cover the person with blankets, coats, newspapers—virtually any insulating material.
- If no insulating material is available, hug the victim to you to share your body warmth.
- Give a conscious person warm, nonalcoholic, decaffeinated drinks. (Alcohol and caffeine dilate the blood vessels, causing a continued loss of body heat.)

Watch for quick changes in body temperature. Rewarming can cause an after-drop syndrome (described in the next section).

Cold Water Drowning

Amazing stories of recovery from 30- to 45-minute exposures to cold water have appeared in media headlines since the early 1970s. The latest information available indicates that if a person drowns, even if all signs of life are absent, CPR must be initiated and continued until the victim reaches an emergency medical facility. Startling as it may seem, children who have been under the surface for up to 45 minutes have been revived, with little or no brain damage, after 4 to 5 hours of CPR and medical attention.

Such survival is possible because the body goes into a form of hibernation. The cold water causes constriction in the blood vessels of the arms and legs and a slowing or stoppage of metabolic activity in the body. Together, these changes partially eliminate the delivery of blood and oxygen to the limbs. This allows blood and oxygen to be diverted to the brain and vital organs.

As the temperature of the major body organs drops, the activity and oxygen utilization of the brain, heart, lungs, and kidneys are also reduced. With this reduction of oxygenation and the cool internal temperatures, the vital organs seem able to survive with the oxygen available in the organ, the surrounding tissues, and the blood.

To provide first aid, you must begin CPR as soon as the victim is removed from the water. Then call the EMS to transport the person to a medical facility. Immediate transportation is vital so that the rewarming and resuscitation processes can be continued and directed by a physician. *Do not* attempt to rewarm such a victim yourself. When the body is rewarmed, the cold blood from the limbs flows back to the internal core, causing the core temperature to drop. This syndrome, called the *after-drop syndrome*, can be minimized by keeping the victim still.

ALLERGIC REACTIONS (ANAPHYLACTIC SHOCK)

Many of us are allergic to something: a food, a certain insect bite, pollen, dust, or one of any number of other elements in our environment. Should a patron have a severe reaction to an allergen, you must know how to handle the situation.

There are several symptoms of extreme allergic reactions or anaphylactic shock:

- Difficulty in breathing
- Fainting or unconsciousness
- Swelling
- Itching or burning skin
- Hives
- Restlessness

If the person has medication for an allergy, help him or her take it. Regardless of how mild the reaction appears, always contact the EMS. You don't know how the body will react. While awaiting EMS personnel, treat the person as you would treat anyone experiencing shock.

- Ensure an open airway.
- Keep the person warm but not overheated.
- Monitor pulse and breathing.
- Do *not* give fluids or food.

ASTHMA

Asthma is a chronic condition that flares up periodically. During an asthma "attack" the person has difficulty getting fresh air into the lungs. The result is a wheezing or forcing of air in and out as the person struggles for air exchange. Attacks may be brought on by strenuous activity, exposure to an allergen, or emotional stress.

Symptoms of an asthma attack include the following:

- Wheezing
- Rapid pulse
- Hunched shoulders
- Pulling on the chest to assist in breathing
- Discoloration of skin, lips, or nailbeds (in severe cases)

Someone with asthma who has been active all day swimming and recreating at an aquatic facility may be susceptible to an attack. Should a patron experience difficulty, take the following steps:

- Position the person for ease of breathing—usually sitting upright.
- Help the person take any prescribed medication.
- Provide reassurance.
- If the episode does not subside quickly, contact EMS.
- Monitor pulse, breathing, and skin color.
- Keep the person warm but not overheated.

EPILEPTIC SEIZURES

Epilepsy is a chronic disorder of the nervous system; abnormal electrical activity in the brain causes a seizure, which may be accompanied by a loss of consciousness. Seizures can be triggered by various conditions or events, including hyperventilation, physical stress, nervous tension, poor regulation of body temperature, lack of sleep, low blood sugar, illness, hormonal changes, fluid and electrolyte imbalances, alcohol, and bright light. Many people with epilepsy can control their seizures through medication or behavioral prevention. Even so, a seizure may occur.

One type of seizure, the "absence" or "petit mal" seizure, is often not noticeable. The person loses awareness for only a few seconds, staring and perhaps fluttering the eyelids. Another type, the "tonic-clonic" or "grand mal" seizure, is more recognizable; the person may have a combination of these symptoms:

- Rigid muscles
- Jerky and convulsive movements
- Clenched teeth
- Drooling
- Loss of consciousness
- Loss of bowel and bladder control
- Biting of the tongue
- Period of apnea (not breathing)

Fortunately, before a grand mal seizure begins, many people with epilepsy will experience a warning in the form of an aura, often described as a bright light, a burst of color, or an odor. Upon recognizing a warning signal, the person can help you provide a safe environment for the seizure.

In a "psychomotor" or "partial complex" seizure, the individual may seem confused or dizzy. He or she may perform unusual motions such as twitching a hand or arm, walking aimlessly, picking at objects, or rubbing the hands together. The person also may speak in a repetitive or incoherent manner. People experiencing such a seizure are sometimes mistaken for drunks.

There is nothing that you can do to stop a seizure. Your role is to protect the person from any injury. If someone has a seizure out of the water, take the following steps:

- Provide an area with as much privacy as possible (many people with epilepsy prefer others not to view their behavior during a seizure).
- Lay the person down in an area where she or he cannot be injured by surrounding hazards.
- Protect the person's head as much as possible, placing a folded towel underneath it.
- Loosen any restrictive clothing.

Not every person about to have a seizure will be able to warn you of it. If an unexpected seizure begins, lay the person down in a location where he or she is not endangered by sharp objects or obstructions, loosen any restrictive clothing, and keep bystanders away from the scene. *Never* attempt to put anything in the person's mouth during a seizure.

If someone in the water has a seizure, you will need to get into the water and move the person away from hazards, such as the side of the pool. Stand behind the victim and grasp both sides of the head. This will help you keep the person's head above the water while the seizure runs its course. In deep water, concentrate on supporting the victim's head above water and move to shallow water as soon as possible. After the seizure, help the person out of the water; she or he will be sleepy.

Whether the seizure occurs in or out of the water, anyone who has had a seizure must see medical personnel; a number of complications could develop as much as an hour after the apparent recovery. Stay with the person until medical assistance arrives.

HYPERVENTILATION

Hyperventilation, or overventilation, is brought about by inhaling and exhaling deeply and rapidly. The goal of this practice is usually to stay underwater for a longer time. You will often see people hyperventilate and then try to swim across the pool underwater. Although such attempts may be fun, hyperventilating can be dangerous.

When you hyperventilate you lower the percentage of carbon dioxide in the air that always remains in your lungs. The carbon dioxide in the bloodstream is what triggers your medulla oblongata (the part of the brain that controls breathing) to initiate taking a breath. By decreasing the available carbon dioxide, you can remain underwater because you delay the point at which the brain signals the need to take a breath. The danger occurs when you delay the trigger point until after the lack of oxygen to the body is so severe that you become unconscious (black out).

You might think that you'd know when you were reaching the point that you would lose consciousness as a result of holding your breath. Unfortunately, research shows that the onset of unconsciousness is like falling asleep—a person really doesn't notice it. Some swimmers who have blacked out have felt beforehand as if they could stay underwater forever.

You may find it difficult to notice when a swimmer has blacked out underwater. Sometimes swimmers continue moving erratically even after losing consciousness. They may also continue kicking until they begin to surface.

You can normally identify people who are hyperventilating because they are taking rapid deep breaths. They may experience tingling in the arms and around the mouth, cramps in their fingers, or sharp chest pains. Prevent them from swimming underwater and explain why you are concerned.

Conscious hyperventilators who are breathing too fast, too slowly, noisily, or painfully may require EMS attention to restore appropriate levels of carbon dioxide in the blood. Even after treatment, you should continue to watch the hyperventilator for any complications that might arise.

If the person is unconscious, contact EMS and monitor breathing. Sometimes normal breathing resumes after the person loses consciousness; if breathing stops, provide rescue breathing.

Hyperventilation or blackouts brought on by deprivation of oxygen can also occur for other reasons, including overexertion—the most common cause of unintentional hyperventilation—and the pressure effect and the position effect, which are less common.

- *Overexertion.* During overexertion the body very quickly uses oxygen stored in the body, which hastens the lack of oxygen. Overexertion also decreases the body's ability to sense the trigger to breathe. Poorly conditioned or overtaxed swimmers are especially susceptible to overexertion blackouts.

- *Pressure effect.* When diving 20 feet or deeper, which is quite unusual for most lifeguards, the increased pressure of the deep water causes increased use of oxygen. Upon surfacing, the lifeguard may lack enough available oxygen and black out.

- *Position effect.* On an extended shallow underwater swim, the oxygen level drops. This drop is not significant enough to reduce the supply of oxygen to the brain, but when the swimmer stands up and the blood supply to the brain is reduced, there is a possibility of insufficient oxygen to the brain, causing a blackout.

For more information on hyperventilation, see page 83 in chapter 5.

FIRST AID QUICK REFERENCE

This chapter has presented important information about providing first aid. Table 9.3 provides a quick guide for you to consult when an emergency arises.

Table 9.3 **First Aid Quick Reference Guide**

Condition	Symptoms	First aid	Necessary to call EMS?
Asthma	Wheezing Rapid pulse Hunched shoulders Pulling on chest Discoloration of skin, lips, or nailbeds	Position person for ease of breathing Help person take medication Reassure Monitor pulse, breathing, and skin color Keep person warm	Sometimes
Allergy (anaphylactic shock)	Difficulty breathing Fainting or unconsciousness Swelling Itching or burning skin Hives Restlessness	Ensure open airway Keep person warm Monitor pulse and breathing Give no fluids or food	Yes

(continued)

Table 9.3 *(continued)*

Condition	Symptoms	First aid	Necessary to call EMS?
Epileptic seizure (grand mal)	Rigid muscles Jerky, convulsive movements Clenched teeth Drooling Loss of consciousness Loss of bowel and bladder control Biting tongue May stop breathing for a period	Provide privacy Provide safe environment Lay victim down/protect head Loosen restrictive clothing Put nothing in mouth Move away from pool side Support head above water Monitor until EMS arrives	Yes
Heart attack	Shortness of breath Chest pains Profuse sweating Pale, sweaty skin Squeezing sensation in the chest Indigestion	Keep person calm Make comfortable Help take medication Monitor condition Be ready for CPR	Yes
Heat cramps	Cramps Sweaty skin Increased heart rate Exhaustion Dizziness	Get out of heat Give water Apply moist towels Do not massage	Only in severe cases
Heat exhaustion	Profuse sweating Cool, clammy skin Dilated pupils Pale color Increased heart rate Weakness Nausea Thirst Fainting Anxiety or apathy	Get out of heat Give water Lay victim down Loosen restrictive clothing Cool with moist, cold towels	Yes Warning: if left unattended can escalate to heatstroke
Heatstroke	Dry or sweaty skin Inability to sweat Increased then decreased heart rate Increased temperature Hot, red skin Rapid, shallow breathing that may then slow Constricted pupils Headache Confusion Disorientation Unconsciousness Seizure	Do not give fluids Get out of heat Lay person down Loosen restrictive clothing Cool immediately using ice packs or ice water-soaked sheets Monitor body temperature and ABCs Be prepared for convulsions	Yes, immediately

Table 9.3 *(continued)*

Condition	Symptoms	First aid	Necessary to call EMS?
Hypothermia	Initially intense shivering Rigid muscles Reduced coordination Slow, labored breathing Bluish color to skin, lips, and nailbeds Reduced blood flow to hands and feet Dilated pupils Loss of logic Difficulty speaking Disorientation Glassy stare Slow, irregular pulse Amnesia Loss of consciousness	Remove wet clothes Dry victim Provide warmth unless cold water drowning Give warm liquids (nonalcoholic, noncaffeinated) If cold water drowning, begin CPR and do not rewarm	Yes
Hyperventilation	Rapid, deep breathing Tingling arms and mouth Cramps in fingers Sharp chest pains Unconsciousness	Administer CO_2 from ambulance Monitor for complications Provide rescue breathing if breathing stops	Yes, if breathing too fast, slowly, noisily, or painfully, or if loss of consciousness
Severe bleeding	External: Bleeding from open wound	For external bleeding: Apply pressure Cover wound with bandage Elevate limb (don't elevate if broken) Apply pressure to pressure point Care for the wound Treat for shock by raising victim's legs 8–12 inches and keeping body warm	External, yes if extensive
	Internal: Bleeding from mouth, rectum, vagina, or blood in urine Visible bruises or cuts Rapid pulse Sweaty, cool skin Dilated pupils Nausea, vomiting Abdominal pain, rigidity, or bruising Chest bruising or rib fractures	For internal bleeding: Call EMS Monitor pulse and breathing Prepare for vomiting Treat for shock	Internal, yes

Review Questions

1. What can you learn from a medical alert tag?
2. What is hepatitis?
3. What is AIDS?
4. List four ways HIV is transmitted.
5. List the nine universal precautionary procedures you can use to prevent contact with body fluids.
6. What should you learn through workplace training regarding OSHA regulations and blood-borne pathogens?
7. List the six guidelines for contacting EMS.
8. List the symptoms and first aid for a heart attack.
9. What are the differences in bleeding from capillaries, veins, and arteries?
10. What are the three steps to control bleeding?
11. List the symptoms and first aid for internal bleeding.
12. What is hyperthermia?
13. List the symptoms and first aid for heat cramps, heat exhaustion, and heatstroke.
14. What is hypothermia?
15. Why are children more susceptible than adults to immersion hypothermia?
16. List the symptoms of hypothermia.
17. What care can you give someone with hypothermia?
18. Why can people survive after being underwater in cold water for a lengthy period?
19. What first aid should you provide a cold water drowning victim?
20. List the symptoms of anaphylactic shock. What first aid is necessary?
21. What can cause an asthma attack? What first aid should you provide?
22. List the symptoms of an epileptic seizure.
23. What assistance can you give to someone having a seizure on land? In the water?
24. Why do people sometimes black out when they hyperventilate?
25. What symptoms will someone have who has hyperventilated but not blacked out? What first aid should you give?
26. List and describe three other reasons people could black out in the water.

ten

Spinal Injury Management

Spinal injuries are a very real concern to all who serve the public at aquatic facilities—and for good reason. According to a 1989 U.S. Consumer Product Safety Commission report, each year approximately 700 people suffer spinal cord injuries while diving into swimming pools, lakes, and other bodies of water. While this number may not be overwhelming, the effects of the injuries can be devastating. All lifeguards must be skilled at handling such injuries, as it can happen in your facility. Your ability to handle the situation may make the difference between an unfortunate accident and lifelong paralysis.

▷ **In This Chapter, You'll Learn About**

- those who experience spinal cord injuries,
- hazardous activities,
- open water diving hazards,
- pool design-related hazards,
- standards for safe diving, and
- No Diving signs.

You'll Also Learn How To

- recognize a spinal injury,
- enter the water and approach a victim,
- perform the head-splint rescue,
- perform shallow and deep water rescues,
- choose a backboard and apply a cervical collar,
- backboard and remove a victim from the water,
- provide rescue breathing and CPR, and
- manage spinal injuries when the victim is in a standing or sitting position, or is in extremely shallow water.

THE VICTIM

Most spinal cord injuries occur in a setting where there is no qualified lifeguard, instructor, or coach present to provide knowledgeable assistance. An overview of data indicates that the typical person who experiences a spinal cord injury has the following characteristics:

- An athletic male 18 to 31 years old
- 6 feet tall
- 175 pounds
- No formal training in diving
- First-time visitor to the location making a first dive there
- Not warned about dangers either verbally or through a sign

CAUSES OF AQUATIC SPINAL INJURIES

Spinal injuries can occur in both pools and the open water. Obviously, equipment and facility design play a larger role in a pool setting than a beach environment. Here are some of the main causes of aquatic spinal injuries.

Injuries in Swimming Pools

Most spinal cord injuries in swimming pools result from a dive into shallow water. This includes diving from

- a deck into an in-ground pool,
- a platform or rim of an above-ground pool,
- adjacent structures (roofs, trees, etc.) into an above-ground pool, and
- competitive starting blocks located in shallow water.

Dives or falls into deep water account for 20 to 25% of spinal injuries in pools. Injuries are caused by dives or falls onto the deck, dives in water 7 feet deep or less, or divers hitting the upslope of the pool bottom that was not far enough away. These dives or falls are from the following equipment:

- Springboards (26 inches or less above the water)
- 3-meter springboards
- 1-meter springboards
- Jump boards 4 to 6 feet long
- The deck into a hopper bottom pool (see page 195)
- The 3-meter stand onto the deck

Water slides located in shallow water also account for spinal cord injuries. These injuries are due to

- sliding head-first,
- diving from the top of the slide, and
- falling onto the deck from the top of the slide.

Injuries in Open Water

Thousands of people enjoy swimming in open water; unfortunately, recreational fun sometimes ends in disaster. Spinal injuries in open water are a result of many factors.

Oceans and Rivers

Currents and tides at ocean fronts and the flow of water in rivers can cause bottom contours to change very rapidly. Sunken logs, debris, and silt or sand build-up on the bottom are some causes of concern for the swimmer who is preparing to run and plunge. Any object underwater can create a danger for the unsuspecting swimmer.

A chief cause of spinal injury in an ocean environment is diving head-first into an oncoming wave. Every swimmer should take precautionary measures to ensure a safe entry into the water. Be sure to warn patrons by posting signs that read "No Diving" or "No Running Dives." In open water, an underwater obstruction could move into the area within minutes; lifeguards should conduct a bottom check each day before the facility opens to the public. Underwater obstructions should be removed or identified with a sign or buoy. Patrons should not run and plunge at any open water facility.

Diving from a dock into water shallower than 9 feet should also be prohibited. Signs that say "Danger—Shallow Water, No Diving" should be located on dock areas with water shallower than 9 feet.

Lakes and Quarries

Although the water in lakes and quarries is not as active as in oceans and rivers, the bottom contour may still change and present hazards. Wind and wave action can carry submerged debris close to shore and deposit it on the bottom. Created lakes or reservoirs may have submerged tree stumps or logs close to shore. Large rocks or boulders may also be under the water in lakes and especially in quarries.

The additional hazards of diving into quarries means it should be prohibited. Boulders, rock slabs, ledges, and even mechanical equipment left behind by former mining operations create hazards for swimmers.

DESIGN-RELATED SPINAL INJURY HAZARDS IN SWIMMING POOLS

Hazards associated with diving into deep water, especially in residential pools, often relate to the configuration of the bottom and sides of the pool and the placement of the diving board. Two specific pool designs present an increased risk for spinal injuries associated with diving from a diving board: hopper bottom and spoon-shaped pools.

Hopper Bottom Pools

The hopper bottom pool slopes on all four sides from the deepest point of the pool up to the break-point (see figure 10.1). There is generally a very limited landing area for diving in the deepest part of the pool; in fact, diving into a hopper bottom pool is like diving into a funnel. The sides of the pool are all angled toward the deepest point, which may only be 2 feet by 2 feet. The depth markers on the deck and sides of the pool indicate the depth at the deepest point, but they don't give any indication of the side depths. The diver may think the depth is safe but find it shallower than expected because of the sloping sides. Diving from the diving board or from the side of the pool in the deep water area could result in striking the bottom or upslope of the pool in water that is shallower than the depth indicated by the markers.

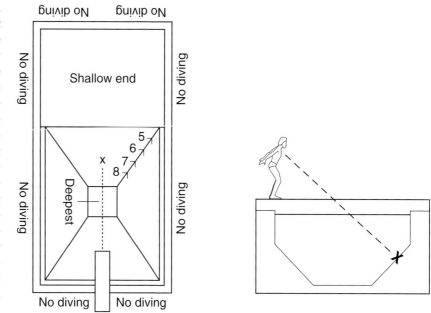

Figure 10.1 Typical residential hopper bottom pool.
Reprinted, by permission, from the American Red Cross, 1996, *American Red Cross Swimming and Diving Handbook.*

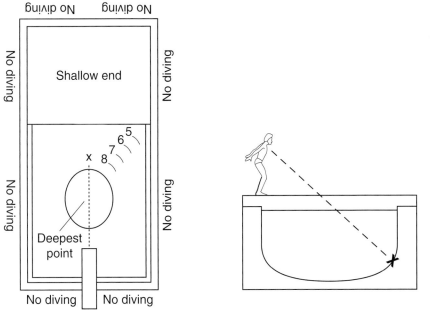

Figure 10.2 Typical residential spoon-shaped pool.
Reprinted, by permission, from the American Red Cross, 1996, *American Red Cross Swimming and Diving Handbook.*

Spoon-Shaped Pools

Another design that creates potential hazards is the spoon-shaped pool (see figure 10.2). The bottom contour of this pool gives a false sense of depth and bottom surface area throughout the deep section of the pool. The distance from the end of the diving board to the upslope of the pool bottom is greatly reduced in spoon-shaped pools, as it is in hopper bottom pools. Striking the slope can cause serious neck and back injuries. The slopes are also found under the diving board and along the side.

FACILITY AND EQUIPMENT HAZARDS IN SWIMMING POOLS

Many safety factors must be considered when a pool is being constructed. The width and depth of the diving area and the angle of the pool bottom are important for safe diving, as are the placement of diving boards and towers. Special features such as water slides, starting blocks, and underwater safety ledges should be built for safe use. Pool rules can be developed to help reduce any dangers inherent to the facility or equipment.

Residential Pools

Not all swimming pools are designed with diving in mind, especially in-ground residential pools. There are many sizes and shapes of in-ground residential pools; their length and depth can create hazards for owners and guests.

Most spinal cord injuries in residential pools result from diving into shallow water. Depths should be marked clearly on the deck near the edge of the pool and on the side of the pool coping itself. The depth on each side of the break-point distinguishing shallow water from deep water should be marked clearly. Signs saying "Danger—Shallow Water, No Diving" should be placed on the deck in shallow water and posted on fences or walls enclosing the swimming pool or on a stand at the entrance to the pool area. If you own a residential pool that is less than 11 feet, 6 inches deep and the distance from the tip of the diving board to the start of the upslope is less than 16 feet, 6 inches, remove the diving board. If your pool is no deeper than 9 feet, don't allow diving from the deck.

Hazards associated with diving into deep water in residential pools primarily relate to the configuration of the bottom and sides of the pool, as previously discussed in "Design-Related Spinal Injury Hazards in Swimming Pools."

If you own a residential pool, do not let divers run on the diving board, attempt to dive for long distances through the air, or dive to the side if there is the slightest chance that they will

- strike the upslope of the pool that rises from the deepest section to the shallow section,
- strike a floating line marking the boundary of the diving area, or
- strike a swimmer inside the diving area.

Hotel/Motel and Apartment Swimming Pools

Many hotel/motel and apartment swimming pools present the same types of hazards as residential pools. Appropriate pool depths and construction are primary considerations for safe and injury-free diving. The lack of professional supervision at these facilities compounds their hazards. Lifeguards and swimmers should carefully assess the dimensions of the pool to assure minimum standards are met before diving is permitted. Catastrophic injuries can be avoided by eliminating diving in facilities that do not meet standards.

Public and Private Swimming Pools

Public and private swimming pools may present some of the hazards already discussed. Owners of these facilities need to be concerned with preventing diving into shallow water and with meeting minimum facility standards for safe springboard diving. Facilities also often maintain 1-meter, 3-meter, or tower-diving facilities that must meet more stringent standards.

All swimming pools with diving equipment should display diving rules and regulations near the boards and towers such as those listed on page 198. These rules should be strictly enforced.

Water Slides Entering Shallow Water

Water slides, which vary in height, shape, and location, can provide safe fun providing proper precautions are met. Several factors need to be addressed regarding water slides. The speed of a swimmer entering the water from a slide depends on the height, friction, and design of the slide and the alignment of the swimmer. A swimmer entering water 3 feet deep at a near vertical angle from a slide 6 to 12 feet high achieves the same velocity as someone diving from a 1-meter diving board, which can cause spinal injury if the swimmer hits the bottom of the pool or another swimmer with his or her head.

The angle of entry from a slide most often is determined by the height of the lip of the slide over the surface of the water. The higher the lip, the greater the angle of entry. To reduce the possibility of spinal injuries, observe the following guidelines:

- Allow no head-first sliding.
- Have patrons cross their legs when sliding to prevent groin or internal injuries.
- Have the lifeguard signal when it is safe for one slider to begin when following another.
- Prohibit deliberate attempts at deep entries.
- Keep the landing area in front of the slide clear of swimmers.
- Provide a minimum water depth of 9 feet in the landing area for drop slides.
- Anchor slides securely to the deck.
- Position the exit lip of the slide at deck or water height.

Competitive Swimming Starting Blocks

Starting blocks are used at the start of races in competitive pools. Competitive pools either have starting blocks permanently installed or have removable platforms. Competitive swimmers are trained in proper techniques for safely diving from platforms. Anyone who has not received training is at risk when diving from this equipment.

An improper dive could result in a spinal cord injury. To prevent injuries, starting blocks must be located in water at least 5 feet deep at the deep end of the pool. Use of the blocks must be restricted to trained swimmers during supervised competitive practices and events. Racing dives, such as the scoop, pike, and shoot start, cannot be allowed. At all other times, starting blocks must be removed or capped off. Safety warnings must be posted regarding starting block use, and access must be controlled by lifeguards. The blocks must be regularly inspected for stability, surface characteristics (traction), and any sign of wear.

Underwater Safety Ledges

Some swimming pools have underwater ledges (see figure 10.3), sometimes called *safety ledges*, constructed so that swimmers can stand up in deep water when next to the side of the pool. These ledges present a hazard related to head and spinal injuries. If it is difficult to see the ledge, a swimmer can dive or jump into deep water and hit it unexpectedly. To reduce or eliminate this possibility, black stripes should be painted on the top side of the ledge with a black line on the border so swimmers can identify the width of the ledge.

Figure 10.3   Underwater safety ledge.

Figure 10.4   No Diving sign.
Courtesy of Recreonics, Inc., Louisville, KY.

NO DIVING SIGNS

To ensure the safety of swimmers, any facility with water shallower than 9 feet should post warning signs indicating that diving is not allowed. Such signs may read "Danger—Shallow Water, No Diving." These signs should be posted on the deck near the edge of the pool and on walls adjacent to shallow water. They should be visible to anyone entering the pool and approaching shallow water.

Signs can be posted in a variety of ways:

- Universal No Diving sign painted on the deck
- Lettering painted on the deck
- Tiled lettering embedded in the deck
- Universal No Diving tile embedded in the deck
- Plastic signs mounted on walls, fences, or stands (see figure 10.4)

Because most spinal cord injuries occur the first time someone is at a facility, it is crucial to warn patrons of hazards. Multiple signs placed in strategic locations will help prevent injuries.

RECOGNIZING SPINAL INJURIES

Because most injuries to the head, neck, and back occur in shallow water, suspect a spinal injury anytime the victim

- is found in an unconscious state (especially in shallow water),
- has been involved in a diving board or water slide accident,
- has fallen from a height, or
- has sustained a blow to the head or neck.

In any of these instances, a serious injury to the spinal cord may have occurred. Because victims with spinal injury require special care, you need to be aware of the signs of spinal injury. However, so you can grasp the significance of such an injury, we'll begin by explaining the structure of the spine.

Structure of the Spine

The spine is a strong, flexible, bony structure that supports the head and trunk (see figure 10.5). The bones of the spine, *vertebrae,* are circular in shape and are separated from each other by cushions of cartilage. This cartilage, called *intervertebral discs,* acts as a shock absorber when a person is walking, running, or jumping. The *ligaments* are the tissues that connect the bones of the spine together. The *spinal cord,* a bundle of nerves that carries vital messages from the brain to be distributed to different parts of the body, runs through the hollow portion of the vertebrae. Nerve branches extend to the various parts of the body through openings on the sides of the vertebrae. The spine protects the nerve center of the body from damage.

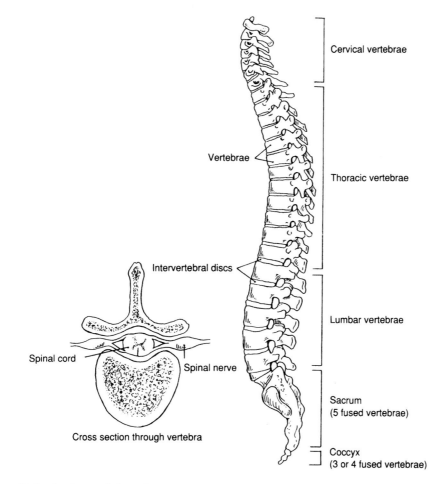

Figure 10.5   Anatomy of the spine.

The spine is divided into five regions. The *cervical* spine is the area around the neck. This region is the most susceptible to injury as a result of an individual diving into shallow water. The *thoracic* spine is located in the middle back, while the *lumbar* region is the lower back. The *sacrum* and *coccyx,* located at the base of the spinal column, complete the structure of the spine.

Signs of Spinal Injury

Injuries to the spine include fractures and dislocations of the vertebrae, sprained ligaments, and compressed or displaced intervertebral discs. Any of these injuries can cause injury to the spinal cord that may result in paralysis or death.

A victim of a spinal injury may exhibit any of the following signs:

- Pain at the site of the injury
- Loss of movement in the extremities
- Loss of movement below the site of the injury
- Tingling or loss of sensation in the extremities
- Disorientation
- Deformity in the neck or back
- Visible bruising over an area of the spinal column
- Difficulty in breathing
- Head injury
- Fluid or blood in the ears and/or nose
- Unconsciousness

Victims with spinal injuries will not necessarily be totally paralyzed after impact with the bottom of the pool or the diving board. They may be able to swim or walk. Spinal injury victims sometimes exhibit signs similar to those of actively drowning victims. They may struggle at the surface momentarily and then sink to the bottom, swim to the side of the pool or shallow water, or even climb out of the water or sit on the edge of the pool.

It will be important for you to identify the cause of the injury to assess if a spinal injury may have occurred. If a victim exhibits any of the signs of spinal injury, regardless of water depth, or has hit the diving board, provide in-line stabilization and perform the backboarding procedures introduced later in this chapter. Your cautious treatment of this victim could truly save a life.

REACHING A SPINAL INJURY VICTIM

As in any rescue, speed is vital to assisting a victim of a spinal cord injury. However, you must take special precautions in entering the water and approaching the victim to avoid causing additional harm.

Entering the Water

Enter the water slowly and carefully. Use a *waveless entry* to prevent water movement that might cause further injury. You can perform a waveless entry in two ways. In shallow water, follow these steps (figure 10.6):

1. Sit on the deck.
2. Place your hands on the deck, one on the outside of each leg.
3. Lower yourself into the water.

a. b. c.

Figure 10.6 Waveless entry into shallow water.

Using the same entry in deep water will create waves. To make a waveless entry in deep water (or an alternative entry in shallow water), follow these steps (figure 10.7):

1. Sit on the edge of the deck.
2. Place one hand on the deck near your leg.
3. Reach across your body with the other hand and place it on the deck or in the pool gutter.
4. As you lower yourself into the water, turn 180 degrees to face the side of the pool, then grab your rescue tube or buoy.

Because your arms have greater flexibility in the forward support position, this entry will allow you to slide into deeper water without creating any unnecessary turbulence.

a. b. c.

Figure 10.7 Waveless entry for deep water.

Approaching the Victim

Whether you are in shallow or deep water, approach the victim slowly, carefully, and with as little water disturbance as possible. If you are in shallow water, walk toward the victim slowly. If you are in deeper water, use the breaststroke or a modified crawl stroke with an underwater arm recovery.

Practice these approach techniques—they take some time to perfect. Remember, they must help you reach the victim quickly without creating waves or disturbing the water.

SPINAL INJURY RESCUE TECHNIQUES

In this section, we describe shallow and deep water rescue techniques, as well as the head-splint rescue, which is common to both types of techniques. While you will be able to rescue and administer rescue breathing or CPR to someone with a spinal injury, remember that you need to call EMS immediately in all situations in which a spinal injury is suspected.

Head-Splint Rescue

The YMCA recommends using the head-splint method for victims with spinal injuries. Research has shown that this method, as described in this chapter, is the most effective one for stabilizing the head and neck during a rescue.

The objective of the head-splint rescue is to stabilize the head and neck. It can be used both when the victim is lying facedown in the water, to stabilize the victim before turning her or him over, and when a victim is faceup in the water. *In-line stabilization* is accomplished by squeezing the victim's arms to trap the head between them.

The head-splint rescue is a part of both shallow and deep water rescues for victims with spinal injuries.

Shallow Water Rescues

The shallow water rescues described here are for a victim who is prone (facedown), supine (faceup), or on the bottom of the pool.

Victim in Prone Position (Facedown)

To apply the head-splint in order to turn the victim to a faceup position (see figure 10.8), use the following steps:

1. Approach the victim from the side and grab the victim's right *upper* arm just above the elbow with your right hand.
2. Grab the victim's left *upper* arm just above the elbow with your left hand.
3. Move the arms sideways, toward the head, to a position in which the victim's upper arms cover his or her ears. This will center the victim's head between the arms.
4. Squeeze both arms against the head simultaneously to trap it in position.
5. After trapping the head between the arms, move the victim forward. The victim's legs will rise. Having the legs ride higher in the water will make it easier to turn the victim.
6. As you roll the victim toward you, turn to face the victim's feet and legs.

7. At the same time, move your top arm (the arm that is over the victim) to a position beneath the victim's shoulder. You will notice that at the end of the sequence the right arm, which was over the victim, is under the victim's right shoulder. Your forearm should be in contact with the shoulder and upper arm of the victim.

8. As you turn the victim, lower yourself into the water to neck depth to avoid lifting the victim during in-line stabilization.

a.

b.

c.

d.

Figure 10.8   Head-splint turnover.

After you have turned the victim over, the victim's arms should be over your shoulder and close to your cheek or neck. Stabilize the victim in a horizontal position by gently supporting the victim's shoulder with your forearm, which is under him or her. Remember, the arm that is under the victim's shoulder is the arm you originally reached over the victim to begin the head-splint. The appropriate stabilization position is illustrated in figure 10.9.

Figure 10.9 Stabilizing position in the head-splint rescue in shallow water.

Keys to the Head-Splint Turnover

1. Grab the victim's upper arms near the elbows.
2. Trap the head between the arms and maintain pressure.
3. Move the victim forward.
4. Roll the victim toward you.
5. Lower yourself to neck depth.
6. Place your forearm under the victim's shoulder for support (right arm under right shoulder or left arm under left shoulder).
7. Check that the victim's arms are over your shoulder, next to your ear.

Victim in Supine Position (Faceup)

Approach the victim from behind. Check to see if the victim is conscious. If the victim is conscious and floating on the surface, ask the following questions:

- Are you OK?
- What happened?
- Do you feel pain anywhere?
- Can you move your fingers?
- Can you move your toes?

This will help you ascertain the condition of the victim.

Let the victim know that you are now going to provide in-line stabilization to protect his or her spine. Explain exactly what you are going to do, then proceed with the following (figure 10.10):

1. Stand behind the victim.
2. Submerge so that the water level is at your neck.
3. Grab the victim's elbows in the same manner as shown previously.
4. Slowly and carefully move the victim's arms laterally (to the side) to a position that will allow you to trap the head between the arms.
5. After the head is trapped, stabilize the victim for backboarding.

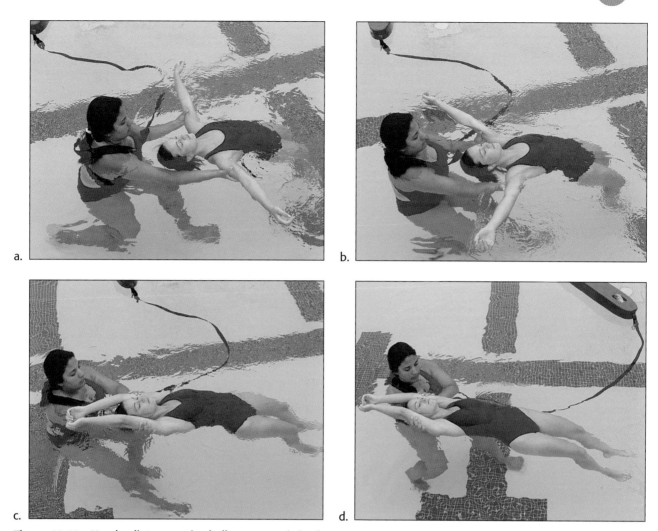

a.

b.

c.

d.

Figure 10.10   Head-splint rescue in shallow water, victim faceup.

Victim on the Bottom

If you are diving to reach a victim on the bottom, you may need to exhale before you submerge in order to reduce your buoyancy. With decreased buoyancy you will be able to position yourself more effectively for the rescue.

If the victim is on the bottom in a faceup position, place your hands in a position to perform the head-splint rescue. You may have to improvise, depending on the victim's position. Trap the victim's head between his or her arms and carefully lift the victim to the surface.

If the victim is on the bottom in a facedown position, trap the head between the arms, lift the victim to the surface, and then turn the victim over.

Deep Water Rescues

Very few spinal injuries occur in deep water, but there is always the potential for such an injury. Hitting the diving board, diving into another swimmer, or striking the head on the bottom or the upslope of the pool in the diving well are all possible ways a spinal injury could occur in deep water. The head-splint technique should be used for in-line stabilization in deep water as well.

Stabilizing the neck in deep water is very difficult. In shallow water, you do not need to support yourself as you work. In deep water, you need a strong kick to keep yourself in position to perform an effective rescue. The YMCA recommends that a pair of fins be stored at all lifeguard stations in deep water areas. With fins, it is far easier to maintain your position using a flutter kick. Without fins, use a breaststroke, scissors, or rotary kick. The rotary kick, or eggbeater, is preferred because it provides a more stable transport of the victim.

Victim on the Surface

As with any spinal injury rescue in deep water, enter the water using a waveless entry. Take a rescue tube to provide flotation for you during the rescue. Use an underwater recovery of the arms to avoid disturbing the water while you approach the victim.

When you reach the victim, perform the head-splint rescue (see figure 10.11), including the turnover if necessary (as described previously). You will need to modify the head-splint technique slightly if you use a rescue tube. You should end up at the victim's side rather than with the victim's arms next to your ears after turning the victim over. Avoid rolling the victim onto the tube.

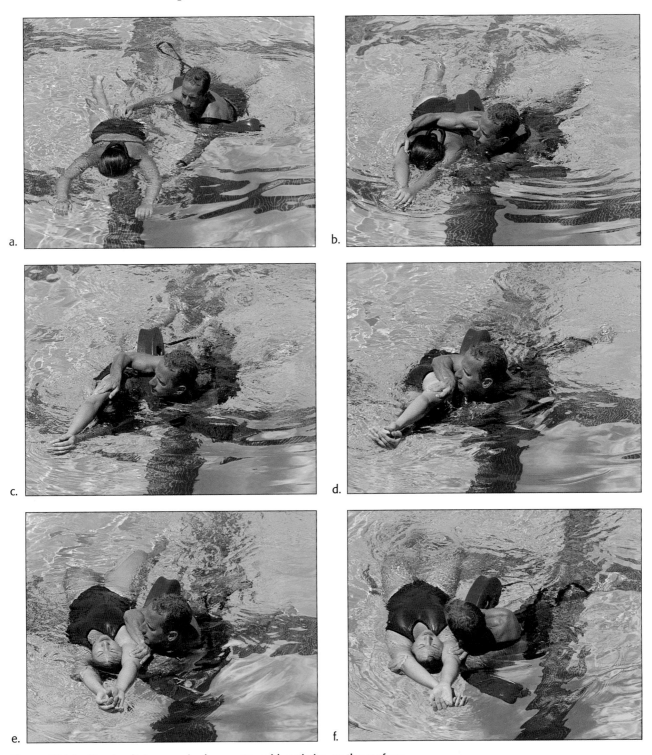

a.

b.

c.

d.

e.

f.

Figure 10.11   Head-splint rescue in deep water with a victim on the surface.

Once you have turned the victim over, transport him or her to shallow water if possible. If you are at a pool or diving well with no shallow section, transport the victim toward the side of the pool and perform the following sequence (see figure 10.17, p. 211).

1. An additional rescuer either lies down on an elevated deck or sits down on the edge of a deck-level pool and verbally guides you toward the corner of the pool. The victim ends up perpendicular to the side of the pool.

2. As you approach the side of the pool, the rescuer on the deck grabs the victim's upper arms and applies the head-splint.

3. Once the rescuer on deck secures the victim's arms and head, release the victim's arms and grab the pool gutter. Support the victim's hips or lower back, if necessary, and then slide a rescue tube under the victim's knees. Then check the victim's breathing.

4. The victim is now ready to be placed on a backboard. The backboarding procedure will be discussed later in this chapter.

Victim Underwater

Unlike when a victim is at the surface, you will not be able to retrieve the rescue tube and place it under your arms during underwater retrieval in deep water. In most cases when the victim is submerged, he or she will not be flat on his or her back on the bottom. Approach the victim from above or behind, depending on the victim's position on the bottom. Trap the victim's head using the head-splint technique described previously and transport him or her to the surface with the face angled toward the bottom to avoid getting water up the victim's nose and possibly into the stomach and lungs. Once you reach the surface, turn the victim to a faceup position as previously described. Transport the victim to the nearest side of the pool, where another rescuer should be located, or to shallow water if possible.

BACKBOARDING EQUIPMENT

Backboarding requires the use of both a backboard and a cervical collar. Here we explain how to choose an appropriate backboard and how to apply a cervical collar. Be sure to learn how to use the backboarding equipment available in your facility.

Selecting a Backboard

A number of types of backboards, like the one in figure 10.12, are available. Any model is acceptable as long as it meets the following requirements:

- It is made of marine plywood or lightweight resins; if an injury results in contamination of the backboard, resin boards are easier to clean than wooden boards.

- It has slats or risers underneath the board or hand grips, which will help prevent rescuers from pinching their fingers when setting the board on the deck.

- It has ample slots on each side of the board to adjust strap placement.

- It has some form of professional head restraint attached to the board that has padding that will prevent the victim's head from dropping too far back onto the board.

- It is long and wide enough to allow rescue of victims of various sizes.

- It has a minimum of four straps connected to the board (one head strap, one chest strap, one waist strap, and one shin strap—a wrist strap is optional).

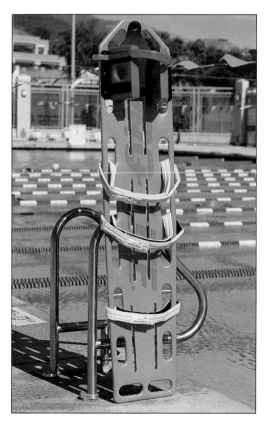

Figure 10.12 A backboard.

Keep backboards on deck and ready for use at all times the facility is open. Have all straps connected to the board in a manner that duplicates how the straps will be connected once the victim is placed on the board.

Applying a Cervical Collar

Cervical collars, when applied correctly, stabilize a victim's head and neck very effectively. Several styles and sizes of collars are available on the market (figure 10.13). Only rigid cervical collars are appropriate for use in an aquatic environment, as foam collars are ineffective in the water. You must have a variety of collar sizes available, ranging from baby collars to adult long-neck collars. Adjustable collars allow the lifeguard to custom fit the collar to the victim.

Figure 10.13 Cervical collars.

Always store cervical collars with backboards. You may attach them to one of the backboard straps or place them in a bag and attach the bag to the board. In this way, the collars will always be available when and where you need them.

Using an improperly sized cervical collar can cause further injury to the victim. For instance, a too-small collar can obstruct the victim's airway. That's why you need to select the correct size collar before applying it.

To some extent, the size will depend on the design of the collar being used. However, you can follow these two steps to determine the proper size (figure 10.14):

1. Put your hand next to the victim's neck. Measure the distance from under the corner of the jawbone to the shoulder (in number of fingers).

2. Choose a collar with the same measurement as the distance from the victim's jawbone to shoulder. Some collars have a black knob that fastens to the collar. Place your fingers beneath the knob and measure to the bottom of the plastic (not the bottom of the foam cushion). If the distance is the same as the measurement you made of the victim, the cervical collar is likely to be the correct size. If the collar doesn't have a black knob, measure the distance from the bottom of the chin cup to the bottom of the plastic. Also, if sizing instructions came with the collar, follow the manufacturer's directions.

If you find you don't have an appropriately sized collar, one that isn't too loose or too tight, use head restraints to immobilize the head instead.

Note that the rigid cervical collar is more of a reminder to the victim to not move the head than it is an actual immobilization device. Instruct the victim not to move his or her head and to answer questions verbally rather than by shaking or nodding the head.

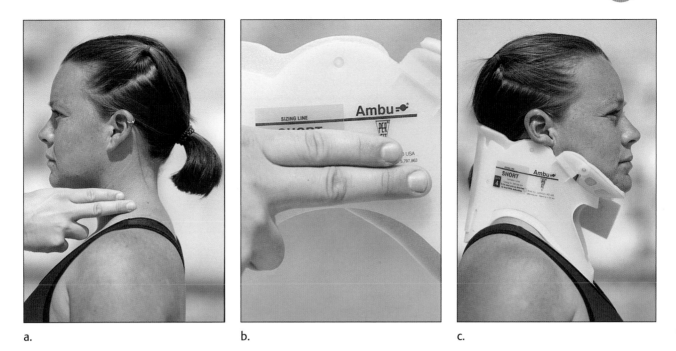

a.   b.   c.

Figure 10.14   Sizing a cervical collar.

All cervical collars have an opening in front of the larynx that you can use in applying the collar. (If the opening is too wide, you may need to modify the following procedures.) Place your middle finger inside the opening, with all other fingers on the outside portion of the collar. Your thumb should be positioned on the side opposite the fingers, as illustrated in figure 10.15. This will allow you to flex the collar to fit it under the chin of the victim.

Some collars can be slipped under the victim's neck and then bent to conform to his or her neck and chin. Other collars, which have preformed curves, need to be placed under the victim's chin and then slid under the neck. Regardless of which style of collar you use, be careful in applying the collar to the victim. If the collar is the wrong size, remove it and try another size. Never try to force a collar into place!

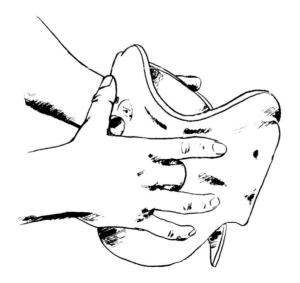

Figure 10.15   Hand position for applying a cervical collar.

Follow these steps to apply a cervical collar:

1. Maintain manual stabilization and avoid overextending the victim's chin when applying the collar.
2. Slide the back of the collar under the victim's neck without lifting or moving the head or neck (see figure 10.16a).
3. Wrap the front of the device around the front of the victim's neck and carefully attach the Velcro strap so the collar fits snugly (see figure 10.16b). In some situations you may have to place the chin cup beneath the victim's chin and carefully slide the chin cup into place. Use the method for holding the collar shown in figure 10.16b for final placement of the collar.

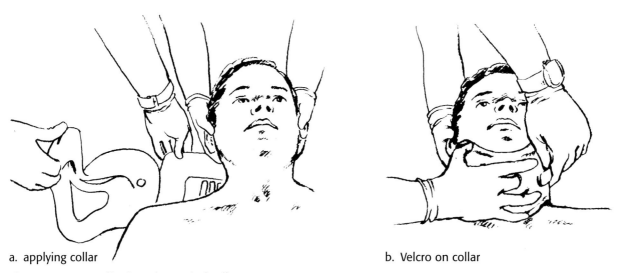

a. applying collar

b. Velcro on collar

Figure 10.16 Application of a cervical collar.

See that the victim's chin rests easily in the collar, allowing the neck to remain in the neutral position. In this position, the victim's head should not be able to turn either side-to-side or up- and-down. Check to make sure that the collar doesn't obstruct the victim's airway.

If goggles are hanging around the victim's neck and interfere with placement of the collar, cut them off or remove them. The original rescuer should be the one to remove the goggles while a second rescuer maintains control of the victim's head. The original rescuer carefully pulls the goggles over the victim's head and around the second rescuer's hands, then traps the head to the backboard as described in backboarding procedures. The second rescuer then carefully removes his or her hands from the victim's head (the goggle strap will be around the second rescuer's hands).

Applying a cervical collar correctly takes a good deal of practice. Be sure you become skilled at it before your season starts. The patrons depend on your ability to keep them safe.

BACKBOARDING PROCEDURES

Putting an individual with a spinal injury on a backboard is not a responsibility to be taken lightly. In this section, we address how to

- position the victim on the backboard,
- strap the victim to the backboard, and
- lift the victim from the water.

Gutter and deck construction and the type of backboard you have may influence the procedures you use while backboarding. For example, the rescuer on deck may need to adjust his or her position to allow the most effective in-line stabilization procedure. Thus, you may have to slightly alter the following procedures in order to make backboarding procedures effective at your facility. Develop procedures that are useful for your facility, using in-service training and rescue drills to establish and test those procedures.

The backboarding procedure described here is for both shallow and deep water. Ideally, two trained lifeguards should be available to perform the backboarding procedure. However, some facilities may not have other lifeguards to assist. In this case, direct another patron or supervisor in the following procedures.

This backboarding procedure requires two rescuers: rescuer 1 in the water and rescuer 2 on the deck. (In all of the procedural descriptions that follow, rescuer 1 is the rescuer in the water providing in-line stabilization at the beginning of the procedure.)

Preparing the Victim for the Backboard

1. While rescuer 1 maintains in-line stabilization and moves the victim to a position perpendicular to the side of the pool, rescuer 2 removes his or her rescue tube and lies down on the deck in preparation to provide in-line stabilization.

2. When rescuer 1 is near the side of the pool, rescuer 2 grasps the victim's arms and applies pressure to trap the head (figure 10.17a). Rescuer 1 releases the victim and rescuer 2 maintains the victim in a horizontal position (figure 10.17b).

3. Rescuer 1 places a rescue tube under the victim's knees to maintain the victim in the horizontal position (figure 10.17c and d) and checks the victim for breathing.

a.

b.

c.

d.

Figure 10.17 Stabilizing the victim at the side of the pool.

Strapping the Victim to the Backboard

4. Rescuer 1 retrieves the backboard and then submerges it under the victim. He or she first turns the backboard on edge and aligns the head-restraint pad with the victim's head; he or she then submerges the board, centers it under the victim, and allows the board to float up under the victim (figure 10.18).

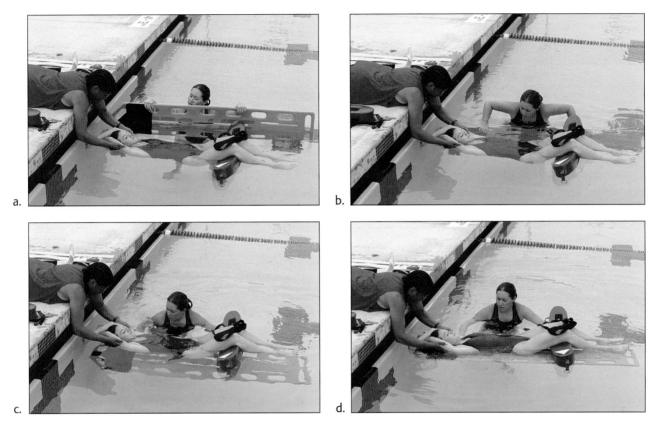

a.   b.

c.   d.

Figure 10.18   Positioning the backboard under the victim.

5. Once the board is in place, rescuer 1 attaches the chest strap, making certain the strap is snug and not under the board. He or she may attach the rest of the straps to one side of the board, but not secure them. At this point he or she places one arm on the victim's sternum and cups the victim's chin, fingers on one side and thumb on the other side, then places the other arm beneath the backboard and traps the victim to the board (figure 10.19).

a.   b.

Figure 10.19   Securing the backboard to the victim.

(continued)

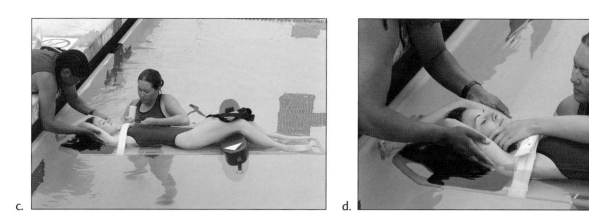

Figure 10.19 *(continued)*

6. Rescuer 2 lowers the victim's arms to his or her sides and then applies the cervical collar (figure 10.20).

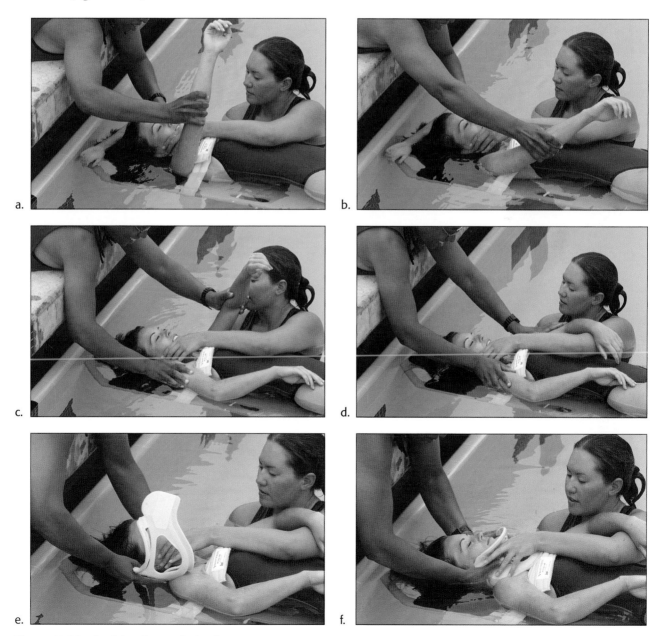

Figure 10.20 Applying the cervical collar.

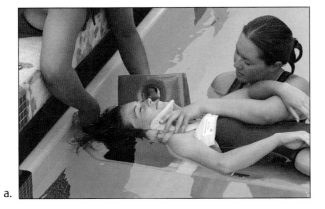

a.

7. Rescuer 2 grabs a head-immobilizer pad and positions it next to the victim's head, then places a thumb in the ear-hole of the pad and grabs the backboard. He or she then positions the second pad in the same manner (figure 10.21). This keeps the pads in contact with the backboard and allows rescuer 2 to stabilize the backboard.

b.

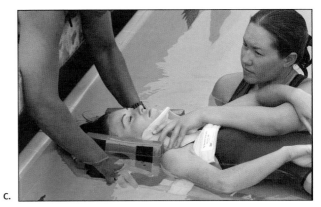

c.

Figure 10.21   Immobilizing the victim's head.

a.

8. Rescuer 1 continues securing the victim to the backboard as follows: Attach the waist strap so that it secures the victim's arms and waist (figure 10.22); move the rescue tube from under the victim's knees to a position under the foot-end of the backboard (figure 10.23); attach the knee/shin strap (figure 10.24); attach the forehead strap (figure 10.25); and place a second rescue tube under the foot-end of the backboard (figure 10.26). (All straps should be snug and should not be under the board.) The victim is now ready to be lifted out of the water.

b.

c.

Figure 10.22   Securing the waist strap.

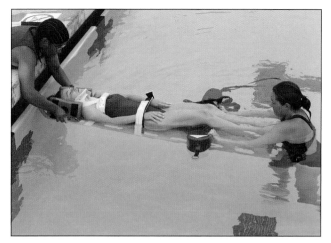

a.

b.

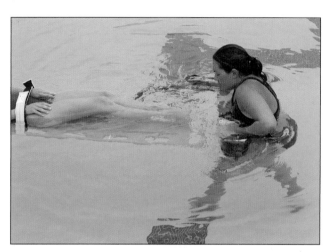

c.

d.

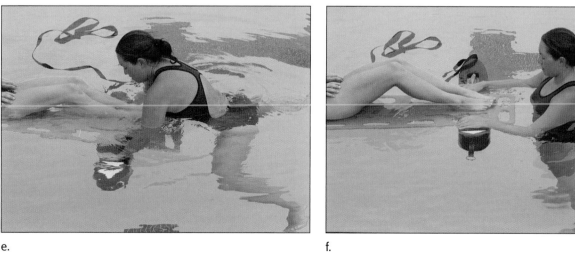

e.

f.

Figure 10.23 Moving the rescue tube from beneath the victim's knees to beneath the backboard.

a.

b.

c.

Figure 10.24 Securing the knee strap.

a.

b.

c.

Figure 10.25 Securing the forehead strap.

a.

b.

c.

Figure 10.26   Placing the second rescue tube under the backboard.

Lifting the Victim From the Water

9. Rescuer 1 stabilizes the backboard while rescuer 2 gets into position to begin the lift from the water.

10. Rescuers 1 and 2 lift the head-end of the backboard onto the deck (rescuers should coordinate efforts for this lifting process). Rescuer 1 can assist from either the water or the deck during removal of the victim from the water.

11. Rescuer 1 and 2 slide the backboard and victim onto the deck (figure 10.27).

a.

b.

Figure 10.27   Lifting the victim from the water.

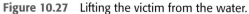

(continued)

c.

d.

e.

f.

g.

h.

Figure 10.27 *(continued)*

RESCUE BREATHING AND CPR

In some situations the victim may require rescue breathing or CPR. When the victim is stabilized on the surface at the edge of the pool, check for breathing. Look for the victim's chest to rise and fall, then listen for breathing. If the victim is breathing, the heart is beating. If the victim is not breathing, remove the victim from the water on the backboard while maintaining the head-splint. Once on deck, move the victim's arms away from the head and begin rescue breathing. Use the modified jaw-thrust technique. Check for a pulse. If the victim has no pulse, begin CPR.

You should have immediate access to a resuscitation mask, latex gloves, and safety glasses for performing rescue breathing and CPR. This is for your protection. Use the resuscitation mask or bag-valve mask during rescue breathing or CPR, as it is highly probable that the victim will regurgitate during rescue breathing. A resuscitation mask with a one-way valve will shield you from contact with the victim's body fluids. If the victim is bleeding, use the gloves and safety glasses to protect yourself from blood-borne pathogens.

An important difference in giving rescue breathing to someone who may have a spinal injury is that you cannot tilt the victim's head to clear the throat. Instead, you can use a technique called the modified jaw-thrust to accomplish this, which we describe next. It also is very likely that the victim will vomit during rescue breathing, so we explain how to clear the victim's mouth after vomiting occurs.

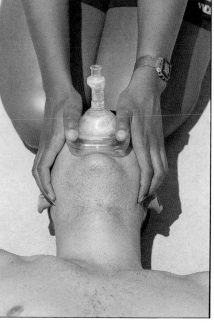

Figure 10.28 Modified jaw-thrust technique.

Modified Jaw-Thrust Technique

If you suspect the victim may have a spinal injury, do not tilt the victim's head back for rescue breathing. This could cause further damage to the spinal column. Instead, use the modified jaw-thrust technique. To perform the modified jaw-thrust, place your thumbs on the cheekbones of the victim as illustrated in figure 10.28. In a real emergency situation, be sure to wear latex gloves. The right thumb is on the right cheek, and the left thumb is on the left cheek. The index and middle fingers of both hands should be positioned on the jawbone so you can lift the victim's jaw forward (you can feel the corners of the jawbone near the victim's ears). This action moves the tongue away from the back of the throat without tilting the head back. Putting light pressure on the cheekbones will help to maintain the victim's head in a neutral position.

Once you have moved the jaw forward, check the victim for breathing. If the victim is not breathing, position the resuscitation mask over the victim's mouth and nose. Press down on the pocket mask with your thumbs while pulling the jaw forward to open the airway (see figure 10.29). Give two full breaths and check the victim's pulse. If there is no pulse, begin giving CPR. If there is a pulse but no breathing, continue rescue breathing. Give one slow, full breath every 5 seconds for an adult; give one slow, full breath every 3 seconds for a child or infant. If you cannot get air into the victim, you may need to tilt his or her head back slightly.

If you have applied a cervical collar to the victim and she or he then stops breathing, work your index and middle fingers down between the cervical collar and the victim's jaw in order to pull the jaw forward. If you cannot work your fingers into position to move the victim's jaw forward, loosen the cervical collar first and then position your fingers.

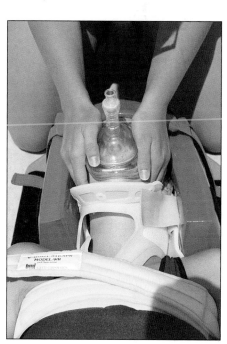

Figure 10.29 Modified jaw-thrust with pocket mask.

Victim Vomiting

If the victim vomits during neck stabilization, rotate the victim to the side and have an assistant clear the mouth of foreign matter while you maintain in-line stabilization. If the victim vomits while strapped to the board, use the following procedure on deck or, with minor modifications, in the water. (see figure 10.30):

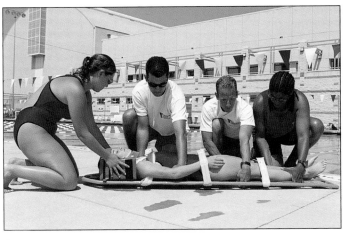

a.

b.

1. Maintain in-line stabilization.
2. Have at least three assistants position themselves on one side of the victim, with the strongest located at the victim's shoulders.
3. Have each assistant reach across the victim and grab him or her. Assistants must be sure to grab the victim, not the board; grabbing the board will result in pinched fingers. They should press the arms that cross the victim against the victim to trap him or her against the board.
4. Coordinate the tilt by counting, "One, two, three, tilt."
5. On the signal, have the assistants lift up on the side of the backboard nearest to them until the victim is angled sideways on the board.
6. Have an additional assistant clear the victim's mouth of vomit, using a clean cloth to wipe it out or a manual suction unit.
7. On a signal, have the assistants lower the victim to a flat position. Continue to monitor the victim's breathing.

c.

Figure 10.30   Turning the victim on a backboard to clear vomit from the victim's mouth.

SPECIAL SPINAL INJURY CONDITIONS

You may have to deal with two special cases of spinal injury: when the victim is in a standing or sitting position, and when the injury takes place in extremely shallow water such as a zero-depth pool. Here are the procedures for each of these cases.

Caring for a Standing or Sitting Victim

Someone who has a spinal injury will not necessarily be paralyzed. A person may sprain or strain the neck or back and be sitting at poolside or in extremely shallow water or standing in shallow water or on the deck. A victim may even walk up to you and complain of neck pain. In any of these situations, follow these general guidelines (figure 10.31):

- Stabilize the victim's head and neck. Grasp the victim's head by placing your hands on each side of the victim's face near or over the ears. Tell the victim not to move until directed to do so.

- Have another rescuer place a cervical collar on the victim; then have him or her retrieve a backboard and place it on the ground, deck, or pool bottom next to the victim.

- Instruct the victim to sit on the backboard while you maintain the head and neck in alignment with assistance from the other rescuer.

- Lay the victim back onto the board, following these steps:

  —Get on one side of the backboard and place one hand on the back of the victim's head and the other hand in the middle of the victim's back.

  —Have the other rescuer get on the opposite side of the backboard and place one hand on the victim's back at shoulder level and one hand on the lower back.

  —On a count of 1, 2, 3, both of you lower the victim to a prone position on the backboard. Maintain alignment of the victim's back, neck, and head during this procedure.

  —Slowly and carefully slide your hands out from underneath the victim. Do not allow the victim's head to drop onto the backboard.

  —Secure the victim to the backboard.

Some agencies advocate placing a backboard behind a standing victim and laying them down. This is an option, but there are some restrictions to the use of this procedure. Regardless of what technique is employed, team practice is critical.

 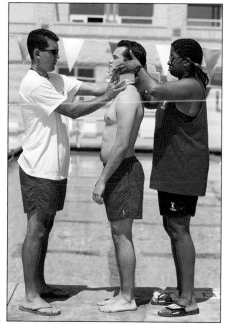

a. b.

Figure 10.31 Helping a standing victim with a spinal injury.

(continued)

c.

d.

e.

f.

g.

h.

Figure 10.31 *(continued)*

Caring for a Victim in Extremely Shallow Water

Many facilities have been built that include an extreme shallow water environment. Zero-depth pools, wave pools, spray pools, and waterfront facilities are just some examples of situations where extreme shallow water exists. Any time there is shallow water, spinal injury is always possible. Here are procedures for spinal injury management if a victim is located in extreme shallow water:

In extremely shallow water (less than 2 feet), the head-splint procedure should be applied (figure 10.32):

1. Apply the head-splint. Approach the victim from the side and move the victim's arms slowly and carefully into position.
2. Grasp the victim's right arm with your right hand and the victim's left arm with your left hand. Trap the victim's head between his or her arms.
3. After the victim's head is trapped between the arms, begin to roll the victim toward you.
4. As you roll the victim, maneuver into a position above and to the rear of the victim's head.
5. As you begin to roll the victim, step from the side of the victim toward the victim's head and turn 180 degrees. You will end up above and toward the rear of the victim's head, looking toward the victim's face and feet.
6. During the rollover, lower your arm and hand on the side of the victim that is closest to you so that the victim's arms go over the top of your arm as you step toward the victim's head.
7. Your hand position must change during this process. Maintain arm pressure against the victim's head during this maneuver.

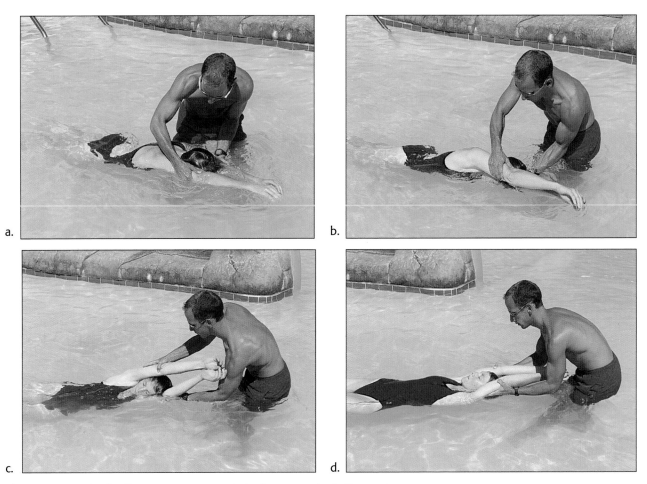

a.   b.

c.   d.

Figure 10.32 Head-splint maneuver on a victim in extremely shallow water.

If a backboard is readily available, you can roll the victim directly onto the backboard. You will need a second rescuer to assist you with this (figure 10.33).

1. The secondary rescuer moves to the victim's side and places the backboard adjacent to the victim.
2. As you begin to roll the victim, the secondary rescuer positions himself or herself near the victim's hips on the same side of the victim as you are.
3. As the victim is rolled to a prone position, the secondary rescuer angles the board to the side and beneath the victim.
4. The secondary rescuer maneuvers into a position at the side of the victim as you step toward the victim's head during the rollover.
5. As the victim is being rolled over, the secondary rescuer assists you by grasping the victim's hip and rolling him or her onto the board.

a.

b.

c.

d.

Figure 10.33   Backboarding a victim in zero-depth water.

If a backboard is not readily available, follow these procedures (figure 10.34).

1. The secondary rescuer retrieves a backboard while you turn the victim to a prone position and maintain in-line stabilization.
2. The secondary rescuer positions the backboard on edge, parallel to and beside the victim, and submerges the board under the victim.
3. If the victim is at zero depth, maintain in-line stabilization while one or more secondary rescuers assist in placing the backboard under the victim, or wait for EMS to perform the backboarding procedure.

a.

b.

c.

d.

Figure 10.34 Backboarding a victim in extremely shallow water.

In extreme shallow water, once the victim has been backboarded remove the victim from the water prior to the strapping process. You have two options for removing the victim from the water prior to strapping.

Option 1: If more than two rescuers are available, follow these guidelines (figure 10.35).

- As primary rescuer, stay at the head of the backboard and continue to apply the head-splint during the entire removal process.
- Have additional rescuers position themselves on each side of the backboard.
- Lift the backboard and transport it to a flat, level surface.
- Lower the backboard and apply the cervical collar, straps, and head restraint (see pages 212–217).

Figure 10.35 Removing the victim from shallow water using three rescuers.

Option 2: If only two rescuers are available, follow these guidelines (figure 10.36).

- The secondary rescuer places the backboard under the victim.
- As primary rescuer, you are positioned at the head and to the rear of the victim. Continue to apply the head-splint.
- Move slightly to one side of the backboard while maintaining the head-splint.
- The secondary rescuer moves next to you at the head end of the backboard.
- The secondary rescuer grasps the head end of the backboard and drags the board and victim out of the water and onto the shore.
- Walk slightly to the side of the backboard and continue to apply the head splint during removal.

a.

b.

c.

d.

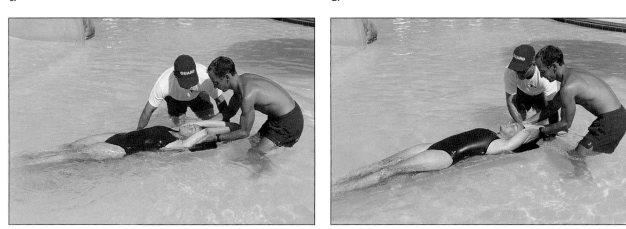

e.

f.

Figure 10.36 Two rescuers backboarding and removing a victim from extremely shallow water.

g.

h.

Figure 10.36 *(continued)*

STRAPPING THE VICTIM TO THE BACKBOARD ON DECK OR SHORE

Once the victim is removed from the water and placed on the deck or shore, follow the same backboarding procedures described earlier (pages 210–217).

PREPARING FOR SPINAL INJURY MANAGEMENT

It is crucial that you practice these spinal injury management skills on a regular basis. Periodic practice of spinal injury procedures will increase your efficiency and response time during an emergency situation. Your ability to perform these skills properly can make a difference in the quality of life a spinal injury victim may have in the future. It can also mean the difference between life and death.

Handle all potential spinal injuries with the utmost care. Your training in and practice of these skills are vital to the standard of care you provide the patrons of your facility. As you practice, follow the sequence of events shown in figure 10.37.

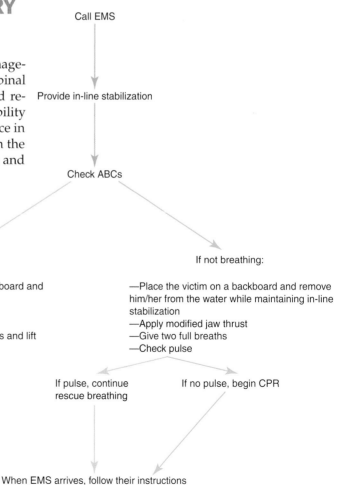

Call EMS

Provide in-line stabilization

Check ABCs

If breathing:

—Place the victim on a backboard and strap the chest

—Apply a cervical collar
—Attach the remaining straps and lift onto the deck

If not breathing:

—Place the victim on a backboard and remove him/her from the water while maintaining in-line stabilization
—Apply modified jaw thrust
—Give two full breaths
—Check pulse

If pulse, continue rescue breathing

If no pulse, begin CPR

When EMS arrives, follow their instructions

Figure 10.37 Sequence of events in a spinal emergency.

Review Questions

1. Describe the typical victim of a spinal cord injury. What is the usual situation leading up to the accident?
2. What hazards lead to spinal injuries in pools? In open water?
3. What swimming pool designs increase the risk of spinal injuries?
4. How deep should water be to allow diving from a diving board? From a starting block?
5. Why are No Diving signs so important?
6. List four conditions under which you should suspect spinal injuries.
7. Define the following: spine, vertebrae, intervertebral disk.
8. List the five regions of the spine.
9. List 11 signs of a spinal injury.
10. Describe the technique used to enter the water when a spinal injury is suspected.
11. How can you reduce water disturbance as you approach a victim?
12. List the eight steps required to turn a facedown victim over using the head-splint technique.
13. How do you stabilize a faceup victim using the head splint?
14. How should you bring a victim to the surface in shallow water? In deep water?
15. List the qualities of a good backboard.
16. Describe how to size a cervical collar.
17. Describe how to apply a cervical collar.
18. Describe how to perform the backboarding procedure.
19. When should you check for breathing and circulation?
20. What should you do if a victim is not breathing?
21. What should you do if a victim has no pulse?
22. What protective equipment should be provided for your use during rescue breathing and CPR?
23. Describe the modified jaw-thrust.
24. What should you do if a victim vomits while strapped to the board?

eleven

Hazards of the Outdoor Environment

Lifeguarding outdoors, whether you're guarding a pool or open water, poses challenges beyond those of controlled environments like indoor pools. This chapter will help you understand the outdoor environment and your responsibilities for protecting patrons from its hazards.

In This Chapter, You'll Learn About

- weather conditions and
- open water conditions.

WEATHER CONDITIONS

Understanding weather conditions is important to providing a safe environment for swimmers in your area. Although you cannot control the weather, you can take necessary precautions to prepare for weather changes and to protect the safety of the swimmers you are guarding.

Storm Conditions

A local weather forecast may warn you that a front is expected to move through your area. Barometric changes and sudden shifts of wind direction and speed are sure signs of weather changes. As warm air meets cooler air, moisture in the form of rain or a thunderstorm usually results. The forecast should be your signal to be on the lookout for storm conditions.

Cloud formations will also alert you to potentially hazardous weather. Figure 11.1 shows three types of clouds you should be familiar with. Cumulonimbus clouds, often called "thunderheads," are dark and thick, seem to have great height, and often take on an anvil shape; they signify a storm. Stratocumulus clouds are continuous, connected globes of clouds that usually occur before and after a storm. Altocumulus clouds are high, white clouds that drift across the sky. As they become larger and darker, they signal a storm.

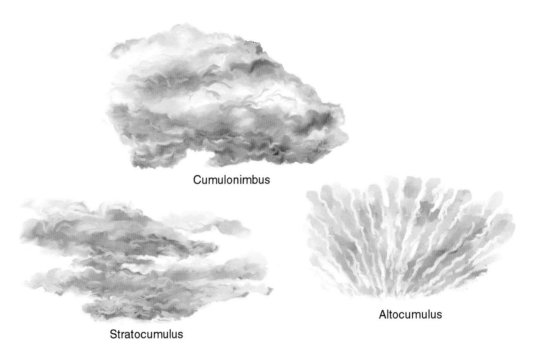

Figure 11.1   Cloud formations.

A squall line is another cloud formation that will help you determine when severe weather is on its way. A squall line usually appears as a gray bank of clouds accompanied by frothy white clouds on the horizon. It is, in fact, the approaching edge of the storm system.

Thunderclouds

As a storm approaches, you are likely to see clouds develop from stratocumulus into the classic anvil-shaped cumulonimbus thunderclouds. The height and darkness of these clouds can be signs of the severity of the associated storm.

Thunderclouds and the lightning that accompanies them are serious weather conditions. The body can act as a natural conductor of electrical current from lightning when someone is in the water or touching it, possibly resulting in death. Pools are connected to electrical equipment such as pumps and filters that can conduct charges from lightning strikes, even if the strikes are outside a building. Pools also are connected to plumbing, which can conduct charges from lightning strikes as well (U.S. Department of Commerce, 1999).

Because of this danger, the National Weather Service and the National Severe Storms Laboratory recommend that both outdoor and indoor pools be cleared during storms under two conditions (U.S. Department of Commerce, 1999): when cloud-to-ground lightning is observed and less than 30 seconds pass between the flash and the thunder; and when in-cloud lightning is occurring overhead. Storms do not have to be severe or even contain large numbers of cloud-to-ground flashes to be dangerous.

Don't take any chances when you see lightning. Follow your facility's procedures and clear the area before a storm hits. You can estimate how many miles away a storm is by counting the seconds between seeing lightning and hearing thunder, then dividing the number of seconds by 5. For example, if you count 10 seconds between lightning and thunder, the storm is about 2 miles away (sound travels 1 mile in about 5 seconds whereas light travels 1 mile almost instantly).

Even when rain-bearing clouds do not contain thunder or lightning, you may want to clear the pool if the rain becomes so intense that it is hard for lifeguards to see. This holds not only for outdoor pools, but also for indoor pools if the rain on the windows or lightning interferes with lifeguards' vision.

Guidelines for clearing swimmers from an outdoor area will depend on the type of facility, the management's policy, and the speed of the approaching storm. If there are no procedures for bad weather, encourage the staff and management to establish them, possibly patterned after similar facilities in your area. Once procedures are established, practice them. The safety of those in your area depends on it. Consider the following procedures for bad weather.

Bad Weather Procedures

- Clear and secure the area (put up equipment, lock up facility), making sure everyone is out of the water.
- Move to shelter, preferably in a building. Avoid standing in an open structure or under a tree.
- Stay away from metal objects, which might conduct electrical current.
- Get down from lifeguard stands; lightning is attracted to the highest objects.
- Don't use showers or use the phone.
- Monitor forecasts by radio or weather radio.
- Don't allow swimmers to return to the water until at least 30 minutes (or as long as is required by your state's guidelines) after you hear the last thunder or see the last lightning of the storm (U.S. Department of Commerce, 1999).

High Winds

High winds often cause changes in water conditions that could present danger for swimmers in the water who are unaware of the change. Swimming pools are not likely to be as affected by the wind as is open water like lakes, rivers, and oceans. Wind can create or enhance the size of waves, influence currents, and reduce water visibility. In any open water area, management must set standards for safe wind levels for aquatic activities.

Tornadoes and Waterspouts

Whatever your aquatic environment, tornadoes and waterspouts pose grave dangers. Tornadoes occur in thunderstorms in which there is a cold downdraft. Before the cloud contacts earth or water, it is known as a funnel cloud. If it contacts land, it is upgraded to a tornado; if it contacts water, it is called a waterspout. These cloud formations are illustrated in figure 11.2.

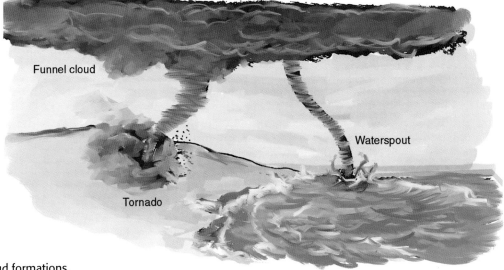

Figure 11.2 Funnel cloud formations.

Tornadoes

Because tornadoes are associated with thunderstorms, they rarely arise without warning. If you are in an area that experiences tornadoes, your local civil defense should have warning systems. Typically there are three stages of tornado alert. The first is a watch, which means that conditions are right for tornadoes to develop, not that a tornado will occur. The second stage is a warning, which means that a funnel cloud has been sighted. Finally, in most areas, a siren means that a funnel cloud has been sighted in your immediate area.

Tornado Safety Procedures

- Clear the water and surrounding area.
- Move patrons to a designated shelter (an approved tornado shelter or a strong structure) immediately.
- Avoid trailers and garage-type structures.
- Stay away from windows and doors. The safest locations are the center or lowest parts of the building or the corner closest to the storm's approach. Interior bathrooms and closets, basements, and spaces beneath stairs are good shelter choices.
- Hide under a strong table, if available, or huddle covered with towels on the floor.
- If no shelter is available, lie flat in a ditch or on a low section of ground. Where there are towers and other large objects, position yourself and others between the approaching storm and those objects. Do not seek refuge in vehicles.
- Monitor a weather station, weather radio, or civil defense frequency for progress reports on the tornado.
- Once you hear a siren warning of the tornado, remain in your safe location until you hear an all-clear signal. Such signals vary; make sure you know the one used in your community.

Waterspouts

Waterspouts are tornadoes over water. They can be weak or strong, but either type is dangerous enough to warrant action.

Weak waterspouts form from one of a line of cumulus clouds when winds are very light. Showers, but not thunderstorms, are usually nearby. Weak waterspouts have winds around 40 knots and lose strength quickly if they come onshore. Most have no particular direction and usually dissipate in about 10 minutes. Despite their weakness and short life, these waterspouts can overturn objects or throw them around, so it's best to evacuate the water and have patrons move inland at least 100 yards. Because weak waterspouts move slowly, there's usually plenty of time to get everyone to safety.

Strong waterspouts are much more dangerous. They form from cumulonimbus clouds and are usually accompanied by lightning and thunder. Usually moving in the same direction as the thunderstorm, they may reach forward speeds of 50 knots or more. Strong waterspouts can spin at up to 200 knots and have been known to damage boats and structures on land and to kill people. If a strong waterspout should occur, quickly clear the water and have patrons move to a solidly constructed, permanent structure.

The National Weather Service issues a Special Marine Warning whenever a waterspout is spotted, whatever its strength. If you hear such an alert, follow your facility's procedures for getting patrons to safety.

Fog

Fog occurs when the ground or water surface is warm and the air is cool and moist. The resulting sensation of being inside a cloud can severely reduce visibility and the safety of those in your aquatic area. If the fog limits your ability to see swimmers or boaters in your area of responsibility, clear the water and close the facility until conditions improve.

Fair Weather

We don't often think of good weather as dangerous, but it holds some uncontrollable hazards for which you should be prepared. Hot summer days usually bring people to the water. Heatstroke, heat exhaustion, and sunburn are just some of the hazards you'll face. First aid for hyperthermia was discussed in chapter 9; it can also affect you and your ability to guard.

Sunburn is not just uncomfortable; it also can be dangerous. The primary cause of skin cancer is prolonged and repeated overexposure to sunlight. The American Cancer Society estimates that 500,000 Americans develop preventable and curable skin cancer each year. To avoid sunburn and to reduce your risk of developing skin cancer, take the following personal precautions.

Sunburn Precautions

- Wear a suitable sunscreen. The American Cancer Society recommends a sunscreen with a sun protection factor (SPF) of 15. Use a higher protection level for sensitive areas, like the face and the tops of the feet.
- No sunscreen is water-resistant; reapply after swimming or sweating.
- Wear a hat.
- Wear sunglasses with a good UV (ultraviolet ray) rating to reduce glare and exposure to ultraviolet sunlight.
- Wear a uniform shirt.

To further protect yourself from the dangers of skin cancers, examine your body regularly for lesions and for changes in moles, freckles, or pigmented areas. If you notice any changes, contact your doctor or a dermatologist.

OPEN WATER CONDITIONS

In contrast with pools, open water environments have particular characteristics and risks. One of the most significant differences is the constantly changing nature of open water environments. The ocean, for example, may be calm one moment and rough and dangerous the next as a squall moves landward. In any open water, currents may shift, debris may wash in or out, and sandbars may move as conditions change. As an open water lifeguard, you need to be aware of the characteristics and dangers of the environment and know how to respond to them.

Water Temperature and Clarity

Water temperature and clarity are common issues of concern in any open water. In most open water areas, water temperature varies greatly depending on the time of the swimming season. The water is generally colder both early and late in the season. As you learned in chapter 9, cold water can increase the risk of hypothermia for swimmers and lifeguards. Figure 9.12 on page 185 provides a graphic review of water temperature and survival time.

Usually water temperature is layered in *thermoclines*, with the warmer water on the top. Normally the warmer water stays at the surface, but a shift in the surface temperature can cause the warmer water to cool and drop. This could take a swimmer who is not used to cold water by surprise, and fatigue and hypothermia can set in more quickly in these conditions.

Shallow lakes or ponds generally turn over due to thermoclines twice each year, once in the spring and again in the fall. This thermocline activity adds to the seasonal water temperature extremes.

Water clarity should be monitored, particularly in an area with nearby industry. In the absence of water circulation, certain conditions could make the water excessively murky and unhealthy. Report factors such as discoloration, temperature changes, dead fish, or a putrid smell to local health officials. These conditions could pose health hazards in your area.

Ocean Environment

A combination of wind and bottom conditions contributes to the size of ocean surf. The stronger the wind and the sharper the drop-off, the larger and stronger the waves. Be familiar with the surf conditions in your area.

Winds

Depending on the wind conditions, waves can take many forms. The fetch is the distance of open water over which any wind blows to develop waves (see figure 11.3). The longer the fetch, the greater the possibility of large waves. (So you expect to see larger waves in an ocean than in a lake.)

Two other wind-related terms are important for your awareness of potential dangers. An *onshore wind*, one that blows toward the shore, brings debris inland. Be alert for objects floating or suspended in the waves. An *offshore wind*, on the other hand, blows toward the water and can carry flotation devices and unsuspecting swimmers from shallow into deeper water. Be aware of these possibilities and act to prevent swimmers from getting into situations they can't handle.

Waves

Several terms are used to describe parts of waves (see figure 11.3). The *peak* (or *crest*) is the highest point of the wave, at which it breaks either from right to left or left to right. When the wind forces the top of the wave into the trough, the wave is said to be *spilling*. *Foam* describes whitewater; air is trapped in the water, giving the wave a foamy appearance. The shallow area where waves break is known as the *surf zone*.

You should become familiar with several different types of waves (see figure 11.3). Gently sloping waves generally found in deep water are called *spilling* or *rolling waves*;

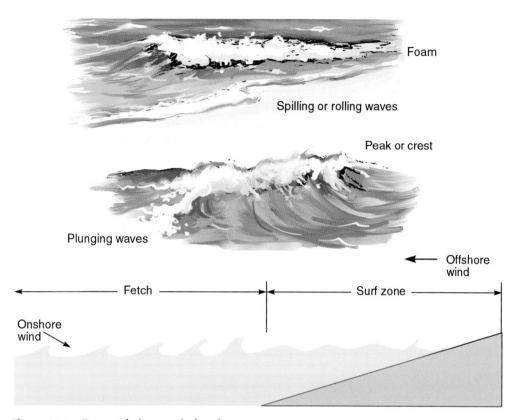

Foam

Spilling or rolling waves

Peak or crest

Plunging waves

Offshore wind

Fetch — Surf zone

Onshore wind

Figure 11.3 Terms relating to wind and waves.

they are not particularly dangerous. *Plunging waves* occur either near shore or in shallow water over a sand bar or reef because the bottom slows the speeding water. The break can be quite strong and is caused by water being pushed over the crest of the wave. These waves can be dangerous, especially to inexperienced bathers, who may jump up to avoid the force of an oncoming wave instead of ducking under it. When lifeguarding, you may want to warn such bathers about this danger.

Running and plunging into waves is dangerous; don't allow patrons in your areas to do so. The waves may contain debris that could cause serious injury.

Sets and Lulls

A series of breaking waves is called a *set*, and the calm between sets is the *lull*. Any wave can be dangerous because it could knock an unsuspecting swimmer down. But lulls are dangerous too; they give swimmers a rest period in which they may become unprepared for the next series of waves or be swept farther out to sea in a rip current.

Tides

Tides are created by the gravitational pull exerted by the sun and moon on the earth's water. Water is pulled away from the shore during low tide (ebb tide), becoming more shallow, and moves toward the shore during high tide (flood tide), making the water deeper. Tidal variations usually are greater on U.S. northern beaches than on southern beaches.

The primary danger associated with the change in tides is that swimmers may inaccurately estimate the depth of the water they are swimming in; a poor swimmer may panic upon trying to stand and finding that the water is too deep. A secondary danger created by tides is variation in prevailing currents. Lifeguards must be aware of these tidal variations in depth and current to protect swimmers in their areas from danger. Take time to learn about how the tides affect any area where you work or swim.

Parallel Current

A parallel current usually is caused by waves that break on the shore at an angle. Also known as a *longshore*, *lateral*, or *littoral current*, these currents can sweep swimmers parallel to the shore. Swimmers or rescuers caught in a parallel current should not try to move straight in to the shore, even though it is the shortest distance. Rather, they should go with the current and gradually angle in; they will arrive on shore safely without having become fatigued from fighting the current.

Runback

The return flow of water from waves that have rolled ashore is a *runback*, often called an *undertow*, or *backrush*. Contrary to popular belief, it does not pull objects out to sea. The strong runback instead moves under the approaching waves, pulling objects down into the water. The strength of the runback, which depends on the slope of the shoreline, usually lessens at a depth of 3 feet.

Rip Currents

A *rip*, or *runout*, is a current created where there is a break in a sandbar or reef just offshore or around structures such as piers, jetties, or other barriers. Such a current forms when water rushes out to sea in a narrow path (Sea Grant, n.d.) (see figure 11.4). It picks up speed as it moves through the channel and dissipates after passing through. Some currents are present a few hours; others are more permanent. They are more prevalent after storms (Sea Grant, n.d.).

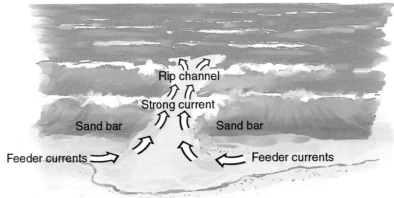

Figure 11.4 Rip current.

Rip currents are the most common surf condition for which beach lifeguards must be prepared. A rip current usually looks different from the surrounding surf and is easy to spot from an elevated position. Learn to spot these currents and keep swimmers away from them. Key characteristics include the following:

- The rip may be a different color than the surrounding water, either because of dirt and sand stirred up from the bottom or because the water is deeper (Sea Grant, n.d.).
- The rip waves may be large and choppy, while the waves in front of the barriers that caused the rip may be smaller and calmer (Sea Grant, n.d.).
- The rip may have an offshore plume of turbid water past the barrier (Sea Grant, n.d.).
- The rip may contain floating debris moving seaward.
- Rip currents have stronger force after a wave set has hit the shore.
- People swimming in or near the rip will be drawn to the sea.
- A rip may have one to as many as three feeder currents.

Many beach areas have permanent rip currents. These areas should be a key point in your watch and should be indicated by posted warnings or warning flags, especially on rough or windy days. A permanent rip is caused when the ocean floor is deeper in one spot than in the surrounding area. Stationary objects projecting into the water, such as rocks or piers, may cause such a rip; they may be present for an extended period or may change from season to season. A flash rip is a temporary rip generated by a sudden wave buildup, generally resulting from unusual wind or water conditions changing quickly. Flow from rip currents continually changes the bottom conditions and causes hazards to those unfamiliar with the danger.

Because the rip current is pulling seaward, it is too tiring for swimmers to try to swim directly to shore to escape it. Instead, a swimmer caught in a rip should signal for help and swim parallel to the shore or drift out with the current until the seaward pull decreases to a level that swimming toward shore is possible. The swimmer should then swim parallel to shore for a short distance to move away from the rip current and finally swim toward shore.

For a rescue, use the rip to your advantage to get to the victim quickly. Waves will seldom break in through a rip, which will make it easier for you to maintain eye contact with the victim as you approach.

Marine life

A final potentially hazardous ocean element is the marine life. Most aquatic creatures are as frightened of swimmers as swimmers are of them; in fact, most are quite passive unless threatened. Still, some injuries are likely to occur. Some aquatic animals, such as jellyfish and the Portuguese man-of-war (see figure 11.5), have long tentacles that inflict painful stings. Some shells and coral can inject venom or inflict sharp cuts. Reactions to these contacts can range from a mild stinging sensation to shock, nausea, and respiratory difficulty. If the reaction is severe, seek medical attention immediately.

Figure 11.5   Stinging marine life: jellyfish (left) and Portuguese man-of-war.

First aid for most jellyfish, Portuguese man-of-war, or sea anemone stings is simple. Rinse the affected area with sea water (not fresh water) and soak the skin with vinegar or isopropyl alcohol. If vinegar or alcohol is not available, meat tenderizer, a baking soda paste, or ammonia diluted with 3 parts water will soothe the skin irritation. Do not use ice or rub the skin. Encourage the injured person to stay out of the water. Contact EMS if the victim doesn't know what stung him or her, if the sting is on the face or neck, or if the victim displays any allergic reaction or difficulty in breathing.

On surf beaches, predatory fish such as sharks, barracudas, and bluefish are threats, and you must be on the lookout for them. Most shark attacks occur near shore, most often between the first sandbar and the shore but sometimes between sandbars where sharks may be trapped at low tide or near steep drop-offs. On southeastern beaches, attacks occur most often in the winter and early spring.

Here is some advice you can give patrons for avoiding a shark attack:

- Always swim in a group. A shark is less likely to attack a group of people than an isolated individual.
- Avoid swimming in darkness or at dawn or dusk, when light is limited and sharks have a competitive advantage.
- Do not enter the water if you are bleeding from an open wound or menstruating.
- Avoid wearing shiny objects, which approximate the sheen of light on fish scales.
- Do not enter the water if a shark is known to be present, and evacuate the water if a shark is seen.
- Do not wander too far from shore.
- Avoid water with known effluents.
- Avoid waters being used for commercial or sport fishing.
- Use extra caution when water is murky.
- Refrain from excessive splashing.
- Exercise caution when occupying the area between sandbars or near steep drop-offs.
- Do not provoke sharks.

As a lifeguard, you have the responsibility to alert patrons to the presence of all dangerous marine life. Learn about the types in your area so you know the proper precautions.

Rivers and Streams

In rivers and streams, as in the ocean, currents can be particularly dangerous because they change so frequently. As currents shift, unsuspecting swimmers can be caught in a current and carried away from shore. Watch for changes in the currents and be prepared to act.

Current strength is very deceptive. If you are caught in a river current, do not try to swim directly against it—you'll only tire yourself out. Swim diagonally across the current until you escape its strength (see figure 11.6).

Never run and plunge into moving water. As in oceans, the current may carry debris, which in addition to being potentially hazardous may change the bottom contour. Such changes make diving very dangerous.

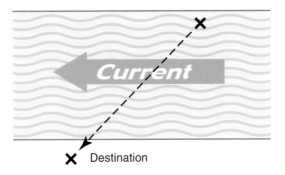

Figure 11.6 Swimming diagonally across a river current.

Lakes, Ponds, and Quarries

In fresh water such as lakes, ponds, or quarries (open, excavated holes created to mine rock), underwater weeds and other plant life pose potential danger. The plants themselves are not dangerous, but they catch swimmers by surprise. A swimmer who panics at contact with weeds could become entangled as a result of frantic and erratic attempts to escape. The panic, not the entanglement, is the real danger.

If you encounter weeds yourself, remain calm and use slow, subtle shaking movements to escape the entanglement. If you must rescue someone who has become entangled, your first task will be to calm the victim and get him or her to stop thrashing about. Give the victim your rescue tube or buoy to provide some flotation assistance; it will provide some security and give you a chance to untangle the victim's feet. When swimming out of an area of underwater weeds, modify your crawl or breaststroke by kicking minimally to avoid entanglement.

Review Questions

1. What conditions indicate that a storm is approaching?
2. What procedures should you follow when bad weather is detected?
3. List the tornado safety procedures.
4. How can you avoid sunburn?
5. What should you look for when examining yourself for possible skin cancer?
6. What two issues are of concern in assessing water conditions?
7. Why are tides of concern to open water lifeguards?
8. List the different kinds of currents you might encounter in an open water environment.
9. How do you provide first aid for a jellyfish sting?
10. How do you reduce your chances of being attacked by a shark?
11. How would you swim out of a strong current in a river?
12. How would you escape from being tangled in weeds?

twelve

Lifeguarding on the Waterfront

Although most YMCA-certified lifeguards work in pool settings, some guard in open water environments, such as oceans, lakes, ponds, or rivers. As you just learned, these environments present some concerns not found in pools. To handle the changing conditions of open water and to cope with disadvantages of lifeguarding outdoors, such as larger areas to guard, greater distances to communicate over, and delays in obtaining EMS assistance, waterfront lifeguards need to know additional special procedures.

▷ **In This Chapter, You'll Learn About**
- waterfront procedures,
- scuba safety, and
- search and rescue operations.

NEED FOR ADDITIONAL TRAINING

As stated in the *United States Lifesaving Association Manual for Open Water Lifesaving* (1995), lifeguarding in open water requires a high level of fitness and additional training. Beach lifeguards need extensive experience in swimming in open water. They may be stationed in remote locations where advanced medical support can be delayed, and they may have other responsibilities such as aiding distressed boaters, law enforcement, cliff rescue, flood rescue, marine firefighting, and scuba search and rescue. In addition, they may need to operate emergency vehicles, rescue boats, and other technical equipment. Because of this, they require more in-depth training.

Open water presents guards with different conditions than a pool:

- Water temperature and clarity depend on the natural environment.
- Long distance swimming in adverse conditions may be necessary.
- Natural hazards, such as surf, currents, and severe weather, can cause problems.
- Attendance levels and hours are not controlled.

The United States Lifesaving Association (USLA) provides a certification specifically for surf lifeguards. For more information, contact the USLA, P.O. Box 366, Huntington Beach, CA 92648. The relationship between the USLA and the YMCA is described in more depth in appendix E.

WATERFRONT PROCEDURES

Having learned about open water environments in the previous chapter, you now need to consider how those environments change your role as a lifeguard. To this point, we have discussed primarily procedures that are most appropriate for lifeguarding at a pool. If you will be working at an open water area, beach areas, conditions, and equipment require some additional specific training. We'll address these in a surf environment, with some variations for lakes, rivers, and ponds.

Selection of a Beach Area

Many beautiful beachfront areas are not acceptable for recreational swimming. For a waterfront area to be designated as a swimming beach, various factors must be considered:

- Shoreline
- Water conditions and purity
- Bottom conditions
- Marine life
- Obstructions (sandbars, shipwrecks, etc.)
- Boat traffic
- Local current and tide conditions

Shoreline
To be selected as a beach site, an open water area must have a relatively unobstructed stretch of shore that allows lifeguards a clear view of all swimming areas and has adequate access for emergency vehicles. Piers, wharfs, and other such obstructions create hazards for both swimmers and lifeguards. The shoreline must have suitable locations for elevated lifeguard stands. On an ocean beach, these stands may be fixed or may be movable to allow lifeguards close access to the water at both high and low tides.

Water Conditions and Purity
Both the height of waves as they come ashore and water depth are factors in selecting a swimming beach. Large crashing waves are certainly not conducive to recreational swimming. The best open water swimming areas are also not very deep. Shallow water offers several advantages:

- Waves tend to break farther from shore.
- More people enjoy shallow water because they know they can stand up if they are knocked over by a wave.
- Area markings are more consistent because tethers anchored to the bottom are not as long, keeping markers from drifting as much.

Water purity is also important—any swimming area should be reasonably free of pollution from nearby industry and shipping channels. The local health department should run appropriate tests over several weeks to gather conclusive data about water cleanliness.

Bottom Conditions

Avoid areas with sharp drop-offs, which in addition to catching swimmers unaware can accentuate the effects of tides, rip currents, and winds. In shallow water, sandbars may build, which can create steep drop-offs and troughs. Gently sloping conditions are best, both for swimmers' comfort and for anchoring lifelines and markers.

Marine Life

Virtually every open water area will have some marine life. People selecting swimming beaches must evaluate the types of life in the area, their effect on swimmers, and the swimmers' effect on the marine life. For example, areas where seaweed is common should be avoided; swimmers could become entangled, panic, and drown. Similarly, areas that tend to collect jellyfish, sea urchins, and microscopic bacteria are not suitable for swimming.

Some marine life will not harm humans, but the presence of people threatens the marine life. For example, swimming areas should not be set up in spawning areas.

Obstructions

Rocks, sandbars, ledges, pilings, piers, and sunken or partially submerged wrecks can be dangerous to swimmers and lifeguards. These obstructions can create rip currents and modify the flow of water unpredictably. Swimmers could be pulled into such obstructions and be injured or entangled, and lifeguards are placed at a disadvantage in dealing with such objects. They obstruct the lifeguard's view and then endanger life during a rescue. Such conditions should be avoided in selecting swimming areas.

Boat Traffic

Any swimming area should be relatively free of intrusion by boats of any size. In addition to the obvious danger associated with a boat moving through a group of swimmers, the pollution from oil and wastes and the wake left as the boat moves on are hazardous.

Currents

The best open water swimming areas are those that are relatively unaffected by currents and tides. Bays and inlets offer excellent conditions, as do protected areas well inside a breakwater. Although some current is unavoidable, try to stay away from areas with a history of strong currents. On rivers, be especially careful of areas near low-head dams.

Other Considerations

Other factors should be taken into account in selecting a beach area:

- The availability of funds and personnel to build and maintain the necessary facilities and equipment
- The age and experience level of those expected to use the area
- The proximity of rescue and first aid facilities and the means to call for assistance (phone, radio links)

Once the decision has been made to create a swimming area, your association will need to develop facility operations. Those operations should conform to all local, state, and federal health and safety codes and ordinances (Aquatic Council, n.d.). For more on safety in waterfront facilities, see appendix F.

Marking the Swimming Area

The swimming area should be marked by flags, buoys, and lifelines. These items serve somewhat standardized roles at all beaches.

Flags

Flags are used to identify boundaries predominantly in ocean settings. The outside boundaries of the guarded area of a beach are marked by flags posted on the beach. The international convention is to plant two flags—at one end a flag with a red horizontal stripe, at the other end a flag with a yellow horizontal stripe—on 12-foot poles to designate the swimming area. The poles are movable and allow lifeguards the flexibility to change the designated swimming area to avoid strong currents.

A second type of flag, to signal the present conditions, should appear on every beach. Such flags are usually attached to posts at the entrance to the beach area and on each lifeguard stand. One example of the flag system operates on the following color coding:

- Red: Dangerous conditions. No swimming allowed.
- Yellow: Lifeguard on duty. Hazardous conditions require some caution; only experienced swimmers should enter the water.
- Green: Lifeguard on duty. It is safe for all swimmers to enter the water.

An explanation of your facility's color coding should be posted.

Buoys and Safety Floats

Brightly colored buoys or safety floats may also be used to mark the swimming area. Large buoys anchored to the bottom can be spaced along the perimeter of the swimming area. On beaches using the buoy system, lifeguards must check a diagram of the swimming area regularly to be sure that wind, surf, and storm conditions have not caused a change in the location of the buoys. Buoys are used not only in surf conditions but also on freshwater beaches. Even in these areas, the lifeguard should regularly verify the placement of the buoys.

Buoys should have legible markings and no sharp edges, and they should be anchored securely (Aquatic Council, n.d.). They also must be maintained properly in ocean environments. If they are not cleaned regularly, various marine organisms will attach themselves to the buoys, making the buoys dangerous to touch.

Buoys and their anchors should be removed from the water at the end of the season. The long winter months can damage the buoys or anchor lines, cutting short their lifespan.

Lifelines

Some beach areas use lifelines to designate the outer boundaries of the swimming area. The lines are generally set to angle in away from shore. As a result, the shoreline boundary is wider than the one opposite. Lines are anchored onshore and attached to a weighted anchor in the water. The angle of the lifeline will vary somewhat due to the wind and tide action.

Although some areas also provide a lifeline at the edge of the swimming area farthest from shore, this demarcation is not recommended because swimmers are often tempted to "swim to the rope." During low tide that may be no problem—the swimmer can still touch the bottom if necessary—but during high tide the water may be considerably deeper, making the swim to the rope unwise.

Lifeguard Stations

In waterfront situations, two types of lifeguard stations may be useful: lifeguard towers and floating lifeguard stands. Each has certain advantages. Regardless of the type, lifeguard facilities must be maintained for safe use and must meet applicable codes (Aquatic Council, n.d.).

Lifeguard Towers

Depending on the prevailing conditions, lifeguard stations may be enclosed or simply elevated chairs. Enclosed lifeguard stations offer protection from the elements, fewer distractions by beach patrons, good visibility, and a storage area for rescue equipment. They are also highly visible to those on the beach who need assistance. Enclosed stations do have a disadvantage, though, in that they are usually erected at a point near the water during high tide, and thus at low tide they are farther from the waterline.

One solution to that problem is to erect a high, sturdy lifeguard chair that is portable—the lifeguard moves the chair to be close to the water's edge. This chair, however, does not offer storage space. In almost all instances a stationary tower is preferable to a portable chair.

Floating Lifeguard Stands

On a waterfront, it may be useful to have lifeguards designated to patrol an area from a paddleboard, boat, or floating deck. The advantage of a floating lifeguard stand is that the guard is already in the water should a problem arise. The guard is also more able to enforce rules if she or he is closer to the swimmers.

Boats are a bit more difficult to use than paddleboards or floating decks, but they have some advantages. Boats can provide a safety barrier by sandwiching swimmers between the guard in the chair and the guard in the boat. They also put the guard in the water in a position to help keep other boats away from the swimming area. Special training is required for using a boat in rescue operations.

Equipment for Open Water Beaches

The equipment required to operate a safe open water beach is significantly different from what is needed at a pool. Besides making sure that each lifeguard has an RFD (rescue tube or buoy) with him or her, your facility will need

- a more sophisticated communication system;
- paddleboards;
- mask, fins, snorkel, skin diving vest, and possibly a weight belt;
- boats; and
- vehicles, in addition to other specialized rescue equipment.

All emergency equipment should be inspected daily (Aquatic Council, n.d.).

Communication System

Because lifeguard stations are more spread out at a beach than at a pool and because the area patrolled there is much larger, it may be impossible to communicate by whistle blasts. For communicating with beach patrons, power megaphones, air horns, and public address systems are excellent options.

On a beach, each lifeguard should have a telephone or a two-way radio to communicate with other guards and emergency personnel. Emergency phone numbers should be posted with each phone (Aquatic Council, n.d.). The radio systems are often linked to a local emergency frequency so that help can be summoned immediately.

In an emergency, the lifeguard should not have to spend much time communicating the problem. For that reason, a code system has been developed by many agencies. Check with your local police and fire departments and EMS to determine how they want you to quickly communicate your needs.

When sending a message on the radio, proceed with guidelines similar to those used in calling for emergency assistance at a pool:

- Give your name and the name of the person or service being called.
- Await acknowledgment by that person or service.
- State your location.
- Speaking slowly, give your message as distinctly as possible.
- Await acknowledgment of your message.
- Sign off with your name.

Figure 12.1   Paddleboard with passenger.

Paddleboards

Paddleboards (figure 12.1), also known as rescue boards or rescue surfboards, are versatile. Because of their buoyancy, they can be used as floating lifeguard stands or for quick transportation to a victim in light to moderate surf. They also can be used to carry a victim back to shore, and their flat surfaces make in-water rescue breathing easier.

Paddleboards are available in a variety of lengths and widths and are made of plastic or fiberglass. A good paddleboard has a tapered nose (front) on the underside to help keep the nose above the water's surface and a skeg or skegs (a type of rudder) to keep the board from slipping sideways due to wind or choppy water.

Paddleboards should be kept near the water and checked daily for any needed repairs. The surfaces should be kept smooth for maneuverability and for the comfort of the rescuer and victim. Boards should be kept waxed to avoid slippage during a rescue.

A paddleboard can be mounted from either side. To mount one, reach across the middle of the board, grab the far side, and kick onto the board while leaning it slightly toward you. To mount it from the rear, grab the stern or back end by placing a hand on each side. Kick and belly up onto the board while pressing it down. Slide up toward the center (beam) to a position where the bow (front) rides just above the water's surface. Be sure to center your torso and hips in order to prevent the paddleboard from rolling over when paddling.

To propel the paddleboard, lay flat with your chin resting on the top surface and use an alternating crawl stroke or a butterfly arm movement. To make a wide turn, use a breaststroke movement with one arm while holding on to the side of the board with the other hand. To make a spin turn, in which the paddleboard turns on its axis, make a backward sweep stroke with one hand and a forward sweep stroke with the other on the surface of the water.

To rescue an active victim using a paddleboard, paddle to the victim as quickly as possible using an alternating crawl-type stroke or butterfly arm stroke, then do the following:

1. Position the board to bring it in front of the victim. As the bow of the paddleboard approaches the victim's face, stop it by placing both hands in the water by your hips.

2. Slide off the board on the side opposite the victim and push the board to the victim until he or she can grab it. You may need to reach across the board to help the victim gain a hold (figure 12.2). Reassure the victim that everything will be all right.

a.

b.

Figure 12.2   Rescuing an active victim using a paddleboard.

3. After the victim calms down, stabilize the board as he or she crawls onto it. Then tell the victim to hold on to each side of the board, centering the body with legs extended back and feet over the side in the water.

4. Once the victim is securely on the board, move to the rear (stern), grab the board with both hands, and slide up onto the board until your chin rests on the victim's buttocks. Be sure to adjust your body position so that the board is balanced with the bow (nose) slightly above the water's surface. Be sure the victim is lying flat with his or her head turned to one side or the other as you paddle to shallow water.

To rescue a passive victim, use the same approach as for an active victim. Then follow these steps (figure 12.3):

1. When the paddleboard is stopped near the victim's head, quickly flip the board upside down, turning it toward you.

2. Crawl back onto and across the paddleboard.

3. Reach over the board and under the water to grab one of the victim's wrists. Bring the victim's entire arm across the top of the board toward you. Position the victim beyond the beam toward the stern (tail end). Hold that arm on the board (be very careful not to hit the victim's face on the side of the paddleboard).

4. Reach down with your free hand and bring the victim's other arm over the board.

5. Place the victim's hands one on top of the other, then place your hand on top of the victim's hands.

a.

b.

c.

d.

Figure 12.3 Rescuing a passive victim using a paddleboard.

6. Reach across the board with your free hand and grab the board's edge. Press down on the victim's hands while you roll the paddleboard over toward you. The victim is now facedown across and on top of the board with her or his arms in the water.

7. Roll the victim onto her or his back toward the stern, or back, of the paddleboard and begin the ABCs. Use your resuscitation mask for rescue breathing if necessary.

8. Transport the victim in this position to shallow water or a dock if he or she needs rescue breathing (one breath every 5 seconds). If the victim does not require rescue breathing, carefully slide the victim's arms and legs onto the board after rolling the victim over. Be sure to center the victim's entire body lengthwise down the middle of the board. Move the victim's feet so one is over each side of the board, then mount the board as you did for the active victim. Paddle carefully so as not to turn the board over.

Be careful when using a paddleboard in a crowded surf zone or a swimming area. Its size and weight can cause serious injury to a patron who is knocked into the board or is hit by it as it cuts through the water. In rough surf you should stay prone to reduce the chances of losing your balance and being knocked off the paddleboard.

Figure 12.4 Skin diving gear.

Skin Diving Gear

In waterfront areas you may have to skin dive in order to rescue victims who are submerged in deep or low-visibility water or to mount an underwater search and rescue. To do this, you will require skin diving gear, including a mask, fins, snorkel, vest, and possibly a weight belt if needed (figure 12.4). Such gear should be standard equipment at lifeguard stations for open water, as well as for deep water pools (pools with depths greater than 12 feet).

You will need special training to learn to skin dive, including the standard hand signals used to indicate whether a diver is OK or is in trouble and needs help. You also will have to learn how to fit the equipment properly and how to clear the mask and snorkel.

Masks.   The air space between your eyes and the water provided by a mask enables you to see clearly underwater. Several styles of masks are available, varying in the amount of peripheral vision they allow and the ease with which you can clear water out of your mask. Avoid masks that do not cover the nose because they do not allow you to equalize pressure in the mask.

Whatever mask you select, try this test to determine whether it fits properly: Without putting the strap over your head, position the mask on your face, enclosing your eyes and nose. Inhale through your nose and hold your breath. If the mask stays firmly in place, it fits your face properly.

Even the best-fitting mask will sometimes become filled with water. Should that happen, don't panic. In some instances you can simply pull the mask away from your face, surface, drain the mask, and start over again. There is, however, no need to surface to clear the mask. Just follow these procedures (figure 12.5):

1. While underwater, position yourself vertically, holding the mask in one or two hands.

2. Place the palm of your hand on the center and top of the mask and press the mask in toward your forehead. Or place both hands on the side of the mask and press the mask toward your forehead.

3. Begin to exhale through your nose. Look up and continue to exhale until all the water is out of the mask.

4. Surface with your hand up and your head up, then give the OK signal.

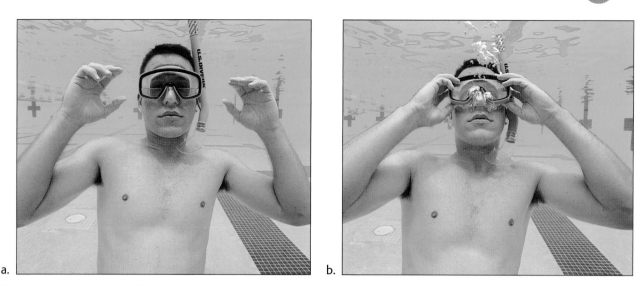

a.   b.

Figure 12.5 Clearing the face mask underwater.

Fins.   Using fins will extend the power and strength of your kick. Fins come in two types, open heel and closed heel (also called a full-foot shoe fin). An open heel fin requires the use of a bootie for better fit and comfort. The closed heel fits over the foot without a bootie. Fins used by open water lifeguards for swimming through rough surf have heel straps and short blades and are fairly rigid. Because more strength is needed for large, rigid fins, most swimmers will want fins with moderate rigidity and medium-size blades.

Put fins on in the water to prevent tripping while on land. To swim with fins, use one of three main kicks: flutter, dolphin, or scissors. Try each of the kicks to see which one gives you the best speed. Fins let you cover more distance in less time while expending less energy. This ability, which is what makes wearing fins fun, also makes them useful in searching for submerged victims.

Snorkels.   The snorkel should be attached to your mask strap with a "snorkel keeper" (see the loop on the snorkel in figure 12.6) to ensure proper positioning when you surface and try to clear the snorkel. As your snorkel goes underwater, water will fill it. Do not breathe in until the snorkel has been cleared.

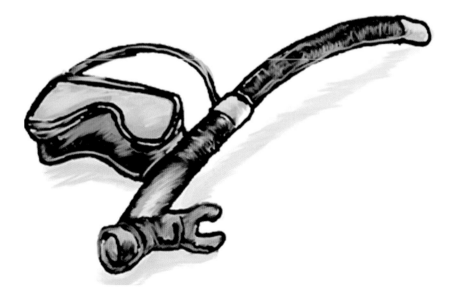

Figure 12.6 Snorkel attached to a mask with a "snorkel keeper."

When water gets into your snorkel, you will need to clear it. The two methods for clearing a snorkel are the blast method (figure 12.7) and the displacement method (figure 12.8). To perform the blast method, surface with your hand up and your head up. At the surface, look down and blow out forcefully to clear the snorkel, breathe in easily and blast again, then give the OK signal. To perform the displacement method, surface with your hand up and your head up. Just before reaching the surface, gently exhale into the snorkel, making sure the top of the snorkel is positioned down. When your head breaks the surface, tilt your head forward and breathe easily using the snorkel. Give the OK signal.

Figure 12.7 Blast method for clearing the snorkel.

Figure 12.8 Displacement method for clearing the snorkel.

Skin diving vests.   Because positive buoyancy can be helpful when you want to rest at the surface or carry something, wear a buoyancy vest whenever you skin dive. The vest fits around your neck and secures with various straps (see figure 12.4, page 248). A standard feature of a skin diving vest is an oral inflation tube. Some vests have a CO_2 detonator. You must care for the detonator at the end of every day of diving or it will not function reliably (Graver, 1999).

Weight belts.   A weight belt is needed for skin diving when a lifeguard would have difficulty achieving negative buoyancy without one. A weight belt is made of 2-inch wide heavy nylon webbing (see figure 12.4, page 248). You can thread the belt through lead weights, wrap pouches of lead shot around the belt, or put weights or pouches of lead shot into pockets on pocket-type belts (Graver, 1999).

Boats

The type of boat needed at a particular beach depends on the kind of service it will see. Boats are often used as lifeguard stands in the water, as rescue tools, and to perform a variety of daily maintenance checks. They are also used in search operations.

If the boat is needed simply to assist swimmers and perform daily checks, an inflatable rescue boat is recommended. In surf situations this craft is less dangerous to swimmers. In lake or river environments, not only is the inflatable rescue boat safe in a swimming area, it is an excellent in-water lifeguard stand.

Personal watercraft, such as jet skis, are also useful rescue tools that allow the lifeguard at any open water area to reach a victim quickly. Because of their size and maneuverability, these vehicles are less dangerous to swimmers than motorboats are.

If the boat is to be used in rescuing other small craft, a motorized boat is necessary. Operation of such power vessels requires additional training. Patrol boats should be equipped with the following:

- Motor
- Gas can
- Oars
- Anchor and extra line
- PFDs
- Rescue equipment
- Bailers and tools
- Fire extinguisher
- Flashlight
- Mask, fins, and snorkel
- First aid kit

For safety, the motor can be equipped with a protective prop guard and a kill switch.

Vehicles

At a pool, a victim can be brought to a first aid station with little difficulty, but on the beach a victim may be quite far from treatment. It is essential that the lifeguard have some sort of vehicle to transport the victim to a first aid center immediately. The vehicle may also be used to transport rescuers, first aid equipment, and a public address system for crowd control to the scene of an accident.

A four-wheel-drive vehicle is most appropriate. The vehicle must be equipped with lifesaving equipment, first aid equipment (including a backboard), a radio for emergency communication, and a siren and flashing lights to identify it as an emergency vehicle and to clear a path during an emergency.

Any lifeguard vehicle should be operated at a low speed for routine duties. In an emergency, however, the siren and lights should alert beach patrons that there is an emergency and that the vehicle is moving fast.

Helicopter

The distance from many open water beaches to an emergency medical facility is considerable. In such instances, helicopters offer speedy transportation. Train with local helicopter services to determine landing zones and transportation procedures before you try to use this option.

Additional Equipment Needs

Here is a checklist of equipment that may be available at open water facilities.

Equipment Checklist

_____ Plastic molded rescue buoy with handle grips (known as a rescue can)

_____ Rescue tube

_____ Area-specific rescue equipment

_____ Megaphone, air horn, or public address system

_____ Telephone or two-way radio

_____ Binoculars

_____ First aid kit (including blood-borne pathogen prevention kit) for minor injuries at each guard post and a more advanced kit at each first aid station

_____ Universal spill kit (for cleaning up blood and body fluids)

_____ Oxygen kit, aspirator

_____ Automated external defibrillator

_____ Blankets

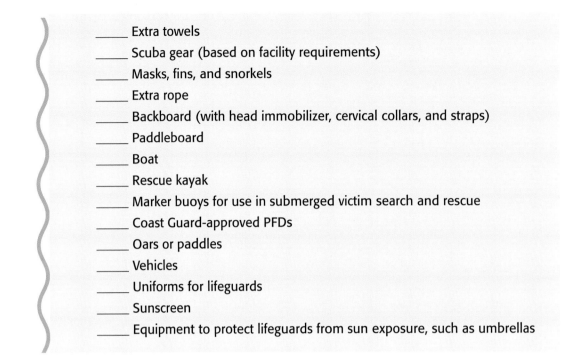

_____ Extra towels

_____ Scuba gear (based on facility requirements)

_____ Masks, fins, and snorkels

_____ Extra rope

_____ Backboard (with head immobilizer, cervical collars, and straps)

_____ Paddleboard

_____ Boat

_____ Rescue kayak

_____ Marker buoys for use in submerged victim search and rescue

_____ Coast Guard-approved PFDs

_____ Oars or paddles

_____ Vehicles

_____ Uniforms for lifeguards

_____ Sunscreen

_____ Equipment to protect lifeguards from sun exposure, such as umbrellas

Accident Prevention

Accidents can be caused by any number of circumstances at any swimming facility. If you will be working at a beach, become familiar with the following causes of accidents in open water and consider how you can help swimmers avoid becoming victims.

15 Frequent Causes of Beach Accidents

- Being unable to swim
- Diving into shallow water
- Rough play in the water and on the shore
- Inability of untrained would-be rescuers
- Hypothermia
- Drop-off from shallow to deep water
- Currents (rips and parallel currents instigate 80% of surf rescues)
- Changing bottom conditions
- Being pulled over rocky areas or into piers and jetties
- Overestimating one's swimming ability
- Being intoxicated
- Using an unapproved flotation device (e.g., air mattress, tube)
- Not wearing a PFD while boating
- Stepping on broken glass or other sharp debris
- Swimming outside the marked area

Your facility is responsible for keeping all public facilities, such as docks, diving boards, ladders, or rafts, in proper repair and safe condition at all times (Aquatic Council, n.d.). It also should post rules, regulations, and hazardous condition warnings in prominent locations. The signs should be legible and adequately secured (Aquatic Council, n.d.). The beach should be inspected daily for unusual hazards, and those hazards should be eliminated or warnings should be posted (Aquatic Council, n.d.).

To help keep the beachfront safe, follow these rules when lifeguarding:

- Do not permit play with rescue equipment at any time.
- Monitor the swimming area for floating debris and periodically check for debris on the bottom.
- Never leave your area of the waterfront unguarded.
- Know what you are to do in the event of an emergency and understand all emergency plans.
- If there is a dock, check it for stability and for protruding sharp objects such as splinters or nails. If springboard diving equipment is present, check it as well (Aquatic Council, n.d.).
- Keep rescue equipment on the swimming dock for immediate access.

If there is a floating dock in your area, suggest that the following regulations be posted:

- Keep the dock clear of all unnecessary equipment (bicycles, gas cans, etc.).
- No running or pushing on the dock.
- No fishing from the dock.
- No swimming under the dock.

Encourage waterfront swimmers to follow these guidelines:

- Swim only in designated areas and only near a lifeguard.
- Always swim with a buddy.
- Stay within your ability.
- Avoid staying in the water too long. When you are cold or tired, get out!
- Avoid long exposure to the sun.
- Never swim in an unlighted area after dark.
- Never go on a long swim without being escorted by someone in a boat or on a paddleboard.
- Never swim during an electrical storm.
- Never call for help unless you need it.
- Dive only in designated diving areas where you know the depth of the water.
- Obey all rules and regulations.

RESCUING SKIN AND SCUBA DIVERS

Interest in the sports of skin and scuba (self-contained underwater breathing apparatus) diving has been growing. YMCAs across the country have had increased involvement in the YMCA Scuba Program and have been training their members to dive, first in swimming pools and later in open water. This has created a greater demand for lifeguards with skills related to skin and scuba diving. As a lifeguard, you may be called upon to guard the pool during skin or scuba classes, asked to accompany a scuba instructor to an open water checkout site, or required to rescue a drowning diver in an open water environment. You will need to understand the rescue procedures for skin and scuba divers, depending on the gear used (see figure 12.9).

Figure 12.9 Scuba gear.

Figure 12.10   Diving flag.

Segregate scuba and skin divers from other swimmers so that all groups of aquatic enthusiasts can enjoy safe, adequately supervised experiences. In open water, make sure that the diving area is marked with a flag as illustrated in figure 12.10. In some states such flags are required where boat traffic is possible. In a pool, remove lane lines before classes and keep the classes separate from other activities in the pool. Whether classes are in open water or in a pool, one lifeguard should be posted next to the water during class.

If you are lifeguarding scuba classes, be aware of these safety procedures that scuba class participants should follow:

- Always lay your tanks down.
- Never place your mask on your forehead. This can signal that you are in distress.
- Before entering the water, make sure no one is swimming where you will be entering.
- If you are skin diving, wear a vest for buoyancy.
- When a diver is exiting the pool on the ladder, don't get behind him or her.

The YMCA and other national organizations have certification standards for scuba divers. Facility management will set policy to determine which "C" (certification) cards will be accepted for admission to their facility. Only divers with current C cards should be admitted.

If you will be guarding a scuba area regularly, you may want to get training in Scuba Lifesaving and Accident Management rescue (SLAM). The YMCA Scuba Program offers such a certification course for certified scuba divers. For more information on scuba certification and training, call YMCA Scuba at 800-872-9622.

Skin and Scuba Diving Emergency Procedures

Scuba diving emergencies require special attention. Air embolism and decompression sickness accidents (see page 256), in which gas bubbles get into tissues or blood, both require immediate treatment in a recompression chamber, so time is of the essence. Where scuba diving is permitted, you may need to know the location of the nearest recompression chamber and how to get a diver there. To obtain this information, call DAN—the Divers Alert Network. This agency runs a 24-hour-a-day hotline to answer questions regarding diving accidents at 800-446-2671.

Special rescue procedures for skin and scuba divers will vary depending on the area where you are guarding, but the basics for determining those procedures can be developed through CARE—cognizance, assessment, rescue, and evacuation.

Cognizance

Watch divers for clues about their diving capabilities. Look for the following early warning signs in these situations.

Pool

- Hesitation to get into the water
- Removal of the mask or the regulator mouthpiece, or both
- Hesitation to descend
- Problems with equipment, such as checking gear frequently

Open Water Checkout Dive

- Assembling equipment wrong
- Talking nervously about fear of the unknown OR being extremely quiet
- Being very slow in getting into the water
- Removal of the mask or the regulator mouthpiece, or both

Open Water Recreational Diving

- Diving alone
- Having difficulty assembling gear
- Being in an environment that is becoming hazardous (perhaps one developing large waves or strong currents)

Assessment

As you guard, you must continuously observe divers so you can recognize problems as they develop. Skin and scuba victims fall into three types: distressed, actively drowning, and passively drowning. (See chapter 6 for more on the three types of victims.)

Distressed divers.   Divers who are distressed cannot make it to safety on their own. Situations that may lead to divers becoming distressed are cramps, losing a buddy, over-exertion, not wearing proper safety equipment (for example, not wearing a vest when skin diving), or wearing equipment that doesn't fit properly. Look for the following characteristics (figure 12.11):

- Arm waving
- Shouting for assistance or blowing a safety whistle
- Kicking to maintain an upright position
- Removal of the mask or the regulator mouthpiece, or both

Figure 12.11   Recognizing a distressed diver: *(a)* waving the arms; *(b)* removing the mask; *(c)* shouting for help; *(d)* kicking to stay upright.

Distressed skin or scuba victims can assist in their own rescue by following instructions to inflate their buoyancy compensators (BCs) or grabbing extended rescue equipment such as a rescue tube or reaching pole.

Actively drowning divers.   Panicked divers can become actively drowning victims in a short period of time. Unlike distressed divers, they may or may not call out for help, as they may be expending all of their energy trying to keep their heads above water. However, you must identify drowning divers quickly; they may have as little as 60 seconds before they slip below the surface. This situation requires your immediate attention. Victims may be unable to assist you with rescue.

Characteristics of actively drowning divers may include the following:

- Victim may or may not call out for help.
- Victim's head is back and the body is very low or very high in the water.
- The victim's mask and/or regulator mouthpiece is removed.
- The victim moves the arms alternately out to the sides and then overhead, raising the body into the air and sinking again, and splashing a lot.
- Victim gets little or no support from kicking.
- Victim is in an upright position, facing the nearest source of assistance.

Many situations can cause divers to actively drown:

- Lack of ability
- Being overweighted
- Lack of physical fitness
- Malfunctioning gear
- A lost buddy
- A frightening occurrence, such as lowered visibility
- Injury from a marine animal
- Cramps
- Entanglement
- Cold water
- Ear problems
- Running out of air (in scuba)
- Air gas embolism (in scuba)
- Decompression sickness (in scuba)

The DAN Dive and Travel Medical Guide says the following about air gas embolism and decompression sickness (Mebane, 1995):

An air gas embolism (AGE) can occur when scuba divers surface while holding their breath. The air trapped in the lungs expands and may rupture lung tissue, releasing air bubbles into the circulatory system. This distributes the bubbles to body tissues, including vital organs such as the heart and brain. If trapped in these organs, bubbles can cause unconsciousness and death. Symptoms of an AGE include dizziness, visual blurring, chest pain, disorientation, and paralysis or weakness. Signs include bloody froth from the mouth and nose, paralysis or weakness, convulsions, unconsciousness (breathing may stop), and death.

Decompression sickness (DCS) is caused by the formation of gas bubbles in the blood or tissues during or following ascent from an open water scuba dive that was too long and too deep. Symptoms include unusual fatigue, skin itch, pain anywhere in the body, dizziness, numbness and tingling, and shortness of breath. Signs include a blotchy rash on the skin, paralysis or weakness, staggering, coughing spasms, and unconsciousness. Symptoms may appear from 15 minutes to 12 hours after the victim surfaces, but in extreme cases the symptoms may appear before the victim surfaces.

If you are caring for a victim who has either AGE or DCS, follow these steps:

- Contact the EMS.
- Check the victim's ABCs.
- Administer oxygen (100% medical grade preferred).
- Contact the Divers Alert Network (DAN) for the nearest recompression chamber.
- Transport the victim to the hospital or a chamber, following the DAN's recommendations.

Passively drowning divers. Those who are drowning passively do not struggle at the surface because they are unconscious, incapacitated, or dead. Such divers are usually found floating at the surface or submerged. They display no active movement. (Actively drowning divers can become passive as a result of fatigue, disorientation, or unconsciousness.) You may have no warning prior to a passive drowning. Situations that can cause passive drowning include the following:

- Air gas embolism (in scuba)
- Decompression sickness (in scuba)
- Oxygen toxicity (in scuba)
- Heart attack or cardiac arrest
- Shallow water blackout
- Stroke
- Alcohol or drug abuse

Rescue

An advantage to rescuing a scuba diver is that you can use the diver's equipment as a flotation device to stabilize the victim at the surface and allow rescue breathing. You also may choose to use a rescue tube during certain scuba rescues and all skin diving rescues.

If you are rescuing a distressed skin or scuba diver, proceed in the following manner:

1. Recognize that the diver is in trouble.
2. Activate your facility's emergency action plan, but do not call the EMS at this point.
3. Enter the water.
4. Tell the diver to inflate the BC and drop the weight belt. If the diver does so, then tell her or him to swim to safety.
5. If the diver doesn't respond to your instructions, perform a front active victim rescue (see pages 116–118).
6. Contact the EMS and DAN if necessary.
7. Fill out an incident report after the rescue is over.

If the victim is actively drowning, take the following steps (figure 12.12):

1. Recognize that the diver is in trouble.
2. Activate your facility's emergency action plan and have someone contact the EMS.
3. Enter the water.
4. Perform a front active victim rescue or a rear active victim rescue (see pages 116–119).
5. Tow the victim to safety.
6. Assess the victim and provide necessary first aid (including oxygen).
7. Contact DAN if further treatment is necessary.
8. Fill out an incident report after the rescue is over.

If the diver is passively drowning at the water's surface, facedown, follow these steps (figure 12.13):

1. Recognize that the diver is in trouble.
2. Activate your facility's emergency action plan, and have someone contact the EMS and DAN.

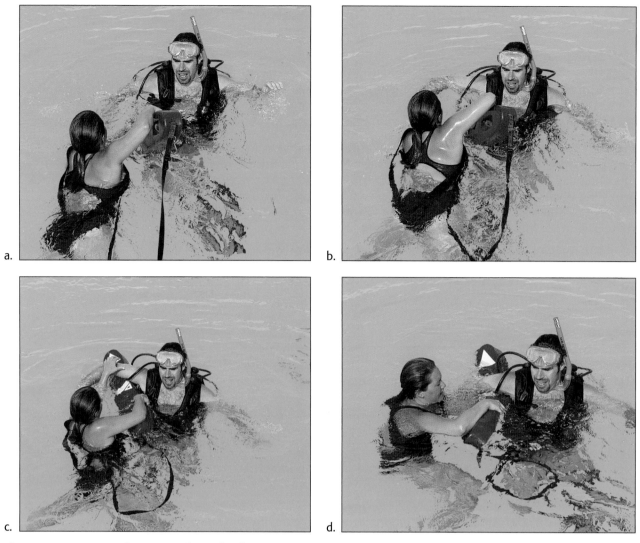

Figure 12.12   Front active rescue of a scuba diver.

3. For a skin diver, use the front passive victim rescue (see pages 121–125).

4. For a scuba diver, grasp the diver's right wrist with your right hand, keeping your thumb on top. Turn the diver face up by pulling the arm down and then back toward the surface (draw a "U") (figure 12.13). Once the diver is faceup, release the wrist.

a.

Figure 12.13   Turning a passively drowning diver faceup.

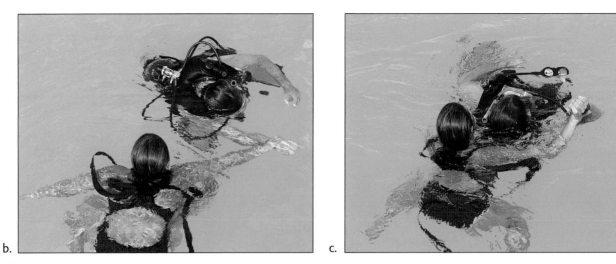

Figure 12.13 *(continued)*

5. Move to the diver's side and release and drop the weight belt. Inflate the diver's BC (using the power inflator or manually) to provide buoyancy to the victim. Do not overinflate the BC, as it can restrict the victim's breathing. Place the arm closest to the diver's head on the diver's forehead. Place your other arm over the diver's arm and under his or her back (do-si-do). Remove the diver's mask and regulator (figure 12.14).

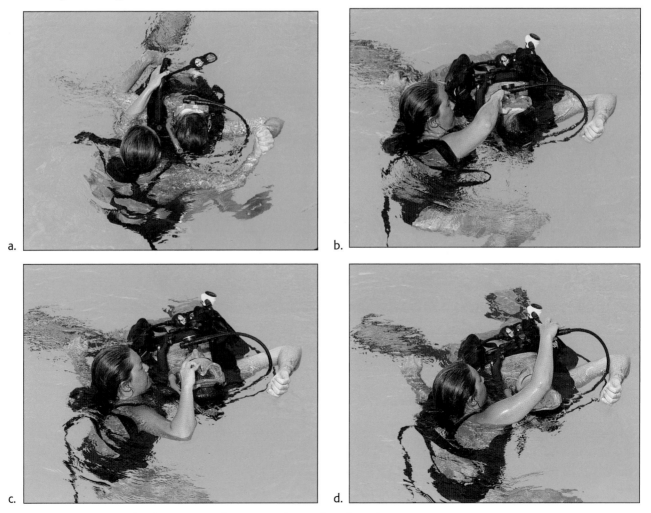

Figure 12.14 Inflating the diver's BC and removing the mask and regulator.

6. Get your resuscitation mask and prepare for rescue breathing, if needed. Using the hand on the victim's forehead, open the victim's airway and check for breathing. Administer rescue breathing if necessary, using a resuscitation mask (figure 12.15).

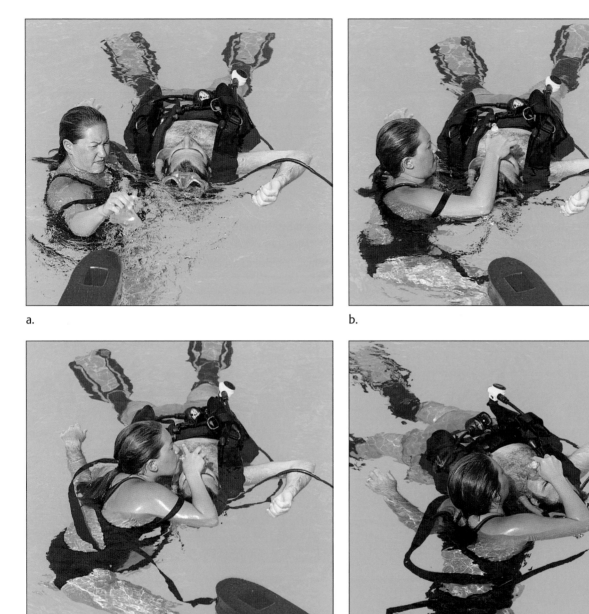

a.

b.

c.

d.

Figure 12.15 Retrieving the resuscitation mask and administering rescue breathing.

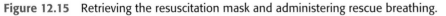

7. Tow the diver to safety (figure 12.16) while providing rescue breathing, if necessary.

a.

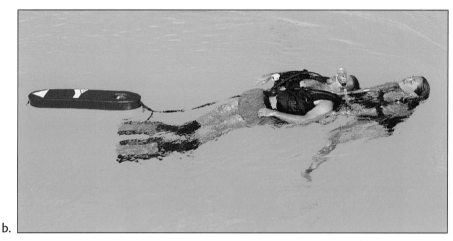

b.

Figure 12.16 Towing the diver to safety.

8. If necessary, remove the diver's gear in this sequence:
   - Unfasten the shoulder clips at the top of the BC.
   - Release the cummerbund.
   - Unclip any gauges that are fastened to the BC (not the tank).
   - While securing the diver, press down on the tank valve and push the gear away from the diver.
   - Remove the diver from the water.
9. Once you have moved the diver to safety, assess his or her ABCs again, then administer oxygen.

Although it is unlikely to happen, you may be called upon to recover and rescue a submerged scuba diver. Thus, you should be trained and prepared for this specialized type of rescue, especially if you guard a pool in which scuba activities are conducted. In most such rescue situations, the use of a mask, snorkel, and fins would help you perform the recovery and rescue.

Be sure to use caution and prudence in doing such a rescue. Don't dive too deep or too long and jeopardize your own safety. Also, don't use scuba equipment to rescue unless you have been properly trained and certified in its use.

If the victim were underwater and unconscious, your priority would be to locate and bring him or her to the surface. The sooner this is accomplished, the better the victim's chances of recovery. Once you bring the victim up to the surface, you can assess the person's ABCs and initiate rescue breathing if necessary.

If you are called upon to rescue a submerged diver, follow these procedures to bring the diver to the surface (see figure 12.17):

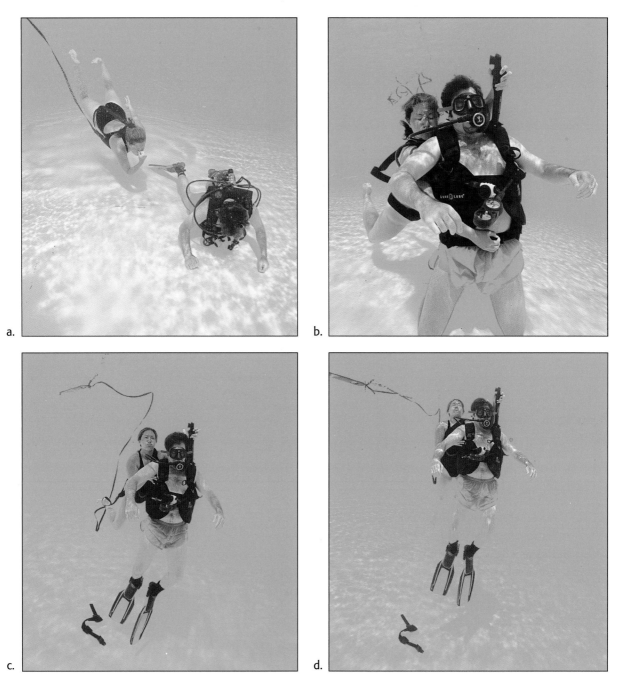

a.

b.

c.

d.

Figure 12.17   Rescuing a submerged scuba diver.

1. Recognize that the diver is in trouble.
2. Activate your facility's emergency action plan and have someone contact the EMS and DAN.
3. Put on a mask, fins, and a snorkel, if necessary.
4. Surface dive to the diver, leaving the rescue tube on the surface. Remove the rescue tube if it doesn't have enough line to allow you to reach the diver.
5. Approach the diver from behind, drop the diver's weight belt, and inflate the diver's BC. If the regulator is in the victim's mouth, leave it there.

6. Make a controlled, slow ascent to the surface.

7. At the surface, stabilize the diver by placing the hand closest to the diver's head on his or her forehead and the other arm over the diver's arm and under his or her back. Remove the diver's mask and regulator.

8. Check the victim's breathing. If necessary, provide rescue breathing.

9. Tow the diver to safety.

10. Remove the diver's gear, in this sequence:
    - Unfasten the shoulder clips at the top of the BC.
    - Release the cummerbund.
    - Unclip any gauges that are fastened to the BC (not the tank).
    - While securing the diver, press down on the tank valve and push the gear away from the diver.

11. Remove the diver from the water, reassess him or her, then administer appropriate first aid.

The skills necessary to successfully complete a rescue of a scuba diver are somewhat different from typical rescue skills. You'll need to practice scuba rescue carefully if you are assigned to an area where scuba diving is done. Be sure to learn the procedures your facility has developed.

Evacuation

Once you have rescued a diver, you must get her or him out of the water as quickly as possible to start emergency first aid. The type of exit you use will depend on the location of the rescue and your proximity to medical assistance; your own size and strength; the assistance available; and the diver's size, condition, and injuries. Exits you can use include the supporting assist, the one-person drag, the one- or two-person lift, or backboarding (see chapter 7 for descriptions of these exits and chapter 10 for backboarding).

Injured or unconscious scuba divers may be suffering from AGE or DCS. Such victims' conditions will worsen quickly, so be sure to activate the EMS immediately. As these victims may need special facilities for treatment, call DAN to locate the nearest recompression chamber.

Keep victims flat while lifting them onto boats or into vehicles for transport to medical facilities. If vomiting occurs, roll victims onto their side and wipe their mouths clean, then maintain open airways. If you are trained to administer oxygen, provide 100% medical oxygen to victims if it is available as you provide other first aid measures.

Missing Diver Procedure in Open Water

If you suspect that a scuba diver is missing and not simply separated from a diving buddy, take the following steps immediately:

1. Determine whether the diver could have left the diving area without notifying anyone.

2. Activate the EMS. This is a medical emergency. Send for additional help (lake patrol, emergency personnel, law enforcement personnel, underwater search and rescue team, or others).

3. Identify the missing diver's buddy; ask the buddy where the missing diver is or where he or she was last seen.

4. Determine from others where the diver was last seen.

5. Move to that area and look for bubbles.

6. Put a search group of at least two certified scuba divers into the water immediately to search the area. Use a predetermined search pattern (see pages 265–266).

Be aware of currents that could alter the missing diver's location. Where currents are present, conduct the search working in a downstream direction.

SEARCH AND RESCUE OPERATIONS

Time is critical when you are searching for a submerged victim. The increased mobility and visibility with mask, fins, and snorkel will allow you to search more area more quickly. In some open water areas, however, the visibility is unavoidably limited. Groups of volunteers or guards can assist in shallow water, and groups of lifeguards can search in deep water.

The following procedures should be used by the person in charge, such as the head guard or lifeguard supervisor, to initiate a search for a swimmer believed to be missing in open water.

1. If a swimmer is suspected to be missing, alert all staff immediately.
2. Encourage the person who reported the missing swimmer to remain calm, to give a complete description of the missing swimmer—including where he or she was last seen—and to stay in one location.
3. Make an announcement specifying the name, description, and last location of the missing swimmer; tell patrons where additional information about the swimmer should be reported.
4. If the swimmer does not report, clear the swimming area and begin search procedures.
5. Instruct designated lifeguards to check the water, bathrooms, showers, locker rooms, snack bars, and adjacent areas.
6. Depending on the personnel available, have someone call the swimmer's home (or check living quarters if the person is vacationing).

Shallow Water Search Method

In shallow water with poor visibility, instruct volunteers or guards to link arms or hold hands and wade in a line across the area. (Volunteers should not be used in water deeper than chest level.) The line should progress forward slowly, with searchers making careful sweeping motions with their feet as illustrated in figure 12.18 and trying not to disturb the bottom. When the shortest member of the search line is unable to continue, the coordinator should reform the search line with lifeguards capable of continuing the search through the use of surface dives. A guard should coordinate each search group.

a.

b.

c.

Figure 12.18 A search line using sweeping foot motions.

Deep Water Search Method

In deeper water, standardized search patterns are suggested for specific circumstances. No search can be completed in an orderly manner without planning and practice, but these standard patterns should simplify the organization of a rescue effort. If a search is prolonged, the chances of a rescue are diminished, and the search instead becomes a recovery.

In searching, adjust the extent of each sweep of the pattern to the current level of visibility in order not to skip any area. Also, keep in mind that the victim may not be lying on the bottom. In a line, guards should surface dive to the bottom and complete a predetermined number of strokes before surfacing. They should use sweeping, semicircular motions with their arms just above the bottom to search. Such movements will avoid stirring up the bottom sediment. To cover low-visibility areas completely, guards must stay close enough together to slightly overlap each other's sweeps.

Guards should complete the designated number of strokes, surface almost straight up, and move back about 6 feet before reforming their line and diving down again. A guide line formed with one guard on the surface will allow directional control because the guards will be able to see the guide when they come to the surface. The guard on the surface is responsible to see that the other guards move back to the designated surface dive location, an important task in ensuring that the entire area is searched thoroughly.

Where visibility is better, extend a rope between rescuers to maintain spacing. In clearer water, rescuers can rely on sight rather than on touch to locate the victim, so they can remain closer to the surface and expand their field of vision and the area covered. Each facility should have a set of hand signals that all guards and experienced rescue personnel know to indicate recovery or the need to surface.

Search Patterns

Using one of four standard search patterns—circular, grid, parallel, and diagonal—lifeguards can search virtually any area efficiently. Each pattern has its own benefits.

Circular Pattern

From a fixed center point, search a progressively widening circle (see figure 12.19) using the surface dive and reforming procedures already described. The distance from the center point of each circular sweep depends on the water clarity. Expand the circle with each revolution, and make certain that a marker is placed at the starting point to assure complete coverage of the circle. The distance from the center can be readily controlled by a line held by the guards that is attached to the center point. In murky water, the hand not holding the line may be used to search by touch. Guards should try not to disturb the bottom while searching.

A post stuck into the river or lake bottom can serve as a center point. The anchor line of the boat also can be used for the center, or a weight may be placed on the bottom, providing it is heavy enough to remain in a fixed position. The rope attached to the center should be kept taut on each sweep at the distance desired for searching.

Grid Pattern

Divide the area into a grid to be searched by tying ropes to fixed anchors. The pattern, illustrated in figure 12.20, allows the area to be covered thoroughly. Guards can search one unit and then move to another. The size of the units should not be greater than twice the visibility distance each guard has on one sweep. Two or more guards can be assigned to search a unit before moving to another sector of the grid.

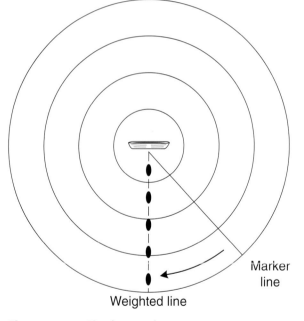

Figure 12.19 Circular search pattern.

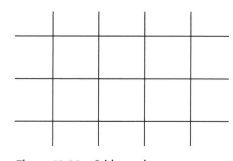

Figure 12.20 Grid search pattern.

Parallel Pattern

The guide or controller should walk along the shore holding a line extended to a guard or line of guards searching the visibility range from the shore. By keeping the line taut and at right angles to the shoreline, the guards can search the area thoroughly. Space each search pass to the limit of visibility and complete the search.

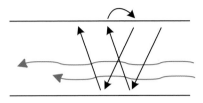

Diagonal Pattern

Swim diagonally to the shore (because the current naturally carries you on an angle, this will eliminate the need to fight the current). After crossing the current, return using a diagonal path (see figure 12.21). Upon reaching the shore, step upstream 6 feet and start a second search. Be sure to keep your search parallel to your initial entry point. It is important to search quickly where currents are involved because the victim may drift.

Figure 12.21 Diagonal search pattern.

Choosing a Search Pattern

It is important that lifeguard staff understand each pattern so that the correct one can be selected in an emergency. Table 12.1 highlights the situations for which each pattern is most valuable.

Table 12.1	Selecting a Search Pattern
Pattern	**Appropriate situation for use**
Circular	Flat-bottomed areas with little current (Large areas can be searched quickly.)
Grid	Areas with irregular bottoms (This method is the surest search method, but it takes a great deal of time and equipment to set up and execute.)
Parallel	Areas of irregular shoreline
Diagonal	Areas where currents are likely to have influenced the position of a victim

Review Questions

1. List seven considerations in selecting a beach site.
2. How are beachfront swimming areas identified?
3. List the additional equipment required on beaches.
4. Explain how to perform a paddleboard rescue for an active victim and for a passive victim.
5. How can you tell if a mask fits you properly?
6. How do you clear a snorkel of water?
7. What's the advantage of wearing a skin diving vest?
8. List 10 of the frequent causes of accidents on beaches.
9. Why do scuba diving emergencies require special attention?
10. Describe the procedures for rescuing a distressed, actively drowning, and passively drowning skin or scuba diver.
11. If you suspect a swimmer is missing, what should you do?
12. Describe the search methods for shallow water and deep water.
13. Briefly explain the search and rescue patterns for a flat-bottomed lake, a lake with an irregular bottom, an irregular shoreline, and a river current.

CHAPTER *thirteen*

Lifeguarding Water Recreation Attractions

Water recreation attractions started to become really popular in the 1970s, and today you may find anything from a single water fume in a camp lake or community pool to multi-attraction indoor water recreation parks and 50-acre outdoor water parks. They are all meant to give patrons fun, thrilling rides, but special lifeguarding precautions are necessary to ensure the ride is safe, too.

▷ **In This Chapter, You'll Learn**

- the main causes of accidents at water recreation attractions;
- the characteristics of specific attractions, along with the most common accident situations on those attractions and the appropriate lifeguarding positions;
- the recommended operational safety guidelines for lifeguarding water recreation attractions;
- the general areas of concern for rules and safety and the use of signs and recorded messages to communicate those concerns to patrons; and
- the recommended installation guidelines and operational safety guidelines for lifeguarding inflatables.

HOW TO GUARD WATER RECREATION ATTRACTIONS

Today, American water recreation areas include not only pools and diving areas but also a wide variety of water recreation attractions (see figure 13.1). In most of these attractions, water helps control the speed of the rider, reduce friction between the rider and the activity surface, and restrain or cushion the rider in a landing area at the end of a ride.

For you to do a good job of lifeguarding water recreation attractions, you need to understand the main causes of accidents on attractions. You also need to learn the characteristics of some specific attractions, the most common accidents on those attractions, and where lifeguards should be stationed on each. We also will give you some fundamental operational safety standards to follow for water recreation attractions, as well as information on how to communicate rules and safety concerns to patrons using signs or taped messages.

Figure 13.1 American water recreation today includes a wide variety of water recreation attractions like this one.

CAUSES OF ACCIDENTS AT WATER RECREATION ATTRACTIONS

Over the past 20 years, enough information has been acquired to provide a clear picture of the primary causes of accidents at water recreation attractions, which include the following:

1. Unsafe design. Many attractions are manufactured and put into use without proper safety testing that uses appropriate research design and experimental testing.
2. Facility operations. After attractions have been installed on site, some owners and operators do not operate them properly. Sometimes owners and operators increase water flow rates or do not maintain proper water depths for slides, runouts, and catch pools. Maintenance may also be substandard.
3. Poor supervision. Lifeguards are sometimes inattentive to their dispatcher and ride supervision, rule enforcement, and catch pool duties.
4. Patron behavior. Water recreation area patrons who come to have fun may have medical problems, such as a heart condition, that may affect their safety on attractions. Many patrons also are first-time visitors, unfamiliar with the rules or the

attraction's characteristics. In their excitement, they often fail to read signs or listen to recorded announcements. Some patrons also choose to disobey rules.

5. Poor communication by management. Often patrons fail to read signs at attractions because of the large number of signs or improper signage. Signs may be difficult to read because of the color of the letters or numbers, background colors, or the height, thickness, or style of the font used. Placing signs where they are hard to read, failing to provide pictorial and bilingual signs, or failing to consistently use signal words such as "Danger," "Warning," and "Caution" often render a sign ineffective; in other words, such signs simply do not communicate properly. Recorded statements played while patrons wait in line may also fail to communicate because the tape wears out, the message is too long or is played too frequently, or the words are not clear.

LIFEGUARDING TIPS FOR INDIVIDUAL ATTRACTIONS

Each attraction has its own specific hazards. As a lifeguard, you need to know the characteristics of each attraction, those situations likely to lead to accidents, and where you and other lifeguards should be stationed. The attractions covered here include wave pools, deep water activity pools, free-fall and speed slides, serpentine slides and rapids, coaster rides, lazy or winding rivers, and interactive playgrounds.

Wave Pools

Waves in wave pools (see figure 13.2) are created by one of two methods: compressed air or moving paddles.

In the compressed air method, air is forced into half of the water chambers located within the end wall simultaneously (the odd-numbered ones), pushing the water out through the bottom of the chambers. After the water has escaped from the odd-numbered chambers, it is then released from the even-numbered chambers.

In the paddle-operated method, a large mechanically operated paddle moves in a chamber in which a cascade of water is released from the back wall to displace water in a filled chamber.

A wave pool may produce waves on a cycle of small waves for 20 minutes followed by a 20-minute off-cycle period or one large wave every 5 to 10 minutes.

Figure 13.2   A wave pool.

Wave Pool Accidents

Wave pool hazards relate directly to the size and frequency of waves, as well as the cement bottom of the pool. Common wave pool accidents include the following:

- Swimmers in the 4- to 5-foot depth zone who are knocked over by waves
- Swimmers or nonswimmers who become buoyant as a wave lifts them off the bottom, causing them to panic
- Swimmers who are injured when waves push them into recessed wall ladders in the deep end
- Patrons in shallow water who are knocked down by people riding the waves on inflatable rafts
- Swimmers floating on inner tubes in deep water who fall off the tube, submerge, and cannot return to the surface due to the number of tubes covering the surface
- Swimmers hanging onto pool railings who are not strong enough to swim safely through the waves to shallow water

Patrons who suffer impact injuries from contact with the bottom or who are struck by other patrons riding on rafts may bleed and have an increased risk of spinal injuries. Be prepared to follow the blood-borne pathogen procedures identified in chapter 9.

Some rules that might help prevent accidents in wave pools are these (Lifesaving Society, 1993):

- Swimmers are not allowed to hold onto one another in the deep zone (to minimize collisions).
- Parents who are holding children are restricted to the shallow zone.
- Swimmers are to keep a safe distance from the walls (to prevent collisions with the walls).
- Body surfing or diving is not allowed in shallow water.
- The size of the waves is limited (to avoid injuries resulting from collisions between swimmers and waves).
- If flotation mattresses and tubes are allowed in the pool, they may interfere with lifeguards' ability to see. Divide the pool into two sections, one for swimmers and one for patrons with flotation devices. Another possibility is to limit the number of flotation devices allowed in the pool.
- Allow only those flotation devices that are provided by the facility (World Waterpark Association, 1989).
- Require patrons to enter the wave pool from the beach area only, not the sides (World Waterpark Association, 1989).

According to the Royal Life Saving Society Canada (Lifesaving Society, 1993), when a rescue is needed, you should stop the waves but not evacuate the wave pool as in a regular swimming pool (figure 13.3). Rescues usually can be completed with just local crowd control. However, when a total evacuation of the pool is necessary, as when bad weather hits, you should use a more detailed crowd control plan. Stop the waves, signal the patrons to leave, and, with the help of the other guards, supervise the departure of the swimmers.

Lifeguard Positions

The number of sitting lifeguards and standing lifeguards depends on the size of the pool and the number of patrons in the water. Lifeguard chairs should be placed only near water depths over 5 feet along the sides of the pool (figure 13.4). Standing or moving guards should be placed between chairs, along the back wall, and in shallow water. Additional guards may be in the water with tubes. The seated guards should handle communication. Teamwork is essential, as overlapping zone coverage is used in wave pools (Lifesaving Society, 1993).

Figure 13.3 When a rescue is needed in a wave pool, stop the waves.

Figure 13.4 Lifeguard chairs should be placed along the sides of the pool.

Deep Water Activity Pools

Deep water activity pools are associated with a variety of attractions. Sometimes they are used as a landing area for patrons exiting from a "shotgun slide" 5 to 6 feet above the surface of the water. They also provide entry areas for diving boards, diving platforms, cable or rope swings, zip lines, nets, or rings on cables, along with inflatables or walking and play surfaces anchored to the bottom. Depending on the activity, the water depth may vary from 11.5 to 18 feet.

Deep Water Pool Accidents

Accidents in this type of pool are related to entries. Entries from objects high above the water are sometimes unplanned falls or sudden drops, and impact with the water can be painful. Accidents common to deep water pools are the following:

- An injured or weak swimmer suddenly entering deep water
- A person losing consciousness who ends up lying facedown in the water due to impact with the water, another person, or some part of the attraction

Be ready to use blood-borne pathogen procedures with impact injuries.

Lifeguard Positions

The number of lifeguards and their locations should be determined by the activity:

- For shotgun slides, a lifeguard dispatcher is needed at the top of the slide. Another lifeguard should be stationed near the drop zone where patrons enter the water.
- For pools with 7.5- and 10-meter platforms, water depths will range from 15 to 18 feet. In case they have to rescue a submerged victim, lifeguards should have mask, fins, and snorkel handy. They should receive in-service training on how to use this equipment in victim recovery from the bottom and practice rescue procedures regularly.

For most of these deep water activities, a lifeguard should be stationed near the entry point. Other lifeguards should be situated where they have an unobstructed view of the sides.

Free-Fall and Speed Slides

Free-fall and speed slides are similar in design. Free-fall slides are long slides with very steep drops. Some are so steep that the top of the slide is enclosed, giving the rider the sensation of falling straight down. Speed slides have a more gentle slope and sometimes have a bump halfway down. These slides may end in a catch pool or a long run-out, which is generally where accidents occur.

Free-Fall and Speed Slide Accidents

Because of the speeds attained on these slides, riders should stay in a position in which their legs are crossed at the ankles and their arms are folded across their chest (see figure 13.5). Injuries on these attractions usually result from a combination of speed and improper body position, as in these situations:

- Soft tissue injuries, such as strains and sprains affecting the limbs, can occur.
- Serious internal injuries can occur from entering the catch pool or run-out with legs apart.
- Broken bones or dislocated joints can occur from impact with the slide after becoming airborne from sliding over a speed bump. Impacting water in the catch pool or hitting the wall or steps at the end of a slide run-out or catch pool that is too short can produce similar injuries.

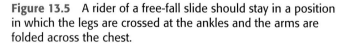

Figure 13.5   A rider of a free-fall slide should stay in a position in which the legs are crossed at the ankles and the arms are folded across the chest.

Lifeguard Positions

Lifeguards for free-fall and speed slides should be stationed at the top of the slide to control the dispatch of riders and at the bottom in the run-out area or adjacent to the catch pool.

Serpentine Slides and Rapids*

Serpentine slides are generally long slides that wind their way down a hillside or super structure much like a rollercoaster (see figure 13.6). They are constructed of fiberglass or cement. Riders slide on mats or in one- or two-person tubes or they body-slide feet-first with arms and legs crossed (as when using a speed slide). Rapids-type rides simulate tubing in a creek or river. Such rides wind downhill and may have one or two catch

Figure 13.6 A serpentine slide.

basins at points between the top and bottom where the ride funnels riders into a cave or to the next drop level.

When your facility management decides to install a slide, they should follow these guidelines:

- Follow the manufacturer's recommendations on water depth for a serpentine slide with a low-grade discharge (a 10% grade is recommended). Slides that do not have a safe deceleration to near zero velocity at the point of discharge should have a minimum depth of 9 feet and would preferably meet one-meter board guidelines for water depth (figure 13.7).
- Some catch pool areas have a pad to help absorb any impact from the landing. Check with your manufacturer on their recommendation based on the slide you are considering.
- Follow the same guideline for pool depth at the mouth of a drop slide as you would use for a one-meter board.
- Install closed steps with landings instead of ladders (according to industry standards).
- Have permanently enclosed sides on the platform.
- Make sure that there is plenty of empty space (at least 9 feet) above the platform.
- Make sure that deck obstructions meet codes.
- If the pool has a diving board and a slide in the deep end, make sure there is a space at least 10 feet wide between them.

* Information on permanent slides taken from *Swimming Pool Slides Safety Standard,* Consumer Product Safety Commission.

Figure 13.7 A low-grade discharge at the end of the slide is recommended.

- Post signs to identify assumption of risk for riders. We recommend you require parental releases before allowing those under 18 years of age to use the equipment.

Serpentine Slides and Rapids Accidents

Accidents may occur anywhere from the top to the bottom of these slides. Common accidents include the following:

- Falling off a mat and losing body control, producing soft tissue injuries, broken bones, or head injuries.
- Stopping on the way down and blocking the following riders, causing impact injuries.

Figure 13.8 Lifeguards in the catch pool should have rescue tubes.

- Riding in one- or two-person tubes and hitting the walls of the slide with the head, arms, or feet. The rider cannot control the tube as it spins and turns on its downhill course.
- Sliding and getting caught in a hydraulic formed at the end of the ride. Hydraulics are the result of water cascading from the slide into the catch pool, which forms a waterfall effect that produces a reverse circular current. A hydraulic can make it extremely difficult to stand up, especially for young children or weak swimmers, and may even hold a person on the bottom.
- An excessive number of tubes collecting in a rapids' catch basin where some tubes may be overturned, causing injury or even drowning.

To help prevent accidents on serpentine slides, your facility's management should follow these guidelines:

- Be aware of conditions in the catch pool, such as currents created from the water flow.

- Require the lifeguards stationed in the catch pool to always have their rescue tubes (figure 13.8). It is also helpful for them to wear deck shoes to minimize slipping.
- Have written emergency procedures for this area and rehearse them.
- Station lifeguards at the top and bottom of the slide. The guard at the top has dispatching duties and the guard at the bottom supervises proper exiting of the participants.
- Don't allow children on the equipment if they are shorter than 48 inches (4 feet). This is because it is recommended that children be 6 inches taller than the water depth in the catch pool, or other modifications should be in place (e.g., deep water swim test, use of lifejackets, or a guard in the catch pool). Be sure to discuss this with the manufacturer to ensure that the slide will be properly positioned so that the groups you want to serve will exit into the appropriate water depth.
- Heed weight limits established by the manufacturers. A weight limit used by some manufacturers is about 250 pounds for a basic serpentine slide.
- Don't use members as safety testers.
- Stop water flow and the dispatch of participants during a major rescue (such as when multiple guards are involved in the assistance and care of an injured swimmer). Have a water shut-off button close by so the guard can stop water flow quickly.
- Allow only feet-first sliding.
- Perform a safety inspection prior to opening each day.
- Keep a detailed log of any maintenance and safety inspections.
- Review and analyze an injury chart and incident reports for any corrective measures that can be taken to reduce the possibilities of repeat occurrences. Note and date any actions taken.

Lifeguard Positions

Riders may need assistance or rescue at any point from the top of the ride to the catch pool. Standing lifeguards need to be stationed at the dispatch positions, the catch pool, and appropriate locations in between. The lifeguard positioned at the bottom of the slide

Figure 13.9 The lifeguard at the bottom of the slide should be in the water.

should be in the water with a tube (figure 13.9). Two guards on deck should be available for communication with the guards at the dispatch position.

Coaster Rides

Coaster rides are similar to, but shorter than, speed slides. They often are constructed in pairs. Riders sit on plastic sleds that glide down on small metal rollers or water-lubricated surfaces. When the rider and sled leave the slide, they skim along the surface of a long catch pool, gradually slowing down until coming to a stop.

Coaster Ride Accidents

Accidents common to coaster rides include the following:

- Collisions between two sleds discharged simultaneously
- Sleds flipping over, resulting in a rider hitting a side wall or the bottom

Lifeguard Positions

Lifeguards assigned to coaster rides should be positioned at the top of the slide to dispatch riders and adjacent to or in the catch pool to assist injured or disoriented riders. Lifeguards in the catch pool should be ready to use blood-borne pathogen protocols.

Lazy or Winding Rivers

The paths of lazy or winding rivers may be oval in shape or they may wind their way through a water recreation area, sometimes encompassing the entire area. They gener-

Figure 13.10 A lazy or winding river.

ally are 3 to 4 feet in depth and float patrons along on inner tubes at 2 to 3 miles per hour (see figure 13.10).

Lazy or Winding River Accidents

Lazy or winding rivers generally have a low incidence of accidents. Those that do occur are often the following:

- Patrons slipping or falling at the point of entrance or exit
- Patrons who injure themselves by getting out of the river and then jumping or diving back in
- Patrons who hit their heads after falling from an overturned tube caused by horseplay and other patrons blocking the progress of riders

Lifeguard Positions

Lifeguards should be stationed at the entrance and exit points in order to assist riders in getting into and out of tubes. They also should be positioned sitting or standing along the river, so that no part of the river is out of the sight of a lifeguard at any time (figure 13.11).

Figure 13.11 Lifeguards should be stationed along the river.

Interactive Playgrounds

Interactive playgrounds (figure 13.12) combine equipment for water fun such as water slides with playground elements such as climbing nets. Often the equipment is designed to follow a theme. The equipment is in water that ranges from zero depth to 18 inches deep.

Figure 13.12 An interactive playground.

Figure 13.13   Post the rules next to pool entrances and equipment.

Your facility should follow these safety precautions for interactive playgrounds:

- Post the rules by each piece of aquatic equipment and at pool entrances (figure 13.13).
- Make sure that the rules are clearly written and easily understood by all.
- Instruct adults to closely supervise their children, and lay out the park so it is easy for them to do so (World Waterpark Association, 1989).
- Have special guarding policies in writing for each piece of equipment.
- Strictly enforce all policies and rules, especially those related to running and horseplay.
- Station an additional lifeguard on a play structure to monitor slides and potentially hazardous play.
- Have smooth surfaces on all objects (walls and pipes).
- Have contour lines to show increases in depth.
- Make sure that it's clear that the playground is intended for children under 4 feet tall.
- Make sure slides have an open tube at the end of the slide so visibility is clear (figure 13.14).
- Ensure that the angle and exit of slides are not dangerous and conform to Consumer Product Safety Commission standards.

Figure 13.14   Slides should have open tubes at the end to help visibility.

OPERATIONAL SAFETY GUIDELINES FOR LIFEGUARDS

As water recreation areas have many different types of activities, ensure that each attraction is supervised and guarded according to its individual characteristics. We recommend the following operational safety guidelines for water recreation attractions:

- Always emphasize accident prevention.
- Get orientation and in-service training specific to each attraction you guard.
- Have some means of communication and signaling provided by your facility, such as an intercom system, FM radio, public address system, signal lights, radio telephones, cell phones, walkie talkies, CB radios, air horns, or whistles.
- Completely inspect and test each attraction according to manufacturer's instructions each day before use. Then fill out a daily checklist specific to the attraction to record findings. After inspection and testing, have a lifeguard ride the attraction as it would normally be used by patrons. If maintenance needs to be performed, do it before the attraction is opened for use or close the attraction until the required maintenance can be completed. Record all maintenance procedures in the log.
- Inspect first aid, safety, and rescue equipment, including first aid kits, HIV precautionary kits, and resuscitation masks, and record the results of the inspection in a log.
- Test and adjust the water chemistry balance each time the filters are cleaned, and test and adjust the disinfectant levels hourly.
- Expect your facility to have developed written emergency and accident management procedures (which should be practiced) specific to each attraction as well as an emergency procedure for an unplanned shutdown of each attraction.
- Remember that the keys to accident prevention are to
  —stay at a high level of physical conditioning,
  —pay constant attention to scanning and lifeguard duties, and
  —consistently enforce rules.
- Use your victim recognition skills and be ready to respond quickly when you see a patron
  —slip and fall;
  —collide with another rider, side wall, end wall, or bottom;
  —lose body control on an attraction;
  —fall from an attraction;
  —become airborne and hit a hard surface;
  —fail to read signs or listen to recorded messages and warnings;
  —act as if he or she is under the influence of drugs or alcohol;
  —appear to be suffering from a medical condition, such as a heart attack, epilepsy, diabetes, or heat exhaustion;
  —fail to heed warnings such as height, weight, or age restrictions; or
  —act disoriented or unstable.

COMMUNICATION AT WATER RECREATION ATTRACTIONS

You should communicate often and clearly with all coworkers and patrons, especially patrons who are visiting for the first time, as they are more likely to be injured than those who frequent the attractions regularly. Keep in mind that patrons are excited and eager to ride as many attractions as possible. As a result, they sometimes don't read the rules and warning signs or listen carefully to recorded messages. Some children may also be unsupervised by an adult. You may have to repeat warnings and rules verbally in a dispatch area, even though patrons have been presented with signs and recorded messages along the way into or up to an attraction. The following list represents general areas of concern for which your facility should develop, communicate, and enforce warning and safety rules. (Warning signs relating to the activities or behaviors identified in this list should be matched to specific park attractions.)

Warning Signs

Personal Health
Fear of heights or sudden immersion
Fatigue and exhaustion
Heart problems

Proper Use of Equipment
Tubes, rafts, mats, sleds, and PFDs

Slowing and Stopping
Extending arms and legs to slow
Extending arms and legs to stop
Holding on to wave pool rails

Rider Behavior
Changing body positions
Multiple riders, trains
Weaving back and forth

Safety Signs

Bathing and Personal Attire
Bathing suits
Clothing—T-shirts
Glasses, sunglasses
Jewelry
Dentures, hearing aids
Prosthetics

Patron Limitations
Age
Height
Weight or overweight
Height and weight for large patrons

Body Position
Head-first
Feet-first

Activity Use Prohibited
For people on certain prescription drugs or those using recreational drugs or alcohol

Water Depth
At entrance and exit of attractions
On the coping of all pools

General Warnings
Failure to follow the rules or instructions can result in paralysis or serious or fatal injury.
Lifeguards must always be obeyed.
Failure to obey can result in dismissal.

Prone position
Supine position
Sitting position

Entry Positions
Jumping
Diving
Running
Swinging
Pushing off

Exit Rules
Approved behavior
Where exit is allowed

Special Rules
Unique to special attractions

As mentioned, besides posting signs, you may want to have recorded messages on warnings and rules announced through loudspeakers located along entrance paths and stairs. When you record such a message, make sure to do the following:

- Speak clearly and slowly.
- Use inflections, avoiding a monotone.
- Make the message brief and concise.
- Use language that everyone can understand.
- Use positive messages, avoiding sarcasm and profanity.
- Consider multilingual messages in languages, such as Spanish, French, German, and Japanese, consistent with the languages and nationalities of those who frequent your facility.
- Be sure the message is loud enough to be heard, but not obnoxiously loud.

INFLATABLES*

Even if pools don't have permanent aquatic equipment like slides or wave pools, they may have inflatables. Inflatables are large objects or animals usually made of a reinforced PVC fabric with a tough polyester mesh bonded between two layers of PVC to allow for stretching and flexing. They come in many models, shapes, and sizes, but are generally one of two types:

- Sealed inflatables are play structures that can support one or more persons above the surface of the water (figure 13.15). They are capped once they are filled with air. There are many different designs.
- Constant-blow inflatables have an air blower permanently connected and constantly running while the inflatable is in use. These tend to be used differently than the sealed inflatables. For example, participants try to run the length of aqua fun runs and use them as obstacle courses. There also are inflatable water slides.

As always, it is your facility's responsibility to ensure the safety of users of this equipment. When using inflatables, consider the following precautions in addition to the manufacturer's safety recommendations and applicable state and local codes.

Figure 13.15 A sealed inflatable.

*Adapted, by permission, from The Institute of Sport and Recreation Management, Melton Mowbray, United Kingdom, *The Use of Play Equipment and Water Features in Swimming Pools: A Recommended Code of Practice.*

Sealed Inflatables

Figure 13.16 shows how a sealed inflatable should normally be anchored. Any inflatable used should not cover a continuous area more than 1 square meter (39 square inches) wide of water and should be no more than 1 meter in height above the water's surface. Wherever possible the depth should be consistent on all sides of the inflatable.

Limited product safety research is available on the appropriate depth at which inflatables should be placed. Due to the variety of activities for which inflatables can be used, a minimum of 5 feet is recommended for sealed inflatables (and an even greater depth would be preferable). We recommend that all swimmers be required to take a deep water swim test before being allowed to play on the structure.

These play structures are not recommended for use by children or adults who cannot swim. If your facility chooses to allow young children and their parents to play on the structure who are not proficient swimmers, try to make parents aware that accidental falls can be frightening for a child and can cause a fear of the water. Your facility might want to consider having the children wear lifejackets and establishing a separate play period for parents and their young children.

Here are some recommendations for the installation and operation of sealed inflatables.

Sealed Inflatable Installation

Figure 13.17 shows the bottom method for anchoring a sealed inflatable. When you install a sealed inflatable, take these precautions:

- Inspect the inflatable each time before it is used. Pay particular attention to seams, anchorage points, and other potential areas of weakness. Record these checks in a log book.
- Prior to using an electric blower for inflation or deflation, check the blower for safety and make sure it is plugged into a conveniently located outlet with a ground-fault interrupter. Make sure that electrical cords do not cross traffic areas. Before each use, check the blower for any damage and make sure that the mesh guards over the air inlet and outlets are secured and that cables, plugs, sockets, and switches are not damaged.
- When you fill the inflatable with air, do not let it obstruct the movement of people onto the pool deck or block emergency exits. If on-duty guards are responsible for inflating or deflating the inflatable, close the pool during that time.

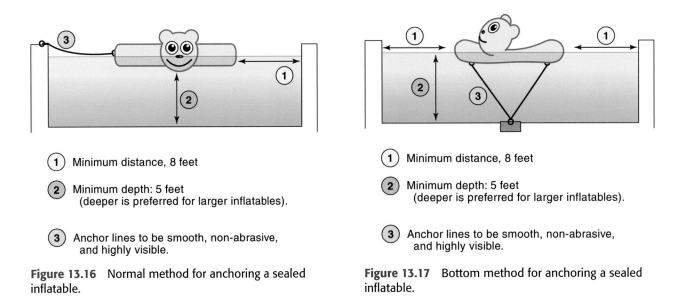

1 Minimum distance, 8 feet

2 Minimum depth: 5 feet
(deeper is preferred for larger inflatables).

3 Anchor lines to be smooth, non-abrasive, and highly visible.

Figure 13.16   Normal method for anchoring a sealed inflatable.

1 Minimum distance, 8 feet

2 Minimum depth: 5 feet
(deeper is preferred for larger inflatables).

3 Anchor lines to be smooth, non-abrasive, and highly visible.

Figure 13.17   Bottom method for anchoring a sealed inflatable.

- Transport the inflatables carefully. Carry them rather than dragging them along the pool deck (figure 13.18). Inflatable lifespans fluctuate due to variations in care, use, and storage, but an average is 3 years. With the proper care, they will last longer.

Figure 13.18 Transport inflatables by carrying them.

- Use nylon or other water-resistant tether lines with a minimum diameter of 3/8 inches to tether all pool inflatables. Place 5-inch "lock-on" rope floats every two feet on the tether line, with a brass swivel clip on one end to attach to the pool side. Do not allow patrons to pull on or play with the tether lines or to use the tether lines to climb on the inflatable. Use anchor lines that are smooth, nonabrasive, and highly visible.
- Leave a minimum clearance of 8 feet on all sides of the sealed inflatable.

Sealed Inflatable Operation

Figure 13.19 illustrates how to position a sealed inflatable. Your facility should take the following steps for safe operation of a sealed inflatable:

- Develop an emergency plan and train staff to use it for the following: dealing with unruly behavior, collapse or partial collapse of the inflatable, failure of the tether ropes, or serious injury of a swimmer.
- Station at least one lifeguard on the deck on each side of the inflatable structure. Use additional guards if needed to help supervise in the water, depending on the number, age, and abilities of the swimmers using the inflatable. This does not include the general duty guards for other swimmers using the pool.

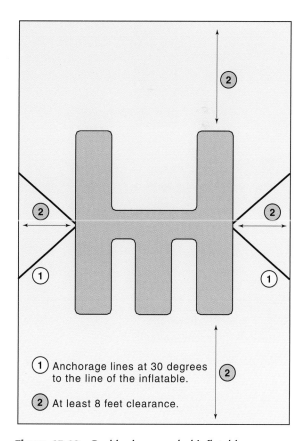

① Anchorage lines at 30 degrees to the line of the inflatable.

② At least 8 feet clearance.

Figure 13.19 Positioning a sealed inflatable.

- Allow only a small age range to play on the inflatable at one time (for example, 10- to 12-year-olds should not play at the same time as 5- to 7-year-olds). Recommended playing time for each group is between 15 and 20 minutes.
- Consider having an age minimum, depending on the size of the inflatable.

When you guard, do not allow patrons to do the following:
- Dismount head-first
- Stand on the object (unless it is specifically designed for this)
- Push or throw each other onto or off of the inflatable
- Deliberately swim under the inflatable or lift it to try to knock others from the inflatable
- Swing, hang, or pull on the anchor ropes
- Bring swimsuit pins or sharp objects near the inflatable

Constant-Blow Inflatables

Two common types of constant-blow inflatables are inflatable slides and aqua runs.

Inflatable Slides

Inflatable slides are attached to a 3-meter diving platform or a customized frame. The active sliding length is about 26 feet. The air blower works continuously so that the proper air pressure is delivered. The user safely slides between two large air-filled side tubes.

The following are guidelines for safe inflatable slide installation and operation.

Inflatable slide installation. The positioning of an inflatable water slide is shown in figure 13.20.

For safety, your facility should install the inflatable slide in the following way:

- Use constant-blower-filled slides that are secured to a platform or frame three meters above the water surface area to ensure the correct angle of descent.
- Establish a designated "splash area" that extends out at least 15 feet from the bottom of the slide. Form the boundary lines of the splash or nonswimming area using ropes with floats or inflatable booms every 2 feet.
- Make appropriate daily inspections of the slide, supporting structure, and electrical equipment. Log and report them properly.
- Use stairs with landings instead of ladders. Provide handrails of a diameter and height that are appropriate for the age group using the slide.
- Leave plenty of empty space above the platform (at least 8 feet ceiling clearance).
- Completely enclose all sides of the platform.
- Place the exit of the slide no more than 12 inches above the surface of the water.
- Do not allow the slide to obstruct the deck in violation of state or local codes.
- If water is needed to operate the slide, have a hose attachment in place. An adequate water flow down the slide is needed to minimize friction burns to users.
- Provide at least 6 feet clearance from either side of the pool tank (10 feet is preferable).

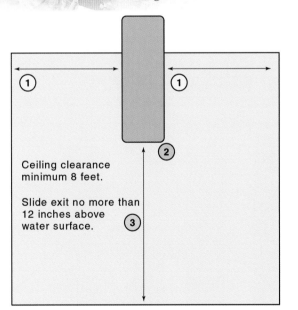

Ceiling clearance minimum 8 feet.

Slide exit no more than 12 inches above water surface.

① Minimum clearance from pool side, 6 feet (more is preferred).

② Minimum landing depth, 9 feet.

③ Minimum distance from base of slide to edge of landing area, 15 feet.

④ Splash area partitioned by ropes or inflatable boom.

Figure 13.20 Positioning an inflatable water slide.

- Place the slide in a pool depth of at least 9 feet (2.8 meters), and leave 15 feet of clearance in front of the exit point of the slide. Limited research is available on the appropriate depth in which to place inflatable slides. As new research becomes available, adjust this depth.
- Be aware that the sliding surface will wear out with usage and require patching and repairing. Some slides have a replaceable sliding surface, which should be inspected and patched or replaced as needed. This can increase the lifespan of the slide.

Inflatable slide operation. When you guard an inflatable slide, do the following:

- Heed weight limits recommended by the manufacturer.
- Do not allow anyone who is less than 4 feet tall to use the slide.
- Allow only one person down the slide at one time.
- Allow only the feet-first sliding position.
- Do not let participants run or jump on the slide.

Position one guard at the top of the slide to make sure the rider is in the proper slide position. This guard should also control the flow of participants using the slide and climbing the stairs. Station another guard on the deck to supervise the exit point of the slide and the swimmers' clearance of the splash area.

Aqua Fun Runs

Aqua fun runs are constant-blow structures that can run up to 40 feet in length and a maximum of 4 feet, 9 inches wide. Aqua fun runs bring up many safety concerns. For instance, fun runs that are more than 1 square meter (39 inches by 39 inches) of covered water surface area shouldn't be used because of the increased risk that someone could become trapped underneath. The play elements of the structure should be no more than 1 meter in height of playable surface above the water. A number of aqua fun runs do meet these recommendations.

The purpose of aqua fun runs is for swimmers to traverse (walk or run) the structure like an obstacle course. We recognize that some facilities will choose to use the structure as a sealed inflatable instead of as a fun run. In this case, different operating procedures and rules need to be established and the sealed inflatable recommendations should be followed. A word of caution: Having two sets of rules can confuse swimmers and make rule enforcement more difficult.

Aqua fun run installation. The proper anchoring for aqua fun runs (constant-blow inflatables) is shown in figure 13.21.

Your facility should follow these recommendations for aqua fun run installation:

- Choose an inflatable that is appropriate to the depths and dimensions of the pool.
- Place the structure in deep water (at least 9 feet) where there will be no other users around the structure.
- Provide at least 12 feet of clearance from the finish to the edge of the pool.
- Provide at least 12 feet of clearance on each side of the pool. The end of the run should allow participants to exit into the deep end of the pool.
- Keep the air blower in constant operation while the structure is in use. Be in full compliance with electrical codes and regulations.
- Clear the pool area when the inflatable is being put in or taken out.

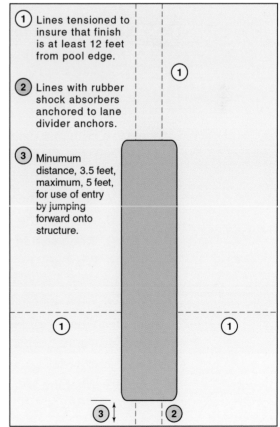

① Lines tensioned to insure that finish is at least 12 feet from pool edge.

② Lines with rubber shock absorbers anchored to lane divider anchors.

③ Minumum distance, 3.5 feet, maximum, 5 feet, for use of entry by jumping forward onto structure.

Figure 13.21 Proper anchoring of an aqua fun run.

Aqua fun run operation.   At least two designated guards are needed—one to supervise participants getting on the inflatable and then dispatching swimmers, the other to supervise the run and dismount and clearing of the dismount area. Lifeguarding is similar to that for sealed inflatables, plus the following:

- Control the flow of participants. Dispatch only one participant onto the inflatable at a time.
- Tell swimmers that, at the far end, they must slide off feet-first and then swim to the nearest side.
- Instruct swimmers to fall off the fun run if they lose their balance, not try to dive off it.
- If the aqua fun run is being used as a sealed inflatable (for play and not as a run), then do not allow participants to stand on it, but only to crawl on it. The type of play on the inflatable should be posted so swimmers understand the designated rules and you can enforce them.
- No substantive research has been done on the best entry of the swimmers onto the run. Until more research is completed, use your best judgment as to how swimmers should get onto the structure. Two methods are possible:
    1. Station a lifeguard at the beginning of the run, with its starting point against the edge of the pool. That lifeguard helps users step carefully onto the structure before they traverse the obstacle course.
    2. Have a lifeguard closely supervise the swimmers as they jump onto the unit (rather than step onto it) to ensure forward projection and to reduce the danger of falling back and hitting the poolside. The unit should be placed so that there is a minimum clearance of 3-1/2 feet and a maximum clearance of 5 feet from the edge of the pool to the start of the structure.

Review Questions

1. What are the primary causes of water accidents at water recreation attractions?
2. What are the common accidents in a wave pool?
3. What are the common accidents in deep water activity pools?
4. What are the common accidents from using a speed slide?
5. What are the common accidents from using a serpentine slide?
6. What are the common accidents resulting from a coaster ride?
7. What are the common accidents from using a lazy or winding river?
8. What are the lifeguard's keys to accident prevention?
9. When should a lifeguard be ready to respond?
10. What are the general areas of concern for which warning and safety signs should be developed, communicated, and enforced?
11. What are the two types of inflatables?
12. Why is it important to carry inflatables?
13. Name two of the rules to enforce when guarding sealed inflatables.
14. How tall does a patron need to be to use an inflatable slide?
15. What are two ways that you can help patrons get onto an aqua fun run?

fourteen

Pool Management Basics

As a lifeguard, you will most commonly be assigned to monitor the pool area to help prevent accidents and to respond to situations as necessary. It is likely that you will also be asked to assist in several other operations essential to the success of the aquatic facility. This chapter is designed to give you an introduction to pool management. For more in-depth coverage, take the YMCA P.O.O.L. (Pool Operator on Location) course.

In This Chapter, You'll Learn About

- safety inspections and precautions,
- signage,
- filtration,
- pool chemistry,
- common water problems, and
- spas.

SAFETY INSPECTIONS

Each facility must be routinely inspected for potential hazards. A complete inspection should be performed regularly throughout the season. The findings of these inspections are the basis for major maintenance work to be completed.

The regulations governing your facility may provide a timetable for systematic inspection of the water and the surrounding areas. Be sure you are aware of the procedures to be followed.

Most inspections cover not only the pool or the waterfront but also include any structures on the facility grounds, and the results should be reported to the managers of the facility. As a general guideline, the following areas should be checked:

Bottom	Diving area
Water clarity	Diving boards
Chemical readings	Diving stands
Air and water temperature	Radio or phone system
Deck	Entry and exit areas
Ladders	Shower and locker room areas
Lifelines and lane lines	Water fountains
First aid and safety equipment	Deck chairs or furniture
Lights	Drain areas
Filtration system	

If a problem is noted in any of these areas, maintenance is required. That maintenance must be performed to remove the risk associated with the conditions and to protect the facility from legal action in the event of a related injury. Patrons should not be allowed in areas with problems until the hazards are removed or fixed.

The inspection forms, together with maintenance reports indicating when and how the noted safety problems were handled, should be filed in a secure location and kept for at least 5 years.

Daily maintenance is also vital to the well-run aquatic facility. Testing pool chemicals, sweeping walkways and locker room floors, emptying trash cans, and disinfecting floors, benches, toilet seats, and fixtures are all important to the cleanliness and healthfulness of your facility.

SAFETY AND SANITATION PRECAUTIONS

Pool chemical safety, electrical safety, and maintenance of nonslip surfaces are all areas of concern in pool management. Pools also must be kept clear of fecal contamination, which can spread many different diseases.

Chemical Safety

Although you are not likely to be solely responsible for the management of pool chemistry, you may be asked to assist in this task. You must be aware of the potential dangers of pool chemicals; mishandling them is hazardous.

To better understand the dangers and proper handling of the chemicals used at your facility, ask your pool operator or manager for copies of the material safety data sheets (MSDS) for those chemicals. By OSHA (Occupational Safety and Health Administration) standards, your employer must have these informational sheets available. Your employer should train you in the handling of pool chemicals before you work with them.

Use the following general safety precautions when handling chemicals:

- Never smoke near chemicals.
- Avoid inhaling the fumes or dust of any chemical.

- Avoid spilling chemicals on your clothes or body.
- Wear a dust mask or breathing apparatus, rubber gloves, and a rubber apron when handling chemicals.
- Never mix chemicals together.
- Always add acid to water—never add water to acid.
- Divide a chemical into three equal units and apply a third of the chemical every 3 to 4 hours.
- Dissolve powders or crystals in water before adding them to the pool.
- Use chemical feed pumps, and change output levels slowly if possible.
- Add chemicals dissolved in water to the pool when the pool is not in use.
- Avoid adding chemicals to vacuum filter tanks, skimmers, or gutters.
- Make sure chemicals are stored properly.

Before you help move or apply any chemical, be sure you know how to work with that substance. Your pool operator should provide you adequate instruction before you attempt to assist in chemical operations.

Your facility should have a plan for chemical emergencies. In the event of a chemical accident, contact EMS immediately. These professionals will provide advanced care for the victim. While awaiting the EMS, you can provide some emergency first aid. The chart here indicates what steps you can take in the event of a chemical accident.

First Aid for Chemical Accidents

For any chemical accident, have someone call EMS immediately.

Chlorine Gas

Remove the victim from the area; keep him or her warm and quiet. Lay the victim on the back with the head elevated. If the victim is breathing, administer oxygen if you are trained to do so. If the victim is not breathing, begin rescue breathing or CPR immediately, supplementing it with oxygen if you are trained to do so.

Liquid Chlorine

Flush skin with cold water. Flush eyes with cold water for 15 to 30 minutes. If clothing is splashed with the chemical, remove the clothing and wash the skin with cold water. If the victim has swallowed the chemical, have someone call the poison control center in your area after calling EMS.

Hydantoin Bromine

If the liquid mixture gets in your eyes, flush with cold water for 15 to 30 minutes. If clothing is splashed with the chemical, remove the clothing and wash the skin with cold water. For contact with skin, flush with cold water. If the victim has inhaled fumes from a dry chemical fire, give oxygen if you are trained to do so. If the victim has swallowed the chemical, have someone call the poison control center in your area after calling EMS.

Dry Chlorine Compounds

For dry chlorine compounds, such as calcium or lithium hypochlorite and chlorinated cyanurates or sodium bisulfate, flush skin with cold water. Flush eyes with cold water for 15 to 30 minutes. For contact with clothing, remove the clothing and flush the skin with cold water. If the victim has inhaled fumes from a chemical fire, give oxygen if you are trained to do so. If the chemical was swallowed, have someone call the poison control center in your area after calling EMS.

Muratic Acid

Flush skin or eyes with cold water for 15 to 30 minutes. If clothing is splashed, remove the clothing and flush the skin with cold water for 15 to 30 minutes.

Soda Ash, Diatomaceous Earth

Flush skin with cold water. Flush eyes with cold water for 15 to 30 minutes. If the victim inhaled large amounts of the substance, have someone call EMS.

Test Kit Reagent

Flush skin with cold water. Flush eyes with cold water for 15 to 30 minutes. For contact with clothing, remove the clothing and flush the skin with cold water. If the chemical was swallowed, have someone call the poison control center in your area after calling EMS.

The phone number of the poison control center in your area should be posted by your phone. Call the center as well as EMS whenever chemicals have been inhaled, absorbed, or swallowed.

Electrical Safety

Any pool environment poses the potential for electrical shock because electrical outlets and fixtures in this area often come in contact with water. For your protection, the National Electrical Code has established stringent requirements for the location of electrical fixtures in pool areas. Outlets are typically required to have covers and ground-fault interrupters.

Your facility must meet safety requirements, but you must also exercise caution and common sense in preventing electrical accidents. Don't use tape recorders, video cameras, or other electronic devices near the water's edge. And don't stand in water as you reach into the electrical box of the pool filter compartment.

Nonslip Surface Maintenance

Pool lifeguards often are required to perform maintenance jobs prior to pool opening, while off duty, or during relief breaks. One job that is frequently performed incorrectly, and which could cause an accident, is the cleaning of nonslip surfaces. Such surfaces can be found on places such as springboards, diving mount steps, starting block surfaces and steps, lifeguard chair steps, steps leading to water slides and flumes, and steps to diving platforms. At outdoor facilities where these surfaces are constantly wet and are shaded, green algae can cause the surface to become slippery. In indoor pools, especially those with high humidity or poor air handling, or in which the air handling system is turned off overnight (which is improper), black mildew may collect on these surfaces, which also can cause slipperiness.

In an effort to clean these surfaces, lifeguards or maintenance personnel often are told to scrub the surface with detergent and a stiff bristled brush. However, frequent scrubbing with such a brush will loosen the silica in the paint or loosen the sand put on top of the wet paint (as is done in homemade resurfacing). If the gritty material is removed by scrubbing, the surfaces become smooth and slippery when wet, and are then hazardous.

A better way to clean nonslip surfaces is to apply household bleach, full strength, to the entire surface to be cleaned. After letting it stand for up to 5 minutes, rinse the bleach off with a hose. This type of cleaning removes the slime while leaving the grit material in place. It also is less effort than scrubbing!

FECAL CONTAMINATION OF POOL WATER

Fecal matter in the water can transmit many different bacteria, viruses, and parasites, including blood-borne pathogens, to others. This is why you must take immediate action if you see feces in the pool. Notify your aquatic director or pool manager so he or she can put your facility's cleanup policy into action.

The YMCA of the USA recommends the following cleanup procedures:

- If the feces are solid and the free chlorine level is above 1.5 ppm (parts per million), remove the fecal matter and check the free chlorine level in three different locations. Samples should be taken from shallow, transitional, and deep water and should not be taken from water in front of inlets.

- If the feces are solid and the free chlorine level is below 1.5 ppm, follow the same steps as in the previous example. However, in this case the pool must be closed and the water treated until the free chlorine residual is 2.0 ppm in three different locations. Do not reopen the pool until 30 minutes after the free chlorine residual has reached 2.0 ppm.

- If the feces are liquid and include particulates, the person who had the fecal accident has had diarrhea in the last two weeks, or your health department has identified your pool as the source of cryptosporidium, use more extensive procedures (detailed in appendix G).

Some steps you can take as a lifeguard to help prevent the contamination of pool water with feces are these:

- Follow your YMCA's procedures for maintaining the correct disinfectant levels.
- If you see someone changing a baby's diaper on deck, ask him or her to move to the bathroom or locker room to change the baby to avoid contaminating the deck.
- If your pool has a rule that infants and preschoolers must wear diapers that keep fecal matter inside the diapers, enforce that rule.

For more information on the prevention and control of fecal contamination in swimming pools, see appendix G.

SIGNAGE

Along with adequate safety inspections, every aquatic facility should have signs with rules, warnings, and information about water depth and other potential hazards. These signs should be large enough to be read from a distance, written in language that is easy to understand, and placed in the proper visible location. Where possible, use universal symbols, and in multilingual areas, signs should be multilingual. All depth markings should be at least 4 inches high and be posted in both feet and meters. They must appear on the pool deck and on the vertical wall at or above the water's surface, and they must be of a contrasting color with the background.

FILTRATION

Each aquatic facility has its own system and procedures for maintaining the water environment. Although these systems vary, all should meet the standards set by the appropriate local and state public health and safety organizations. Additional information regarding your facility's system can be obtained from your manager. You also can receive additional training by taking the YMCA P.O.O.L. (Pool Operator on Location) course. Be sure to follow manufacturer's instructions relating to care and use of the equipment.

Filtration Equipment

In general, the filtration system in a pool is designed to recirculate the water continuously, keeping it clean, safe, and enjoyable for all swimmers. The system serves a number of important functions:

- Removes hair, lint, leaves, and other items that would otherwise interfere with the water treatment process
- Adds fresh water to replace water lost through leakage, splashing, evaporation, cleaning, and skimming

- Recirculates water so that all pool water is filtered every 6 to 8 hours (check your state code on required filtration rate)
- Adds chlorine or bromine to disinfect the water
- Adds soda ash or acid when necessary to maintain the appropriate pH level
- Filters out any materials suspended in the water
- Cleans itself with a backwash system

The catcher that removes foreign matter from the water protects the pumping unit. Having debris flow through the system would cause unnecessary wear and reduce the pump's effectiveness.

Repairs on the pumps and motors that run the filtration system should always be made by competent technicians who are familiar with the manufacturer's instructions for the equipment. Normal maintenance consists of:

- protecting the pumps and motors against water and chemical corrosion,
- lubricating the pumps and motors, and
- adjusting the pump packing to ensure a slight water leak, thus avoiding over-tightening the adjustment bolts.

Most pools use one of two types of filtration systems: sand-and-gravel or diatomaceous earth.

Sand-and-Gravel Filtration Systems

Dirt and other suspended particles must be removed from pool water to provide maximum clarity. Sand-and-gravel filters are one type of filter system used in many pools. There are three common types of sand-and-gravel filters.

- Vacuum sand filters consist of a bed of several layers of gravel topped with sand in an open tank. Water flows through the layers of sand and gravel, which trap the dirt, and is recirculated by a combination of gravity and vacuum forces.
- Pressure sand filters are closed filter tanks containing several layers of sand and gravel. Water is forced through the layers, which trap the dirt, usually in the first layer of sand.
- High-pressure or high-rate sand filters combine two or more small closed filter tanks, usually consisting of a few feet of sand. This setup is used to speed the filtration. Dirt particles are removed throughout the entire bed of sand as the water moves through the filter from top to bottom.

Diatomaceous Earth Filtration Systems

These filters also remove small particles from the water, but diatomaceous earth differs from sand in being made up of fossilized marine plant life, or diatoms. When diatomaceous earth is applied to the system's filter elements, water passes through and around the tiny spaces in the diatoms, which trap the dirt particles. Diatomaceous earth filters, because of the size of their individual particles, can remove smaller particles than sand-and-gravel filters.

Cleaning the Pool Bottom

Filters remove the fine dirt that is suspended in the water, but a certain amount of matter settles to the pool bottom. Removing this residue takes some of the strain off the filters and makes for a more attractive pool.

The extra dirt can be picked up by a pool vacuum. Two common types are a portable pump and motor, which can be rolled to the edge of the pool, and a vacuum line hooked directly to the filter system.

The vacuum line is perhaps the most popular method because it operates without any loss of water. Connections to the vacuum hose are made at various points around the pool by outlets a few inches under the surface. Other models and methods for cleaning the pool bottom are on the market.

The best time to vacuum is in the morning when no one is in the pool, after the sediment has settled overnight. In smaller pools, the operation can be done from the deck by using a long pole with a vacuum head attached to vacuum along the bottom of the pool. In larger pools, automatic vacuums move across the pool bottom.

POOL CHEMISTRY

Maintaining safe, clean water for swimming requires the use of chemicals to kill bacteria and to keep the proper pH balance. The correct balance helps ensure that water isn't irritating to swimmers and, in outdoor pools, that algae won't form in the water and on pool surfaces. The amount of chemical to be used is determined in part by the facility's capacity.

Disinfecting Water

Chlorine is the most common water disinfectant, although bromine has become more popular recently. They work in similar ways. For our purposes, we'll consider how chlorine functions. If your facility uses bromine, ask about proper testing procedures.

Chlorine acts quickly and can be maintained in the water to provide for continuous disinfection. Although chlorine can be corrosive and poisonous, it does not pose any great difficulty in distribution or handling.

Water can be chlorinated in several ways. One method is using pure chlorine gas contained in cylinders under pressure. A chlorinator is needed to feed the gas into the pool in a controlled manner. Another common method of chlorination is using hypochlorites in liquid, granular, or powder form. Such substances are applied by a chemical feeder that must operate constantly to maintain a steady amount of chlorine suspended in the water, or a residual.

Water must be tested for the residual value of chlorine; it is considered safe if a minimal value of 0.4 ppm can be maintained. The recommended level is 1.0 ppm. The acceptable level of chlorine residual varies among states, so check with your health department to learn about local standards.

One common method used to test residual chlorine is the colorimeter test. A sample of water to be tested is mixed with the test solution in a test tube, and the coloring immediately produced indicates the amount of residual chlorine present. By comparing the color to a fixed scale, you can make an accurate reading in seconds. Another test uses a test strip, whose coloration is also compared to a fixed scale.

Acid-Base Balance

Water molecules are constantly breaking up into positive or negative ions. An excess of positive ions make the water more acidic, which can cause skin irritation and corrode metal surfaces. An excess of negative ions makes the water more basic, which can lead to cloudy water and form scale on filters and plumbing. Thus, a proper balance of acidic to base is sought for effective filtration, for effective use of chlorine, and for swimmers' comfort.

This balance is maintained by testing for pH, a measurement of how basic or acidic the water is. A pH test is used to monitor the water. You can determine the pH with a colorimeter test or test strips: A rating below 7.0 is considered acidic; above 7.0, basic. The recommended pH range is 7.4 to 7.6. At this level the water is suitably alkaline (basic) for the filtration system to operate. Soda ash (sodium carbonate), added through a chemical feeder, is the generally accepted material used to raise the pH level when necessary.

Algae Control

Algae is slimy-looking green or brown plant life that makes pools look and smell uncared for. Because wind and rain can introduce algae to water, growth of algae is more of a problem in outdoor than indoor pools. If conditions are right, algae can multiply enough within 24 to 48 hours to grow on the pool walls and make water appear green or brown.

Warm water encourages the growth of algae as well as of bacteria. Control of algae has been a perplexing problem for outdoor pool operators. The best method to control algae is to prevent its growth. Once algae begins its growth cycle, the chief method for control is superchlorinating the water. During this procedure, which must be done when the pool is not in use, the chlorine residual is raised to 3.0 ppm, three times the recommended amount of residual.

Pool Volume

Whatever chemical is to be applied, the pool volume (sometimes known as facility capacity) is an important determinant of the amount to be used. A variety of formulas exist to determine the volume of water in the pool. Once you know the capacity, check the manufacturer's instructions for proper chemical application.

In general, you can determine the volume of a rectangular pool by using the following formula:

$$\text{Volume in gallons} = (\text{length} \times \text{width} \times \text{average depth}) \times 7.5$$

where 7.5 is the number of gallons in a cubic foot of water.

WATER TESTING

It is vital that the water in any aquatic facility be tested systematically. Faulty procedures or lack of adherence to standards can increase the risk of spreading communicable diseases, damaging the filtration system, and promoting algae growth. Your facility should have a commercial grade testing kit (figure 14.1) available for testing disinfectant levels, pH, alkalinity, and calcium hardness (hard water). The facility should also test for the amount of total dissolved solids in the water—the sweat, body lotion, hair spray, disinfectant, and other solids that would be left if all of the pool water evaporated. If the chemicals used in testing the water are over 1 year old (6 months for phenol red), they should be replaced; they must be fresh to ensure valid testing. In fact, chemicals stored incorrectly may not last even 2 weeks.

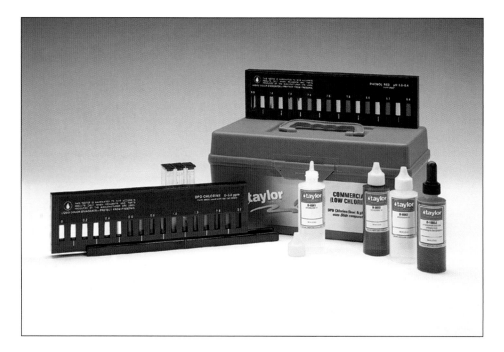

Figure 14.1   A commercial grade water testing kit.

Your facility procedures should call for the water to be tested at regular intervals during the day (figure 14.2). The need for more frequent testing depends on the number of swimmers, the temperature, and numerous other factors.

Figure 14.2 Test the water several times a day.

Table 14.1 identifies six tests that should be conducted, what tests should be used, and acceptable levels for each.

Table 14.1   **Water Quality Tests**

Element tested	Type of test	Appropriate level
Residual chlorine	Colorimeter or test strip	1.0 ppm
Residual bromine	Colorimeter or test strip*	2.0 ppm
pH	Chemical tests or test strips	7.4–7.6
Alkalinity	Chemical test kit	80–100 ppm
Calcium hardness	Chemical test kit	80–200 ppm
Total dissolved solids	Chemical test kit	200–600 ppm

* You can also use chlorine colorimeters and test strips to determine the amount of residual bromine by doubling the chlorine reading.

You may also calculate the Langelier Saturation Index weekly to ensure pH balance at a specific pool temperature. This index is important because the pH can affect both patron comfort and the pool system. Ideally, the Langelier Saturation Index should equal zero. A positive index means that a deposit may form on the valves, pipes, and pumps. A negative index means that the water may begin to corrode metal surfaces. Both circumstances can be corrected by adding corrective chemicals: muriatic acid or sodium bisulfate for positive readings and soda ash, bicarbonate of soda, or calcium chloride for negative readings.

The Langelier Saturation Index uses five variables to calculate water balance: pH, temperature, calcium hardness, alkalinity, and total dissolved solids. Temperature, calcium hardness, and alkalinity must be converted to factor weightings for use in the formula. Factor information is presented in table 14.2. Simply look up your test scores and use the related factor weighting in the formula.

$$\text{Saturation index} = \text{pH} + \text{temperature factor} + \text{calcium hardness factor} + \text{alkalinity factor} - \text{total dissolved solids}$$

For additional information about the saturation index, consult the *YMCA Pool Operations Manual (2nd edition)*.

Table 14.2 **Langelier Saturation Index**

Section 1		Section 2		Section 3	
Temperature (°F)	Temperature factor	Calcium hardness (ppm)	Calcium factor	Total alkalinity (ppm)	Alkalinity factor
32	0.0	5	0.3	5	0.7
37	0.1	25	1.0	25	1.4
46	0.2	50	1.3	50	1.7
53	0.3	75	1.5	75	1.9
60	0.4	100	1.6	100	2.0
66	0.5	150	1.8	150	2.2
76	0.6	200	1.9	200	2.3
84	0.7	300	2.1	300	2.5
94	0.8	400	2.2	400	2.6
105	0.9	800	2.5	800	2.9
128	1.0	1,000	2.6	1,000	3.0

COMMON WATER PROBLEMS

Water problems begin when the water is not tested systematically and adjusted to maintain proper disinfectant levels. When the water chemistry becomes unbalanced, the following problems may result:

- Low levels of disinfectant
- Algae growth
- Turbidity or cloudiness
- Colored water
- Hard water

The first letters of each of these problems make up the acronym LATCH.

Low Levels of Disinfectant

You must maintain an appropriate level of disinfectant in the water. The amount of free residual chlorine or bromine in the water may decline for a number of reasons:

- Increased bather load
- Old chlorine or bromine being used

- Slow circulation at the end of the filter cycle
- Sunlight and air temperature increases
- Wave and water action from pool activities

Algae Growth

Although algae themselves are not life-threatening, they should be eliminated immediately to avoid odors, slippery surfaces, decreased visibility, and a stale taste to the water. Good pool maintenance—routine superchlorination and meticulous attention to filtration and vacuuming—will reduce the likelihood of developing algae problems.

Turbidity

Cloudy water means that impurities have not been filtered out. The problem may be caused by water contamination, a malfunctioning filter, or unbalanced water chemistry. The best solution is to prevent turbidity in the first place. If it does occur, check to see that you have maintained the pool according to the recommended water chemistry values. Here are the steps to preventing and overcoming cloudy water:

- Maintain appropriate water chemistry levels (see the "Water Testing" section on page 294).
- Maintain the appropriate water level.
- Backwash filters on a systematic schedule.
- Keep pool entrances and deck areas clean.

Colored Water

Colored water is caused by the presence of metallic ions. Each metal gives a different color; for example, copper makes the water appear more blue, and iron gives a reddish-brown tint. You can remove the coloration by adjusting the pH to the appropriate level, superchlorinating, vacuuming the pool, cleaning the filter system, and readjusting the residual chlorine levels.

Hard Water

In many areas of the U.S., hard water—water high in calcium—is a typical complaint. Although it doesn't negatively affect patrons, the water damages plumbing and filtration systems. You can avert hard water problems easily by treating the water with sodium hexametaphosphate or a water softener when the pool is filled.

SPAS

Hot tubs and whirlpools, which are becoming popular at many aquatic facilities, pose some hazards—electrocution, drowning, and the transmission of disease seem to be the most common. A few rules and common sense will help make spas safe for patrons to enjoy. Review the rules listed on page 88 for some suggestions to make the spa at your facility hazard-free.

The health-related problems associated with spas can be reduced if the management

- maintains the spa at a temperature between 98 degrees and 104 degrees Fahrenheit,
- keeps the water chemistry balanced, and
- tests for the presence of bacteria and treats the water as necessary.

Review Questions

1. How often does the YMCA recommend safety inspections be conducted?
2. What steps should you take in the event of a chemical accident?
3. What are the procedures for cleanup of solid feces in the pool?
4. What is the role of the filtration system?
5. Describe how a vacuum sand filter functions.
6. What chemicals are used to disinfect water?
7. Define residual chlorine.
8. What is pH? What pH level is deemed appropriate for a pool?
9. What are algae?
10. What factors are included in the Langelier Saturation Index?
11. What is the best way to avoid water problems?
12. What six water tests should be conducted?

CHAPTER fifteen

Job Training and Opportunities

It is often a challenge to the newly trained lifeguard to get that first lifeguarding job. In this section you'll learn how to prepare for a job search. Once you have been hired, there are still ways to improve your skills.

In This Chapter, You'll Learn About
- getting a job and
- additional training opportunities.

GETTING A JOB

Like everything else you have done in preparing to become a lifeguard, getting a job requires some systematic work. Many qualified people are looking for the same kind of position as you. Fortunately, the skills you learn in preparing to find your first lifeguarding job will be helpful as you look for jobs in the future.

Preparing a Resume

The first step in getting a job is to prepare your resume, a brief history of your background. This information tells prospective employers what kinds of experience you have and forms the basis for their decisions on who to interview and what questions to ask.

Your resume gives a prospective employer a first impression about you, so you need to be very careful in your presentation. In general a resume should

- be neat;
- be as complete as possible;
- use accurate grammar, spelling, and punctuation;
- provide your name and address prominently;
- organize information into clear categories; and
- be as short as possible (two pages maximum).

Include the following information in your resume:

- Name, address, and phone number
- Birthdate
- Educational background, including dates of attendance and grade average
- Awards and honors you have earned
- Current certifications and their expiration dates
- Job-related experience, including employers' names, dates of employment, and positions or roles (listed with the most recent job first)
- Volunteer activities
- References

The people you select as your references are very important. First, think about the people you know who could tell a prospective employer about your reliability and your ability to perform the tasks the position would require. Teachers, previous employers, and ministers are commonly listed as references (don't use family members).

Before you list someone as a reference on your resume, as a courtesy ask if she or he is willing to be one for you. It will save you embarrassment if the answer is no, and it will alert your references to your job search. Most people serving as references want time to formulate what they would say about you to a prospective employer.

On your resume list your references' names, addresses, telephone numbers, and how they know you. You want to make it easy for employers to reach people who will tell them about your abilities. Listing how the reference knows you helps tell what kind of information the reference can supply. A neighbor will provide different information than a previous employer.

Job Searching

Once your resume is ready, you can begin looking for job opportunities. Think about where you want to work, then contact your local YMCA, park district, county recreation department, or other aquatic facilities to see if they have openings. Talk with current lifeguards or aquatic supervisors if you can to let them know you are interested in working at their facility. Ask friends who have connections with aquatic facilities you are interested in whether they know of any positions.

Check newspaper ads for job listings, but don't stop there. You can also find job listings in places such as community bulletin boards and the public library or through school counselors, public or private employment agencies, and personnel offices at large companies.

Applying for a Job

The first time you apply for a job, you'll be nervous. Don't worry—you're in good company. What is important is that you leave a positive first impression. Most job applications are done in person, so dress neatly for your visit to a prospective employer and use your best manners.

Although job application forms differ from employer to employer, most include the same types of information. Bring your resume with you to the employer's office. You'll find it helpful in completing the form. Some employers may even accept your resume rather than having you complete the application. When you arrive at the employer's office, ask about the job requirements to make sure you can meet them.

When you complete an application form, keep the following guidelines in mind:

- Complete any application in ink.
- Write or print neatly so the employer can read your application easily.
- Fill in all blanks to the best of your ability. Leaving an area unanswered may make the employer think you were careless.
- If a question does not apply to you, mark it NA (not applicable).
- Be honest; don't try to present yourself as someone you are not.

Preparing for an Interview

When a prospective employer contacts you for an interview, you must then prepare for it. Consider the interview an opportunity to learn more about the position and the employer as well as to present yourself and your abilities.

Before any interview, take these steps:

- Learn all you can about the employer and the type of facility he or she operates.
- Think about the qualities you have that will make you a good employee at such a facility.
- Prepare a list of questions you would like to ask about your responsibilities and the procedures at the facility.
- Practice answering interview questions. Ask a parent or an adult friend to play the role of the interviewer and to conduct a practice interview (figure 15.1). Typical questions include these:
  —What led you to apply for this job?
  —What do you think you can add to our organization?
  —What would you consider your greatest strength?
  —What do you think your weaknesses are?
  —What have you learned from your previous work experiences?
- Select a neat outfit to wear to your interview.

Figure 15.1 A practice interview will help you prepare for the real interview.

Interviewing

The most important thing to remember as you enter an interview is that you want to present yourself in a favorable light. Arrive a little early—it tells the prospective employer that you will be on time if you are hired. Dress neatly, and don't chew gum when you enter the office.

When the interviewer comes to get you, stand up and greet him or her with a firm handshake. Establish eye contact and smile. It's amazing how confident those actions can make you feel. They also present the image of a confident candidate. Try to maintain your eye contact throughout the interview. And try to avoid any distracting habits you might have. Biting your fingernails, drumming your fingers, scratching your head, and tapping your feet are not good ways to present a positive image!

Listen carefully to the interviewer's complete question—never interrupt. Then think before you speak. Provide a clear answer to the question without rambling. When your opportunity to ask questions arises, be sure to ask questions that show you are interested in the job and that you are interested in progressing with the organization.

As you leave, thank the interviewer for contacting you. Indicate that you are interested in the position and hope that you will be considered. Then simply shake the interviewer's hand, thank him or her, and leave in a dignified manner. When you get home, write a note thanking the interviewer for the opportunity to interview.

You may not get the first job you apply for. Learn from each experience and your interviewing skills will improve. Eventually you will land your first job. Congratulate yourself—you're on your way. But don't get complacent. Be a good employee—keep trying to learn as much as you can about your position and about the facility.

KEEPING A JOB

Jobs held early in your career are important learning opportunities. You learn work habits and responsibility. What you learn about yourself and the world all comes from your working life. How you challenge yourself and demonstrate the values of caring, honesty, respect, and responsibility are all important in your job. Here are some ways you can show these values:

- Show up for your shift on time.
- Provide constant and dedicated attention to your duties.
- Attend staff meetings and in-service training when scheduled.
- Plan for recertification in CPR, first aid, and lifeguarding to maintain your certification as a lifeguard.
- Stay in good physical condition.
- Minimize the number of times you need a substitute for your duty shift.
- Be friendly and courteous to patrons.

TRAINING OPPORTUNITIES

Remember that your certification as a lifeguard depends on keeping your CPR and first aid certifications current. More importantly, your moral and legal duties call for you to have adequate first aid and CPR training. Your local American Heart Association, National Safety Council, and American Red Cross branches offer programs that can be of value to you.

The YMCA also offers a variety of aquatic leadership and management courses that you might find valuable. For example, certification courses are available for the following positions:

- Pool Operator on Location
- Competitive Swim Coach

- Competitive Swim Official
- Aquatic Facility Manager
- Specialist Instructor/Trainer (Preschool and Parent/Child, Youth and Adult, Arthritis, Water Exercise, Water Polo/Wetball, Synchronized Swimming, Individuals With Disabilities, Lifeguard)

In-service training at your facility is also a valuable tool in your ongoing training and development (figure 15.2). Each time you review a procedure or learn a new technique, you are becoming more valuable as a professional lifeguard and more capable of taking on additional responsibility.

Figure 15.2 In-service training sessions will keep you up-to-date with the policies and procedures of your facility.

All lifeguards should practice their rescue and backboarding skills regularly. Practice on your own, and participate in the in-service training held at your facility. Such training may include the following:

- Review of CPR and first aid skills (figure 15.3)
- Backboarding skills, both in the water and on the deck

Figure 15.3 Review your CPR skills regularly and keep your certification current.

- Conditioning workouts
- Suggestions for providing service to patrons
- Practice of emergency procedures
- Discussion of lifeguarding scenarios
- Practice of evacuation procedures (in case of fire, chemical spills, power outages, inclement weather, medical emergencies, missing persons, etc.)

Your facility manager should document your participation in any in-service training.

Keep in mind, too, that if you enjoy aquatics or just working with people, you can have a lifetime career at the YMCA. YMCAs across the country offer full-time job opportunities in many different aspects of aquatics and other areas of social service and recreation. If you care about others and want to make a difference in their lives, consider working for the YMCA.

Review Questions

1. List the steps to getting a job as a professional lifeguard.
2. What should you do to prepare yourself for an interview?
3. What should you do during an interview?
4. List other training you can get to improve your lifeguarding and aquatic skills.

Child Abuse Identification and Prevention: Recommended Guidelines for YMCAs

STATEMENT OF THE YMCA OF THE USA MEDICAL ADVISORY COMMITTEE

Child abuse is damage to a child for which there is no "reasonable" explanation. Child abuse includes nonaccidental physical injury, neglect, sexual molestation, and emotional abuse.

The increasing incidence of reported child abuse has become a critical national concern. Child abuse reporting levels increased 41% from 1988 to 1997. It is a special concern of the YMCA because of the organization's role as an advocate for children and its responsibility for enhancing the personal growth and development of both children and adults in all YMCA programs.

Each YMCA is encouraged to develop a written policy that clearly defines management practices related to prevention of child abuse. This policy should include approved practices for recruiting, training, and supervising staff; a code of conduct for staff relationships with children; reporting procedures for incidents when they do occur; and the responsibility to parents on this issue.

To assist YMCAs, the YMCA of the USA has developed a *Child Abuse Prevention Training* manual. This manual includes two, 3-hour training designs—one for staff who hire and supervise and a second for front-line program staff. Sample policies and procedures are included in both designs. Each YMCA received a copy of the manual in 1994. The manual, revised in 1998, now includes an additional piece titled *The Next Steps in Child Abuse Prevention*. This section includes a "how am I doing" checklist, refresher training outlines, a justification for policies limiting staff contact with children, confidentiality and responsibility recommendations, information on screening volunteers, and more. The revised manual is available from the YMCA Program Store, item no. 0-7360-0754-7. The Next Steps document (included in the manual) is available as a stand-alone piece from the YMCA of the USA, Program Development Unit, 800-872-9622. YMCAs are encouraged to offer child abuse prevention training on a regular basis for all staff.

The following guidelines have been developed to stimulate thinking about the potential for child abuse in YMCA programs and the need to develop a YMCA policy related to this important issue. Common sense and good judgement should guide the development of required procedures. Good management policies and practices will vary based on local situations. Laws differ from state to state. YMCA administrators need to be aware of changing state and local requirements and monitor YMCA programs to ensure that they are in compliance.

GUIDELINES FOR LOCAL YMCAS FOR STAFF RECRUITMENT, TRAINING, AND SUPERVISION

1. Reference checks on all prospective employees and program volunteers will be conducted, documented, and filed prior to employment.

2. Fingerprinting and/or criminal record checks of adults who work in programs that serve children, youth, and teens, especially those authorized or required by state law, are included in the employment process.

3. Photographs will be taken of all staff and attached to their personnel records for identification at a later time if needed.

4. All new staff and volunteers must participate in an orientation program including written materials explaining YMCA policies, procedures and regulations. They should be aware of legal requirements and by their signature acknowledge having received and read appropriate policies, standards, and codes of conduct. Documentation of attendance in the child abuse prevention training should be added to the employee's personnel file. Staff should periodically read and sign again the Code of Conduct and participate in refresher trainings in child abuse prevention.

5. Staff and volunteers working directly with children will be provided information regularly about the signs of possible child abuse. They should be educated about "high-risk parents" and "high-risk families" (for example, drug addicted, alcohol addicted, mentally ill, or unemployed parents; teenage parents; and parents who were abused themselves as children). Staff training will include approved procedures for responding to the suspicion of abuse.

6. Administrative staff supervising programs involving the care of children will make unannounced visits to each program site to assure that standards, policies, program quality, and performance of staff are being maintained. Written reports on these visits will be completed.

GUIDELINES FOR STAFF RELATIONSHIPS WITH CHILDREN

7. In order to protect YMCA staff, volunteers, and program participants, at no time during a YMCA program may a program leader be alone with a single child unobserved by other staff.

8. Young children will never be unsupervised in bathrooms, locker rooms, or showers.

9. Staff may not be alone with children they meet in YMCA programs outside of the YMCA. This includes babysitting, sleepovers, and inviting children to their homes. Any exceptions require a written explanation before the fact and are subject to administrator approval.

10. Staff may not date program participants under the age of 18 years.

11. YMCA staff and volunteers will not discipline children by use of physical punishment or by failing to provide the necessities of care, such as food and shelter.

12. YMCA staff or volunteers will not verbally or emotionally abuse or punish children.

13. Staff and volunteers providing direct care for very young children will be identified by a badge/name tag or uniform that is familiar to the children with whom they work. Children will be instructed to avoid any person not so identified.

14. Staff and volunteers should be alert to the physical and emotional state of all children each time they report for a program and indicate, in writing, any signs of injury or suspected child abuse.

15. Invite parents to serve on interview committees to screen and select staff and volunteers. Caution should be taken in the selection of parents for this function. They should have a through understanding of, and be in agreement with, the YMCA's philosophy and operating procedures.

16. Ask parent(s) to sign a Parent Statement of Understanding, which includes a statement limiting staff and program volunteers in their contact with children and families outside of the YMCA program and which informs parents of the YMCA's mandate to report suspected cases of child abuse or neglect.

17. Conduct an intake/orientation with all parents to share the program's policies and procedures. Be sure to include the pre-employment screening, supervision, code of conduct, training, and other child abuse prevention policies established to protect children.

18. Daily communication should inform parents of their child's health, behavior, positive anecdotes from their day, etc.

19. The YMCA should maintain an open-door policy that encourages parents to drop by and observe or share in the program with their child—at any time.

20. The YMCA should offer information on child abuse and parenting and assistance to parents through workshops, counseling, book and video lending libraries, etc.

21. The YMCA should try to identify families in stress and offer referral information to agencies that can assist them.

22. Through newsletters, conferences, and modeling appropriate interaction skills, the YMCA should inform and educate parents about age-appropriate expectations and discipline.

23. The YMCA curriculum should stress children making choices, solving problems, developing a positive self-esteem, sharing feelings, and practicing their assertiveness skills. The YMCA should encourage parents to reinforce these skills at home as they leave children less vulnerable to maltreatment.

24. The YMCA should sponsor guest speakers who address the issues of child abuse, child abuse prevention, teaching personal safety to children, etc. Administrators should screen all individuals and their materials before allowing them to present.

REPORTING PROCEDURES

In the event that there is an accusation of child abuse, the YMCA will take prompt and immediate action as follows:

25. At the first report or probable cause to believe that child abuse has occurred, the employed staff person it has been reported to will notify the program director, who will then review the incident with the YMCA executive director or his/her designate. However, if the program director is not immediately available, this review by the supervisor cannot in any way deter the reporting of child abuse by the mandated reporters. Most states mandate each teacher or child care provider to report information they have learned in their professional role regarding suspected child abuse. In most states, mandated reporters are granted immunity from prosecution.

26. The YMCA will make a report in accordance with relevant state or local child abuse reporting requirements and will cooperate to the extent of the law with any legal authority involved.

27. In the event the reported incident(s) involve a program volunteer or employed staff, the executive director will, without exception, suspend the volunteer or staff person from the YMCA.

28. The parents or legal guardian of the child(ren) involved in the alleged incident will be promptly notified in accordance with the directions of the relevant state or local agency.

29. Whether the incident or alleged offense takes place on or off YMCA premises, it will be considered job related (because of the youth-involved nature of the YMCA).

30. Reinstatement of the program volunteer or employed staff person will occur only after all allegations have been cleared to the satisfaction of the persons named in #25 and 26 above.

31. All YMCA staff and volunteers must be sensitive to the need for confidentiality in the handling of this information, and therefore should discuss the incident only with supervisory staff and the appropriate legal authority.

32. All full-time and part-time employees and program volunteers must read and sign the Child Abuse Reporting Procedures Policy.

POSSIBLE INDICATORS OF ABUSE

Sexual Abuse—Behavioral Indicators

1. Is reluctant to change clothes in front of others
2. Is withdrawn
3. Exhibits unusual sexual behavior and/or knowledge beyond that which is common for his/her developmental stage
4. Has poor peer relationships
5. Either avoids or seeks out adults
6. Is pseudomature
7. Is manipulative
8. Is self-conscious
9. Has problems with authority and rules
10. Exhibits eating disorders
11. Is self-mutilating
12. Is obsessively clean
13. Uses or abuses alcohol and/or other drugs
14. Exhibits delinquent behavior such as running away from home
15. Exhibits extreme compliance or defiance
16. Is fearful or anxious
17. Exhibits suicidal gestures and/or attempts suicide
18. Is promiscuous
19. Engages in fantasy or infantile behavior
20. Is unwilling to participate in sports activities
21. Has school difficulties

Sexual Abuse—Physical Indicators

1. Has pain and/or itching in the genital area
2. Has bruises or bleeding in the genital area
3. Has venereal disease
4. Has swollen private parts
5. Has difficulty walking or sitting
6. Has torn, bloody, and/or stained underclothing
7. Experiences pain when urinating
8. Is pregnant

9. Has vaginal or penile discharge
10. Wets the bed

Emotional Abuse—Behavioral Indicators

1. Is overly eager to please
2. Seeks out adult contact
3. Views abuse as being warranted
4. Exhibits changes in behavior
5. Is excessively anxious
6. Is depressed
7. Is unwilling to discuss problems
8. Exhibits aggressive or bizarre behavior
9. Is withdrawn
10. Is apathetic
11. Is passive
12. Has unprovoked fits of yelling or screaming
13. Exhibits inconsistent behavior at home and school
14. Feels responsible for the abuser
15. Runs away from home
16. Attempts suicide
17. Has low self-esteem
18. Exhibits a gradual impairment of health or personality
19. Has difficulty sustaining relationships
20. Has unrealistic goal setting
21. Is impatient
22. Is unable to communicate or express his/her feelings, needs, or desires
23. Sabotages his/her chances of success
24. Lacks self-confidence
25. Is self-depreciating and has a negative self-image

Emotional Abuse—Physical Indicators

1. Has a sleep disorder (nightmares or restlessness)
2. Wets the bed
3. Exhibits developmental lags (stunting his/her physical, emotional, and/or mental growth)
4. Is hyperactive
5. Exhibits eating disorders

Physical Abuse—Behavioral Indicators

1. Is wary of adults
2. Is either extremely aggressive or withdrawn
3. Is dependent and indiscriminate in his/her attachments
4. Is uncomfortable when other children cry
5. Generally controls his/her own crying
6. Exhibits a drastic behavior change when not with parents or caregiver
7. Is manipulative
8. Has poor self-concept
9. Exhibits delinquent behavior, such as running away from home
10. Uses or abuses alcohol and/or other drugs
11. Is self-mutilating

12. Is frightened of parents or of going home
13. Is overprotective of or responsible for parents
14. Exhibits suicidal gestures and/or attempts suicide
15. Has behavior problems at school

Physical Abuse—Physical Indicators

1. Has unexplained bruises or welts, often clustered or in a pattern (or explanation is inconsistent or improbable)
2. Has unexplained and/or unusual burns (cigarettes, doughnut-shaped, immersion-lines, object-patterned) (or explanation is inconsistent or improbable)
3. Has unexplained bite marks (or explanation is inconsistent or improbable)
4. Has unexplained fractures or dislocations (or explanation is inconsistent or improbable)
5. Has unexplained abrasions or lacerations (or explanation is inconsistent or improbable)
6. Wets the bed

Neglect—Behavioral Indicators

1. Is truant or tardy to school often or arrives early and stays late
2. Begs or steals food
3. Attempts suicide
4. Uses or abuses alcohol and/or other drugs
5. Is extremely dependent or detached
6. Engages in delinquent behavior, such as prostitution or stealing
7. Appears to be exhausted
8. States frequent or continual absence of parent or guardian

Neglect—Physical Indicators

1. Frequently is dirty, unwashed, hungry, or inappropriately dressed
2. Engages in dangerous activities (possibly because he/she generally is unsupervised)
3. Is tired and listless
4. Has unattended physical problems
5. May appear to be overworked and/or exploited

Family Indicators

1. Extreme paternal dominance, restrictiveness, and/or overprotectiveness
2. Family isolated from community and support systems
3. Marked role reversal between mother and child
4. History of sexual abuse for either parent
5. Substance abuse by either parent or by children
6. Other types of violence in the home
7. Absent spouse (through chronic illness, depression, divorce, or separation)
8. Severe overcrowding
9. Complaints about a "seductive" child
10. Extreme objection to implementation of child sexual abuse curriculum

Note: These indicators can also be indicative of emotional dysfunctions that merit investigation for emotional problems and/or being the victim of abuse.

Becca Cowan Johnson, 1992. *For Their Sake: Recognizing, Responding to and Reporting Child Abuse*. Martinsville, IN: American Camping Association. Reprinted by permission of the publisher. For permission to reprint please contact the publisher at (764) 342-8456 or msnider@ada-camps.org. A brief staff training handbook is also available from the publisher.
"Family Indicators" taken from Committee for Children, 2203 Airport Way S., Suite 500, Seattle, Washington 98134-2027; 800-634-4449; **http://www.cfchildren.org/**.

YMCAs are urged to share copies of their management policies related to child abuse with other YMCAs and the YMCA of the USA. A bibliography of printed and audiovisual educational resources for use with parents and children is included in *The Next Steps in Child Abuse Prevention* available from the YMCA of the USA, Program Development Unit, 800-872-9622, or the 1998 edition of the *Child Abuse Prevention Training Manual* available from the YMCA Program Store, 800-747-0089.

June, 1989
Revised April, 1996
Revised October, 2000

EMPLOYEE CODE OF CONDUCT

1. In order to protect YMCA staff, volunteers, and program participants, at no time during a YMCA program may a staff person be alone with a single child where he or she cannot be observed by others. As staff supervise children, they should space themselves in such a way that other staff can see them.

2. Staff shall never leave a child unsupervised.

3. Restroom supervision. Staff will make sure the restroom is not occupied by suspicious or unknown individuals before allowing children to use the facilities. Staff will stand in the doorway of the restroom while children are using the restroom. This policy allows privacy for the children and protection for the staff (not being alone with a child). If staff are assisting younger children, doors to the facility must remain open. No child, regardless of age, should ever enter a bathroom alone on a field trip. Always send children in pairs, and whenever possible, with staff.

4. Staff should conduct or supervise private activities in pairs—diapering, putting on bathing suits, taking showers, etc. When this is not feasible, staff should be positioned so that they are visible to others.

5. Staff shall not abuse children, including the following:
    - Physical abuse—striking, spanking, shaking, slapping
    - Verbal abuse—humiliating, degrading, threatening
    - Sexual abuse—inappropriately touching or speaking
    - Mental abuse—shaming, withholding kindness, being cruel
    - Neglect—withholding food, water, basic care, etc.

6. Staff must use positive techniques of guidance, including redirection, positive reinforcement, and encouragement rather than competition, comparison, and criticism. Staff will have age-appropriate expectations and set up guidelines and environments that minimize the need for discipline. Physical restraint is used only in predetermined situations (necessary to protect the child or other children from harm), is only administered in a prescribed manner, and must be documented in writing.

7. Staff will conduct a health check of each child each day as they enter the program, noting any fever, bumps, bruises, burns, etc. Staff will direct questions or comments to the parent or child in a nonthreatening way. Any questionable marks or responses will be documented.

8. Staff will respond to children with respect and consideration and treat all children equally regardless or gender, race, religion, or culture.

9. Staff will respect children's rights to not be touched in ways that make them feel uncomfortable and their right to say "no." Other than diapering, children are not to be touched on areas of their bodies that would be covered by a bathing suit.

10. Staff will refrain from intimate displays of affection towards others in the presence of children, parents, and staff.

11. While the YMCA does not discriminate against an individual's lifestyle, it does require that in the performance of the job, he or she will abide by the standards of conduct set forth by the YMCA.

12. Staff must appear clean, neat, and appropriately attired.

13. Using, possessing, or being under the influence of alcohol or illegal drugs during working hours is prohibited.

14. Smoking or use of tobacco in the presence of children or parents during working hours is prohibited.

15. Profanity, inappropriate jokes, sharing intimate details of one's personal life, and any kind of harassment in the presence of children or parents is prohibited.

16. Staff must be free of physical and psychological conditions that might adversely affect the children's physical or mental health. If in doubt, an expert should be consulted.

17. Staff will portray a positive role model for youth by maintaining an attitude of respect, loyalty, patience, courtesy, tact, and maturity.

18. Staff may not be alone with children they meet in YMCA programs outside of the YMCA. This includes babysitting, sleepovers, and inviting children to their homes. Any exceptions require a written explanation before the fact and are subject to administrator approval.

19. Staff are not to transport children in their own vehicles.

20. Staff may not date program participants under the age of 18.

21. Under no circumstances should staff release children to anyone other than the authorized parent, guardian, or other adult authorized by the parent or guardian (written parent authorization on file with the YMCA).

22. Staff are required to read and sign all policies related to identifying, documenting, and reporting child abuse and attend trainings on the subject, as instructed by a supervisor.

23. Staff will act in a caring, honest, respectful, and responsible manner.

I understand that any violation of this Code of Conduct may result in termination.

Employee signature _____

Supervisor signature _____

Date_____

APPENDIX B

New Aquatic Guidelines for Resident Camp, Day Camp, Child Care, and Waterfront Operations

The following is a document with updated aquatic guidelines released by the YMCA of the USA in June 1998.

INTRODUCTION

Conducting quality programs that meet both industry standards and local needs is an ongoing task for YMCA staff and volunteers. The New Aquatic Guidelines for Resident Camp, Day Camp, Child Care, and Waterfront Operations will help local YMCA staff and volunteers assess the quality of their aquatic programs. These more detailed guidelines about aquatics in child care, day and resident camps, and along the waterfront expand upon the basic guidelines that were previously published in *Principles of YMCA Aquatics* (1st edition) in 1997. They were further developed for child care, day and resident camping, and waterfront operations because local YMCA leaders asked us to do so. Used as a tool for self-assessment, the guidelines can point out both areas that need improvement and areas of excellence. Meant to be used in conjunction with YMCA of the USA aquatic program manuals, the guidelines have been compiled from suggestions and evaluation instruments contributed by many local YMCAs.

It is important to differentiate between guidelines and standards. Guidelines are recommendations from the YMCA of the USA to be considered by local YMCAs. Standards are rules or policies governing any particular program that can only be set by the local association. In developing those standards, each YMCA can customize these guidelines to conform to their methods of operation and to the needs and legal requirements of their communities. Input from every level of your organization—staff, volunteers, and members—is crucial to developing your own standards; quality should be everyone's concern.

When developing your standards, keep in mind that there may be local or state regulations with which your YMCA *must* comply. Because regulations vary from place to place, each instructor is responsible for knowing and abiding by the requirements in her or his locale. The local YMCA director should be able to provide the necessary information about those requirements. Instructors who aren't knowledgeable about them should be sure to ask.

But instructors also need to be aware that state and local standards may only be minimum requirements for operation and may not fully address the quality of the program desired by participants and the YMCA. The goal of a YMCA should be to offer programs of the highest possible quality.

Development of standards is only a starting point. Once that is done, your YMCA will need to create a process to regularly assess programs using the standard benchmarks. The following is a recommended six-step approach, which should be conducted by an outside validation team:

1. The association CEO or branch executive explains the assessment process to staff and volunteers.
2. The aquatic director, with the help of other staff, conducts a review of all programs using the standards and addresses areas needing improvement.
3. A validation team is recruited from the community. This team may include program participants, experts in aquatics, directors of other aquatic facilities, YMCA board members, or staff from other YMCAs.
4. An orientation is conducted for the validation team to review the association's aquatic program standards.
5. The validation team conducts a review of each program.
6. The validation team reports its findings to the YMCA Board of Directors through the appropriate channels and process.

Using a validation team provides good community publicity for your YMCA. It familiarizes key people with YMCA aquatic programs and impresses upon them your concern for quality.

During assessment, each standard should be considered important and should be addressed at the appropriate staff level. Self-assessment should not only provide an overview of each program but also reinforce the specific standard.

After the assessment is completed, staff and volunteers should determine what corrective action, if any, is needed to bring programs in line with the standards. A realistic timetable should be established for implementation, and a monitoring system that focuses on achievement should be put in place. Maintaining high quality in programs is an ongoing job; assessment needs to be done regularly to maintain the standards.

CHILD CARE AND CAMPING AQUATIC ACTIVITIES AND PROGRAMS

The child care/camp director should meet with the aquatic director to plan a safe, developmentally appropriate program for the children. The discussion should include the following:

- What is the length of each swim session?
- What type of program (lessons, structured games, recreational swimming) will be offered?
- What are the ages of the children (needed to help determine instructor-to-student ratios)?
- Will all children participate in the aquatic program, and how will you identify who will participate in the swim program? Determine alternate activities for the children who do not swim.
- Discuss how children will be identified as swimmers/nonswimmers (using, for example, wrist bands, colored swimming caps), as well as usage of diving board, floatation devices, inflatables, toys, etc.
- How many lifeguards will be needed? (Consider state and local ordinances, licensing requirements, and local YMCA policy.) How many instructors will be needed?
- What will child care/camp staff be expected to do during aquatic activities (for example, help children change, supervise children in the water, act as "safety assistants" on deck, conduct restroom runs, supervise locker rooms)?
- When will joint staff training and in-service training sessions be held?

- What are the emergency procedures?
- What are the emergency procedure roles/responsibilities for child care/camp staff?
- What safety orientation and pool/waterfront rules will be reviewed with children?
- Which department pays for expenses related to the camp/child care use of the pool?
- If the pool/waterfront is to be shared with others, how it will be scheduled?
- Review all applicable state and local regulations related to swimming pools/waterfronts, child care, and camping.

Make sure a written plan is in place for safety considerations (depth of water, starting blocks, number of children in the water, identification of swimmers who cannot swim, staff placement in and out of the water, etc.). Make sure everyone is aware of the plan and emergency procedures (including lost swimmer drills).

A deep water test should be administered to all children, and a record of results should be kept at the YMCA and with camp/child care staff if you are using another swimming facility.

A camp/child care supervisor should be on duty during all aquatic activities, in addition to an on-site aquatic supervisor. This is in addition to the appropriate number of lifeguards and other staff necessary to protect the safety of the children. If a center is licensed, required ratios must be maintained.

Games and activities should be conducted if the plan for swimming does not include instruction. *Notes:* When children are involved in activities, rather than allowed to play freely in the water, they are safer and learn additional skills.

Well-trained and experienced aquatic staff members should conduct an aquatic safety orientation and training session for all camp/child care staff who will assist in swimming activities. A session should be conducted prior to the camp/child care program and continue throughout the season.

A lost swimmer policy and drill should be established and part of the aquatic plan. The lost swimmer drill should be reviewed with all staff and practiced on a regular basis throughout the season. Refer to *On the Guard II: The YMCA Lifeguard Manual (4th edition)*.

Childrens' emergency information, medications, first aid supplies, and local emergency numbers should be readily accessible. If you travel to another site for swimming, the records should accompany the director (or appointed supervisor) to the off-site location.

Define responsibilities for day camp/child care staff, swim instructors, lifeguards, and children. For example, for recreational activities, these are suggested responsibilities:

Camp/Child Care Staff

Watch children at all times, whether in water, locker rooms, or otherwise.

Pair up buddies (if buddy system is used).

Guide children's behavior and help to enforce pool/waterfront rules.

Supervise in locker rooms and on deck.

Ensure children take thorough soap showers before entering the pool.

Help children keep track of their clothing.

Follow your YMCA's policy for proper attire on deck.

Follow all rules and regulations.

Alert the lifeguard if assistance is needed.

Keep track of swimmers who leave the pool/waterfront area.

Conduct head counts.

Obey lifeguard decisions and instructions.

Supervise children not participating in programmed aquatic activities.

Collect lost and found articles; clean up deck/beach area.

Inform aquatic staff if any child has a disability or requires special attention.

Know emergency procedures and lost swimmer policy.

Children

Take care of their clothing and towel.

Take a thorough soap shower before entering the pool.

Follow all pool/waterfront rules and procedures.

Ask permission to leave the pool/waterfront area.

Be quiet on a signal: "When the whistle blows, mouths close."

Stay with their buddy (if buddy system is used).

Lifeguards

Guard the pool/waterfront and enforce the rules.

If not on guard duty at the time, test children, assign them to a swimming area, and give them identifiable bands or other items to identify their swim level.

If not on guard duty at the time, orient swimmers to rules and procedures to follow when in the pool/waterfront area.

Swim Instructors

Teach classes.

Are certified in the aquatic specialist (YMCA Swim Lessons Instructor) area in which they are instructing.

Maintain complete records and complete end-of-session progress reports.

Table 1 shows recommended staff ratios for children in the water.

Table 1	Instructional Swimming	
Classification	**Age (years)**	**Ratio to instructor**
Child	0 to 3	1:1 in the water, unless state child care licensing regulations are stricter. Follow the YMCA of the USA aquatic guidelines for children under the age of 3.
Preschool	3 to 5	6:1
Youths	6 and up	8:1 for Polliwog and Guppy levels 10:1 of Minnow level and up

Ratios do not include the lifeguards or supervising child care/camp staff members.

RECREATIONAL SWIMMING

The facility size and water depth, equipment, and participants' ages and ability levels may require additional supervision. As a general rule, have one lifeguard to every 25 campers (age 6 and over) plus one additional trained day camp staff member who serves as "safety assistant" on deck to observe swimmers.

Other camp/child care staff should still be involved with the children playing in the water or assigned to children on deck or those not swimming. *Note:* Pool design and water depth may affect the number of staff needed. For example, if the pool is too deep for children to stand, additional staff may be needed and/or flotation devices may be required for children.

Children under the age of 6 and those with special needs will require additional supervision.

During recreational swims, the number of nonswimmers (for example, preschoolers in the water at one time without flotation devices) should be limited or additional staff assigned to increase supervision. All nonswimmers who cannot touch the bottom of the pool should wear flotation devices.

Day camp/child care staff members designated as *safety assistants* should be under the direct supervision of aquatic personnel; oriented to procedures for aquatic safety, the activity, and the site, as well as elementary emergency assistance, CPR, and first aid certification; and stationed to observe participants, quickly assist them, and signal lifeguards if necessary. *Note:* We recommend that these individuals be certified as YMCA aquatic safety assistants.

Plan entry to and exit from the pool/waterfront to ensure staff always know how many children they have with them and where the children are at all times. An assigned staff member should check head counts and/or attendance before children enter the water and prior to the children's leaving the pool/waterfront area. Use a standard location where all children are seated before and after aquatic activities.

Camp/child care staff must be aware of and follow each individual pool's/waterfront's operating procedures (if the program utilizes several sites).

A head count system should be used during recreational swimming. During regular periods, all swimmers should be called out of the water and the number of swimmers counted. For example, every 15 minutes, after three loud whistle blasts, the children must sit on the side of the pool or deck with their buddies so they can be counted. Follow any state or local codes on the frequency with which head counts are needed.

If children leave to use the restroom, make sure they check in with staff before re-entering the water. Children should be supervised in the restrooms or locker rooms by more than one adult as a child abuse prevention practice.

Children should pass a swim test before being allowed in the deep end of the pool or water. The test should include the ability to swim the length (20 to 25 yards) of the pool/waterfront comfortably without the use of flotation devices. There should be some means of identifying swimmers who are allowed in the deep end (such as wrist bands, caps, etc.). Document the results of testing, such as which children can swim and where they can go in the water. All other children should be classified as nonswimmers.

SWIMMING FACILITIES AND WATER PARKS NOT OWNED BY THE YMCA

Day camp and child care programs should only use public/private waterfronts that have a qualified lifeguard or lifeguards on duty. If the programs use waterfronts without lifeguards on duty, the YMCA should provide its own lifeguard or lifeguards, ones who hold proper certification and have received training in that aquatic environment.

Prior to the trip, the day camp/child care director should visit with the park staff to walk through the facility to review parking areas, entrances and exits, bathrooms, vending areas, proper use of slides and other equipment, emergency procedures, missing child procedures (including intercom announcements available for lost children), lifeguard-to-swimmer ratios, first aid stations, etc. Staff should write a plan based on this meeting.

Discuss the responsibilities of the day camp/child care staff while at the facility and any other facility rules. Emphasize that staff must supervise the children at all times and detail how the children will be grouped and allowed to move around the facility with their group leader. Discuss the system that will be used to identify YMCA staff and children by employees at the host facility.

When the group arrives, they should check in with the facility manager or head lifeguard. Any child with a disability or otherwise requiring special attention should be brought to the attention of the staff of the aquatic facility. A head count or attendance should be checked regularly, and day camp/child care staff should give children a rest period every hour.

Children should have identification bands or other means of identifying them as members of the YMCA group. Children should stay with a buddy from the time they leave the YMCA until they return. Staff should wear the same identifying YMCA attire (T-shirts, visors, etc.) so they can be easily identified as YMCA staff.

To prepare for medical emergencies and the need for first aid, do the following:

- Bring emergency information about the children (for example, special conditions) to the facility.
- Take a first aid kit to the facility.
- Transport medication for children by a designated adult. If the medication is administered, the person administering it should make notes on medical forms for parents to review.
- If possible, have a YMCA lifeguard or designated "first responder" (in charge of first aid) travel with the group to increase group safety. This person can be in charge of the medical information forms and group first aid kit.

Rules about the facility and the attractions (for example, water slides) should be reviewed with the children. Also give an introduction to the attractions so children are aware of what to expect during the ride. A meeting point should be designated in case anyone gets separated from the group. At all times, a YMCA staff person should be at a designated spot known to facility staff and children. If feasible, a tour of the facility should be given to the children prior to allowing them to play. Children should be shown the designated swimming and picnicking areas, as well as what is off limits to them.

All other field trip guidelines should be followed.

WATERFRONT SAFETY

In these guidelines, the term *waterfront* will refer to any place where open water meets land. This includes surf and inland aquatic environments, such as rivers, ponds, lakes (natural or artificial), quarries, reservoirs, and ocean beaches.

Waterfront program and facility operations must conform to all local, state, and federal health and safety codes and ordinances. YMCA of the USA aquatic guidelines (where applicable) and applicable American Camping Association standards should also apply. Based on these guidelines, develop your own association policy

A written policy explaining aquatic operating and emergency procedures should be available and reviewed with all camp and aquatic leadership staff regularly throughout the season. See *On the Guard II: The YMCA Lifeguard Manual (4th edition)*.

All waterfront program and facility operations should have the following equipment readily available in an appropriate quantity based on the size of the facility and attendance. All equipment should be inspected daily.

Emergency Equipment

Keep the following emergency equipment nearby: telephone with emergency numbers posted; first aid kit; personal protective equipment, such as latex gloves, resuscitation mask and equipment, eye shield, and pocket masks; backboard; head restraints, cervical collars, and backboard straps; rescue boat; paddleboard; and rescue tubes/buoys, masks, fins, and snorkels. A rescue boat or motorized rescue craft is recommended for larger facilities.

Remote and rural locations should seriously consider having the following available: supplemental oxygen (O_2); an automatic external defibrillator (AED); a first aid room with bed; refrigeration or ice; splints, blankets, and a suction respiration bag-valve mask. The time and distance away from advanced life support services should be used to determine the necessity of this equipment. A helicopter landing zone location and emergency procedures for helicopter evacuation should be established. Also, there will be a need of advanced trained staff (EMT/RN) on site in these areas. Staff on duty should be trained and certified to administer additional medical equipment (O_2 or AED) if available.

A telephone or cellular phone should be readily accessible to waterfront staff for emergencies. We recommend that rescue drills be practiced and reviewed with local EMS personnel to maximize efficiency in these procedures if needed.

Communication Equipment

Staff should have immediate access to communication equipment. Examples include flags, a public address system, a walkie-talkie, a bullhorn, an intercom, a cellular phone, and a telephone. Whistles can be used as means of communication to swimmers. For example, one blast can mean "Listen," two blasts can mean "Resume activity," and three blasts can mean "Get out of the water immediately."

Rules and Warnings

Rules for behavior and warnings should be clearly stated on signs that can be understood by swimmers. The signs should be adequately secured and done in accordance with ANSI sign standards.

Beach, Water, and Dock Conditions

Beaches should be inspected each day for unusual hazards and action taken to mitigate hazards, such as emptying trash cans to minimize the number of bees in the area.

Identify water and bottom conditions such as the following: depth (check the accuracy of depth markers); debris on the bottom; holes or sandbars on the bottom; currents; tides; drains; open storm sewers; wave size, direction, and type; and thermocline conditions and water temperature. Identify how to deal with these conditions. Water and bottom conditions should be inspected daily.

For docks, check the following: stability; slickness of the surface; protruding splinters, nails, or other sharp objects; springboard diving equipment; and the height of the dock and springboards above the water (look for variations of water depth due to evaporation, tides, or dams).

SUPERVISION AND PERSONNEL

Lifeguards who are currently YMCA certified should be on duty at all times while the facility is open. Lifeguards should not be given duties unrelated to their public safety function of water surveillance. Sufficient breaks should be provided (per aquatic guidelines) throughout shifts.

In-service training, including child abuse prevention and training specific to the facility, must be provided.

Lifeguards should practice the facility's emergency action plan(s) prior to the opening of the facility and periodically during the season. Lifeguards at any aquatic facility that offers swimming should practice lost swimmer and submerged victim drills (with mask and fins) regularly in the water with zero visibility.

Lifeguards should be positioned so all areas of the beach, water, docks, and floats are easily observable. Lifeguards should be staffed at a level adequate to ensure that a distressed person in a protected swimming area can be quickly recognized and a rescue immediately initiated. Zone coverage should be set by policy and clearly stated to all lifeguards via training procedures, policies, and posted directions. Zones should require lifeguards to scan no more than 180 degrees and should allow them to reach any victim in no more than 10 seconds. (This means no more than 180 degrees and no farther than a 10-second swim to the farthest point in their zone.) Specific guidance and continuous observation must be given to persons swimming underwater, diving, or surface diving.

International staff working in U.S. camps should "crossover" their aquatic and safety certifications to receive a U.S. course certification. If U.S. certification is not obtained, those staff should be assigned to other duties.

WATER ENVIRONMENTS

Swimming areas should be roped off (with lines running parallel to shore so swimmers can stay in similar depth). Swimmers should be informed of the potential hazards and rules of the area. An orientation for all swimmers should be given prior to their first aquatic experience, including a deep water test. If the water is over 15 feet deep, masks and fins should be available for lifeguards and an additional line attached to a rescue tube. Swim tests should be required before swimmers are allowed in the deep area. The swimming area should have limited access. It should be fenced and locked appropriately.

"No Diving" signs should be posted when the area does not meet minimum diving depths as indicated in YMCA of the USA aquatic guidelines.

Rules and warning signs should be clearly stated and easy to understand, adequately secured, and in accordance with ANSI sign standards. Incompatible activities, such as boating, water skiing, and fishing, should be prohibited near swimming areas, and areas should be constantly monitored for violations.

Waves and currents can create hazards in a short amount of time. Practice preventive lifeguarding, directing potential victims away from beach hazards or waves caused by boats. Similarly, currents can shift, creating potential danger. Educate swimmers on how to identify currents and how to get out of them. Practice preventive lifeguarding by identifying rip currents and directing swimmers away from them. Post clear, understandable warning signs where appropriate. Backwash can also create a hazard. Practice preventive lifeguarding during times of dangerous backwash by actively warning beach patrons.

Post signs on piers and issue warnings from piers and mobile units to keep swimmers away from dangerous areas. Actively warn swimmers away from areas where the ocean bottom is dangerous. Discourage dangerous activities, such as skim boarding "aerial dismounts," shallow diving, horseplay pier jumping, or diving under docks.

Flotation devices, such as boogie boards, surfboards, skim boards, and air mattresses, can be used if reasonable precautions are taken. Educate swimmers on the hazards of these devices and the problems they face if they lose their flotation devices. Take steps to segregate swimmers from surfers. Educate swimmers on the local aquatic life and potential hazards. Post warning signs during appropriate seasons.

BOATING AND SMALL CRAFT

Designate a specific area for small craft. Do not allow swimming in that area. Do not allow small craft in the swimming area. A swim test and a personal flotation device (PFD) should be required when using any small craft. Staff supervising this area should be trained by a nationally recognized organization in small craft safety or in the specific crafts used at the waterfront.

Instructors for boating activities should be certified for their craft as an instructor by a nationally recognized organization.

All boating activities should require that all users wear a PFD that is appropriate to the activity and in good condition. Rescue equipment, such as reaching and throwing devices, should be appropriate to the activity on the craft.

Staff and boaters should be trained to identify hazardous water and weather conditions and to implement appropriate actions. All staff and boaters using small craft should be trained in handling, trimming, loading and moving on the craft; the use of life jackets; and self-rescue in case of capsizing or swamping situations. Boaters should not be allowed beyond the sight of waterfront guards, unless the trip has been planned and approved in advance.

Aquatic facilities with intensive equipment use, such as boats, should create an equipment checklist to be used daily to protect against damaged or faulty equipment. A properly equipped rescue boat should be available and in good working order for emergency retrieval purposes. During small craft trips, campers must have appropriate training in packing small craft, propelling a loaded boat, and hooking the boat to the trailer. Safety systems, such as buddy checks, tag boards, and equipment checkout, should be used to help enable lifeguards and safety assistants to quickly account for all participants in swimming and boating activities. All swimmers should be evaluated and classified as to their swimming ability. Water tests should be given, and swimmers should be assigned to a designated area or to wear appropriate flotation devices.

REFERENCES FOR ADDITIONAL INFORMATION

American Camping Association, 5000 State Road 67 North, Martinsville, IN 46151-7902; 765-342-8456; **www.acacamps.org**

Pohndorf, Richard. 1960. *Camp waterfront programs and management.* New York: Association Press (National Board of Young Men's Christian Associations).

The Royal Life Saving Society Canada. 1993. *Alert: Lifeguarding in action.* North York, ON: The Royal Life Saving Society Canada.

United States Lifesaving Association.1995 *Manual of open water lifesaving.* Upper Saddle River, NJ: Prentice Hall.

Waterfront safety: A position paper of the Aquatic Council; American Association for Active Lifestyles and Fitness; American Alliance for Health, Physical Education, Recreation and Dance. 1997. Reston, VA: American Alliance for Health, Physical Education, Recreation and Dance.

YMCA of the USA. 1997. *On the guard II: The YMCA lifeguard manual.* 3d ed. Champaign, IL: Human Kinetics. [Available from theYMCA Program Store, Item No. 0-88011-815-6.]

Risk Management Involving Starting Blocks or Platforms, Water Depth, Deep Diving Starts, and Supervision

Research has proven that it is dangerous to dive in water less than 5 feet deep. Key factors in preventing diving injuries are swimmer/diver supervision, correct training and instruction, and participant awareness of the hazards of diving in shallow water.

STARTING BLOCKS OR PLATFORMS

Starting blocks or platforms

- are to be placed at the deep end of the swimming pool only. They are never to be placed in the shallow end or in water less than 5 feet deep.
- are removed from the pool area, capped off to avoid any unintended use, or use is regulated by signage.
- are inspected regularly for stability, surface characteristics (traction), and any sign of wear.
- are considered competitive swimming equipment ONLY, to be used with proper supervision and safety instruction. They are not to be used as recreational devices or toys.
- are to have safety warnings posted regarding starting block or platform use.

WATER DEPTH

In order to minimize the risk of injury, conduct diving instruction from the deck in no less than 9 feet of water* and from a 1-meter board in no less than 11 feet, 6 inches of water.

Long shallow dives should be taught in no less than 9 feet of water. Once participants are proficient in such dives, warn them that they are allowed to perform these dives only in water at least 5 feet deep and when participating in a competitive swimming or lifeguard training program. Standing front dives should be performed in no less than 9 feet of water.

---

* Height and weight of the participant and the design of the pool bottom are factors to be considered in determining the safety of the diving area.

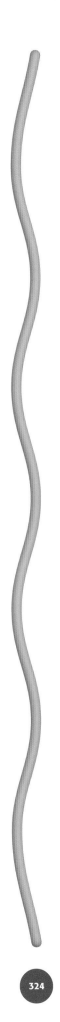

DEEP DIVING STARTS

This type of dive has been called the scoop start, pike start, spoon start, hole-in-the-water start, and no-resistance start. This start causes a swimmer to enter the water at a steeper angle than the traditional long shallow water dive or flat start.

This particular dive is being used more frequently by competitive swimmers. It is of questionable value and presents a potentially dangerous dive unless the water is 5 feet deep or more.

The water, unfortunately, may be deep enough in one pool, but not in another. This presents a problem for swimmers and coaches in determining when the scoop dive can be safely used. During the excitement of a swimming meet, the competitor may forget, use the scoop start in a shallow pool, and suffer injury. **Due to the potential danger of serious injury, the scoop dive should be eliminated in water less than 5 feet deep.**

SUPERVISION

Starting blocks or platforms are to be used only by trained swimmers under supervision in the deep end and in water at least 5 feet deep. They are removed or capped off to prevent use in all other situations or their use is regulated by posted rules.

Coaches and instructors will use proper sequential training techniques and enforce safe starting skills. Swimmers will be instructed not to abort a poor start during its execution. Somersaulting, tucking, or jerking to one side may increase the risk of hitting the pool bottom.

Shallow water areas and starting blocks are controlled by lifeguards, instructors, and aquatic personnel. Lifeguards will be alert and strictly enforce all rules.

REFERENCES

American Red Cross basic water safety. 1988. Oklahoma City: American National Red Cross.

American Red Cross safety training for swim coaches. 1988. Oklahoma City: American National Red Cross.

Aquatics. 1988. *YMCA Risk Report.* Winter, page 2.

BFS Architectural Consulting and Interior Design. 1988. *Pool depth.* [Memorandum, December 7.]

Bunnell and Company. 1984. *Safety group warns swimmers about Labor Day diving accidents.* [News release, August 21.]

Counsilman, J., Nomura, T., Endo, M., and Counsilman, B. 1988. A study of three types of grab start for competitive swimming. *National Aquatic Journal* Spring: 2-6.

Gabriel, J., editor. 1992. *Diving safety, a position paper.* Indianapolis: U.S. Diving, Inc.

Gabrielsen, M.A. 1984. *Diving injuries: A critical insight and recommendation.* Indianapolis: Council for National Cooperation in Aquatics.

Gabrielsen, M.A. 1987. *Swimming pools: A guide to their planning, design, and operation.* Champaign, IL: Human Kinetics.

Hunsaker, D.J. 1986. *Design compendium for competition swimming and diving pools.* San Antonio: National Swimming Pool Foundation.

National Collegiate Athletic Association. 1990. *1991 NCAA swimming and diving men's and women's rules.* Overland Park, KS: Author.

Pennsylvania Interscholastic Athletic Association. 1990. *Major rule revisions in swimming and diving.* [Memorandum, April 12.]

Pennsylvania Interscholastic Athletic Association. 1990. *Water depth requirement in swimming.* [Memorandum, April 20.]

Pennsylvania Interscholastic Athletic Association. 1990. *Swimming and diving rule revisions for 1990-91.* [Memorandum, April 24.]

Prigitano, A. 1988. The cost of poor diving safety: Great incidence of paralysis. *Perspective* September: 30–31.

Think twice before you dive. 1989. *For Kids' Sake* 7(2):5.

YMCA of the USA. 1986. *On the guard: The YMCA lifeguard manual.* Champaign, IL: Human Kinetics.

YMCA of the USA. 1986. *YMCA progressive swimming instructor's guide.* Champaign, IL: Human Kinetics.

YMCA of the USA Aquatic Director. 1989. *Warning notice.* [Memorandum, July 7.]

Sample Accident Report Form

Date of report: _____

Name of injured person: _____ Age: _____ Sex: _____

Address: _____

Date of accident: _____ Time: _____ Number of people in water: _____

Water condition: _____ Weather condition: _____

Describe the accident. Include where the accident occurred, what happened, and how many people were involved in the accident.

List the names of those involved in the accident and comment on their swimming skills if such skills contributed to the accident.

Did those involved disregard rules or orders of the lifeguard? _____ If so, explain.

Identify who, if anyone, was injured and describe the injuries.

Describe the first aid given.

Was CPR used? _____ For how long? _____

Were law enforcement or EMS squads called? _____ What time did they arrive? _____

Was additional medical attention required? _____ If so, indicate where individuals were taken, who provided treatment, and what treatment was given.

Blood-Borne Pathogen Program Exposure Incident

Employee name: _____ Soc. sec. no.: _____

Was the source the injured person listed above? _____ Yes _____ No

If not, give source's name: _____

Address: _____ Phone no.: _____

Document route of exposure: (mucous membrane, puncture, etc.) _____

_____

Was protective equipment used? _____ Yes   Describe equipment. _____

_____

_____

Was protective equipment used? _____ No   Give reason it was not used. _____

_____

_____

Describe postexposure cleanup procedures that were used: _____

_____

Lifeguard Information

Name: _____ Position: _____

Years of experience: _____ Assignment location: _____ Hours on/off duty: _____

List names, addresses, and phone numbers of at least two witnesses on the back of this sheet.

Sketch the area of the accident, showing unusual conditions (if any) and assignments of personnel.

General comments of employees:

Signature: _____ Date: _____

YMCA Lifeguarding and the United States Lifesaving Association

The YMCA of the USA is proud of its heritage in lifeguard training and water safety. It began with the first lifesaving corps, organized at Camp Dudley in 1904, the first National Lifesaving Service in 1912, and the first lifesaving textbook, *Water First Aid*, by George Goss in 1913. For almost 100 years YMCA-certified lifesavers and lifeguards have staffed America's swimming pools, lake and river beaches, and camp waterfronts. However, training has not included surf lifeguarding.

After briefly attempting to certify surf lifeguards in the mid-1970s, the YMCA soon discovered that they lacked the surf beach facilities to train and certify surf lifeguards. However, many students who complete YMCA lifeguard courses would like to use their lifeguarding skills at surf beaches. That is why the YMCA aquatic program is pleased to have developed a linkage with the United States Lifesaving Association (USLA).

The USLA is the oldest, most experienced surf lifeguard training agency in America today. Its mission is to establish and maintain high standards for open water (beach) lifeguards, to educate the public, and to promote actions intended to result in the saving of human life in and around the aquatic environment. The USLA is made up of groups of individuals who form chapters locally. The chapters then join together to create regions of the USLA within which they can exchange local and regional information relevant to their activities and needs. Currently there are eight regions of the USLA.

This appendix was developed in cooperation with the USLA to provide YMCA lifeguards with the information and fundamental steps necessary to link up with USLA programs from coast to coast. Because USLA training includes the use of cervical collars for spinal cord injury victims, the use of a rescue buoy in rescue skills, and the use of in-water assessment and rescue breathing, just as YMCA training does, YMCA-trained lifeguards have an advantage in training for surf lifeguarding.

If you are a certified YMCA lifeguard with an interest in becoming a surf lifeguard at a USLA-certified beach, you must satisfy the following basic requirements to be eligible for entry-level open water lifeguard training:

1. Age—Be a minimum of 16 years of age.
2. Swimming ability—Demonstrate the ability to swim 500 meters over a measured course in 10 minutes or less.
3. Health and fitness—Possess adequate vision, hearing acuity, physical ability, and stamina to perform the duties of an open water lifeguard, as documented by a medical or osteopathic physician.
4. First aid certification—Be certified as having successfully completed a first aid course accepted by the federal government or by the state government in the state of employment. Total formal first aid training, including the certified first aid course, shall be no less than 21 hours.
5. CPR certification—Be certified as having successfully completed a course in providing one-person adult, two-person adult, child, and infant CPR, including

obstructed airway training, accepted by the federal government or by the state government in the state of employment.

6. Lifeguard training—Be certified as successfully completing a course consisting of no less than 40 hours in open water lifesaving that meets the curriculum requirements of USLA. This shall not include the minimum training hours required for first aid and CPR.

7. Scuba training—Any lifeguard who will be required to utilize scuba in the course of employment must, at a minimum, be certified as a scuba diver at the basic level by a nationally recognized certifying agency.

Because the USLA realizes that differences in environmental conditions will impact specific training issues, variations to the USLA curriculum requirements may be permitted under very specific situations.

If you can meet the first six requirements of the seven just identified, then you are considered to be a viable candidate for USLA surf lifeguard training. Your next step would be to obtain and study a copy of *The United States Lifesaving Association Manual of Open Water Lifesaving*, as well as other USLA publications. In the meantime, you should stay in peak physical condition by swimming and participating in a resistive exercise program, and you should contact the USLA chapter in the beach town where you would like to gain employment as a beach lifeguard.

Other standards exist for Open Water Lifeguard Trainees, Full Time Open Water Lifeguards, and Open Water Lifeguard Instructors. Information on the USLA's certification programs may be obtained by ordering their *Lifeguard Agency Certification Program* booklet which, along with *The United States Lifesaving Association Manual of Open Water Lifesaving*, is the association's response to the need for standardization in the profession of open water lifesaving.

To order copies of *The United States Lifesaving Association Manual of Open Water Lifesaving* (ISBN: 8359-4919-2), write or call Brady Publishing at

Brady Publishing (Division of Prentice-Hall)
113 Sylvan Avenue
Englewood Cliffs, NJ 07632
800-374-1200
(For customer service, call 201-767-4993.)

APPENDIX **F**

Waterfront Safety

A Position Paper of the Aquatic Council, American Association for Active Lifestyles and Fitness, and the American Alliance for Health, Physical Education, Recreation and Dance

Aquatic activities at waterfront beaches are very popular throughout the United States. Nonetheless, natural hazards presented by the open water environment can cause injury or death. Many of these hazards differ significantly from those in swimming pools, although drowning remains a paramount concern. For these reasons, the establishment of appropriate safety procedures and policies is critical to the health and enjoyment of participants in waterfront activities. This position paper establishes guidelines and standards for safety at waterfront facilities.

The term waterfront has been used in many different ways. For purposes of this paper, a waterfront is any place where open water meets land. Waterfront facilities consist of both public and private aquatic related venues that cater to the recreational enjoyment of participants. They include surf and inland venues, such as rivers, ponds, lakes (natural or artificial), quarries, reservoirs and ocean beaches.

Waterfront facility operation should at all times conform to local, state, and federal health and safety codes and ordinances. All waterfront beaches should have the following equipment readily available in a quantity appropriate to the geographic size of the facility and attendance. All emergency equipment should be inspected daily.

• Emergency equipment: telephone and emergency numbers posted nearby; first aid kit; personal protective equipment (e.g., latex gloves, resuscitation mask, eye shield); resuscitation equipment; spine-board, head restraint, cervical collars, and straps; rescue boat; paddleboard; rescue tube/buoy; mask, fins, and snorkel.

• Equipment recommended for larger facilities: rescue boat, motorized rescue craft.

• Communication equipment: should be readily available for use; examples include flags, public address system, walkie-talkies, bullhorn, telephone.

• Rules and warning signs: Make sure they are legible and adequately secured.

• Beaches: Beaches should be inspected each day for unusual hazards and the hazards mitigated.

• Identify water/bottom conditions: accuracy of depth markers; debris on bottom; holes and sandbars; currents; tides; wave size, direction, and type; and thermocline conditions.

• Docks: Check stability, protruding splinters, nails or other sharp objects; springboard diving equipment

• Buoys and safety floats: properly secured; no sharp edges; markings legible.

• Lifeguard facilities: maintained safe for lifeguard use and meeting applicable codes.

• Whenever public facilities such as docks, diving boards, ladders, rafts, etc., are provided, they should be in proper repair and in a safe condition at all times.

To ensure appropriate supervision, a lifeguard who has been fully trained under a nationally recognized program appropriate to the facility should be on duty at all times the facility is open. All lifeguards should be fully trained by a nationally or state recognized agency in emergency provider first aid and CPR. Lifeguards should not be given duties unrelated to their public safety function, and lifeguards assigned to water surveillance should be given no other duties whatsoever. In-service training specific to the facility should be provided. Lifeguards should practice the facilities emergency action plan(s) prior to the opening of the facility and periodically during the season.

To provide for proper levels of safety in the designated swimming area and adjacent areas, lifeguards should be positioned so all areas of the beach, water, docks, and floats are easily observable. Lifeguards should be staffed at a level adequate to ensure the distress of any person in a protected swimming area can be quickly recognized and a rescue immediately initiated. Zones of coverage should be set by policy and clearly stated to all lifeguards via training procedures, policies, and/or posted directions.

The waterfront environment poses many safety concerns. Keep the beach-going public informed as to the potential hazards of the facility. This can be accomplished by creating Junior Lifeguard programs and public information outreach programs to educate the public. The facility should address safety in the following manner:

• Diving: Shallow water diving can cause serious injury and death. It should be discouraged through public education efforts, preventive actions, and appropriate signs. Place accurate depth markings on docks, retaining walls, and/or bulkheads; prohibit diving where water depth is less than 9 feet. (Water depth beneath 1 meter diving boards should be adequate for safe diving. Many aquatic organizations identify a minimum depth of 11 feet beneath and 16 feet in front of the tip of the diving board as adequate.) Place No Diving signs where diving is prohibited. Rules and warning signs should be clearly posted, legible, and adequately secured. Incompatible activities such as boating, water skiing, and fishing should be kept away from swimming areas.

• Waves: Practice preventive lifeguarding, directing potential victims away from beach hazards.

• Currents: Educate the public on how to identify currents and how to get out of them. Practice preventive lifeguarding by identifying rip currents and directing swimmers away from them. Post warning signs where appropriate.

• Piers: Post signs on piers and issue public address warnings from piers and mobile units to keep swimmers away from danger areas.

• Ocean bottom: Actively warn swimmers of dangers in the area. Discourage dangerous activities (i.e., skim boarding "aerial dismounts," shallow diving, horseplay pier jumping, etc.).

• Flotation devices (boogie boards, surfboards, skim boards, air mattresses, etc.): Educate the public as to the hazards of flotation devices and the problems they face if they lose their own flotation device. Take steps to segregate surfing and swimming populations.

• Backwash: Practice preventive lifeguarding during times of dangerous backwash by actively warning beach patrons.

• Aquatic life: Educate the public on the local aquatic life and the hazards they present. Post warning signs during appropriate seasons.

• Alcohol and drugs: Follow federal, state, or local laws and ordinances.

• Small craft: Designate a specific area for small craft. Do not allow swimming in that area. Do not allow small craft in the swimming area.

Most drownings in the United States occur in unsupervised areas. Do not enter the water in areas where supervision by a fully and properly trained lifeguard in not provided. Public safety at waterfront facilities can be greatly enhanced if proper precautions are taken. Implementation of such precautions, in turn, can result in better educated users who can help themselves and others avoid injury and increase their enjoyment of the aquatic environment.

Reprinted, by permission of the American Association for Active Lifestyles and Fitness (AAALF), Aquatic Council. AAALF is an association of AAHPERD, *A Position Paper of the Aquatic Council.*

Prevention and Control of Fecal Contamination in Swimming Pools

STATEMENT OF THE YMCA OF THE USA MEDICAL ADVISORY COMMITTEE

With the large number of swimming pools and participants in YMCA aquatic programs, it is not uncommon for YMCAs to experience fecal accidents in those pools periodically. Until recently it was thought that removal of the fecal matter with a skimmer and the addition of extra doses of chlorine was a sufficient procedure to use when this occurred. There was a level of confidence that chlorine would kill any bacteria or virus in the pool. A free residual chlorine level of 1.0 ppm (parts per million) has usually been considered adequate to kill amoebic dysentery, herpes, hepatitis, impetigo, and thousands of other water-borne diseases, realizing that some bacteria, such as staphylococcus auereus, can develop a resistance to normal chlorine levels.

However, recent reports from health authorities across the United States indicate that disease organisms previously not associated with swimming pools have been identified in pool water and have caused significant public health problems. These outbreaks stemming from fecal contamination in pools include nematodes, giardia lamblia, and cryptosporidium parvum, all of which can become intestinal parasites. The difficulty with these three organisms is that they cannot be removed from any type of sand filter, and normal chlorine levels (1.0–2.0 ppm free residuals) will not eliminate them. Because of this, lifeguard and aquatic directors must take aggressive action to prevent the possible development of disease among members and participants when fecal contamination occurs.

The best defense against an outbreak of intestinal disease in a pool is to establish a series of preventive measures. The following procedures for prevention of fecal contamination are recommended for all YMCA aquatic facilities. YMCAs should also refer to local bathing codes if additional procedures are required. These recommendations are:

- Be sure your staff is trained and certified in the YMCA P.O.O.L. (Pool Operator on Location) course.
- Maintain all components of the circulation, filtration, and disinfection system in good working condition.
- Use some form of chlorine as a disinfectant (i.e., CL2, gas, sodium hypochlorite, or calcium hypochlorite).
- Maintain an effective chlorine residual: pool 1.5–2.0 ppm, whirlpool/spa 3.0–5.0 ppm, wading pool 2.0–3.0 ppm. Keep the pH between 7.4–7.6.
- Use a chemical feeder to dispense chlorine into the pool 24 hours a day. Never batch or hand feed chlorine.
- Operate the pool, whirlpool, and wading pool circulation system 24 hours a day.

- Test, adjust, and record chlorine and pH levels every 2 hours for pool and wading pools; whirlpools once an hour.
- Calculate a Langelier Saturation Index once a week and adjust the balance to 0.
- Drain the pool and scrub the walls and pool bottom once a year. If the pool cannot be drained because of a high water table, then dilute the old water from the pool by draining 1/3 of the pool water and refilling. Repeat this procedure 6 times to achieve the best result.
- Superchlorinate the pool once a month to a free residual of 5.0 ppm and then reduce the level back down to 1.5–2.0 ppm by using sodium thiosulfate penta hydrate (granular form) and adjust the pH to 7.4–7.6. Use the following formula to reduce the chlorine level:

  1.7 lb/100,000 gallons reduces free CL2 by 2.0 ppm

  2.7 oz/10,000 gallons reduces free CL2 by 2.0 ppm

  0.017 lb/1,000 gallons reduces free CL2 by 2.0 ppm
- Avoid the use of stabilized chlorine if possible.
- Establish and enforce personal hygiene rules for the pool and whirlpool:
  1. A soap and warm water shower is required before using the pool or whirlpool.
  2. After using the whirlpool, a soap and warm water shower is required before entering the swimming pool.
  3. Infants, preschool children, and adults who may experience incontinence must use some form of diaper that keeps fecal material inside the diaper.
- Provide diaper changing stations in both the men's and women's dressing rooms for parents with infant responsibilities.
- Install "child acceptable" toilet facilities and strongly recommend to parents that they encourage their use before bringing toddlers and preschool age children into the pool for instruction and recreational swimming.
- Add a rule to facility behavioral signs requesting that anyone currently experiencing diarrhea not use the pool, wading pool, or spa.
- When rehabilitating an old pool or building a new pool, spa, or wading pool, install a circulation system with a maximum of a 6 hour turnover for pools, 2 hours for wading pools, and 30 minutes or less for spas. Give strong consideration to the installation of any form of diatomaceous earth filter (vacuum, pressure, or regenerative cycle).
- Be sure that spray pools for toddlers and preschoolers do not have any standing water or untreated recirculating water.
- Educate patrons on prevention of disease transmission and water safety. The Center for Disease Control recommends the following educational tips*:
  1. Do not swim if you have diarrhea (people can spread germs in the pool without having an "accident").
  2. Do not drink the pool water. (Remember: it's everybody's bath water and chlorine doesn't kill all germs.)
  3. Do wash your hands thoroughly with soap and water after using the bathroom. (Germs on hands end up everywhere, including the water.)
  4. Do notify the lifeguard if you see feces in the pool or if you see behaviors, such as changing a diaper at poolside, that may spread disease.
  5. If you're a parent:
     —Do take your child on bathroom breaks often.
     —Do change diapers in a bathroom, not at poolside. (Germs can contaminate surfaces and objects around the pool and spread disease.)
     —Do wash your hands thoroughly with soap and water after changing diapers and make sure that your child's hands are washed.

—Do wash your child thoroughly (especially his or her bottom) with soap and water before swimming.

—Do not count solely on swim diapers or pants to stop accidents from leaking into the pool. (These products are not leakproof.)

—If you have questions about the diseases or think you have a parasitic infection, consult a health care provider.

* From Centers for Disease Control and Prevention; National Center for Infectious Diseases; Division of Parasitic Disease. "Prevention tips: Invisible pool guests can cause kids to get sick", August 1999.

STRATEGIES FOR DEALING WITH A VISIBLE EPISODE OF FECAL CONTAMINATION

When dealing with a visible incident of fecal contamination, the type of bacteria, virus, or parasite that might be in the water will not be known.

If the feces is solid material and your free chlorine level is above 1.5 ppm

- remove the fecal matter, and
- check free chlorine levels in three different locations (samples should be taken in shallow water, transitional water, and deep water and not from in front of inlets).

If the feces is solid material and your free chlorine level is below 1.5 ppm

- remove the fecal matter,
- check free chlorine levels in three different locations (samples should be taken in shallow water, transitional water, and deep water and not from in front of inlets), and
- close the pool until the free chlorine residual is 2.0 ppm in three different locations. (Samples should be taken in shallow water, transitional water, and deep water and not from in front of inlets.) The pool should remain closed for 30 minutes after achieving the 2.0 ppm level and then reopened.

If the feces is liquid and particulates, or you are informed that the person who had the fecal accident has been sick or has had diarrhea in the last two weeks, or your health department has identified your pool as a source of cryptosporidium, then comply with the following procedures:

1. All pool users should be required to leave the pool, and the pool should be closed.

2. As much fecal material as possible should be removed from the pool. Adjust the pool water level so that skimming takes place through the skimmers or over the gutters. Next vacuum the pool bottom. Wastewater should be channeled directly to a sewer or approved waste disposal system, not through the filtration system. Any components of your vacuum sweeping equipment exposed to contaminated water, self-contained vacuum cleaner filters, intake areas, and internal channels must be cleaned and disinfected with sodium hypochlorite before reuse.

3. The free chlorine residual should be raised to 20.0 mgL (ppm), and a pH level of 7.2 should be maintained for at least 9 hours (540 minutes). This is the equivalent of an approximate CT value (chlorine × time) of 10,000 (20 ppm × 540 minutes = 10,800). A higher or lower chlorine residual can be used, provided a CT value of 10,000 is achieved. The 9 hour time period begins when the three free chlorine tests are verified by readings at three locations: shallow water, transition water, and deep water areas. Be sure your chlorine reagent (i.e., DpD 1 and 2) is no more than 6 months old.

Note: In order to eliminate the organisms, two factors must now be considered: the concentration of the disinfection in mgL (ppm) and the time in minutes necessary to eliminate 99.9% of the organism (the formula CT [chlorine × time] is used to express this relationship). The disinfectant used in the process is chlorine. Cryptosporidium has a CT time of 9,600. 20 ppm × 540 minutes = 10,800, which exceeds the value of 10,000.

4. The filtration system should be operated for a minimum of three to six complete turnovers. The turnover rate at public swimming pools is usually 6 to 8 hours; therefore, three turnovers can be achieved within 24 hours. In general, sand filters are more effective when they are slightly dirty or use an alum floc. If a sand filter is not in need of backwashing at the time of the fecal accident, do not backwash the filter.

5. After three to six turnovers, thoroughly clean or backwash the filter.

6. If the pool is a low volume pool, such as a spa or wading pool, drain the pool at this point.

7. Disinfect the filter tank and filter media by applying a 20:1 solution of sodium hypochlorite (20 parts water to 1 part 12% sodium hypochlorite) directly to the filter.

8. Restart the filtration system

9. Neutralize any excessively high chlorine residual with sodium thiosulfate penta hydrate. Balance the water with a Langelier calculation, adjust your chemical levels as needed, and then reopen the pool.

10. Be sure to formulate these recommendations into an emergency response procedure and incorporate the procedure into your facility operations manual.

11. Develop a step-by-step time response log for a fecal incident. Record the time and each action step taken to eliminate any potential health problem since a serious illness or death could result in legal action.

It is important that YMCA pool operators discuss this matter with state or local health departments for their recommendations and to determine procedures to follow. Additionally, it is recommended that YMCAs review the procedures with their medical advisory committee.

BIBLIOGRAPHY

Buchanon, J.D., Juranek, D.D., Parkin, W.E., Porter, J.D., Ragazzoni, H.P., and Waskin, H.A. 1988. Giardia transmission in a swimming pool. *American Journal of Public Health* 78(6):659–662.

Centers for Disease Control. 1994. Assessing the public health treatment associated with waterborne *Cryptosporidiosis* [Workshop Report, September]. *Morbidity and Mortality Weekly Report* 44(RR-6):1–19.

Centers for Disease Control. 1994. *Cryptosporidium* infections associated with swimming pools. *Morbidity and Mortality Weekly Report* 43:561–563.

Centers for Disease Control. 1996. Foodborne outbreak of diarrheal illness associated with *Cryptosporidium Parvum*. *Morbidity and Mortality Weekly Report* 45(36):783–784.

Centers for Disease Control. 1996. Outbreak of *Cryptosporidiosis* at day camp. *Morbidity and Mortality Weekly Report* 45(21):442–444.

Ewert, D. 1995. *Giardiasis* outbreak associated with the Arlington Heights pool [Memorandum, March 2]. Indiana State Department of Health, pages 1-5.

Frost, F., Grunenfelder, G., Harter, L., Libby, J., and Perkins Jones, K. 1984. *Giardiasis* in an infant and toddler swim class. *American Journal of Public Health* 74(2):155–156.

Frost, F., Johnson, R.L., MacDonald, S.C., Ongerth, J.E., and Stibbs, H.H. 1989. Backcountry water treatment to prevent *Giardiasis*. *American Journal of Public Health* 79(12):1633–1637.

Indiana State Department of Health. 1995. Prevalence of pathogens raises interest. *Indiana Epidemiology Newsletter* 3(2):1-6.

Indiana State Department of Health. 1995. Survey looks at testing for *Cryptosporidium* in Indiana. *Indiana Epidemiology Newsletter* 3(3):1-6.

Johnson, R.L. 1997. Fecal contamination: An old swimming pool problem with new concerns. Research paper presented at the 1997 National Convention of the American Alliance of Physical Education, Health, Recreation and Dance, St. Louis, MO.

Kebabjian, R.S. 1995. Disinfection of public pools and management of fecal accidents. *Journal of Environmental Health* 58(1):8-12.

Sinclair, C.L. (no date). Intestinal parasitism: A brief overview. *Indiana State Department of Health* 40(SS-3).

November, 1997
Revised April, 2000

REFERENCES

American Academy of Orthopaedic Surgeons and National Safety Council. (1999). *Professional rescuer CPR.* Sudbury, MA: Jones and Bartlett.

American Red Cross. (1995). *Head lifeguard.* St. Louis: Mosby Lifeline.

Bechdel, L., and Slim, R. (1997). *River rescue: A manual for whitewater safety.* Old Saybrook, CT: Globe Pequot.

Brewster, B.C. (1995). *The United States Lifesaving Association Manual of Open Water Lifesaving.* Englewood Cliffs, NJ: Prentice Hall, Brady Emergency Care.

Canadian Red Cross Society. (1983). *Cold water survival.* Victoria, BC: Author.

Dworkin, G.M. (1998, October 31). *Rescue from submerged vehicles.* **www.lifesaving.com/articles/subveh.htm**

Fenner, P., Leahy, S., Buhk, A., & Dawes, P. (1999). Prevention of drowning: Visual scanning and attention span in lifeguards. *The Journal of Occupational Health and Safety – Australia and New Zealand, 15*(1), 61-66.

Gabriel, J.L., Leas, D.E., & George, G.S. (1999). *U.S. diving safety training manual (2nd ed.).* Indianapolis: U.S. Diving Publications.

Graver, D.K. (1999). *Scuba diving (2nd ed.).* Champaign, IL: Human Kinetics.

Lepore, M. (2000). E-mail to author.

Lifesaving Society. (1993). *Alert: Lifeguarding in action.* North York, Ontario, Canada: The Royal Life Saving Society Canada.

Maas, T., & Sipperly, D. (1998). *Freediving.* Venture, CA: Blue Water Freediving.

Mebane, G.Y. (1995). *DAN dive and travel medical guide.* Durham, NC: Divers Alert Network.

Modell, J.H. (1997, September). 22. Modell, Dr. Jerome H. In *International medical-rescue conference,* edited by B. Chris Brewster. San Diego: International Life Saving Federation Americas Region.

National Safe Boating Council and U.S. Coast Guard. (1997). *Wear your life jacket! Boat smart from the start.* U.S. Coast Guard.

National Safety Council. (1997). *First aid and CPR standard.* Sudbury, MA: Jones and Bartlett.

Pennsylvania Fish and Boat Commission. (2000). *Dams.* **www.state.pa.us/PA_Exec/Fish_Boat/boatbkgg.htm**

Personal Watercraft Industry Association. (n.d.). *Riding rules for personal watercraft.* Winter Park, FL: PWIA Communications.

Pia, F. (1997, September). 25. Pia, Frank. In *International medical-rescue conference,* edited by B. Chris Brewster. San Diego: International Life Saving Federation Americas Region.

Porter, R.R. (1997). Comparison of the American Red Cross and Young Men's Christian Association Rescue Procedures for a passive near-drowning victim. Master's thesis. Indiana University of Pennsylvania, Indiana, Pennsylvania.

Richardson, W.J. (1997, September). 26. Richardson, Capt. (ret.) William J. In *International medical-rescue conference,* edited by B. Chris Brewster. San Diego: International Life Saving Federation Americas Region.

Royal Life Saving Society Canada. (1994). *The Canadian lifesaving manual.* Ottawa, ON: The Royal Life Saving Society Canada.

Royal Life Saving Society Canada. (1995). *10 water smart moves for PWC riders.* **www.interlog.com/~jlogan/rlss/rlssc.html**

Royal Life Saving Society Canada, Alberta and Northwest Territories Branch. (n.d.). *Water smart tips, ice safety, how thick is thick enough?* The Royal Life Saving Society Canada Web site.

Sea Grant. (n.d.). *Rip currents: Don't panic.* Raleigh, NC: N.C. Sea Grant.

U.S. Department of Commerce. National Weather Service Forecast Office. (1999, December 16). Letter to Cleveland County YMCA.

United States Coast Guard, Department of Transportation. (1977). *Hypothermia and cold water survival – Instructor's guide.* Washington, DC: Government Printing Office.

United States Lifesaving Association. (1995). *Training guide for USLA safety tips.* **www.usla.org/publicinfo/safety_guide.html**

World Waterpark Association. (1989). *Considerations for operating safety.* Lenexa, KS: World Waterpark Association.

YMCA of the USA. (1999). *The youth and adult aquatic program manual.* Champaign, IL: Human Kinetics.

INDEX

Note: The italicized *f* and *t* following page numbers refer to figures and tables, respectively.

Additional Resources for Lifeguarding and Aquatic Safety

See the YMCA Program Store catalog for details about these additional items for your lifeguarding or aquatic safety programs, or contact the Program Store, P.O. Box 5076, Champaign, IL 61825-5076, phone 800-747-0089. To save time, order by fax, 217-351-1549. Please call if you are interested in receiving a free catalog.

Lifeguarding

0-7360-3976-7	On the Guard II (Fourth Edition)	$31.00
0-7360-3989-9	On the Guard II – Instructor Manual (Fourth Edition)	$95.00

Aquatic Safety

0-88011-742-7	YMCA Splash	$37.00
0-7360-0308-8	YMCA Splash (video)	$21.95
0-7360-3311-4	Staff Aquatic Safety Training (video)	$21.95

Aquatics

0-87322-656-9	YMCA Pool Operations Manual (Second Edition)	$25.00
0-88011-670-6	Principles of YMCA Aquatics	$24.00
1-887359-00-1	Aquatic Games	$21.95
0-87322-501-5	Water Fun and Fitness	$14.95

Scuba

0-393-31944-X	Scuba Diving: A Trailside Guide	$18.95
0-87322-132-X	Scuba Lifesaving and Accident Management (Second Ed.)	$14.00
0-7360-4476-0	YMCA Scuba Diving Log	$7.00
0-7360-4408-6	YMCA Scuba Sport Diving Tables	10/$35.00

For a complete listing of all the aquatics resources please refer to the Program Store catalog.

Prices shown are subject to change.